THE TIMES | Mapping History

Queens
of the British Isles

Thomas Cussans

Times Books

Paperback Edition
Published in 2004 by
TIMES BOOKS
HarperCollins Publishers
77-85 Fulham Palace Road
London W6 8JB

The HarperCollins website address is
www.collins.co.uk

First published by Times Books 2002

British Library Cataloguing in Publication Data:
A catalogue record is available from the British Library

Printed and bound in Singapore by IMAGO

ISBN 0 0071 9279 7

The Times Kings and Queens
of the British Isles
By Thomas Cussans

Maps conceived and compiled by:
András Bereznay

HarperCollins Publishers:

Editorial Direction:
Philip Parker

Editorial and Picture Research:
Ceire Clark

Cartographic and Design Direction:
Direction: Martin Brown
Cartography: András Bereznay

D&N Publishing

Editorial and Design Direction:
David Goodfellow

Editorial:
Elizabeth Mallard-Shaw

Design:
Shane O'Dwyer

Proof-reading:
Michael Jones

Index:
Chris Howes

Additional Cartography:
Cosmographics, Watford, England

The publishers would also like to thank Janet Larkin
(Department of Coins & Medals, The British
Museum), Colin Brown, The Bank of Ireland Group,
Old Royal Naval College, Roxburghe Estates

of the British Isles

Kings &

CONTENTS

INTRODUCTION 7

1 MYTHS AND ORIGINS 8

BRITAIN: THE ROMAN CONQUEST 10 | THE FIRST ANGLO-SAXON KINGDOMS 12
WALES TO 1284 16 | SCOTLAND TO C.842 20 | SCOTLAND TO C.842–1034 22
IRELAND TO 1183 24

2 PRE-CONQUEST ENGLAND 871–1066 26

VIKING INVASION AND SETTLEMENT 28 | ALFRED THE GREAT 871–899 30
THE HEIRS OF ALFRED 899–975 32 | THE HEIRS OF ALFRED: AETHELRED II 978–1016 34
CORONATION RITES 36 | THE DANISH KINGDOM OF ENGLAND: CNUT AND HIS SONS 38
EDWARD THE CONFESSOR 1042–66 40 | HAROLD II 1066 42

3 ENGLAND: THE NORMANS 1066–1154 44

WILLIAM THE CONQUEROR 1066–1087 46
MONARCHY IN THE AGE OF FEUDALISM 50 | WILLIAM II 1087–1100 52
HENRY I 1100–35 54 | STEPHEN 1135–54 56

4 SCOTLAND: FROM DUNKELD TO BRUCE 1034–1329 58

THE HOUSE OF DUNKELD 1034–1153 60 | THE HOUSE OF DUNKELD 1153–1296 62
ROBERT I·THE BRUCE 1306–29 64 | THE AULD ALLIANCE, 1295–1560 66

5 ENGLAND: THE ANGEVINS AND PLANTAGENETS 1154–1399 68

HENRY II 1154–89 70 | THE EVOLUTION OF THE ROYAL COURT 74
RICHARD I 1189–99 76 | JOHN 1199–1216 78 | HENRY III 1216–72 80
THE KING-IN-PARLIAMENT 82 | EDWARD I 1272–1307 84 | EDWARD II 1307–27 88
EDWARD III 1327–77 90 | RICHARD II 1377–99 94 | PROJECTIONS OF ROYALTY: ONE 96

6 ENGLAND: LANCASTER AND YORK 1399–1485 98

HENRY IV 1399–1413 100 | HENRY V 1413–22 102 | HENRY VI 1422–61/1470–1 104
THE WARS OF THE ROSES 106 | EDWARD IV 1461–70/1471–83 108
RICHARD III 1483–85 110

6 Contents

7 **SCOTLAND: FROM BRUCE TO STUART 1329–1625** *112*

David II to James II 1371–1460 **114** | James III to James V 1461–1542 **116**
Mary, Queen of Scots 1542–67 **118**

8 **ENGLAND AND WALES: THE TUDORS 1485–1603** *120*

Henry VII 1485–1509 **122** | Henry VIII 1509–47 **124**
Edward VI 1547–53 **128** | Mary I 1553–58 **130**
Elizabeth I 1558–1603 **132**

9 **ENGLAND, WALES, SCOTLAND AND IRELAND: THE STUARTS 1603–1714** *136*

James I 1603–25 **138** | Charles I 1625–49 **140**
The Commonwealth 1649–60 **144** | Charles II 1660–85 **146**
James II 1685–88 **148** | The Glorious Revolution 1688–89 **150**
William III and Mary II 1689–1702 **152** | Anne 1702–14 **154**

10 **GREAT BRITAIN AND IRELAND: THE HANOVERIANS 1714–1917** *156*

George I 1714–27 **158** | The Jacobite Uprisings 1689–1745 **160**
George II 1727–60 **162** | George III 1760–1820 **164**
George IV 1820–30 **168** | Projections of Royalty: Two **170**
William IV 1830–37 **172** | Victoria 1837–1901 **174** | The Development
of Constitutional Monarchy to 1901 **178** | Edward VII 1901–10 **180**

11 **GREAT BRITAIN: THE WINDSORS FROM 1917** *182*

George V 1910–36 **184** | The Growth of Royal Ceremony **188**
Edward VIII 1936 **190** | George VI 1936–52 **192**
Elizabeth II from 1952 **194**

Bibliography *198* | **Index** *199* | **Picture Credits** *208*

THE AIM OF THIS BOOK IS TO ANSWER A SERIES OF simple questions of the sort that an interested reader might want to ask about the kings and queens of Britain. Who were they? When did they rule? What was noteworthy – or not – about their reigns? What, to the extent that this can be known, were they like as individuals? At the same time, the book attempts to explain in straightforward terms the changing nature of monarchy. Why were there monarchs in the first place? How did monarchy as an institution evolve? How did today's limited, constitutional monarchy come about? It is not a specialist work; it is aimed at the general reader, although the bibliography should help readers in search of more detailed information.

The reasons for believing this a worthwhile exercise are clear-cut. First, the histories of Britain's kings and queens are interesting in themselves. Whether sordid or heroic, indolent or industrious, foolish or far-sighted, each ruler, by virtue of their office, tells us a great deal not just about themselves but about their times. The tragedy of the poor mad Henry VI in the 15th century is no less absorbing than that of the triumphs of the greatest of the Plantagenet kings, Henry II, three centuries earlier.

Second, it is impossible to understand Britain without also understanding at least the outlines of its monarchy. It is no exaggeration to claim that Britain has been defined by monarchy. The shortlived republican experiment of the Commonwealth between 1649 and 1660 aside, the monarchy as an institution has been the foundation of political life in the British Isles for over 1,500 years. Today, Elizabeth II can trace descent from Egbert, the 9th-century king of Wessex. Other than that of Denmark, no other European royal family can lay claim to anything like the same continuity.

The nature of today's monarchy may be very different from that of its medieval counterparts, its actual powers long since given up to Parliament. But it retains a key feature in common with its precursors as the ultimate guarantor of the nation's political legitimacy and stability. Republicans may take the view that the monarchy is anachronistic and a barrier to reform. Yet it is precisely the political stability of Britain that has made it one of the most dependably democratic and conspicuously free countries in the world; it is this political stability that the monarchy underpins. It is no trivial matter.

Almost inevitably, the balance of the coverage of individual rulers is canted in favour of England. This is a reflection of political reality: at least since the emergence of Anglo-Saxon Wessex in the 9th century, England, as it subsequently became, has been the dominant power in the British Isles. Wales, permanently threatened by an expansive England, whether Anglo-Saxon, Norman or Plantagenet, only briefly developed as a separate kingdom until its hold on independence was extinguished by Edward I's remorseless conquest at the end of the 13th century. Ireland, too, despite a marked cultural and religious vibrancy from as early as the 4th century, was always politically fragmented. The Norman takeover of the island after 1169 brought an effective end to Ireland's own kingships, a point rammed home in 1541 when Henry VIII imperiously proclaimed himself King of Ireland.

Even in Scotland, which could claim a continuous existence as an independent kingdom from the 9th century until its formal union with England in 1707, its kings were almost permanently in thrall to their English neighbours. That said, between the deaths of Elizabeth I in 1603 and Anne in 1714, the Stuart kings and queens of Scotland were also – albeit if only by dynastic accident – the rulers of England, the 11 years of the Commonwealth apart. Stuart rule also conveniently highlights a little-remarked fact of English and later British monarchy: that it was scarcely ever English. England as a coherent political entity may have emerged in the reign of Alfred (871–899), but it was ruled by a native Anglo-Saxon dynasty (itself originally Germanic) for less than 180 years. Even this was not continuous. Between 1016 and 1042, Cnut, a Dane, and his sons were kings of England.

Between the Norman Conquest in 1066 and the overthrow of Richard II in 1399, every king of England was clearly and unambiguously French. If it is stretching a point to claim that the Lancastrian and Yorkist kings who followed were French in the same way – time alone had made them English – their dynastic French origins are undeniable.

The following dynasty, the Tudors, who ruled for 118 years, was Welsh, while the Stuarts, who ruled England for 101 years, were Scottish. Thereafter, the Hanoverians, who came to the throne in 1714 and whose direct descendants, the Windsors, remain Britain's ruling family 288 years later, were German. In the 1,131 years since Alfred became king of England, there have been only 169 years when the monarchy has been unambiguously English.

None of this detracts from the unique influence the throne has had not just on the history of England but on that of Britain as a whole. It is a remarkable story, one whose interest only deepens on closer inspection. I hope this modest attempt to sketch its highlights will provoke some readers to look at it more closely.

THOMAS CUSSANS, *London, July 2002*

MYTHS AND ORIGINS

IN HIS *HISTORY OF THE KINGS OF BRITAIN*, COMPLETED PROBABLY IN 1139, THE WELSH CLERIC GEOFFREY OF MONMOUTH TRACED AN UNBROKEN LINE OF 76 BRITISH KINGS WHO RULED BETWEEN ABOUT 1100 BC AND THE FIRST ARRIVAL OF THE ROMANS UNDER JULIUS CAESAR IN 55 BC. ALL, ACCORDING TO GEOFFREY, WERE DESCENDED FROM A TROJAN, BRUTUS, WHO WAS THE GREAT-GRANDSON OF AENEAS AND FROM WHOM BRITAIN TOOK ITS NAME. AMONG THEM WERE LLUD, AFTER WHOM LONDON WAS NAMED, AND LEIR, THE ORIGINAL OF SHAKESPEARE'S LEAR.

Despite his claims to have based his genealogy on "a certain very ancient book", every one of these pre-Roman kings is fictitious. Geoffrey conjured them into being through an ingenious combination of recycled legend and his own invention.

Similar myths, in this case the product of the Celtic bardic oral tradition, chart the origins of Ireland's high kings. Between the reign of Slaigne the Firbolg (literally "bog man") and AD 1, Ireland was said to have been ruled by 107 high kings, 89 of them called Milesian (or "Son of Mil"). Another myth maintains that the name Scotland is derived from Scota, daughter of the Pharaoh Cingris, who married an early Irish traveller to Egypt. Moses, it is claimed, healed their infant son Goidel, who in turn gave his name to the Gaels.

Such myths are not confined to remote prehistory. Almost all the Anglo-Saxon kings of England claimed descent from the Norse god, Woden. With the coming of Christianity, their origins were often extended even further.

Alfred the Great's contemporary biographer, Bishop Asser, traced Alfred's ancestry, via Noah and Methuselah, to Adam himself.

All countries lay claim to foundation myths. In Europe, most stem from similar pagan, Hebrew, classical and later Christian sources. In most cases, however, these myths are all that is known. This is certainly so of Britain, none of whose pre-Roman rulers is documented. Though the archaeological record highlights the existence of Celtic tribal leaders, a number possibly with pretensions to kingship, individually they are lost in impenetrable obscurity.

It was only as a result of the conquest of Britain by the literate Romans that the first documentary evidence of Britain's rulers is available. Cassivellaunus, leader of the Catuvellauni, enjoys the unique status of being the first Briton whose name is known. Even so, the record is never more than partial. In addition, it is presented in exclusively Roman terms. All the names of tribes and rulers that have come down to us are known only in their Latin forms. The Celtic originals are a matter for arcane speculation at best.

With the slow disintegration of Roman Britain from the early 5th century, the documentary record disappears again. Later histories, often of shadowy, semi-mythical figures, are all that remain. This was the age of the "proud tyrant" Vortigern, who precipitated the Anglo-Saxon takeover of England by recruiting the Saxon mercenaries Hengest and Horsa in his wars against rival Britons. It was also the age of King Arthur, perhaps a local Welsh ruler, certainly not the heroic figure of later legend.

By the early 7th century, however, the picture becomes clearer. And it was then that "kingship" in the sense understood today began, fitfully, to develop. The most important influence in this was Germanic. The word "king" itself, from *cyning* or *kuning*, is of Germanic origin, imported by the Anglo-Saxons who, in the wake of Hengest and Horsa, migrated across the North Sea to the east coasts of Britain. Over the next 150 to 200 years, as they drove the native Britons into the mountainous western extremities of the country – Devon and Cornwall, Wales and southwest Scotland – dozens of Anglo-Saxon kingdoms were created.

If the broad chronology of these events can be reconstructed with some certainty, very little is known of the early rulers themselves. In some cases, only their names have survived; in others, not even that: the existence of many kings can only be inferred. The same is true even of some kingdoms. Of the presumed kingdom of the Middle Saxons (or Middlesex), so named because it lay between the South Saxons (of Sussex), the West Saxons (of Wessex) and the East Saxons (of Essex), not a single documentary source exists.

This was a world of near permanent instability, dominated by warrior aristocracies, in which the fate of kingdoms was almost entirely dependent on the often transient achievements of their rulers. As kings rose, their kingdoms rose with them; as they fell, their kingdoms fell too.

Nonetheless, a new idea was taking shape: that the right to rule depended as much on legitimacy as on pure force. Whatever their actual route to the throne, rulers increasingly sought to justify their kingship by reference to a higher right, generally an hereditary claim, however bogus, or "designation" by their predecessor.

It was a process crucially reinforced by the spread of Christianity. By encouraging literacy and promoting ideals of Roman law, the Catholic Church introduced the notion of an external authority vested in the person of the king himself. Kings came to be seen as divinely appointed, uniquely equipped to interpret God's will.

In practice, Anglo-Saxon kingship was still an uncertain and brutal business, above all in the permanently vexed matter of succession. That said, the stages by which a chaotic patchwork of competing statelets had given way by the 7th century to just a handful of much larger if still rival kingdoms was the product of – and further stimulus to – the development of a new form of government: kingship.

BRITAIN: THE ROMAN CONQUEST

CELTIC BRITAIN WAS SUCKED INTO ROME'S ORBIT WELL BEFORE ITS FORMAL CONQUEST AFTER AD 43. FROM AT LEAST 100 BC, EXISTING TRADING LINKS ACROSS THE CHANNEL WERE SUPPLEMENTED BY GROWING ECONOMIC AND POLITICAL CONTACTS WITH ROME. ALL THE EVIDENCE SUGGESTS THE PRESENCE OF AN INCREASINGLY SOPHISTICATED SOCIETY, ESPECIALLY IN SOUTHERN BRITAIN.

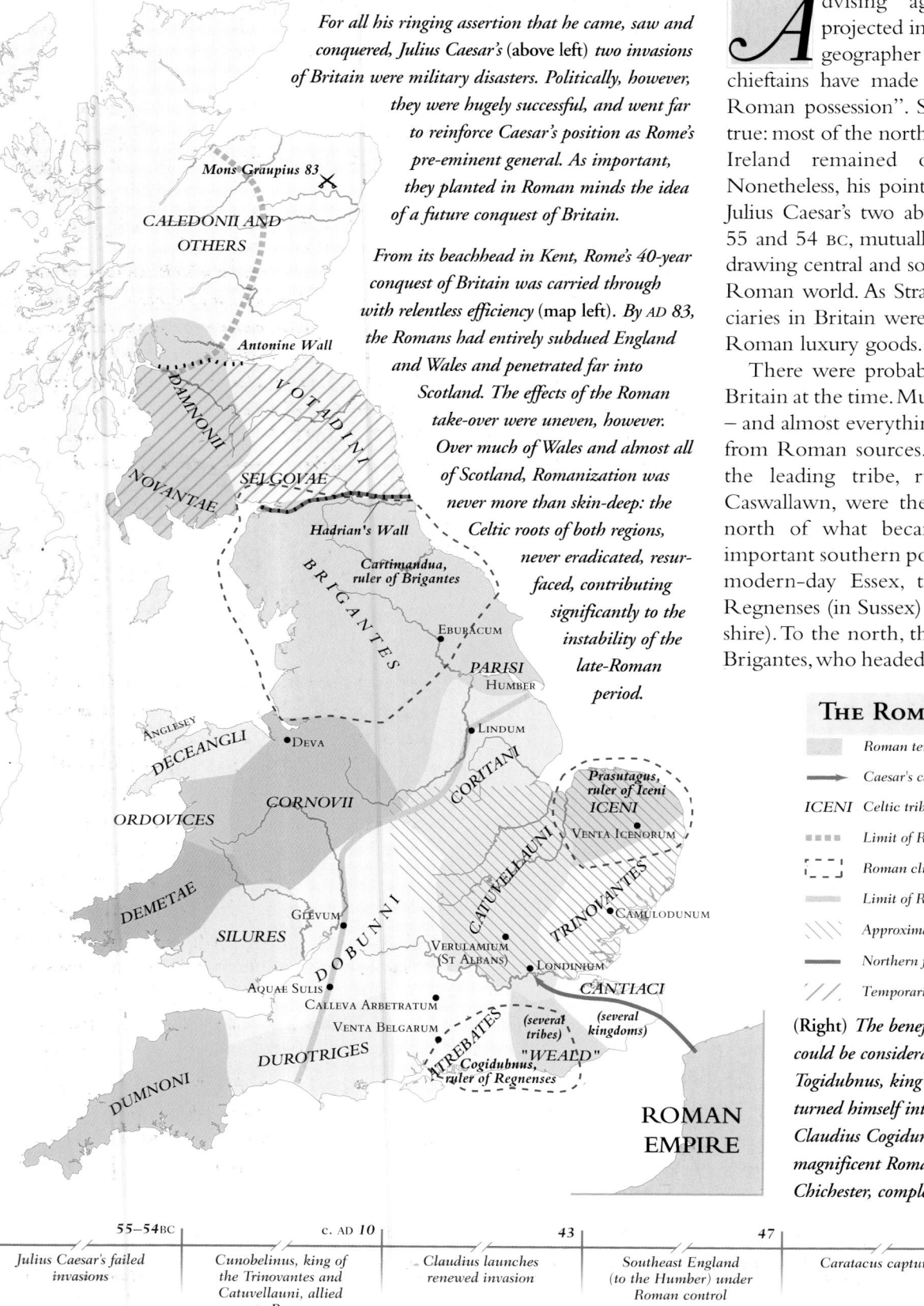

For all his ringing assertion that he came, saw and conquered, Julius Caesar's (above left) two invasions of Britain were military disasters. Politically, however, they were hugely successful, and went far to reinforce Caesar's position as Rome's pre-eminent general. As important, they planted in Roman minds the idea of a future conquest of Britain.

From its beachhead in Kent, Rome's 40-year conquest of Britain was carried through with relentless efficiency (map left). By AD 83, the Romans had entirely subdued England and Wales and penetrated far into Scotland. The effects of the Roman take-over were uneven, however. Over much of Wales and almost all of Scotland, Romanization was never more than skin-deep: the Celtic roots of both regions, never eradicated, resurfaced, contributing significantly to the instability of the late-Roman period.

Advising against Emperor Claudius's projected invasion of Britain in AD 43, the geographer Strabo pointed out that "local chieftains have made virtually the whole island a Roman possession". Strictly speaking, this was not true: most of the north and west of Britain and all of Ireland remained outside Roman influence. Nonetheless, his point was well made. Even before Julius Caesar's two abortive invasions of Britain in 55 and 54 BC, mutually lucrative trading links were drawing central and southern Britain into the wider Roman world. As Strabo implied, the chief beneficiaries in Britain were its rulers, avid consumers of Roman luxury goods.

There were probably 20 major Celtic tribes in Britain at the time. Much of what is known of them – and almost everything about their rulers – comes from Roman sources. According to Julius Caesar, the leading tribe, ruled by Cassivellaunus, or Caswallawn, were the Catuvellauni, based to the north of what became London. Among other important southern powers were the Trinovantes in modern-day Essex, the Cantiaci (in Kent), the Regnenses (in Sussex) and the Atrebates (in Hampshire). To the north, the dominant power were the Brigantes, who headed a loose confederation of sub-

THE ROMAN CONQUEST

	Roman territory by 54 BC
→	*Caesar's campaign, 54 BC*
ICENI	*Celtic tribes c. AD 43*
▪▪▪▪	*Limit of Roman conquest by AD 43*
⌐ ¬	*Roman client kingdoms in c. AD 40–50, with details*
	Limit of Roman conquest by AD 83
\\\\	*Approximate extent of Boudicca's revolt AD 60–61*
——	*Northern frontier of the Roman Empire from AD 105*
///	*Temporarily added to Roman Empire, 142–85*

(Right) *The benefits of embracing Roman rule could be considerable. Even so, few went as far as Togidubnus, king of the Regnenses, who in effect turned himself into a Roman, styling himself Tiberius Claudius Cogidumnus and building himself a magnificent Roman palace at Fishbourne outside Chichester, complete with intricate mosaic floors.*

55–54BC	c. AD 10	43	47	50	60
Julius Caesar's failed invasions	Cunobelinus, king of the Trinovantes and Catuvellauni, allied to Rome	Claudius launches renewed invasion	Southeast England (to the Humber) under Roman control	Caratacus captured	Druids on Anglesey defeated; revolt of Iceni under Boudicca

tribes. Further north still were the Caledonii, the most numerous tribe in what would become Scotland.

It was Cassivellaunus who spear-headed the resistance to Julius Caesar. But this is not to suggest that the Celts were in any sense united against the Roman invaders. They had little sense of a wider Celtic identity, and intertribal rivalry was a permanent fact of life. In fact, there is a strong probability that Caesar was invited to Britain by tribes resentful of Cassivellaunus's aggressive expansionism and who saw an alliance with Rome as the best means of reasserting their local rule. It is known for example that Caesar was accompanied on his first invasion by Commius, the king of the Atrebates,

Close on a century followed before the Romans attempted to conquer Britain again. This time, the invasion was mounted with overwhelming force, upwards of 50,000 men. Resistance was sporadic. Most rulers chose co-operation rather than confrontation, only too happy to become client-kings of Rome. The Iceni under Prasutagus, the Brigantes under Queen Cartimandua, and the Regnenses under Togidubnus, all committed themselves to Roman rule. Even the king of distant Orkney is said to have acknowledged Roman supremacy.

Those who did resist were ruthlessly pursued. Caratacus, the son of Cunobelinus (see box), was driven progressively further west until, finally defeated in AD 50, he fled north to the Brigantes where Queen Cartimandua promptly handed him over to her new allies. In AD 60 the Iceni, led by

their formidable queen, Boudicca, rose almost as one, laying waste to Colchester and St Albans before moving on London. In the ensuing battles, 70,000 – the vast majority of them Britons – are said to have been slain. The Roman response was remorseless. Boudicca and her army were utterly destroyed.

As the Romans under Julius Agricola pushed their rule north and west, the remaining resistance was gradually crushed in campaigns that took place between AD 77 and 84. They climaxed in the Highlands of Scotland at Mons Graupius, where the Caledonii were defeated. Scotland may never have been fully incorporated into the Roman Empire and Roman rule in Wales and large parts of northern England never have penetrated very deeply, but Britain had been brought definitively within the Roman world.

Among the most striking evidence for Britain's economic links with Rome in the 1st century BC was the appearance of coins. As well as highlighting the increasing economic sophistication sparked by contact with Rome, they are uniquely revealing about Celtic kings and tribes. The first British monarch to appear on a coin (above right), minted in about 10 BC, was Tasciovan, successor to Cassivellaunus as the king of the Catuvellauni. Twenty years later, his successor, Cunobelinus, produced a series of gold coins bearing not only his name but the inscription AUGUSTUS DIVUS, the "Divine Augustus" being the Emperor Augustus, with whom the Catuvellauni were clearly allied. A further 20 years later, his coins (below) were marked simply CUNOBELINUS REX or CUN CAMU (a reference to the tribe's name), equally strong evidence of a break with Rome and the assertion of his own kingship. A number of other Celtic rulers, Volisios of the Coritani and Bodvoc of the Dobunni, for example, are known only through surviving coins.

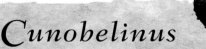

Cunobelinus

Cunobelinus, king of the Trinovantes from AD 1 and of the Catuvellauni from AD 10, both of whom he conquered by force, ranks high as one of the great mythical figures of the immediate pre-Roman age. He figures strongly in Geoffrey of Monmouth's always unreliable History of the Kings of Britain, apparently influenced in this instance by the Roman writer Suetonius, who called Cunobelinus "Rex Britannorum". This he certainly wasn't, for all that he was the most powerful ruler of his day. The Tudor author Raphael Holinshead glamorized Cunobelinus further, claiming that he was brought up in Rome, "and there made knight by Augustus Caesar, vnder whome he serued in the warres, and was in such fauour with him, that he was at libertie to pay his tribute or not…". Whatever the inaccuracies of this account, they were the stimulus for Shakespeare's play Cymbeline in which he is described as the king of Britain. Cunobelinus's sons Togodumnus and Caratacus were in the forefront of resistance to the invasion in AD 43. Caratacus was paraded in chains through Rome after his capture in AD 50, his dignity impressing the emperor so much that he was pardoned and allowed to live in Rome until his death. Togodumnus was killed in battle against the Romans, possibly in Hampshire, soon after Claudius's invasion.

68	71	77–84	85	122	142
Southwest England and central Wales under Roman control	Uprising of Brigantes under Venutius crushed	Campaigns of Julius Agricola subdue Wales, northern England and southern and eastern Scotland	Progressive evacuation of southern Scotland (to 105)	Hadrian's Wall begun	Progressive reoccupation of southern Scotland (to 163); Antonine Wall begun

THE FIRST ANGLO-SAXON KINGDOMS

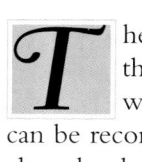

THE DEPARTURE OF THE LAST ROMAN LEGIONS IN 407 PLUNGED BRITAIN INTO CHAOS. THERE WERE RENEWED INVASIONS FROM SCOTLAND, WHILE IN ENGLAND AND WALES RESURGENT CELTIC LEADERS STRUGGLED WITH THOSE TRYING TO MAINTAIN A SEMBLANCE OF ROMAN ORDER. INTO THIS VOLATILE MIX A NEW ELEMENT WAS ADDED AS GERMANIC PEOPLES MIGRATED ACROSS THE NORTH SEA TO BRITAIN.

Gold purse lid discovered at Sutton Hoo (above). The level of craftsmanship of many of the objects discovered at Sutton Hoo transformed understanding of the Anglo-Saxon kingdoms.

The exact process by which the chaos of the immediate post-Roman period gave way to a Germanic Anglo-Saxon England can be reconstructed only tentatively. That said, it is clear that by about the mid-6th century a series of more or less stable Anglo-Saxon kingdoms were taking root across England.

The arrival of the Anglo-Saxons was just one part of the general westward migration of peoples into the former territories of the West Roman Empire. But it was also a response to the unfolding chaos in Britain itself, in which Celts fought Celts, Romano-Britons fought Romano-Britons and each fought the other. Among those struggling for supremacy was the Welshman Coel Hen, immortalized much later as "Old King Cole", who was possibly a Roman commander. Another such Roman commander-turned-warlord was Vitalinus, known variously as the Vawrtighern or Vortigern, the "Supreme Leader".

Sutton Hoo

The excavation in 1939 of a ship burial at Sutton Hoo, at the head of the river Deben, transformed understanding of Anglo-Saxon England. Not only did the burial accord closely with the description of a royal funeral in Beowulf – "Rime-crusted and ready to sail, a royal vessel with curved prow lay in harbour. They set down their dear king amidships, close by the mast" – but it revealed a treasure hoard of astonishing richness, by far the most extensive and important archaeological discovery of the period ever made. The sumptuousness of the objects makes it clear that this was the resting place of a king: among the candidates, Raedwald, king of East Anglia and listed by Bede as the fourth Bretwalda, is favourite. The magnificent armour, not least the king's helmet (right), with its bronze, silver and gold overlays, underline his warrior status. Objects such as the gold purse lid, with stone, garnet and glass inlays, display exquisite craftsmanship. Equally intriguing in what was clearly a pagan burial was the presence of two spoons, one bearing the name Paul, the other Saul. The Christian reference is clear – as is the fact that early 7th-century Anglo-Saxon England was a world straddling a pagan past and a Christian future.

449 In this year Mauricius and Valentinian obtained the kingdom and reigned seven years. In their days, Hengest and Horsa, invited by Vortigern, King of the Britons, came to Britain at a place called Ypwines fleot at first to help the Britons, but later they fought against them. They then sent to Angeln, ordered [them] to send more aid and to be told of the worthlessness of the Britons and of the excellence of the land. They then sent them more aid. These men came from three nations of Germany: from the old Saxons, from the Angles, and from the Jutes.

The Anglo-Saxon Chronicle

It was Vortigern who at some point around 430 may have recruited the Saxon mercenaries Hengest and Horsa to help repulse the Picts. Having arrived, Hengest and his followers simply stayed, establishing a kingdom in Kent. At much the same time, other Germanic settlers were arriving – the Angles on the east coast, the "South Saxons" along the Channel. They, too, began to establish their own territories, which in time became kingdoms. The net result was a gradual northward and eastward infiltration of Germanic rule into England.

The process was by no means certain or clear-cut. The Germanic settlements were piece-meal and uncoordinated, and the newcomers were

c.430	477	c.500	597	c.616	617	c.625	664
Saxon mercenaries Hengest and Horsa recruited by Vortigern	Reputed landing of Aelle, first king of Sussex, on south coast	Saxons defeated at Mount Badon	Christian mission under St Augustine, sent by Pope Gregory, lands in Kent	Northumbria united under Edwin	Conversion of Edwin to Christianity	Burial of King Raedwald at Sutton Hoo	Synod of Whitby accepts Roman authority in matters of Church doctrine

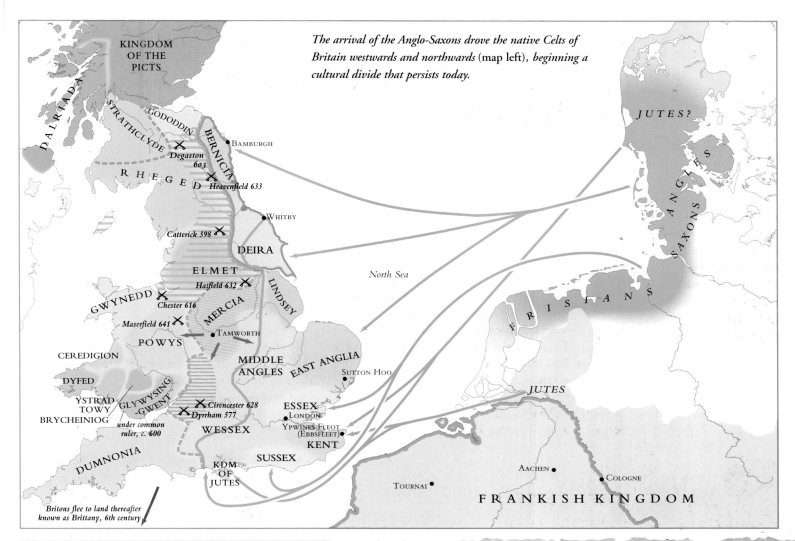

The arrival of the Anglo-Saxons drove the native Celts of Britain westwards and northwards (map left), beginning a cultural divide that persists today.

THE FIRST ANGLO-SAXON KINGDOMS, TO C.AD 600

	Roman Empire c. 450
	Approximate Anglo-Saxon homeland
→	Presumed direction of Anglo-Saxon emigration to Britain, c.5th–6th centuries
	Frankish Empire, 532
	Approximate limit of Anglo-Saxon control, late 5th century
	United as Northumbria, 604
	Approximate western limit of Anglo-Saxon control, late 6th century
	Added to Northumbria under Ethelfred and Edwin, by 632
→	Mercian expansion under Penda
	To Mercia 628: sub-kingdom of Hwicce from mid-7th century
	Approximate northern limit of expansion of Northumbria under Oswald, 642

King Arthur

Even if it is now generally accepted that Arthur was a real figure, possibly a Welsh prince who fought against the Anglo-Saxons in the late 5th and early 6th centuries, few rulers have loomed larger in popular imagination on more meagre evidence. The earliest reference to him dates from over 400 years after his presumed lifetime. The 12th-century writer Geoffrey of Monmouth was the man most responsible for launching the cult of Arthur, conflating a series of legends to produce an extraordinary story in which, having conquered the Anglo-Saxons, Arthur subdued Scotland and Gaul. "Britain," wrote Geoffrey, "had reached such a standard of sophistication that it excelled all other kingdoms in its general affluence, the richness of its decorations and the courteous behaviour of its inhabitants." Arthur then defeated the Roman emperor before having to return hurriedly to Britain to deal with the traitor Mordred. It was an improbable epic that later writers — seeing in Arthur the epitome of medieval, above all French, chivalry — embroidered even further. Sir Thomas Malory's 15th-century work, Le Morte D'Arthur, remains the best-known example.

often as hostile to each other as they were to the Britons, a rivalry that would persist well into the 9th century. Furthermore, native resistance, however sporadic, could be effective. A major reverse was suffered by the Anglo-Saxons in about 500 at the battle of Mount Badon, later claimed to have been won by the elusive if not wholly mythical figure of King Arthur (see box). Nonetheless, by the end of the 6th century, Anglo-Saxon kingdoms were established across the whole of England, Cornwall apart.

Seven kingdoms – the so-called "Heptarchy" – are traditionally identified. Three were clustered in the southeast: Sussex, Kent and Essex. To the west was Wessex. The Midlands were dominated by the kingdoms of East Anglia and Mercia, which abutted the patchwork of Celtic territories in Wales and included the sub-kingdoms of Lindsey, Hwicce and

655	from 716	731	from 756	780	787	825	829
King Penda of Mercia defeated and killed by Northumbrians under Oswy at Battle of Winwaed	Mercian supremacy under Aethelbald begins	Bede's Ecclesiastical History of England completed	Mercian supremacy extended under Offa	Offa begins the construction of his defensive barrier between Mercia and Wales	First Viking raid, on south coast	King Egbert of Wessex breaks Mercian supremacy at Battle of Ellendun	Northumbria acknowledges supremacy of Wessex

Magonsaete. To the north was Northumbria, literally the kingdom "north of the Humber", which was an amalgam of two earlier kingdoms, Bernicia and Deira.

In very general terms, the subsequent development of these kingdoms was that of the domination – under a succession of powerful rulers and through a maze of confused power-struggles – of three of these kingdoms: Northumbria and Mercia in the 7th century, Mercia by itself in the 8th century, and Wessex in the 9th. Under Edwin (d. 633), Oswald (d. 642) and Oswy (d. 670), Northumbria not only extended

IN SEARCH OF ANGLO-SAXON UNITY c.650–850

Northumbria to c.750

- *Northumbria under Oswiu, 657*
- *Annexed temporarily by Northumbria (with dates)*
- *to Northumbria, 750*

Mercia to c.800

- *Sub-kingdoms of Mercia during parts of 7–8 centuries*
- *Southern and eastern limit of direct rule by Mercia under Aethelbald, 757*
- *Mercia at the end of Offa's rule, 796*
- *Offa's dyke, completed by c.790's*

Wessex to c.850

- *Wessex, Mercian dependency 789–802; Egbert's kingdom, from 802*
- *Added to Wessex by 825*
- *northern and eastern limit of area acquired by Wessex, 829–30*

- → *Anglo-Saxon campaign, with details*
- *Revolt, with details*
- ✕ *Battles*

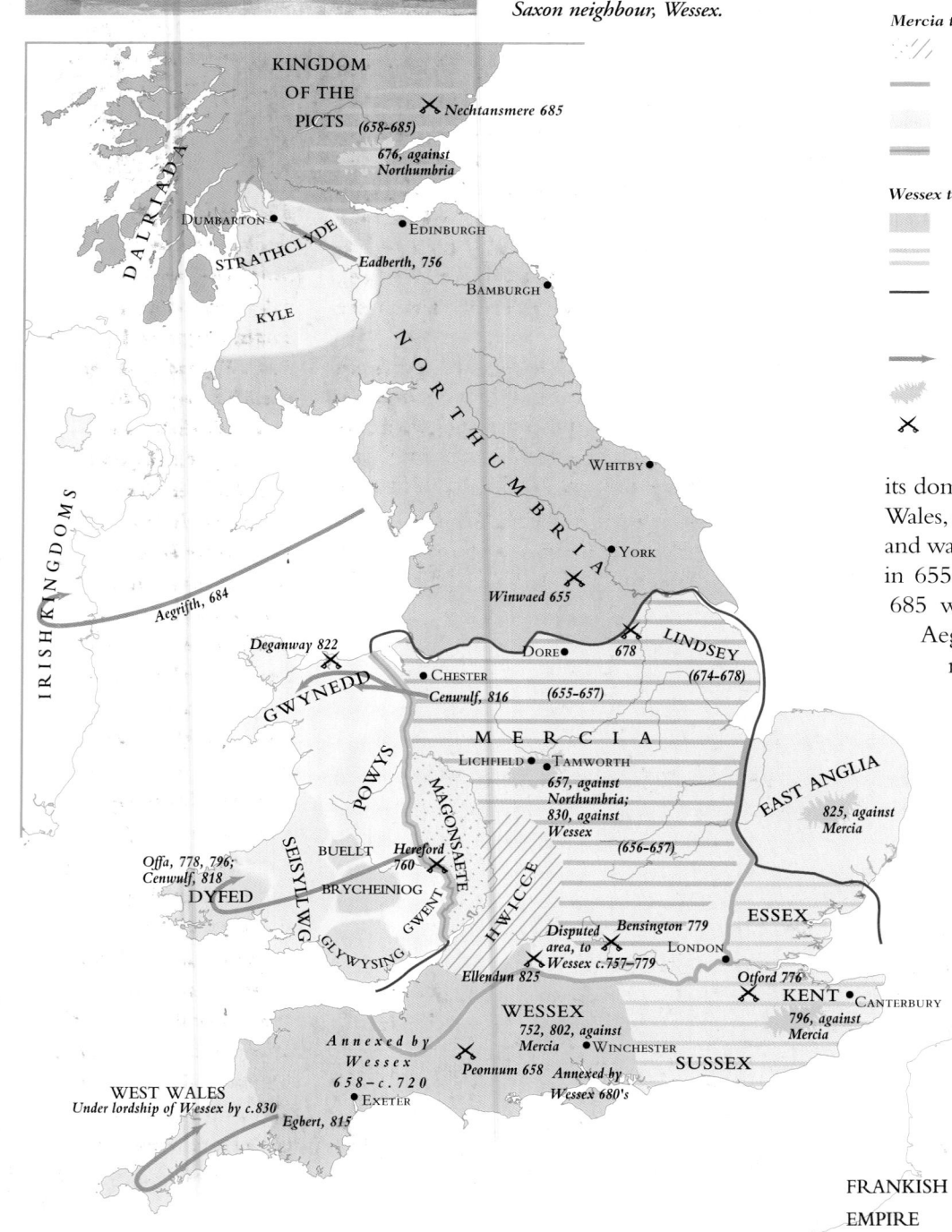

KINGDOM OF THE PICTS
(658-685)
✕ Nechtansmere 685
676, against Northumbria

DALRIADA

DUMBARTON
STRATHCLYDE
EDINBURGH
Eadberth, 756
KYLE
BAMBURGH

NORTHUMBRIA

IRISH KINGDOMS

WHITBY

YORK
✕ Winwaed 655

Aegristh, 684

Deganway 822 ✕
GWYNEDD
Cenwulf, 816
CHESTER
DORE ✕ 678
LINDSEY
(674-678)
(655-657)

POWYS
MERCIA
LICHFIELD ● TAMWORTH
657, against Northumbria; 830, against Wessex

Offa, 778, 796;
Cenwulf, 818
SEISYLLWG
BUELLT
Hereford 760 ✕
MAGONSAETE
EAST ANGLIA
825, against Mercia

DYFED
BRYCHEINIOG
GWENT
HWICCE
(656-657)
ESSEX

Disputed area, to Wessex c.757–779
Bensington 779 ✕
LONDON

Ellendun 825 ✕
Otford 776 ✕
KENT ● CANTERBURY
796, against Mercia

WESSEX
752, 802, against Mercia ● WINCHESTER
SUSSEX

Annexed by Wessex 658–c.720
✕ Peonnum 658
Annexed by Wessex 680's

WEST WALES
Under lordship of Wessex by c.830
● EXETER

Egbert, 815

FRANKISH EMPIRE

its domination deep into Scotland and westwards to Wales, it also subdued Mercia, whose first great king and warlord, Penda, was defeated and killed by Oswy in 655. Northumbrian power began to wane after 685 with the defeat and death of its then king, Aegfrith, at the hands at the Picts. Mercian power reached its apex under Offa, who from the mid-780s was effectively exercising hegemony over most of Anglo-Saxon England. From Offa's death, in 796, the supremacy of Wessex was established under Egbert, who extended West Saxon control into Cornwall before defeating the Mercians at the Battle of Ellendun in 825. Four years later, he received the submission of the Northumbrian king, Eanred.

This may still have been an unstable, often violent world, but it was one increasingly dominated by a more sophisticated ideal of kingship in which a single king ruled a single more or less well-defined territory. To the traditional role of the king as warrior chief a new notion was added: that of the king as dispenser of justice and source of a

> *We have come to the conclusion that the temples of the idols ... should on no account be destroyed. He [Augustine] is to destroy the idols, but the temples themselves are to be aspersed with holy water, altars set up, and relics enclosed in them ... In this way, we hope that people may abandon idolatry ... They are no longer to sacrifice beasts to the Devil, but they may kill them for food to the praise of God ... If the people are allowed some worldly pleasures ... they will come more readily to desire the joys of the spirit.*

Instructions from Pope Gregory the Great to Augustine on the conversion of the Anglo-Saxons

Offa's Dyke

*I*n about 780 – in an effort both to delimit the border of his kingdom with Wales and to prevent Welsh infiltration into it – King Offa of Mercia began one of the most remarkable building projects in medieval Europe. It was a dyke, or earth barrier, running the full length of Mercia's 149-mile border with Wales. It was not an entirely original idea. A hundred years earlier, King Wat (or Wade) had undertaken the construction of a similar dyke. But Offa's was to be on an altogether different scale: 11 feet high and 22 yards wide. Given the limitations of the technology available to him, it is an extraordinary achievement, for all that some northern sections were never completed. It remains a testimony not just to the energy and determination of Offa but to the organizing ability of his kingdom. Thousands of peasants were employed over many years to create the barrier. Substantial sections survive today.

body of external wisdom to which he alone, sanctioned by his royal birth and office, had access.

Consciousness of this new role is evident at least in part in the title Bretwalda, variously translated as "Power Wielder" or "Ruler of Britain". According to the 8th-century Northumbrian monk, Bede, whose *Ecclesiastical History of England* is the most complete and reliable contemporary source for Anglo-Saxon England, the first Bretwalda was Aelle, king of Sussex, at the end of the 5th century. Bede lists a further six Bretwaldas, ending with the Northumbrian, Oswy, in the 7th century.

In reality, any such claim to rule all Britain would have been at odds with the still confused condition

of the country. Nonetheless, kings such as Oswy, Offa and Egbert were slowly coming to preside over kingdoms that were increasingly better governed and prosperous and that were also capable of disposing of considerable resources. These resources were not just military might and manpower, though the building of Offa's dyke after 780 is a graphic illustration of the great extent to which such means were available to the Mercian king (see box). This was also an increasingly literate and artistically advanced society with contacts well beyond the narrow confines of Anglo-Saxon England. The Sutton Hoo treasure demonstrates levels of craftsmanship and access to precious metals and jewels that can scarcely be said to be the products of a "primitive" society. A similarly vivid amalgam of pagan and Christian forms is represented by the Lindisfarne Gospels, produced from 698 onwards at the Northumbrian monastery of Lindisfarne and incontestably among the great works of early-medieval European art.

The Lindisfarne Gospels highlight a further essential feature of Anglo-Saxon England: that it had become Christian, the result of a two-pronged missionary push southwards from Scotland by Irish missionaries, and northwards, after 597, on the initiative of Pope Gregory the Great. Though England's pagan roots would occasionally resurface, by 664 and the Synod of Whitby (called by Oswy to determine the supremacy of Roman or Irish Christian practice), Christianity was accepted by the great mass of the Anglo-Saxon population.

The Christian conquest of Britain was significant less for doctrinal reasons than because it encouraged literacy – a fundamental requirement of good government – and brought the Anglo-Saxons into contact with a wider European world that was itself rediscovering the essentials of stable government. But like the Anglo-Saxons themselves, Christianity was to be threatened by a new and terrible threat: the Vikings.

Offa was amongst the first Anglo-Saxon monarchs to mint silver coins. The lettering on this coin (above) is characteristically elegant and clear. Though otherwise obscure, the early 9th-century East Anglian king, Athelstan, seems to have been the first monarch to produce coins describing himself as REX ANG, or King of the English. (below).

The magnificent objects of the kind unearthed at Sutton Hoo were not the only manifestation of the creative energies of Anglo-Saxon England. From the late 7th century, at the remote Northumbrian monastery of Lindisfarne (founded by St Aidan, a monk from the Irish monastery at Iona in Scotland), an exceptional series of illustrated books were produced. Collectively known as the Lindisfarne Gospels, they are uniquely revealing of the profound spirituality and learning that infused these early northern outposts of the Church (left). Though many of the same swirling, spiralling motifs seen at Sutton Hoo are used, here they are unambiguously pressed into the service of the Christian Church. It is likely that the books were meant for the shrine of the mystic St Cuthbert on the even more remote island of Farne.

WALES TO 1284

THE COLLAPSE OF ROMAN RULE SPARKED A RESURGENCE OF NATIVE CELTIC KINGDOMS ACROSS BRITAIN, ABOVE ALL IN AREAS SUCH AS WALES THAT HAD BEEN ONLY LIGHTLY ROMANIZED. YET MUCH SUBSEQUENT WELSH HISTORY WAS ONE OF INTERNAL DIVISION AND OF SUBJUGATION BY ITS LARGER ENGLISH NEIGHBOUR. DESPITE A SUCCESSION OF STRONG LEADERS, BY 1284 WALES HAD FALLEN UNDER PERMANENT ENGLISH CONTROL.

The 10th-century Welsh king Hywel Dda (above) held sway over a kingdom even greater in extent than that of his 9th-century predecessor Rhodri Mawr. His rule encompassed Deheubarth, Gwynedd and Powys. He sought to impose stronger central control and in 945 codified the Welsh laws.

No less than Anglo-Saxon England, Wales between the 5th and 9th centuries saw the growth of a shifting mosaic of competing states ruled by a rapidly changing cast of kings and sub-kings, clan and tribal leaders. Though the external difficulties facing these territories were often formidable – Irish settlers, Viking raiders and, above all, the expansionist Anglo-Saxons to the east – by the 10th century four dominant kingdoms had emerged: Gwent and Deheubarth in the south, and Gwynedd and Powys in the north. Wales seemed poised to develop as a centralized, unitary state.

In the event, this apparently nascent statehood proved stillborn. Critically, the Welsh never developed the more sophisticated mechanisms of government that underpinned Anglo-Saxon and Norman England. In addition, while providing strong local identities, Welsh tribal origins worked against the formation of an overarching national identity.

The country was also handicapped by geography. There was little to distinguish the south from neighbouring England – in many places the two merged seamlessly. The mountainous north, by contrast, had always been something of a land apart, with little more in common with south Wales than with its English neighbours. Crucially, north–south communication was exceptionally difficult.

Welsh law provided a further inhibiting factor. Until its repeal in the 13th century, partible inheritance – by which a king's holdings had to be divided among all his sons – made dynastic consolidation all but impossible. It is no accident that the achievements of strong rulers were rarely sustained in the following generation.

That said, Welsh disunity and, ultimately, domination by England were never a foregone conclusion. In 633, for example, Cadwallon, the ruler of Gwynedd, aided by Penda, king of Mercia, inflicted a devastating defeat on the great Northumbrian king, Edwin. Had Cadwallon brought Northumbria into his own kingdom, he would have made himself the greatest ruler in Britain. Instead, he spent the next year laying waste to Northumbria until he was killed in further fighting with the Northumbrians.

Welsh hopes revived in the 9th century under Rhodri Mawr, "the Great", who united Gwynedd, Powys and the smaller kingdom of Seisyllwg, in the process triumphing in a series of near simultaneous campaigns against the Danes and the Anglo-Saxons. But his gains were frittered away with his death in 878.

A more lasting contribution was made in the 10th century by Hywel Dda, "the Good". By 942, his rule covered Deheubarth, Gwynedd and Powys. Hywel recognized early that Wales was best served by co-operation with the Anglo-Saxons. The price was high, however. In 918 Hywel secured peace for Wales by acknowledging Edward the Elder, king of Wessex, as his feudal master. As a result, all subsequent English monarchs would claim the overlordship of Wales, a claim they would back up with force whenever they were strong enough. Nonetheless, Hywel had understood a central truth: that England was strong because it was well governed. His own attempts to introduce more efficient government to Wales focused on a far-sighted revision of the country's myriad local laws in 945. Significantly,

The Marcher Lordships

The creation of the Marcher lordships by William the Conqueror had a profound impact on Wales. William's goal was to isolate the potentially troublesome Welsh by allocating the Anglo-Welsh border to a number of his key nobles, William Fitz Osbern, Roger Montgomery and Hugh d'Avranches, who became the earls of Hereford, Shrewsbury and Chester respectively. In turn, they were allowed to take over whatever Welsh territories they could grab and administer them in any way they saw fit. Though the Marcher lords themselves were feudal subjects of the king, their territories were not technically part of his kingdom. A series of lesser Marcher lordships were created soon afterwards. A second wave of Marcher settlement followed in the reign of William Rufus. Though unable to penetrate the mountainous north, the Normans, with the Earl of Shrewsbury to the fore, carved out huge new territories in South Wales, subjecting them to a colonial conquest that was brutal even by Norman standards. The Normans' failure to conquer northern Wales had the unintended side-effect of partitioning Wales into what became known as Marchia Walliae, the March, and Pura Wallia , "deep" or "proper" Wales.

c.440	633	c.780	844–78	918	945	1055	1063	after 1066	1093
Irish settlers expelled by Cunedda, legendary founder of Gwynedd	Northumbria laid waste by Cadwallon	Construction of Offa's Dyke begun	Hegemony of Rhodri Mawr over Wales	Hywel Dda submits to Edward the Elder	Codification of Welsh laws by Hywel Dda	Gruffydd ap Llywelyn effective sovereign of Wales	Anglo-Saxon invasion overthrows Gruffydd ap Llywelyn	Marcher Lordships established	Second wave of Marcher settlement launched

Hywel remains the only Welsh king to have issued his own coinage.

The subsequent history of independent Wales was a paradoxical mixture of internal fragmentation and English conquest – by Anglo-Saxons, Normans, Angevins and Plantagenets alike – accompanied by near simultaneous regeneration and self-assertion under a number of exceptional rulers. Ultimately, however, whatever their achievements, the kings of Wales would prove no match for the increasingly powerful rulers of medieval England.

The career of the fearsomely warlike Gruffydd ap Llywelyn is a case in point. By 1055, Gruffydd had not merely destroyed his rivals in Wales: his military grip was such that he was effectively able to oblige Edward the Confessor's England to recognize him as sole ruler of Wales. In 1057 the Anglo-Saxons duly came to terms; in turn, Gruffydd acknowledged Edward as his feudal lord. The respite was brief. A whirlwind Anglo-Saxon campaign was launched against Gruffydd in 1063 under Harold Godwine. Having destroyed Gruffydd's armies, Harold demanded that the Welsh hand over their sovereign. Rather than risk further Anglo-Saxon depredations, Gruffydd's erstwhile supporters cut off his head and sent it to Harold as a sign of their submission.

The Norman Conquest in 1066 was no less a disaster for Wales than for England. Determined to pen the Welsh into their ancestral homelands, William the Conqueror turned the Anglo-Welsh border, the "March", into a series of private principalities under the control of his most important nobles (see box). There they were free to do much as they pleased. The result was the imposition of voracious Norman rule across the eastern border of the country and all of the south.

Welsh resistance centred around Owain ap Gruffudd, king of Gwynedd (1137–70), and the long-lived Rhys ap Gruffydd (1155–97), king of

Early coins are not just a significant source of information about early British rulers, they are a certain sign of political as much as of economic stability. It remains a striking fact that, whatever the pretensions to nationhood and overlordship of a number of Welsh kings, only one, Hywel Dda in the 10th century, issued his own coins (left).

Deheubarth. Both not only reconquered substantial territories from the marcher lords but withstood major campaigns by the otherwise formidable Henry II. The resulting stalemate culminated in a rapprochement in 1163. Owain was allowed to take the title Prince of Wales at the cost of reaffirming Henry's overlordship. A further rapprochement, between Henry and Rhys, in which Henry acknowledged

Fragmented and remote, Wales never emerged as a unified state. Although strong kings such as Hywel Dda and Gruffydd ap Llywelyn did temporarily unite large parts of the country (map below), after their deaths these holdings fell away or were divided between their children. Wales was also persistently threatened by the Anglo-Saxons as well as by the Norman conquerors of Anglo-Saxon England. The means to turn its fierce local identities into an overarching state remained elusive.

WALES TO 1100

——	Frontiers of Welsh states, c. 800
▨	Possessions of Rhodri Mawr, 872
☐	Limit of area held by Hywel Dda, 942–50
▨	Possessions of Maredudd ap Owain, 999
▨	Possessions of Gruffydd ap Llywelyn, c. 1057
→	Norman campaigns, 1067–94
⟍⟍	Welsh control, 1094
▧	Core area of Welsh revolt, 1094
→	Welsh counterattack, with dates
——	Western limit of area retained by the Normans, 1100

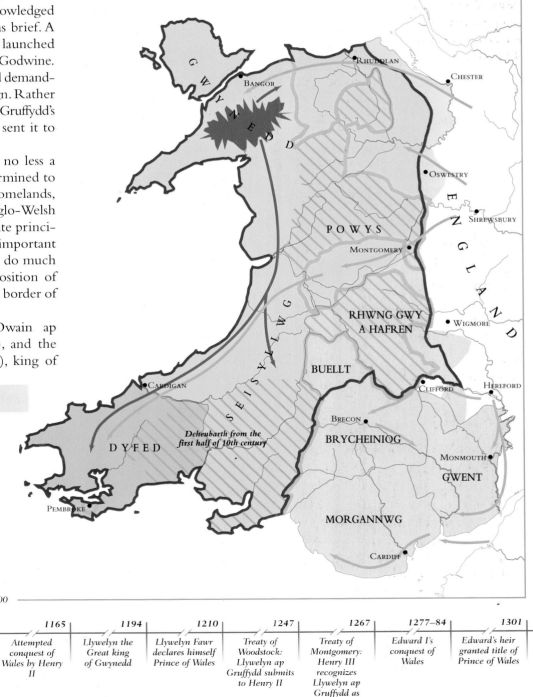

Deheubarth from the first half of 10th century

GWYNEDD · RHUDDLAN · BANGOR · CHESTER · OSWESTRY · ENGLAND · SHREWSBURY · POWYS · MONTGOMERY · WIGMORE · RHWNG GWY A HAFREN · BUELLT · CARDIGAN · CLIFFORD · HEREFORD · BRECON · BRYCHEINIOG · MONMOUTH · GWENT · SEISYLLWG · DYFED · MORGANNWG · PEMBROKE · CARDIFF

1137	1155	1163	1165	1194	1210	1247	1267	1277–84	1301
Owain ap Gruffudd King of Gwynedd	Rhys ap Gruffudd King of Deheubarth	Owain ap Gruffudd submits to Henry II and is recognized as Prince of Wales	Attempted conquest of Wales by Henry II	Llywelyn the Great king of Gwynedd	Llywelyn Fawr declares himself Prince of Wales	Treaty of Woodstock: Llywelyn ap Gruffydd submits to Henry II	Treaty of Montgomery: Henry III recognizes Llywelyn ap Gruffydd as Prince of Wales	Edward I's conquest of Wales	Edward's heir granted title of Prince of Wales

Edward I's massive military campaigns against the Welsh were followed by a programme of castle building that amounted to the largest and most expensive construction projects in Britain since the erection of Hadrian's Wall (such as Kidwelly Castle, above). In addition to their obvious military purpose, these immense structures – "the badge of our subjection" – had a crude psychological role in that they served as permanent reminders to the Welsh of their oppression.

WALES 1100–1284

—— Frontiers of Welsh states, c. 1188

░░ Gwynedd under Llywelyn the Great, c.1212

░░ Brought under control of Llywelyn the Great by 1234

→ Campaigns of Llywelyn the Great (with date)

▭ Welsh states, vassal to England under Treaty of Woodstock, 1247

➡ Campaigns of Llywelyn ap Gruffydd, 1255–57

⋯⋯ Frontier of Llywelyn ap Gruffydd's Welsh principality under Treaty of Montgomery, 1267

➡ Edward I's campaigns 1277–78

▨ Welsh states, vassal to England under Treaty of Aberconway, 1277

Wales in the 13th century, first under Llywelyn the Great, then under Llywelyn ap Gruffydd, had never seemed to be more likely to assert itself as a unified, independent state (map right). Edward I's brutal campaigns against the Welsh in 1277–8 established an English domination it has never been able to escape.

Gruffydd ap Llywelyn

Fanning the flames of inter-Welsh rivalries to ensure the country's instability was a long-standing English tactic. In 1241, for example, the Welsh king Dafydd ap Llywelyn was holding his half-brother and rival claimant to his throne, Gruffydd, prisoner. Henry III forced Dafydd to release his brother and in turn imprisoned him in the Tower of London. His aim was to make Dafydd hand over territories won during the reign of his father, Llywelyn Fawr. If he refused, Henry threatened to release Gruffydd knowing he would immediately set about the overthrow of his brother. Such was the stuff of medieval realpolitik. In the event, Henry's scheme came to nothing. Gruffydd, in trying to escape from the Tower by climbing down a knotted sheet, fell to his death (left).

> King Henry [II] gathered a mighty host ... planning to carry off or destroy all the Britons [Welsh]. And against him came Owain Gwynedd and his brother and all the host of Gwynedd, and the Lord Rhys ap Gruffudd and all Deheubarth and many others ... a few picked Welshmen who knew not how to admit defeat, manfully fought against him, and many of the bravest fell on both sides. Then ... [the king's] provisions failed and he withdrew to the plains of England. And filled with rage he blinded his hostages, two sons of Owain Gwynedd and a son of the Lord Rhys and others.

Chronicle of the Princes or Brut y Tywysogyon, 1165

Rhys as his "justiciar" in Deheubarth, took place in 1172. The net result, however, was that the minor Welsh princes and Norman Marcher lords alike felt themselves undermined. The last years of Rhys's reign saw a series of inconclusive campaigns against him by elements of his former Welsh followers and the Marcher lords, often in uneasy alliance.

A dramatic revival of Welsh pride occurred under Llywelyn Fawr, "the Great", who by 1212 had not only firmly established himself as Prince of Wales but had faced down an attempted English invasion by King John. As important, and in the face of substantial Welsh resistance, he also overturned the long-established principle of partible inheritance. In 1240 his son Dafydd inherited a united crown whose prospects had never been more promising.

Within 27 years they were more promising yet. Llywelyn's grandson, Llywelyn ap Gruffydd, having decisively rebuffed an attempt by Henry III of England to fragment his grandfather's gains, was reluctantly recognized by Henry as the country's sole ruler. It was the first time a single Welsh king had ruled a single Welsh state. It was also the last.

It was Llywelyn's misfortune to come up against the most implacable of England's medieval rulers, Edward I. His first invasion of the country, in 1277, reduced Wales to little more than a rump state centred on Gwynedd. His second, in 1282, exterminated it. Llywelyn himself was killed in a chance skirmish towards the end of the campaign. Had he survived, it would probably have made no difference. Under the 1284 Statute of Wales, the independent existence of Wales was formally ended.

In 1301 Edward I (above) appropriated the ancient Welsh title of Prince of Wales and bestowed it upon his 17-year-old son and heir, Edward, in the very un-Welsh setting of Lincoln. The gesture may have been deliberately contemptuous, but the eldest son of the monarch has taken the title ever since.

SCOTLAND TO *c.*842

LACK OF NATURAL BORDERS TO ITS SOUTH, THE ABSENCE OF ALL BUT THE MOST BASIC MECHANISMS OF CENTRAL GOVERNMENT, AND THE RIVAL AMBITIONS OF DISPARATE PEOPLES – PICTS, IRISH, BRITONS AND ANGLES – MADE THE EMERGENCE OF A UNIFIED SCOTTISH KINGDOM AN UNCERTAIN AND USUALLY VIOLENT PROCESS. BY THE 9TH CENTURY, HOWEVER, THE OUTLINES OF WHAT WOULD BECOME SCOTLAND WERE HARDENING.

Fergus Mor, traditionally the first king of Dal Riada (above), *migrated from the north of Ireland to the area around present-day Argyll around AD 498. He is said to have brought with him the Stone of Destiny upon which subsequent Scottish kings would be crowned.*

Dunadd Fort (below) *was the capital of the Irish kingdom of Dal Riada, established at the end of the 5th century around Argyll. The stone, bearing the footprint of a boar* (left) *and an ogham inscription* (right) *may have played a part in the inauguration rituals of the Dal Riadan kings.*

A t the time of the collapse of Roman Britain in the early 5th century, by far the largest group in Scotland were the Picts, who may have arrived in Scotland in the middle of the first millennium BC. Divided loosely into northern and southern Picts, the Caledonii and the Maetae respectively, their territories extended over most of the Highlands and Islands. Though later king lists and other legends clearly indicate the antiquity of Pictish rule, almost nothing is known of individual Pictish rulers before the mid-6th century.

By this point the Picts had long been engaged in a power struggle with the Irish kingdom of Dal Riada, which was beginning to be established – possibly from as early as the 4th century – in what is now Argyll (from Ar-gael or "the eastern Irish"). In time, the Irish settlers would be given another name, the Scotti, from the Latin name for the Irish. It was the ultimate success of the Dal Riadans in subsuming their much larger Pictish neighbours to form a new kingdom that would in turn give Scotland its name. Hardly surprisingly, Dal Riadan–Pictish rivalry would form a key strand of early Scottish history, one that would last into the 9th century.

From about 500 they were joined by a new group, the native Celtic Britons, who began to establish kingdoms of their own in southwest Scotland much as their counterparts were establishing Celtic kingdoms elsewhere in Britain. The two most important were Rheged, which extended southwards into Cumbria, and Gododdin, to the north.

By about 600, a fourth group had arrived, the Angles, part of the great wave of Germanic settlers who were establishing themselves across eastern and central Britain. Pushing north and west from their kingdom of Bernicia, shortly to become part of the much more powerful Northumbrian kingdom, they drove the Britons before them.

The net result of this slow coming together of rival peoples was a predictable pile-up in which all four found themselves variously allied with and against each other in a state of near permanent warfare. Though Northumbrian ambitions were severely checked by the Picts at the Battle of Nechtansmere in 685, which thereafter restricted Northumbrian rule in Scotland to Lothian, the Britons fared worse. By 700, Rheged and Gododdin had been wiped from the map. They were replaced by the much smaller kingdom of Strathclyde, the most northerly outpost of Celtic rule in Britain and consistently on the defensive.

Two further factors were significant. One was the unifying impact of Christianity, specifically the Irish or Gaelic variant. The Picts had been Christians since St Columba himself had converted their king, Brude I, in 565. However tentatively, this common religious heritage would in time provide an overarching identity, one reinforced by increasing political contracts and alliances.

The other factor was the Vikings. As their raiding increased, it was the Picts who came to bear its brunt. In 839, they suffered a crushing defeat at Forteviot. It is possible that they were betrayed by a Dal Riadan prince, Kenneth Mac Alpin, who had negotiated a secret pact with the Vikings.

Kenneth was able to exploit the Picts' disarray and, by about 842, had made himself undisputed ruler of a joint Dal Riadan–Pictish kingdom. The Britons of Strathclyde and the Angles had yet to be subdued. Similarly, the Vikings were building enduring kingdoms in the Orkneys and Hebrides. But Kenneth's kingdom, which would be called Alba, was poised to form the heart of a new, much more powerful kingdom: Scotland.

297	c.400	424–53	c.498–501	563	565
Earliest surviving (Roman) reference to the Picts, the "painted people"	St Ninian builds first known stone church in Britain, Whithorn Priory, Galloway. Earliest Pictish symbol stones	Rule of Drust Mac Erp, first known king of the Picts	Rule of Fergus Mor, legendary first king of Dal Riada	Columba's monastery at Iona established	Pictish king, Brude I, converted to Christianity by Columba

Pictish Symbol Stones

The Picts are among the most mysterious of Britain's early inhabitants. Opinions are divided as to whether they pre-date the Celts or were, at least partly, a Celtic people. But as a resolutely non-literate people whose culture and language were in any case effectively obliterated after the Dal Riadan/Scottish take-over in the 9th century, much of the little that is known is inevitably hedged around with qualifications. The so-called Symbol Stones, the most tangible evidence of the Picts, if anything only deepen the mystery. These are a series of about 200 incised stone slabs, all found in the east of Scotland and most dating from between the 4th and 7th centuries. Though it is presumed that their purpose was religious, their meaning remains almost completely obscure. Their elaborate symbols, some human, some animal, many abstract, are unlike any produced elsewhere in Britain or Ireland. A number of the later stones are clearly Christian, though these, too, also use some of the same elaborate abstract forms of earlier stones.

Map

Orkney Islands

580–81

CAITHNESS

WESTERN ISLES

KINGDOM OF THE PICTS

CIRCINN

Nechtansmere 685

• Dunkeld

741

FORTRIU

Scone •

Forteviot 839

IONA •

676; Southern Picts' rebellion defeated by Angles despite assistance by Northern Picts

DALRIADA

MAEATAE

DUNADD •

756

744

• DUMBARTON

GODODDIN

Approximate western limit of Bernicia c.550

TARBERT •

STRATHCLYDE

Degastan 603

NORTHUMBRIA

DUNAVERTY •

RHEGED

• DUNSEVERICK

IRISH KINGDOMS

582–3

Isle of Man

THE FORMATION OF SCOTLAND TO c.842

- Core Dal Riada, from 5th century; lost 640
- Added from late 5th century
- Known campaigns of Aidan (574–608)
- Approximate extent of British kingdoms c. 615
- Approximate extent of Northumbria c. 632
- Approximate extent of Northumbrian expansion under Oswald, 642
- Occupied by Northumbria, 658–85
- Unified under Brude III (672–93)
- Attacks by Oengus macFergus, with date
- Controlled by Oengus macFergus (729–61); finally united by Mac Alpin, c.842
- To Northumbria, 750 (approximately)
- Early Viking incursions around 800

The emergence of the core of the Scottish kingdom under Kenneth Mac Alpin after 840 (map above) *was made in the face of rival Anglo-Saxon, Pictish, British and Irish Dal Riadan ambitions, all of them also subject to Viking deprivations. Even after 842, Scottish control was more apparent then real, however, largely concentrated in the Pictish heartlands around Fortriu.*

603	685	c.700	795	839	c.842
Dal Riadans under Aidan routed by Northumbrians under Athelfrith at Degastan in Borders	Northumbrian expansion into Pictland halted at Nechtansmere	Effective disappearance of British kingdoms of Rheged and Gododdin	Earliest Viking raids on Scotland	Picts crushed by Vikings at the Picts' capital, Forteviot	Dal Riada and Pictland united under Kenneth Mac Alpin

SCOTLAND *c.*842–1034

THE DESCENDANTS OF KENNETH MAC ALPIN RULED SCOTLAND FOR 176 YEARS IN AN UNBROKEN LINE OF SUCCESSION. BUT THOUGH THEY SUCCESSFULLY OVERCAME MOST PICTISH RESISTANCE, THEIR RULE WAS THREATENED BY VIKINGS, BRITONS AND ANGLES, AS WELL AS BY PERMANENT DYNASTIC FEUDING. NONETHELESS, BY 1034 THEIR KINGDOM COVERED MUCH OF PRESENT-DAY SCOTLAND.

Sarcophagus of Constatine II (below right). Constantine's more than 40-year rule (900–43) saw some of the most decisive moments in the consolidation of the newly formed Scottish kingdom. Squeezed by aggressive Viking and Anglo-Saxon assaults – and variously allied with and against both – and despite a series of defeats, notably at the hands of the Anglo-Saxons at Brunanburh in 937, Constantine managed not just to preserve the core of his kingdom but to further the Scottish claim to Strathclyde.

Kenneth Mac Alpin's kingdom of Alba – Pictavia in Gaelic – contained the kernel of a nascent Scottish state but not much more. Northumbria still held sway over Lothian; the British kingdom of Strathclyde, though shrinking, remained a threat; and the Picts, especially those in the distant north, the "men of Moray", were far from reconciled to Kenneth's takeover of the joint Scottish-Pictish throne. There was also the danger posed by the Vikings, whose kingdoms in the Western Isles, Orkney and Shetland as well as on the mainland in Caithness and Sutherland were all taking firmer shape in the 9th century. The Viking presence in Ireland was hardly less of a threat.

Scottish rule also took place against a background of persistent dynastic instability. This was the result not just of the endemic political turmoil of the period but of a curious succession arrangement whereby the crown alternated between the sons of Kenneth's own sons, Constantine I (863–7) and Aed (877–8).

Against this unpromising background, the 8th

The Stone *of* Destiny

*A*s a mark of his overlordship of the Picts, Kenneth Mac Alpin was crowned in 843 at Scone, in the east of Scotland, long a royal Pictish site. Significantly, he had transported there the so-called Stone of Destiny, ever since known as the Stone of Scone. It was a key symbol of Celtic and Irish sovereignty, said to have been brought to Ireland from the Holy Land, via Egypt and Spain, long before the birth of Christ. Until Fergus, traditional founder of Dal Riada, reportedly brought it with him to Scotland in about 500, it had been at Tara where all the high kings of Ireland are claimed to have been crowned on it. Nonetheless, from the time of Kenneth onwards, the Stone of Destiny became as fundamental a mark of Scottish kingship as it had once been of Irish kingship. Every Scottish monarch, up to and including John Balliol in 1292, was crowned on the Stone. Until 1120, the ceremony took place in the open air, thereafter, it was held in Scone Abbey. After his conquest of Scotland, and as a mark of Scottish subjection, Edward I of England removed the Stone and installed it in Westminster Abbey, placing it under what became in effect the first throne of England's monarchs (picture right). Every subsequent ruler of England (and later of Britain) has since been crowned on the same throne over the Stone of Scone. Despite the absence of the Stone, Scottish rulers continued to be crowned at Scone until James II in 1434 when the ceremony was moved to Hollyrood in Edinburgh. Symbolically, in 1651, Charles II, excluded from his throne in England during the Commonwealth, was nonetheless crowned in Scotland at Scone. In 1996 the Stone was returned to Scotland.

Other than in the far north and west, effective Scottish rule had been more or less successfully established by 1034 (map below). Yet conflict with the Anglo-Saxons to the south, which would continue well into the 16th century, as well as the presence of well-established Norse settlements to the west inevitably limited the actual political control of Scotland's rulers.

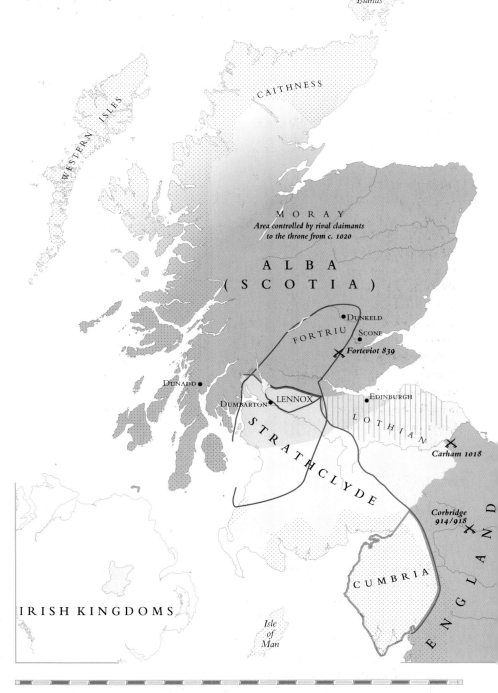

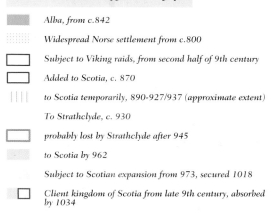

SCOTLAND 849 – 1034

- Alba, from c.842
- Widespread Norse settlement from c.800
- Subject to Viking raids, from second half of 9th century
- Added to Scotia, c. 870
- to Scotia temporarily, 890-927/937 (approximate extent)
- To Strathclyde, c. 930
- probably lost by Strathclyde after 945
- to Scotia by 962
- Subject to Scotian expansion from 973, secured 1018
- Client kingdom of Scotia from late 9th century, absorbed by 1034

and 9th centuries nonetheless saw a gradual but significant consolidation of Scotland's power and, with it, the power of her rulers. The major feature was the almost complete elimination of the Picts other than in the far north. In part, this was as much a linguistic and cultural process as a political one. The supplanting of the Pictish language by Gaelic and, later, English inevitably signalled a slow end to Pictish cultural life. But at the same time there is no question that it was principally military conquest, made possible by a kaleidoscopic series of shifting alliances and enmities – with Vikings, Britons and Anglo-Saxons alike – that ensured the elimination of most of Scotland's rivals.

It was far from a straightforward business. The Scots suffered major defeats at the hands of the Vikings in 866 and again in 871. They were to be further rebuffed by the Vikings in 914 and 918. In the same year, King Constantine II was forced to "submit" to the king of a resurgent Wessex, Edward the Elder, beginning the English claim to overlordship of Scotland. The English claim was pressed again in 934 when Athelstan mounted a punitive expedition against the Scots. The long-running Anglo–Scots rivalry had been decisively begun. Salt was rubbed in Scottish wounds in 973 when Kenneth II was obliged to promise his fealty to a new English king, Edgar.

Nonetheless, Scotland's burgeoning strength was confirmed in 899 under Donald II when Strathclyde, which included much of present-day Cumbria, became in effect a dependency of the Scottish kings. By 1018, much the same mix of conquest and coercion had been exploited by Malcolm II to confirm Scottish control over the former Northumbrian territory of Lothian. However, Malcolm's attempts to extend Scottish rule further south into Northumbria in 1031 and 1032 were firmly halted by Cnut, Danish ruler of England. Cnut not only obliged Malcolm to submit to him but definitively established English rule in Northumbria. In the process, Cumbria aside,

937 In this year King Athelstan, Lord of Nobles, dispenser of treasure to men, and his brother also, Edmund Aetheling, won by the sword's edge undying glory in the battle around Brunanburh … There lay many a man destroyed by the spears, many a Northern warrior shot over his shield and likewise many a Scot lay weary, sated with battle.

The Anglo-Saxon Chronicle

the Anglo-Scottish border was permanently fixed.

The territorial core of Scotland may have been established but, dying in 1034 with no agreed heir, Malcolm had left a kingdom that was to be plunged into a round of dynastic turmoil.

934	937	945	973	1018	1031–2	1034
Athelstan of Wessex leads punitive raid against Scotland	Combined Irish, Celtic, Viking and Scottish army defeated by Wessex at Battle of Brunanburh	Scotland's right to Cumbria recognized by Edmund of Wessex	Kenneth II swears fealty to Edgar of Wessex; Scotland's right to Lothian recognized	Lothian annexed by Scotland	Scottish expansion into Northumbria by Malcolm II halted by Cnut	Death of Malcolm II

IRELAND TO 1183

IRELAND, NEVER PART OF THE ROMAN EMPIRE, ESCAPED THE CATASTROPHIC CONSEQUENCES THAT OVERTOOK BRITAIN WITH THE EBBING OF ROMAN RULE AFTER 410. BUT THOUGH THE COUNTRY HAD AN ENDURING TRADITION OF CELTIC KINGSHIP, IT NEVER COALESCED INTO A CENTRALIZED STATE. FROM THE 9TH CENTURY, IT FELL VICTIM TO VIKING INVADERS; IN THE 12TH, TO NORMAN CONQUERORS.

Dermot MacMurrough (above), defeated by Rory O'Connor for the High Kingship of Ireland, in 1169 turned to Henry II of England for assistance. The consequences were dramatic, if unintended by Dermot. The Normans, under the earl of Pembroke, came as conquerors, not allies, and in 1177 Prince John of England was proclaimed Lord of Ireland.

By the end of the 5th century, Ireland was the most stable territory in the British Isles. If the origins of Irish kingship can never be properly disentangled from the myths surrounding them, it is clear that by the time of the partly legendary high king Niall Noígiallachi (Niall of the Nine Hostages) in the late 4th century its broad outlines were established. Dominating it, and eulogized in Celtic bardic traditions, was the notion of the high king himself, whose traditional seat was at Tara.

In reality, early medieval Ireland was divided into as many as 150 tribal kingdoms, which by the 6th and 7th centuries were gradually hardening into five centres of power, all variously claiming over-lordship: Ulster, Connaught, Meath, Leinster and Munster. Of these, the rulers of Ulster, the Uí Néills, who claimed the hereditary title of kings of Tara, were consistently the most dominant, howev-er unlikely they may have been to have exercised overlordship in practice.

However politically fragmented, Celtic Ireland was still a fundamentally dynamic entity whose hori-zons were by no means restricted to its home island. From the 5th century to as late as the 10th, there were significant Irish kingdoms in many parts of western Britain – for example, in Cornwall, in Wales and, most enduringly, in Scotland. Far from hem-ming in the Irish, the Irish Sea was the highway that led to the creation of a wider Irish world.

It was this maritime world that the Vikings, first recorded in Ireland from the 790s, sought to exploit. Norse raiders may have founded what would become Ireland's first towns – Dublin, Waterford, Wexford and Cork among others. Similarly, Turgeis, the Norse founder of Dublin in 841, may have styled himself "King of Dublin". Nonetheless, unlike the more settled Danes in eastern England, the Norsemen in Ireland were at least as concerned to construct a trading empire across the Irish Sea as they were to establish a permanent land-based kingdom.

As the Normans would later discover, the grow-ing political instability created by Ireland's feuding kings in any case made effective control impossible. In a familiar pattern of alliance and counter-alliance,

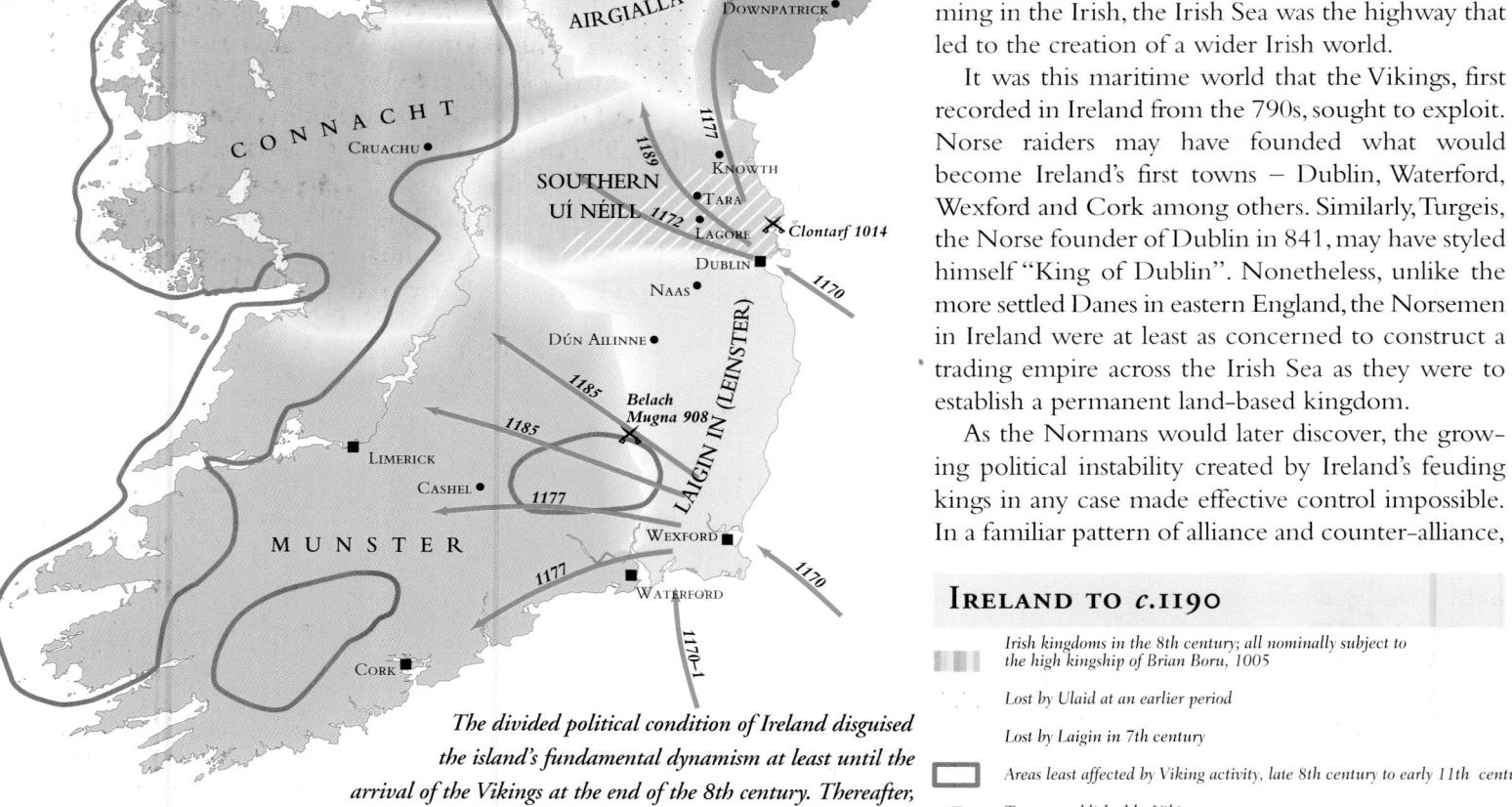

The divided political condition of Ireland disguised the island's fundamental dynamism at least until the arrival of the Vikings at the end of the 8th century. Thereafter, Ireland fell victim not just to internal political divisions but to the growing numbers of Viking settlers (map above). Whatever existence it may still have claimed as an independent state was ended after 1170 with the arrival of the Norman invaders sanctioned by Henry II of England.

IRELAND TO *c.*1190

Irish kingdoms in the 8th century; all nominally subject to the high kingship of Brian Boru, 1005

Lost by Ulaid at an earlier period

Lost by Laigin in 7th century

Areas least affected by Viking activity, late 8th century to early 11th century

■ Towns established by Vikings

→ Norman attack

✕ Battle

c.400	435	795	841	866–73	902	908
Niall Noígiallachi, legendary first high king, leads raids against Britain	St Patrick's Irish mission begun	Earliest Viking raids on Ireland	Foundation of Dublin (the "Black Pool") by Vikings	Rule of Ivar the Boneless: presides over joint Irish-Jorvik kingdom; Ireland becomes major Viking slaving centre	High King Flann Sinna forces Vikings out of Dublin (return 917)	Battle of Belach Mugna: kings of Cashel destroyed by Flann Sinna

Ireland and the Church

From perhaps even as early as the end of the 4th century – certainly from significantly before St Patrick's first mission in 435 – Ireland had benefited from the activities of a series of inspired Christian missionaries, of whom St Patrick is merely the best known. Fusing Celtic lore with Christian teaching, they sparked a distinctive and rich tradition of learning and piety that, in time, a new generation would carry to Scotland and northern England.

It was in Ireland's early monasteries that the country's Celtic mythology, until then an oral tradition only, was first written down, a process that went hand in hand with an explosion of literature: poetry, history, law codes and bible studies that embraced classical, Christian and Celtic sources in equal measure. The dominant figure after Patrick was the ascetic and mystical St Columba (c.521–97), almost certainly a member of the Uí Néill. It was Columba who in the mid-6th century spearheaded the missionary drive into Scotland that resulted in the conversion of the Picts and, famously, in the foundation of the monastery at Iona in 563, which became not just a powerhouse of learning but a depository of astonishingly rich artefacts. The cross of St Martin at the monastery (left) dates from the 8th century. Equally intrepid was St Columbanus (c.543–615), who founded a series of monasteries in France and Switzerland. Despite its isolation on the fringes of the European world, Ireland played a crucial role in the early medieval European rediscovery of Christianity and scholarship.

---

the Norse were sucked into Ireland's turbulent power-struggles. In 902, Flann Sinna, high king from 879, even managed briefly to force them from Dublin altogether.

Whatever their maritime domination, the Norse hold on Ireland became increasingly precarious throughout the 10th century. The sacking of Dublin in 999 by Brian Boru, king of Munster, high king of Ireland (from 1002), and self-proclaimed "Emperor of the Irish" from 1005, was followed by his decisive victory over a combined Norse–Leinster army at Clontarf in 1014. The Norse kingdom of Dublin limped on until 1170, but the Viking role was increasingly peripheral.

Clontarf was important for other reasons as well. His army may have triumphed but Brian himself was killed in the battle. The consequence was a power vacuum that destabilized Ireland well into the 12th century when, in 1169, Dermot MacMurrough, overthrown by his rival, Rory O'Connor, high king from 1166 to 1183, sought help from the Plantagenet king of England, Henry II.

By 1170 a substantial Norman force, led by the earl of Pembroke, had arrived. It rapidly became clear that Pembroke saw in his role chiefly an opportunity for conquest in his own right. With the enforced submission of Rory to Henry II in 1175, independent Ireland had effectively come to an end and, with it, the high kingship.

> *The power of the Irish over the Britons was great, and they had divided Britain between them into estates ... and the Irish lived as much east of the sea as they did [to the west], and their dwellings and royal fortresses were made there. Hence is Dirid Tradui ... that is, the triple rampart of Crimthann, King of Ireland and Britain as far as the ... Channel. From this division originated the fort of the sons of Liathan in the lands of the Britons of Cornwall ... and they were in that control for a long time, even after the coming of St Patrick*
>
> The Glossary of Cormac of Cashel, c.900

The Shrine of the Cathach (left), is one of six early Irish book shrines containing the manuscript of the Gospels known as the "Cathach" or "Battler". The original manuscript was written c.550 and was said to have been copied by St Columba before he left Ireland for Iona in 563.

965	999	1002	1014	1170	1175	1177	1183
Viking Limerick sacked by king of Cashel	Dublin sacked by Brian Boru, king of Cashel	Brian Boru high king of Ireland	Norse–Leinster army defeated by Brian at Clontarf; potential Irish unity shattered	First Norman invaders arrive in Ireland, invited by Dermot MacMurrough, deposed king of Leinster	Treaty of Windsor: Rory O'Connor submits to Henry II	Prince John of England proclaimed Lord of Ireland	Abdication of last high king, Rory O'Connor

PRE-CONQUEST ENGLAND 871–1066

ALFRED THE GREAT 871–99

EDWARD THE ELDER 899–924

AELFWEARD 924

ATHELSTAN 924–39

EDMUND I 939–46

EDRED 946–55

EADWIG 955–59

EDGAR 959–75

EDWARD THE MARTYR 975–78

AETHELRED II 978–1016

CNUT 1016–35

HAROLD I 1037–40

HARTHACNUT 1040–42

EDWARD THE CONFESSOR 1042–66

HAROLD II 1066

THE FIRST RECORDED VIKING RAIDS AGAINST ENGLAND, A COUNTRY WHICH BARELY EXISTED, OCCURRED IN 787. HOWEVER FIRMLY ESTABLISHED AS A WHOLE, THE PATCHWORK OF CHRISTIAN ANGLO-SAXON STATES THAT DOMINATED THE COUNTRY WERE STILL VYING WITH ONE ANOTHER FOR SUPREMACY. IN ADDITION, THEIR KINGS, WHATEVER THE RELATIVELY MORE SOPHISTICATED MECHANISMS OF GOVERNMENT THEY WERE AMASSING, STILL LOOKED BACK AT LEAST AS MUCH TO THE GERMANIC TRADITION OF KING AS WARRIOR-LEADER AND RING-GIVER AS FORWARD TO THE LATER MEDIEVAL IMAGE OF KING AS DIVINELY SANCTIONED AND IMPARTIAL FOUNT OF JUSTICE PRESIDING OVER A CLEAR-CUT NATIONAL POLITY.

Yet within about 100 years, England and a self-consciously English people had evolved. The first actively English king was ruling an actively English people.

The key figure in this transformation was the late 9th-century king of Wessex, Alfred, who withstood and then reversed the Danish assault that had seemed likely to destroy Anglo-Saxon England.

Alfred's achievements were clear and remarkable – not just in resisting the Vikings but in then creating a self-sufficient kingdom distinguished by just administration and an apparently clear sense of its own Anglo-Saxon English destiny, the whole backed by an unprecedented surge in learning and literature. The achievements of his successors over the next 75 years – Edward, Athelstan, Edred and Edgar pre-eminently – were equally striking. Not merely were the previously warring Anglo-Saxon kingdoms united under one obviously English rule, but the Danish threat, if not entirely banished, was at least contained. The creation of an English nation, whatever its Germanic origins, had become a fact.

This "golden age" of Anglo-Saxon rule remains alluring. It is easy to understand why 19th-century historians had little difficulty in identifying in it not just the "real" England but the seeds of what they saw as England's future greatness.

But in reality, even at its height Anglo-Saxon England was no less fragile than any other early medieval European kingdom. The mechanisms of its government may have been more sophisticated and more firmly embedded than most, but its kings and thus its underlying stability were always vulnerable.

Paradoxically, the strength of early medieval kingship was also a major source of its weakness. That the king occupied a uniquely powerful position inevitably meant that any kingdom was only as strong and as stable as the king himself. If this provided enormous scope for strong rulers to create or consolidate strong kingdoms, it provided just as much scope for ineffective rulers to undermine even the strongest kingdoms.

At the same time, the institution of kingship itself was compromised by the lack of agreed rules of succession. If a more or less plausible hereditary claim to rule was essential, the legitimacy of a successor was at least as dependent on his having been "designated" by the existing king as on his having an hereditary right. It was also no less important that the new king should enjoy the support of the country's leading subjects in the assembly known as the Witan ("wise men"), who at least in theory "elected" the new king; in practice this meant no more than acknowledging

his right to rule after the fact of his succession. (It was only in 1216, with the death of King John, that primogeniture – the right of the eldest male heir to succeed – was generally accepted as the determining factor in the succession.)

This vagueness almost invariably ensured that disputed successions, with force of arms the ultimate deciding factor, were the norm not the exception. Even in the immediate aftermath of Alfred's reign, when Wessex and its kings had never been more apparently secure, the succession was never a foregone conclusion.

In the first half of the 11th century, England was dominated by these inherent instabilities. They would come to a head with the Norman Conquest in 1066, when the England created by Alfred and his heirs was effectively exterminated.

Between about 990 and 1016, the nightmare of total Danish conquest so well resisted by Alfred had returned, this time in redoubled strength. Aethelred II, well intentioned but weak, presided over a country that was the focus of overwhelming Danish attacks. He was able neither to defeat the Danes nor to bribe them to leave, and his kingdom sank into what in the end felt like inevitable capitulation. In 1016, with the accession of a Danish king, Cnut, England seemed to have been drawn definitively within the Scandinavian orbit. The Anglo-Saxon dream of a sturdily independent England had apparently died for good.

In fact, the Danish supremacy would prove short-lived. The accession of Edward the Confessor in 1045 seemingly signalled a return to Anglo-Saxon stability and native good government. In reality, this led to a characteristically confused succession, which opened the way for a further conquest of England by a further group of Northmen, the Normans.

If Anglo-Saxon England can be said to have been the best-governed kingdom in early medieval Europe, its sudden and total overthrow in 1066 is the clearest example not just of the inherent political turbulence of the period but of the obvious limitations of early medieval kingship. Strong kings could create strong kingdoms but they could never guarantee their subsequent survival. It is a theme that one way or the other would dominate English kingship at least until the 16th century.

VIKING INVASION AND SETTLEMENT

THE VIKING INVASIONS AND SUBSEQUENT SETTLEMENT OF THE BRITISH ISLES FROM THE END OF THE 8TH CENTURY WERE JUST ONE PART OF A LARGER, FEARSOME EXODUS OF SCANDINAVIAN WARRIORS AND CONQUERORS — EAST ACROSS THE BALTIC AND EVENTUALLY TO THE BLACK SEA, AND SOUTH ALONG THE COASTS OF WESTERN EUROPE AND FROM THERE TO THE MEDITERRANEAN.

That even a conqueror as violent as Eric Bloodaxe – twice the ruler of Jorvik (947–8 and 952–4) – understood the need for orderly government is clear from his issue of coins. This example (right) is from his second reign. His aspiration to legitimacy is underlined by his designation of himself as "Rex", while the reality of his rule is illustrated in his symbol of an unsheathed sword.

Norse ships proved astonishingly seaworthy. They were manoeuvrable, fast and tough. The largest could hold up to 200 men. One would have been terrifying; collectively, their capacity to strike terror would have been overwhelming. In 850, The Anglo-Saxon Chronicle claims a fleet of 350 ships landed in Kent. The one that brought the "Great Army" in 865 was reportedly even larger. This illustration (below) is from a 10th-century Anglo-Saxon manuscript.

THE IMPACT OF THE VIKINGS ON BRITAIN was sudden and terrible. Impelled by overcrowding in their Scandinavian homelands, the Vikings exploited to the full the ocean-going abilities of their ships, and by the end of the 9th century, Viking raids were becoming a brutal fact of life in Britain. They came in two main waves. Raiders from Norway – "Viking" meant simply "pirate" or "raider" – made their way via the Shetlands, the Orkneys and the Hebrides south to the Irish Sea. Those from Denmark generally attacked the east and south coasts of England.

Their early goals were plunder, their favoured targets the rich undefended monasteries of the Western Isles and northeast England. Lindisfarne was the first to be sacked, in 793. It was followed by Jarrow in 794 and Monkwearmouth and Iona in 795. (Iona was attacked again in 802, 806, 807 and 825.) For the pagan Vikings, these repositories of treasure were irresistible. For Christian Anglo-Saxons, such desecration and slaughter could only have been a punishment from God. Alcuin, the Northumbrian-born scholar at Charlemagne's Frankish court, lamented after the sacking of Lindisfarne: "Behold the church of St Cuthbert, spattered with the blood of the priests of God." Where there were no such obvious targets to pillage, the Vikings extorted or simply stole money and slaves.

From about the 830s, as their fleets became larger, Viking goals began to change from outright looting to settlement. As early as about 800, the kernel of what would become the Norse earldom of Orkney had been established. Dublin was first settled by Norwegian Vikings in 841. Then, from about 850, Danish Vikings took to overwintering in Kent.

793 Here terrible portents came about over the land of Northumbria, and miserably frightened the people: there were immense flashes of lightning, and fiery dragons were seen flying in the air. A great famine immediately followed these signs: and a little after that … the raiding of the heathen men miserably devastated God's church in Lindisfarne by looting and slaughter.

The Anglo-Saxon Chronicle

The climax came in 865 when a Danish "Great Army" invaded England. In less than four years, almost the whole of Anglo-Saxon England had capitulated, Wessex aside. Viking-occupied England, the Danelaw, became an established fact.

Thereafter, Viking rule in England was dominated by two contrasting developments. One was its gradual overthrow by Wessex, which ended with the death of Eric Bloodaxe, the last Viking king of York (Jorvik), in 954. The other was a parallel confused power-struggle between Danish and Irish-based Norwegian Vikings for control of Jorvik itself, which variously sucked in the Celts of Strathclyde, the Scots and the English in a shifting series of alliances and counter-alliances, as each sought to exploit weaknesses in the other.

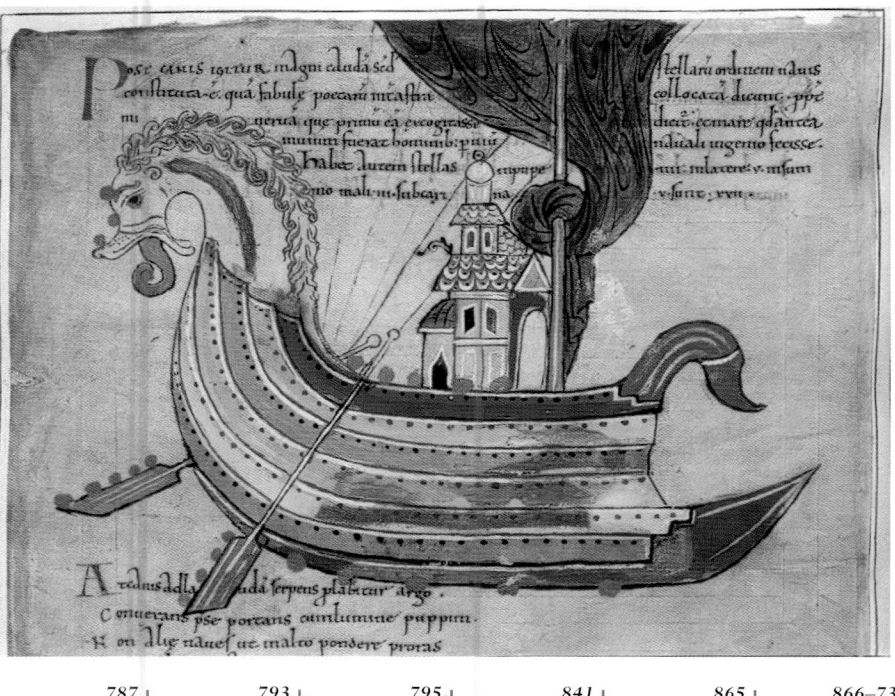

787	793	795	841	865	866–73	c.874	878	892	902
First recorded Viking raid on England (Portland)	Lindisfarne sacked	Earliest Viking raids on Ireland and Scotland	Foundation of Dublin (the "Black Pool") by Vikings	Invasion of East Anglia by Danish "Great Army"; conquers Northumbria (867), East Anglia (869) and Mercia (875)	Rule of Ivar the Boneless: presides over joint Irish–Jorvik kingdom; Ireland becomes major Viking slaving centre	Viking earldom of Orkney established	Danes under Guthrum defeated by King Alfred at Edington	Wessex resists renewed Danish invasions (to 897)	High King Flann Sinna forces Vikings out of Dublin (return 917)

THE VIKINGS OF THE BRITISH ISLES

- → Viking attacks before the arrival of the Danish Great Army, 865
- → Campaigns of the Great Army to 870
- → Campaigns of the Great Army, 870–3
- → Campaigns of Halfdan's section of the Great Army, 874–76
- Northumbria, Danish dependency, 867–72; Independent to 876, when southern part settled by Danes
- Mercia, Danish dependency, 873–79; Eastern part settled by Danes 877, under agreement of 874
- Guthrum's kingdom under treaty with Alfred, 879/886; settled by Danes, 879
- Occupied by Danes later in contravention of treaty
- Danish Mercia or Five Boroughs, subsequent to agreement with Alfred
- Under Anglo-Saxon control by c. 900
- Dependencies of Alfred and his successors
- Viking Kingdom of Dublin c. 920–80
- Viking states, at times loosely connected with Dublin
- Other areas of Norse settlement by mid-10th century
- Olaf Gothfrithson's kingdom, 941
- Frontiers, c. 900
- ✕ Battles

Almost no part of the British Isles escaped the Vikings (map left). Once early raiding had given way to long-term settlement, their major centres were along the west coast of Scotland, the east and south coasts of Scotland, Jorvik (York), capital of a maritime trading empire centred on the Isle of Man, the East Midlands of England, the so-called Five Boroughs.

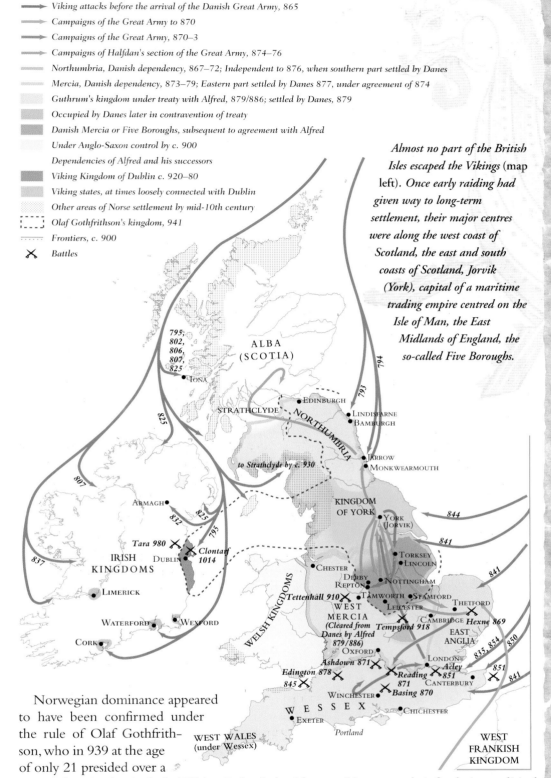

Norwegian dominance appeared to have been confirmed under the rule of Olaf Gothfrithson, who in 939 at the age of only 21 presided over a united domain that included Viking Ireland, the Isle of Man, the kingdom of Jorvik and the previously Danish "Five Boroughs" (Leicester, Lincoln, Derby, Stamford and Nottingham). But with Olaf's early death in 941, Viking hegemony was rapidly undermined. Conquest by Wessex combined with Viking infighting – Jorvik changed hands no less than five times between 941 and 954 – led to the incorporation of Jorvik into Anglo–Saxon England.

However brief their political dominance, the Vikings' cultural impact on England was enduring. But just as important was the memory of Viking settlement, a memory that would spark renewed Danish invasions at the end of the 10th century, in turn leading to the collapse of Anglo–Saxon rule in 1016 and the establishment of a new Danish kingdom in England.

The Earldom of Orkney

*V*iking political control in Ireland and England may have been transient but in the 9th century a much longer-lasting Norwegian kingdom was established that extended south across northern and western Scotland to the Irish Sea: the earldom of Orkney. At its height in the 10th century it included the Shetlands, Orkneys and the Hebrides, Caithness and Sutherland on the mainland and the Isle of Man.

The impetus behind its foundation by the Norwegian king, Harald Fine-Hair, was to stamp out rogue Vikings who were using the Shetlands as a base for raids not against Britain but against Norway itself. It soon developed as the focus of the pan-Irish-Scottish-English Viking maritime empire that grew up in the 10th century and for control of which so many rival Norwegian rulers struggled.

The final Anglo-Saxon conquest of Viking York in 954, and ebbing of Viking political control in Ireland towards the end of the century, shifted the focus of Norwegian ambitions back to the Isle of Man and the Western Isles. The earldom endured until 1266 when, under the Treaty of Perth, and minus the Orkneys, it was ceded by Norway to Scotland. In 1290, the Isle of Man was annexed by Edward I of England. The Orkneys themselves remained under shared Danish/Norwegian rule until 1469. Not surprisingly, this was the only part of the British Isles where Norse dialects took root: Norn was spoken in parts of the Western Isles as late as the 18th century.

910-17	923	927	937	940	947	952	954	965	981	1014
Edward the Elder defeats Danes at Tettenhall, Wednesfield and Tempsford	Viking kings of Jorvik and kings of Northumbria, Strathclyde and Scotland swear loyalty to Edward	Conquest of Viking Jorvik by Athelstan	Battle of Brunanburh: Viking power in northern England destroyed by Athelstan	Jorvik retaken by Vikings under Olaf Gothfrithson	Eric Bloodaxe seizes Jorvik; expelled by Eadred	Eric Bloodaxe retakes Jorvik	Death of Eric Bloodaxe; Eadred retakes Jorvik	Viking Limerick sacked by king of Cashel	Viking Dublin sacked by king of Tara (and again in 999 by Brian Boru, king of Cashel)	Norse–Leinster army defeated by Brian at Clontarf; effective end of Norwegian control in Ireland

853	854–5	865	868	871	878
Four-year-old Alfred sent to Rome	Second visit to Rome	Invasion of Danish "Great Army", led by Halfdan and Ivar the Boneless	Marriage of Alfred to Mercian princess, Ealhswith	Hit-and-run campaigns by Aethelred and Alfred climax in West Saxon victory at Ashdown. Death of Aethelred, Alfred proclaimed king	New Danish attacks, led by Guthrum, on Wessex

ALFRED THE GREAT 871–899

ALFRED THE
GREAT
BORN: c.849
ACCEDED: April 871
King of Wessex

THE FRAGILE STABILITY OF ANGLO-SAXON ENGLAND WAS BRUTALLY SHATTERED BY THE DANES. BY THE TIME A DANISH "GREAT ARMY" LANDED IN EAST ANGLIA IN 865, THE NORSEMEN HAD BEEN RAIDING ACROSS THE NORTH SEA FOR ALMOST 80 YEARS. IT FELL TO ALFRED, KING OF WESSEX, TO HALT AND THEN REVERSE THE DANISH ADVANCE.

IN 867, NORTHUMBRIA FELL TO THE DANES; in 869, East Anglia was overrun. The following year, the Great Army was at Reading preparing to invade Wessex. Though the West Saxons managed at least to contain the Viking attack – in the process inflicting an important defeat on them at Ashdown in 871 – their's could be no more than a defensive campaign against a much stronger enemy that had been bolstered by the arrival of a second invading army. At much the same moment, Aethelred, king of the West Saxons, died. Though he had two young sons, it was Aethelred's younger brother, Alfred, who became king.

Alfred's reputation as the greatest of the Anglo-Saxon kings – who not only withstood the seemingly invincible Danes but decisively helped create the conditions in which a unified English kingdom could emerge – resulted in his being the only English monarch ever to be called "the Great". However, such a lofty and exceptional title belies not only the shadowy circumstances of his actual life but the relative inactivity of his early years on the throne. If his overall achievements are impossible to deny, it is clear that he was nothing if not a late developer. For the first five years of his reign, Alfred did little more than buy off the Danes, who as a result turned their attentions to Mercia, which they conquered in 875. The respite for the West Saxons was purely temporary. Though many of the Danes then concentrated their energies on establishing permanent settlements elsewhere in England, a new force, led by Guthrum, overwhelmed the West Saxons at Chippenham in a surprise attack in January 878. It was only now, with the fate of the last Anglo-Saxon kingdom hanging by a thread, that Alfred emerged not just as a great warrior leader but as an administrator of rare talent, possessed of an unusual combination of foresight, energy and intelligence.

Literacy in the Age of Alfred

In common with every British king of the period, Alfred was illiterate when he came to the throne. In fact, the ability to read and write would not be thought an essential requirement of kingship until the reign of John in the early 13th century. Alfred, however, was the exception to many rules and, at 38, he learned to read. In part, he was consciously emulating the Frankish court, which he had visited as a child on his way back from Rome (which he had visited twice) and where the effects of the great revival of learning initiated by Charlemagne in the early 9th century were still evident. Though much more modest in scale, a significant revival of learning and the arts was begun by Alfred, the first English king to see how learning could be sparked by royal patronage. Among its most lasting achievements was The Anglo-Saxon Chronicle, a remarkable record of contemporary events that would continue until the 12th century. In part, Alfred was also driven by the realization that wisdom and knowledge were essential elements of just kingship. Among a people still only hesitantly emerging from their origins as Germanic warrior tribes whose kings and tribal leaders could enforce laws only by recourse to custom and the strength of their own arms, the idea that justice was dependent on learning (in the king's subjects as well as in the king himself) was of revolutionary importance.

Alfred was eager not merely to introduce greater literacy to Wessex – he established a school for sons of the nobility as well as bringing scholars from many parts of Europe to England – he was anxious to translate classical and biblical texts into Anglo-Saxon so as to make them as widely accessible as possible. An important feature of The Anglo-Saxon Chronicle, for example (below), unlike most other written works of the day, was that it was written solely in Anglo-Saxon.

Map labels:

DUBLIN
ELAND (IRELAND)

summer 894
CHESTER
autumn 893
GWYNEDD
POWYS
late summer 893
LINCOLN
NOTTINGHAM
summer 893
LEICESTER
EAST ANGLIA
THETFORD
CAMBRIDGE
M E R C I A
RHWNG GWY A HAFREN
SEISYLLWG
DYFED
BRYCHEINIOG
GWENT
MORGANNWG
summer 895
GLOUCESTER
CIRENCESTER
OXFORD
autumn 894
895
MALMESBURY
878
CRICKLADE 875
WALLINGFORD
893
892
to Fulham
Ashdown
871
Reading
871
CHIPPENHAM
BATH
LONDON
886
SOUTHWARK
CANTERBURY
AXBRIDGE
Edington 878
X
S
E
Eashing
X
892
Countisbury Hill 878
WATCHET
GLASTONBURY
TISBURY
Farnham 893
WILTON
871
WINCHESTER
spring 893
BOULOGNE
PILTON
LYNG
ATHELNEY
LANGPORT
877
E
876
SOUTHAMPTON
BURPHAM
LEWES
HASTINGS
LYDFORD
EXETER
BRIDPORT
WAREHAM
PORCHESTER
CHICHESTER
CHRISTCHURCH
892
WEST WALES
(under Wessex)
HALWELL
ENGLISH CHANNEL
WEST FRANKISH KINGDOM

Alfred's crushing victory over the Danes at Edington in 878 may have provided a respite for Wessex – crucially buying time to allow the construction of fortified towns along the key strategic areas of the Channel coast and the Thames – but the Viking threat remained persistent (map left). To a large extent, containment was the best Alfred could hope for, as the renewed Danish attacks after 892 made clear. Alfred may appear on contemporary coins as Rex Anglorum (King of the English), but the whole of the north and east of the country remained under Danish control while relations with Anglo-Saxon Mercia always demanded the utmost tact.

WESSEX UNDER ALFRED THE GREAT 871–99

Wessex under Alfred the Great, 871

under Danish control by 871 (overrun by Great Army since 865)

attack of the Great Army on Wessex, 871

attack of the Great Army on Wessex, 875–8 (with date)

other Danish attacks on Wessex, 878

English Mercia liberated by Alfred from Danish control by 886 (dependency of Wessex)

Welsh principalities, vassals of Alfred from 878–81

Danish campaigns 892–6 (with date)

X battle

principal burghs fortified by Alfred

attacks by Alfred with date

As important, Alfred built on the new stability of Wessex to overhaul its law codes. Royal justice, as impartially administered as the inherent instabilities of the period would allow, became a hallmark of Alfred's reign and, in time, of Anglo-Saxon England as a whole. Of equal importance, whatever the latent rivalries simmering beneath the surface of Wessex-Mercian relations, Alfred also began to be widely recognized as the king of "all the English people not under the subjection of the Danes". Whatever the pretensions of the 6th to early 9th-century *bretwaldas* to be "kings of Britain", Alfred's unique achievement was as the first English king who could legitimately claim to rule over, in his own phrase, the *Angelcynn* ("the English folk").

Forced into hiding in the marshes of Athelney in Somerset he devised the strategy to defeat the Danes.

In May 878, he inflicted a defeat on the Danes at Edington that was so complete he was able to force Guthrum to accept Christian baptism as well as to withdraw east of a line running from London to Chester, in the process bringing Mercia definitively under West Saxon control. Alfred then immediately set about strengthening the defences of Wessex: he reorganized the *fyrd*, the Anglo-Saxon army, so that troops were always available to defend the kingdom; he built a new navy of 60-oared ships; and he constructed a series of fortified towns or *burhs*. These *burhs* rapidly developed into important economic centres, in turn sparking an economic revival.

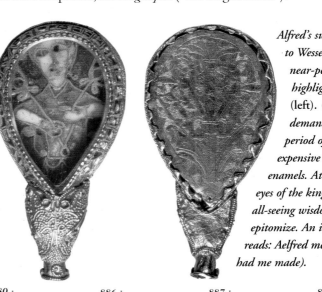

Alfred's success in bringing stability to Wessex in a period of otherwise near-permanent turbulence is highlighted in the Alfred Jewel (left). Craftsmanship of this order demanded not just a sustained period of peace but access to expensive materials: gold and enamels. At the same time, the staring eyes of the king-like figure symbolize the all-seeing wisdom that the king came to epitomize. An inscription on the reverse reads: Aelfred mec heht gewyrcan (Alfred had me made).

878	879	c.880	886	887	892	899
Alfred defeated at Chippenham; regroups to defeat Danes in May at Edington; begins reorganization of West Saxon defences	Mercia brought under West Saxon control	Alfred begins to recruit scholars	Alfred proclaimed "King of all the English"	Alfred begins to learn to read	Wessex resists renewed Danish invasions (to 897)	Death of Alfred

THE HEIRS OF ALFRED 899–975

IN ENSURING THE SURVIVAL OF WESSEX AGAINST THE DANISH THREAT, KING ALFRED HAD LAID THE FOUNDATIONS OF A NASCENT ENGLISH KINGSHIP. BUT IT FELL TO HIS HEIRS TO CONSOLIDATE HIS ACHIEVEMENTS. IN 60 YEARS THEY NOT ONLY DOUBLED THE SIZE OF THE KINGDOM, BUT EXTENDED ROYAL POWER TO AN EXTENT UNPARALLELED IN EUROPE.

Building on his father's, Alfred the Great's, legacy, Edward the Elder (899–924) – picture left – helped to consolidate and expand the territories of the newly formed kingdom of Wessex.

The extension of Wessex rule was as rapid as it was dramatic (map below). By 975, for the first time since the Roman withdrawal in 410, England was effectively under the control of a single power. Yet whatever their successes, the Anglo-Saxon kings remained vulnerable.

WHATEVER THE ADMINISTRATIVE AND military successes of Alfred, early 10th-century Wessex faced a number of pressing dangers. Though dynastic marriage had made Mercia an ally, the long-standing rivalry with Northumbria had scarcely diminished. At the same time, there was the permanent prospect of further invasion from the great swathe of Viking-held territory that stretched from East Anglia to the Lake District.

But in fact most of the period saw sustained expansion by the kings of Wessex, chiefly by Edward the Elder and his son Athelstan. Decisive victories by Edward over the East Anglian Danes in 910 and 911 were followed by an equally crushing victory at Tempsford in 917. Military success on this scale made the incorporation of Mercia into Wessex the following year something of a formality. At the same time, the Danish kingdoms of East Anglia and the Five Boroughs were also added. Edward then set about reinforcing his northern borders, which by 920 had been set at the Humber.

Edward's rapid conquests ensured the primacy of Wessex not just in England but across much of Britain. In 918 the Welsh rulers of Gwynedd and Dyfed had already taken oaths of loyalty to Edward. They were followed in 923 by the rulers of the Viking Kingdom of York and the kings of Northumbria, Strathclyde and Scotland, all of whom acknowledged Edward as their "father and lord". It was a crucial moment. The notion of a centralized kingdom under a single royal authority was taking shape.

899	910–17	918	919	920	923
Accession of Edward the Elder	Edward the Elder defeats Danes at Tettenhall, Wednesfield and Tempsford	Mercia incorporated into Wessex. Welsh princes swear loyalty to Edward	Danish East Anglia incorporated into Wessex	Northern border of Wessex established at Humber	Viking kings of York and kings of Northumbria, Strathclyde and Scotland swear loyalty to Edward

THE EXPANSION OF WESSEX 899–975

- Wessex under Edward the Elder and dependent Mercia under his sister Athelflæd, 899
- Frontier of Wessex and Mercia, to 911
- Independent Mercia, 911–18 and 957–59
- Under Danish rule, 899
- Limit of conquest by Edward the Elder by 916
- Conquered by Edward the Elder by 924
- Forts built by Edward the Elder and Athelflæd
- Campaigns of Athelstan in 927 and 934
- Conquered by Athelstan by 939
- kingdom of York under Olaf Guthfrithsson, king of Dublin, at its greatest extent, 941
- Further area of Norse settlement by early 10th century
- Borders of Wessex by 954
- States partly acknowledging overlordship of Wessex in 10th century
- ○ The "Five Boroughs"
- 911 Date of annexation by Edward the Elder
- → Important Danish campaigns, with date

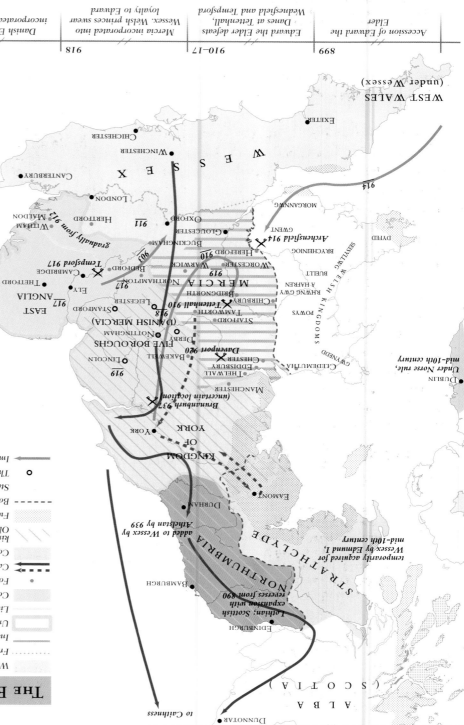

One of Edgar's (959–75) – *picture left* – *most significant achievements was the reform of England's counties, which helped to make the exercise of royal power more effective in an age of turmoil and unrest.*

The dominance of Wessex was reinforced by Edward's successor, Athelstan, who in 927 extended its borders again when he drove the Danes from York. In 934, he demonstrated the military superiority of Wessex even more dramatically, leading a combined land and naval force into Scotland. Three years later, he decisively repulsed a Scottish–Danish attempt to re-take York at the battle of Brunanburh.

The apogee of Wessex power was reached under Edgar, who came to the throne in 959. In an age of almost permanent unrest, the degree of control exercised by Edgar was exceptional. If he was the beneficiary of the military success of his predecessors, it was nonetheless a measure of his intelligent rule that he recognized that peace with his still potentially dangerous Danish subjects, for example, was best preserved by allowing them considerable autonomy.

But Edgar's most important legacy was his continuation of the administrative reforms introduced by Alfred. By his death, Wessex was the most stable and, in many respects, best governed kingdom in Christendom. Among Edgar's most significant achievements was the reorganization of England's counties – they remained essentially unchanged until 1974 – which made the exercise of royal power all the more effective. He also overhauled the coinage, authorizing new mints and, in 973, a new currency. The Witan, or royal council, also continued to grow in influence (see box).

As important, Edgar set in train a series of monastic reforms, important not just because they helped fuel a lavish artistic revival but because, in encouraging the monasteries to reform, Edgar made clear that they did so only because he permitted it. Military might may have made possible the spread of Wessex, but the view was growing that the authority of England's kings ultimately stemmed from their role as Christ's vicar on earth.

EDWARD THE ELDER 899–924

(BORN 870) SON OF ALFRED
First of the great consolidators of Alfred's legacy who enormously extended the territories under the rule of Wessex and its military strength.

AELFWEARD

17 JULY 924–2 AUGUST 924

(BORN 899) SON OF EDWARD THE ELDER
Little is known about the shadowy Aelfweard but a reign of only 16 days suggests his death is unlikely to have been natural or accidental.

ATHELSTAN 924–39

(BORN 895) SON OF EDWARD THE ELDER
Another of the great conquering kings of Wessex who not only further extended the kingdom's borders but greatly enhanced the prestige of the monarchy.

EDMUND I 939–46

(BORN 921) SON OF EDWARD THE ELDER
Presided over the only serious setback to Wessex hegemony in the period, the successful re-taking of York and invasion of Mercia by Olaf Gothfrithson in 940. Olaf's death the following year allowed Edmund to recover most of the lost territories. He was murdered by a follower in 946 after an argument.

EADRED 946–55

(BORN 924) SON OF EDWARD THE ELDER
Continued the re-conquest of the north after Edmund's death, leading a successful campaign against Eric Bloodaxe, who had seized York, in 947. Erik re-took the throne in 952 but his death in 954 allowed Wessex to re-establish its control over the region.

EADWIG 955–59

(BORN 942) SON OF EDMUND I
A four-year reign notable for intrigue and incompetence, which threatened to destroy Wessex's hard-won control of Mercia and Northumbria.

EDGAR 959–75

(BORN 943) SON OF EDMUND I
Saw the consolidation of Wessex's gains over the previous 60 years. Numerous reforms and firm rule made his reign the high-water mark of Wessex domination. His nickname, the "Peaceful", was testimony to his strength, not his weakness.

The Witan

*I*f in no sense a parliament-in-the-making, the Witan, or royal council, was nonetheless fundamental to the growing stability of Anglo-Saxon England. Though its precise role, like its membership, was vague – it met only when summoned by the king, for example – it nonetheless acted as a valuable source of advice and counsel to the monarch, even if it was always subject to him. Its two major responsibilities were to "elect" the king, which in practice meant confirming his right to the throne after the fact rather than in any sense choosing him in the first place, and to give assent to royal measures. Again, this in no way implied a veto over the king's decisions.

On the other hand, it did provide an additional layer of legitimacy. It was this reinforcement of the rule of law that was the Witan's most lasting significance. It may have taken conquest to establish Anglo-Saxon rule, but once in place Anglo-Saxon kingship was deeply concerned to bolster its position by the spread of royal law. That the king, supported by the Witan, should increasingly come to be regarded as the sole source of authority was a development of lasting importance.

Edgar's reign saw an important reform of the coinage, with new currency being introduced in 973. This silver penny (left) was minted in Shrewsbury by the moneyer Hildic.

927	937	940	947	954	959	973
Conquest of York by Athelstan	Battle of Brunanburh: Viking power in York destroyed by Athelstan	York re-taken by Vikings under Olaf Gothfrithson; Mercia invaded	Eric Bloodaxe seizes York; expelled by Edred	Death of Eric Bloodaxe; Edred re-takes York	Accession of Edgar leads to further consolidation of Wessex rule and administrative reforms	Ceremonial double coronation of Edgar (at Bath and Chester); Edgar receives homage of eight "British kings"

KING

AETHELRED II
BORN: *c.*968
ACCEDED: March 978;
crowned April 978,
Kingston-upon-Thames

King of the English

THE HEIRS OF ALFRED: AETHELRED II 978–1016

AETHELRED II HAS LONG BEEN WRITTEN OFF AS ONE OF THE MOST DISASTROUS OF ENGLISH KINGS. IN 978 HE INHERITED AN ANGLO-SAXON KINGDOM THAT WAS PROSPEROUS, UNIFIED AND EXCEPTIONALLY WELL GOVERNED. BY THE TIME OF HIS DEATH IN 1016 HE HAD LOST IT ALL. YET, WHATEVER HIS OWN FAILINGS, IT WAS ULTIMATELY A WAVE OF RENEWED AND IRRESISTIBLE DANISH ATTACKS THAT UNDERMINED HIS RULE.

In 991 a raiding party of Danes made their headquarters on Northey Island. The English general Byrhtnoth blocked the narrow entrance to the causeway (above), but the Danes over-whelmed the defenders. This defeat at the Battle of Maldon led to the first payment of Danegeld.

Pre-eminently, Aethelred was a victim of circumstances. Even his nickname "Unraed" – meaning not "unready" but "bad counsel", a pun on Aethelred, meaning "noble counsel" – suggests a rule that seems to have been consistently at the mercy of events. In many ways, his kingship was blighted from the beginning.

Aethelred came to the throne, aged only 10, when his elder brother, Edward – himself just 16 but already king for three years – was murdered by Aethelred's supporters while visiting Edward. However much an innocent bystander, Aethelred never quite shook off the stain of implication in the murder of his brother, who within a matter of years was being venerated by Aethelred's opponents as "Edward the Martyr".

Even after his majority, Aethelred remained the victim of Anglo-Saxon power politics, unable either to cow his senior subjects or to win their trust. But his overriding weakness was military. No great general, he had the overwhelming misfortune to rule England at exactly the moment that a resurgent Denmark was not merely determined to regain its lost territories in England but had the clear military capacity to do so.

From the early 980s, under two formidable Danish kings – Harold Bluetooth and, after 988, his equally fearsome son, Sweyn – a series of Danish invasions were launched against England. Early Danish successes climaxed in 991 in a devastating Anglo-Saxon defeat at Maldon in Essex. Danish attacks followed throughout the decade. With each Danish victory, Aethelred progressively lost the support of his most powerful nobles, who were increasingly dismayed by his inability to defend the kingdom.

Aethelred's response was logical but flawed. If he was unable to defeat the Danes, he could surely buy them off. For almost 20 years, he paid increasingly large sums to the Danes in an attempt to halt their depredations. Called "Danegeld", these payments became a central feature of Aethelred's rule. Rich though it was, Anglo-Saxon England risked being bled dry within a matter of years. The Danes predictably came back for more.

Anglo-Saxon Administration

Aethelred's reign contained a number of enduring ironies. Though he was without question the least successful of Alfred's principal successors, he was, by some way, the longest reigning. Similarly, despite the increasing chaos caused by the Danish raids, the administrative efficiency of Anglo-Saxon England, crucially important in extending the range of royal authority, was significantly strengthened under Aethelred. Among the most important developments was the creation of new representatives of the king in each shire. These representatives were called bailiffs or "reeves", from which the term "shire-reeve", later sheriff, came. It was the sheriff's task to implement royal decisions in each shire and to preside over the new shire courts, where royal pronouncements and decisions were announced. The sheriffs were also instrumental in the much more efficient tax system that developed under Aethelred. This itself was more than just an administrative convenience but the direct consequence of having to raise huge extra taxes across the country to meet the payments of Danegeld. In a further irony, in the reign of Cnut, this greatly improved tax system was used not to buy the Danes off but to meet the costs of a new Danish standing army in England.

c.980	982	991	997	1002	1003–5
Renewed Danish raids under Harold Bluetooth	London sacked by Danes	Anglo-Saxon defeat at Battle of Maldon heralds further Viking invasions (994, 997, 1002) – Danegeld payments begin. Anglo-Saxon–Norman anti-Danish alliance formed	Wantage Law Code: major revision of Anglo-Saxon laws by Aethelred	Massacre of all Danes in England ordered	Major Danish reprisals against England led by Sweyn

991 This year was Ipswich plundered: and very soon afterwards was Ealdorman Byrhtnoth slain at Maldon. In this same year it was resolved that tribute should be given, for the first time, to the Danes, for the great terror they occasioned by the sea-coast. That was first £10,000. The first who advised this measure was Archbishop Siric.

The Anglo-Saxon Chronicle

Anglo-Saxon successes in containing and then rolling back the Vikings depredations were dramatically undone in the reign of Aethelred II (map right). For over 30 years after 980, Anglo-Saxon England was subjected to a series of devastating Danish attacks that left only the northwest untouched. With the accession of Cnut in 1016, the Viking triumph was complete.

Fatefully, Aethelred also tried to outflank the Danes by allying himself with the French dukedom of Normandy, an alliance strengthened in 1001 with his marriage to Emma, daughter of the Duke of Normandy. Though he could scarcely have known it, the consequences of his diplomatic marriage would later open the way to an even greater disaster.

He committed a much more immediate and avoidable blunder in 1002, however, when, determined to assert his authority, he ordered the massacre of all the Danes in England. His scheme had the triple disadvantage of being barbaric, unenforceable and of provoking Sweyn yet further. A decade of devastating Danish invasions was unleashed in which much of the north of England, swayed partly by its Danish population but above all by its eagerness to see an end to the conflict, threw itself behind Sweyn. By late 1013, Oxford, Winchester and London had also fallen and Aethelred had fled to Normandy.

The denouement followed swiftly. By 1014, Aethelred was back in England confronting Sweyn's successor, Cnut. To his existing military incapacity, he now had an additional handicap in the shape of his son, Edmund "Ironside", who had defied his father by taking control of the remaining Anglo-Saxon forces in the north. What was left of the king's royal authority was undermined further.

In the event, it hardly mattered. In early 1016, Aethelred suddenly died. In October, Cnut inflicted an overwhelming defeat on Edmund. Within a month, Edmund, too, was dead and Cnut was king.

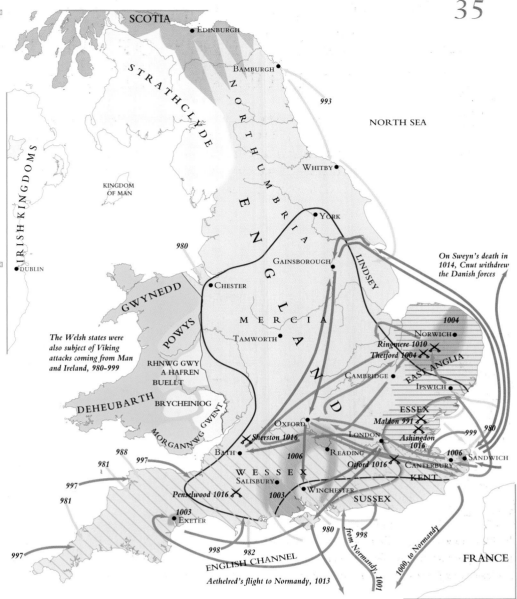

The Welsh states were also subject of Viking attacks coming from Man and Ireland, 980-999

On Sweyn's death in 1014, Cnut withdrew the Danish forces

Aethelred's flight to Normandy, 1013

WARS WITH THE DANES, 980–1016

→	*Early Danish attacks*
—	*Area attacked by Sweyn and Olaf Tryggvason, 994*
→	*Danish campaigns, 997–1001*
▨	*Areas attacked by Sweyn, 1003–6*
→	*Thorkell the Tall's campaigns, 1009–10*
▨	*Area attacked by Sweyn, 1011–12*
→	*Sweyn's campaign, 1013*
—	*Approximate limit of Cnut's campaign/s, 1015–16*
⫽	*Awarded to Edmund "Ironside" under Treaty of Olney, 1016*
≡	*Other areas possibly forming part of Edmund's kingdom*
✕	*Battles*

This coin of Aethelred II (left) shows the king bare-headed and was minted in London by the moneyer Leofnoth.

1006–7	1009	1012	1013	1014	1015	1016
Further Danish invasion bought off by payment of £30,000	*Renewed Danish invasions under Thorkell the Tall*	*Thorkell's troops murder Alphege, the Archbishop of Canterbury*	*Sweyn leads army of conquest against England; gains immediate Northumbrian submission; Aethelred flees to Normandy*	*Danish army led by Cnut after death of Sweyn; Aethelred leads renewed attack against Cnut*	*Further Danish invasion of England under Cnut; Edmund "Ironside" heads English forces in the north*	*Death of Aethelred; Cnut defeats Edmund at Ashingdon (Oct.) and under Treaty of Olney restricts Edmund's rule to Wessex. Death of Edmund (Nov.)*

CORONATION RITES

THE GROWING POWER OF ANGLO-SAXON KINGSHIP IN THE 10TH CENTURY WAS CRUCIALLY REFLECTED IN A MORE ELABORATE FORM OF EXPLICITLY CHRISTIAN CORONATION. THIS CONFIRMED NOT JUST THE SECULAR POWER OF THE KING BUT HIS STATUS AS THE LORD'S ANOINTED. IN UNDERLINING THAT THE KING WAS NOT AS OTHER MEN, THE CORONATION IN TURN REINFORCED HIS AUTHORITY.

*I*f a formal ceremony of inauguration had been a part of the ritual whereby a new ruler was proclaimed since perhaps as early as the 6th century, it was only with the coronation of Egfrith of Mercia in 787 that the outlines of the ceremony as it would subsequently evolve first seem to have emerged. The details of Egfrith's coronation may be known only vaguely, but it is clear that the ceremony held an important new religious dimension.

In fact, this religious element had an obvious political goal: to reinforce Egfrith's legitimacy, a fact clearly seen in Egfrith's being crowned during the lifetime of his father, Offa. Anxious to secure an orderly succession for his son, Offa arranged that the papal legates then visiting the country anoint Egfrith as king. In subsequently being able to proclaim himself as divinely sanctioned, Egfrith's eventual right to his father's throne was significantly strengthened.

By the coronation of Edgar in 973, itself apparently influenced by that of the German emperor, Otto the Great, in 952, the ceremony had taken on essentially the same form and significance it retains today as a solemn, public confirmation of the new monarch's divine right to the throne and of his responsibilities. It is striking that Edgar's coronation was the first at which the anthem used in every subsequent coronation, "Zadok the Priest and Nathan the Prophet" was sung; it is best known in Handel's arrangement of it, composed for the coronation of George II in 1727.

The ceremony itself was divided into five principal elements. First, the recognition, in which the new monarch was presented to the congregation by the presiding cleric, from the coronation of Henry II in 1154 always the Archbishop of Canterbury. It was followed by the oath, in which the monarch swore to safeguard his people and the church, to uphold justice and to be merciful. Then followed the most sacred moment of the ceremony, one which confirmed the king's semi-divine status: the anointing of the monarch with holy oil. (It was precisely the religious character of the anointing that made Elizabeth II in 1953 reluctant to have this part of the ceremony televised).

The monarch was then handed the regalia, essentially symbols of the secular character of kingship: a ring; sword, symbol of his protection of his kingdom; and the crown itself, sceptre and rod, the whole standing for "the glory, virtue, equity and justice reposing in an anointed king". Finally, now crowned and as a mark of his status at the head of the feudal chain, the monarch received the homage of his leading subjects. (Until the coronation of William IV in 1831, there was then also generally a banquet at which the king's champion offered to take on any rival claimant to the throne. William IV discontinued the practise as the conspicuous luxury of his predecessor, George IV's, banquet had been thought so excessive).

Anointed and proclaimed in this way "by the grace of God", a form of words used by every monarch since William Rufus in 1087, normally with as much magnificence as could be mustered, the legitimacy of the new monarch's rule was emphatically established and the principal of hereditary succession reinforced. Needless to say, where the succession was disputed, the sooner the coronation was held, the sooner the legitimacy of the new rule could be asserted. It is no coincidence that in 1066 Harold II, whose succession was among the most disputed in medieval England, was crowned only the day after the death of Edward the Confessor.

In much the same way, in 1170 Henry II had his eldest son, also Henry, the "Young King", crowned king of England, the clearest possible indication that it was the Young King who would succeed Henry in England while his other lands, in France and Ireland, were to be divided among his three younger sons. Further, at least until the succession of Edward I in

The coronation of Henry IV in 1399, taken from the late-15th century Froissart's **Chronicles** *(below). This was the first occasion where holy oil was used for the anointing. For Henry, who had deposed his predecessor Richard II just two weeks previously, the coronation, with its near-sacerdotal aura was a prime opportunity to display to his subjects God's blessing on his succession to the throne.*

The Royal Regalia

The royal regalia, assembled over several hundred years, and including a number of pieces, a crown and several sceptres among them, dating from the reign of Edward the Confessor, were melted down or sold on the orders of Parliament after the execution of Charles I in 1649. The motive was partly the need to raise cash. But it was also a deliberate attempt to destroy for good the most symbolic of objects representing the monarchy. With the Restoration of Charles II in 1660, it was decided in an act of equally deliberate symbolism that the entire regalia should be re-created as precisely as possible. In fact, one item had survived, the 12th-century anointing spoon. All the rest, however, triumphantly used for the first time at Charles's coronation in 1661, was entirely new. Importantly, within years it was being widely assumed that the reconstituted regalia were the original items, a state of affairs the monarchy itself was keen to promote. The first printed guide to the collection, published in 1710, described the centre-piece of the collection, the so-called St Edward's Crown as "The Imperial Crown, which all the Kings of England have been Crown'd with, ever since Edward the Confessor's Time".

1172, by which point the automatic right of the eldest son to the throne had become established, in an important sense the reign of a medieval king began only with his coronation. The sooner it could be held, the sooner his reign could be properly said to have begun.

Similarly, whatever his rather shrill claims to have been designated his heir by Edward the Confessor, William I, Norman or not, deliberately retained the Anglo-Saxon form of the ceremony, the better to emphasise the continuity (non-existent in fact) of his reign with that of Edward's. In very much the same way, the coronation of Henry IV in 1399 after the overthrow of Richard II was not only deliberately magnificent, it was also the first occasion in which the anointing was done with holy oil said to have been given to Thomas Becket by the Virgin Mary. Having usurped the throne, it was essential for Henry IV to legitimize his rule by every means available to him.

Until the consecration of Westminster Abbey in 1065, most Anglo-Saxon monarchs were crowned at what appropriately came to be called Kingston, on the Wessex–Mercia border. Thereafter, beginning with Harold II, every English and later British king other than the uncrowned Edward V in the 15th century and Edward VIII in the 20th century, was crowned at Westminster Abbey. From the coronation of Edward II in 1308, the monarch has always been crowned on the throne constructed by Edward I and incorporating the Stone of Scone, appropriated by Edward I in 1296, on which the kings of Scotland had traditionally been crowned (though not anointed, a practise begun only with the coronation of David II in 1331 after papal recognition of the independence of Scotland was granted).

St Edward's crown is replaced by the lighter Imperial State Crown (above) for the closing procession of the coronation service. It is worn by the Sovereign on leaving Westminster Abbey after the coronation ceremony. This crown was originally made for Queen Victoria in 1838 and was used at the coronations of Edward VII and George V. It was remade with similar stones for George VI in 1937 and is set with 2,868 diamonds, 17 sapphires, 11 emeralds, five rubies and 273 pearls.

The 12th-century anointing spoon (above left), is the only item of the royal regalia to survive the destruction of the original regalia in 1649. It is used to anoint the new monarch with holy oil; this conscious use of Christian symbolism reinforces the legitimacy and status of the newly-crowned monarch.

The coronation of King George VI and Queen Elizabeth at Westminster Abbey (12th May, 1937, left). A comparison with the coronation of Henry IV in 1399 (far left) shows how many elements of the ceremony and the sense of sacred ritual have remained intact over the centuries.

THE DANISH KINGDOM OF ENGLAND: CNUT AND HIS SONS

CNUT WAS AMONG THE GREATEST KINGS OF HIS DAY, RULER OF A POWERFUL NORTH EUROPEAN MARITIME EMPIRE THAT INCLUDED DENMARK, NORWAY AND PARTS OF SWEDEN AS WELL AS ENGLAND. YET HIS RULE DEMONSTRATES THE TRANSIENT AND PERSONAL NATURE OF EARLY MEDIEVAL KINGSHIP. HIS EMPIRE DISINTEGRATED WITH HIS DEATH AND, WITHIN SEVEN YEARS, ENGLAND WAS ONCE MORE UNDER ANGLO-SAXON RULE.

KING CNUT
BORN: c.995
ACCEDED: November 1016; crowned January 1017, London

King of England (from 1016) and King of Denmark (from 1018) and King of Norway (from 1028)

C NUT'S TAKEOVER OF ENGLAND IN 1016 WAS A conquest in every sense. Vigorous, determined and harsh (if not unduly so by the standards of the time), the new Viking king was quick to assert his authority. His principal Anglo-Saxon rivals, including Edmund Ironside's brother Eadric (and probably his eldest son, Edwy) as well as the earls of Mercia and East Anglia, were summarily executed. Edmund's other son, Edward, was exiled, reputedly to Novgorod with orders to its Viking rulers that he be murdered on arrival. (In the event, he made his way to Hungary.) At the same time, substantial numbers of Cnut's Danish followers were granted English lands and titles. In 1017, to underline his claim to the throne more strongly still, Cnut married Aethelred's widow, Emma.

Unlike William the Conqueror 50 years later, Cnut went no further. The large majority of the Anglo-Saxon nobility were left in place. In much the same way, the key figure of Wulfstan, Archbishop of York under Athelstan, was allowed to remain in office. As important, the mechanisms of government were left essentially undisturbed.

Cnut's motives were pragmatic. His focus was at least as much on his Scandinavian homelands as on England. Once he had inherited the Danish throne in 1018 and begun a successful ten-year conquest of Norway, a stable England was fundamental to the control of his North Sea empire. Not only would a ruler – even one as capable as Cnut – have been unable to cope with simultaneous unrest in England and Scandinavia, but a prosperous England could be used to fund his Scandinavian campaigning. It was essential that England be allowed to recover from the quarter-century of invasion and war that preceded the final

> **King Cnut greets in friendship his archbishops** and his diocesan bishops, and Earl Thorkell and all his earls, and all his people... And I inform you that I will be a grateful lord and a faithful observer of God's rights and just secular law ... [and] that I [will] everywhere exalt God's praises and suppress wrong and establish full security, by that power which it has pleased God to give me ... Now I thank Almighty God for his help and his mercy, that I have so settled the great dangers which were approaching us that we need fear no danger to us ...
>
> *From a proclamation to the people of England, c.1019*

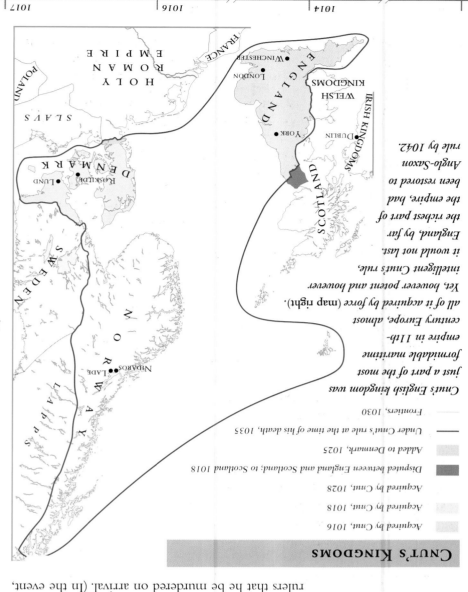

Cnut's English kingdom was just a part of the most formidable maritime empire in 11th-century Europe, almost all of it acquired by force (map right).

Yet, however potent and however intelligent Cnut's rule, it would not last. England, by far the richest part of the empire, had been restored to Anglo-Saxon rule by 1042.

CNUT'S KINGDOMS

Acquired by Cnut, 1016
Acquired by Cnut, 1018
Acquired by Cnut, 1028
Disputed between England and Scotland, 1018
Added to Denmark, 1025
— Under Cnut's rule at the time of his death, 1035
--- Frontiers, 1030

1014	1016	1017	1018	1018–20
Cnut marries Aelfgifu	Assumes throne of England	Marries Emma, widow of Aethelred. Creates earldoms of Wessex, East Anglia, Mercia and Northumbria	Godwine created Earl of Wessex. Cnut inherits Danish crown on death of his brother, Harold. Scots under Malcolm II invade Northumbria	Cnut in Denmark; launches conquest of Norway

Cnut's Successors

However well established at the time of his death, Cnut's empire was undermined by dynastic uncertainty. Ever the Viking, Cnut had two wives at the same time: Aelfgifu, daughter of the former ealdorman of Northumbria, whom he married in 1014; and Emma, the Norman-born widow of Aethelred. After his second marriage, Aelfgifu was sent to Denmark, where she was recognized as Cnut's legitimate queen. Emma meanwhile ruled as Cnut's queen in England. Even by the standards of early medieval Europe, it was an unusual arrangement.

Aelfgifu had two sons by Cnut, Sweyn, king of Norway until his death in 1036, and Harold; Emma had one son by him, Harthacnut. Though designated his successor by Cnut, Harthacnut was in Norway when his father died in 1035. Harold, however, was in England and Harthacnut accordingly appointed him regent. Two years later, with Harthacnut still in Norway, Harold, supported by the all-powerful pirate-turned-nobleman, the rapacious Earl Godwine of Wessex, claimed the throne for himself. Emma fled to Flanders.

By the time Harthacnut returned to England in 1040 Harold was dead, possibly murdered. Just in case there should be any doubt as to who was now king, Harthacnut had Harold's body exhumed, beheaded and "cast into a marsh". His reign, every bit as oppressive as his half-brother's, ended suddenly after two years when, drinking a toast at a wedding, he died "with terrible convulsions".

Of the possible heirs, the two with the strongest claims were the new king of Norway, Magnus I, and Aethelred's and Emma's sole surviving son, Edward. Magnus, though powerful, was in Norway; Edward, by contrast, in England. He also had the support of Earl Godwine, who almost certainly believed that with Edward on the throne he, Godwine, would constitute the real authority in the kingdom. In June 1042, cowed by Godwine's usual crude mixture of threats and bribes, the Witan agreed to Edward's succession and Cnut's short-lived royal line was ended. The Anglo-Saxons had been restored.

Danish conquest. The celebrated proclamation to his leading subjects issued in about 1019 was a clear statement of intent to govern with the support of his nobles and the Church as well as to maintain order.

But Cnut introduced one major innovation that, however sensible in his terms, would in the longer run prove seriously destabilizing to Anglo-Saxon England. In 1017, he divided England into four earldoms – Northumbria, East Anglia, Mercia and Wessex. His intention was to centralize power in these regions and thereby ensure consistent government during his long spells overseas. In effect, he was acknowledging a key limitation of early medieval kingship: that the king could rule only with the support of his nobles. However, by concentrating power in the hands of just four magnates, he created power bases of sufficient strength to challenge the rule of the king himself.

Under Cnut at least any latent conflict was held firmly in check. His rule was increasingly marked not just by his personal dominance but by clear, capable government, among it legal reforms that further reinforced the country's reputation for efficient administration. At the same time, the one-time pagan Viking marauder became an enthusiastic supporter of the Church. In 1027 and 1031, he even journeyed to Rome. A 12th-century chronicler would admiringly describe Cnut's transformation "from a wild man into a most Christian king".

That he was still a warrior king, however, was obvious not just from his conquest of Norway but from the submissions he was able to force from the Scottish king, Malcolm II, and the Norse ruler of Dublin, Margad Ragnallson, in 1031. As king of Denmark, Cnut's authority also extended over the earldom of Orkney. By his death in 1035, Cnut was unquestionably the most powerful ruler in northern Europe.

St Andrew's church (right) at Ashingdon in Kent was founded by Cnut c.1020 after the battle of Ashingdon (1016), "for the souls of the men who were slain".

KING EDWARD THE CONFESSOR

BORN: *c.*1005
ACCEDED: June 1042;
crowned April 1043,
Winchester

King of England

EDWARD THE CONFESSOR 1042–66

FEW ENGLISH KINGS CAME TO THE THRONE BY A MORE CIRCUITOUS ROUTE THAN EDWARD THE CONFESSOR. NONE LEFT A MORE UNCERTAIN OR DAMAGING DYNASTIC DISPUTE. EDWARD'S CLAIMS TO BE KING WERE ENTIRELY LEGITIMATE, HIS REIGN AT LEAST AVERAGELY COMPETENT. BUT LIKE HIS FATHER, AETHELRED, EDWARD WAS TRAPPED IN CIRCUMSTANCES FROM WHICH HE WAS LARGELY UNABLE TO ESCAPE.

The Cult of the Confessor

Despite being universally known as "the Confessor" the evidence for Edward's piety is thin and mostly dates from after his reign. As a young man, he seems to have been typically dissolute. Even in his early years as king his fondness for hunting was considerably more obvious than any latent holiness. Yet almost from the moment of his death Edward was being venerated as a miracle worker and healer of the sick. In 1161, the cult reached a climax when Edward was canonized. The cult of the Confessor seems to have been created partly through nostalgia for a lost Anglo-Saxon past and partly through Edward's apparent simplicity of dress and celibacy (even if his and his queen's failure to have children was almost certainly just because they were unable to). But overwhelmingly, he was remembered as the builder of a great abbey church just outside London, the West Minster of St Peter. Its original construction was fired as much by Edward's desire to establish a new centre of royal authority, preferably one that echoed the great Norman churches being built on the other side of the Channel, as to glorify God. It was consecrated in 1065, just in time for Edward to be buried there. By the time Henry III rebuilt the Abbey in the 13th century, Edward's cult was unchallenged and Henry constructed a new, impressively lavish tomb for the last of the 15 English kings to be made a saint.

IN 1014, AGED ONLY NINE, EDWARD AND HIS brother Alfred had been sent to Normandy for safe keeping from what looked like the increasing probability of a Viking conquest of England. There they were brought up. Whatever its own Viking origins and political turbulence, early 11th-century Normandy deeply coloured Edward's outlook. It is clear that for Edward, England took on the appearance of an alien land.

Nonetheless, the dynastic uncertainties caused by the death of Cnut in 1035 raised the prospect that either Alfred or Edward could reclaim the throne of England. In 1036, both returned to England. Alfred made his way to Earl Godwine's semi-court in Guildford. There, Godwine, crime boss as much as nobleman, ritually submitted to Alfred and then arranged his murder.

In the circumstances, Edward's subsequent distrust of Godwine was hardly surprising. More surprising is that in 1041 Edward allowed himself to be persuaded to return to England again by the new king, Harthacnut. Once in England, Edward was the obvious candidate to succeed Harthacnut after the latter's sudden death in 1042, not least in order to forestall a rival Scandinavian claim by Magnus I of Norway.

The first years of Edward's reign were dominated by a struggle for supremacy between him and Godwine. The latter struck an early blow when he manoeuvred Edward into marrying his daughter, Edith, raising the prospect of a future Godwine claim to the throne. But in 1051, in what must have seemed his apotheosis, Edward succeeded in banishing Godwine. Within a year, however, having mounted almost an invasion of England, Godwine was back stronger than ever.

Godwine's personal triumph was shortlived: he died the following year. But his dynasty seemed assured. By 1055, his sons Harold, Tostig and Gyrth

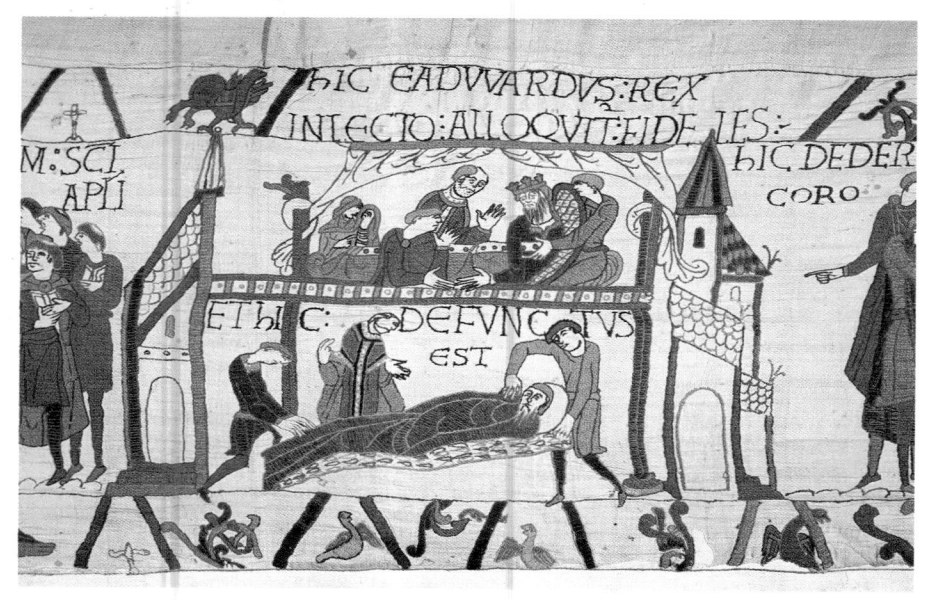

The Bayeux Tapestry is the single most vivid and compelling pictorial account of the Norman Conquest. The scene here (left) is divided in two. The upper panel shows the death of Edward the Confessor, who reaches out his hand to Harold, designating him his successor. In the lower scene, the body of the dead king is prepared for burial.

Edward the Confessor's rule was dogged by the rival ambitions of his leading subjects, Earl Godwine and his sons, Harold, Tostig and Gyrth, pre-eminently, from whose rapacity the beleaguered king was largely unable to escape (map left). Of greater significance was the damaging succession dispute left by the increasingly feeble king. In less than a year, Anglo-Saxon England was violently overthrown.

ENGLAND UNDER EDWARD THE CONFESSOR

Harold's earldom, 1056
Ralph's earldom, 1056
Leofric's earldom, 1056
Tostig's earldom, 1056
Aelfgar's earldom, 1056
Temporary Welsh conquests, 1057–62
Harold's campaigns against Gruffydd ap Llywelyn, with dates
Revolt, with details
Advance of anti-Tostig rebels, supported by Edwin, 1065
Frontiers of the earldoms, 1066, with name of earls

The shrine of Edward the Confessor (above) in Westminster Abbey was built by Henry III in the 13th century when the cult of the Confessor was at its peak.

were respectively the earls of Wessex, Northumbria and East Anglia. Their dominance was reaffirmed in 1063 when Harold and Tostig routed the hitherto invincible Welsh king Gruffydd ap Llywelyn. However secure on his throne, Edward seemed to have been comprehensively outplayed.

The difficulty facing Edward was not just humiliation but rather the succession. His marriage to Edith, often claimed never to have been consummated, had left him with no heir. Given his Norman sympathies, as well as his need to outflank the Godwines, it is credible that he should have nominated his cousin William, duke of Normandy, as his successor – as William steadfastly maintained. If so, he later seems to have changed his mind. In 1056, he arranged for Edmund Ironside's son, another Edward, banished as a baby by Cnut in 1016, to return to England. He would have made a credible successor had he not died the following year.

William meanwhile had never forgotten his designation as successor. At any rate in his own mind, he dramatically strengthened his claim in 1064 when

he secured – or so he asserted – a promise from Harold Godwine, who was in Normandy on a mission that remains mysterious, to support his succession. Nonetheless, within a day of Edward's death in January 1066 it was Harold who was hurriedly crowned. His hereditary right may have been non-existent, but as the man on the spot and in the absence of an obvious native heir his candidature was compelling. When he heard the news, William "… became as a man enraged".

1052 There took up Earl Godwine his burthen, and cleared himself there before his lord King Edward, and before all the nation; proving that he was innocent of the crime laid to his charge, and to his son Harold and all his children. And the king gave the earl and his children, and all the men who were with him, his full friendship, and the full earldom, and all that he possessed before.

The Anglo-Saxon Chronicle

1052	1053	1056	1057	1063	1064
Godwine returns in triumph. Construction of Westminster Abbey begun	Godwine dies; Harold Godwine becomes earl of Wessex	Edward invites Edward "the Atheling" to England and probably designates him as successor	Death of Edward the Atheling	Victorious campaigns against Welsh strengthens Harold Godwine's position	Visiting Normandy, Harold possibly upholds William's claim to the throne of England

Harold II 1066

KING
HAROLD II
BORN: c.1022
ACCEDED: January 5
1066; crowned
January 6 1066,
Westminster Abbey
King of England

HAROLD II WAS KING FOR LESS THAN A YEAR, YET HIS RULE WAS AMONG THE MOST DRAMATIC AND FATEFUL OF ANY RULER OF ENGLAND. IT WAS DOMINATED BY HIS DISPUTED SUCCESSION. HAROLD HARDRADA IN NORWAY, AND WILLIAM, DUKE OF NORMANDY, BOTH BELIEVED THEIR CLAIMS WERE SUPERIOR AND BOTH MOUNTED INVASIONS TO SUPPORT THEM.

O NLY ONE OF THE FOUR CANDIDATES FOR THE English throne in 1066 had a clear hered-itary right: Edgar the Atheling (or prince), the great-grandson of Aethelred the Unready. Neither Harold nor the Norwegian king, Hardrada, had any hereditary claim; duke William in Normandy had only the most tenuous – through his great-aunt, Emma, second wife of King Cnut.

Nonetheless, for the majority of England's lead-ing subjects, Harold was always the most likely choice. The threatened invasions by William and Hardrada made it essential that the country had a strong king to defend it. As its leading native sub-ject and the country's most outstanding general, Harold had obvious advantages. The Atheling, by contrast, as an untried 14-year-old, had none of Harold's political or military strengths. It seems clear, too, that Harold had been lobbying for the throne for some years, building up substantial sup-port. He also seems to have secured the ailing King Edward's designation as his successor. At any rate, that he was crowned the day after Edward's death in a ceremony that immediately followed the old king's funeral strongly suggests the culmination of a careful, long-term strategy.

The rival claims of Hardrada and duke William both rested on their assertions that they (or, in the case of Hardrada, his predecessor, Magnus) had been designated successors by Harthacnut and Edward the Confessor respectively. Both were prepared to use force to back their claims. William in particular, before and after his successful invasion, consistently stressed the legitimacy of his right to the throne, damning Harold as a perjurer and usurper.

There was in fact a further threat to Harold, his brother Tostig. As earl of Northumbria, Tostig had acquired a reputation as an incompetent tyrant, harrying his subjects while simultaneously unable to stop border raids by Malcolm III of Scotland. The previous autumn, Harold had arranged for Tostig's replacement by Morcar, brother of the earl of Mercia. Harold may have acquired a valuable new ally in Morcar but he had made an unforgiving enemy in Tostig.

The first months of Harold's reign were almost entirely given over to strengthening his defences.

Harold and William

Central to William the Conqueror's claim to the English throne was not just that Edward had designated him his heir in 1051 but that Edward had sent Harold Godwine to France to confirm the fact in 1064. It seems unlikely that Harold, whose own designs on the throne were clear, would have been prepared to act so obviously against his own interests in this way. On the other hand, there is no question but that he did go to France and that once there swore to uphold William's claim. The scene is vividly portrayed in the Bayeux Tapestry (below).

VBI[HAROLD]:SACRAMENTVM:FECIT: HIC HAROLD:D... WILLELMO DVCI:

Though it was commissioned by a Norman (William's half-brother, Bishop Odo) and was in general a faithful reflection of the post-Conquest Norman view, the tapestry was actually produced by English embroiderers. So far as Harold's oath is concerned, they seem to have slipped in a particularly subtle contradiction of the official Norman line. The scene immediately following Harold's oath-taking shows Harold and his party leaving the Norman court. The implication is clear: that Harold was William's prisoner and the oath the price of his freedom.

It is possible that Harold went to France not on Edward's initiative but his own to propose that he would support William in his struggles against the king of France if William would support Harold's claim to the English throne. If so, it was a disastrous misjudgement. Nothing would deflect William from his absolute conviction that the throne of England was his by right. Further, having extracted the oath from Harold, he would – and did – do everything in his power to see it honoured.

1053	1063	1064	1065
Harold Godwine becomes earl of Wessex	Defeat of Gruffydd ap Llywelyn in Wales confirms Harold as pre-eminent military leader in England	Harold journeys to Normandy, forced to uphold William's claim to English throne	Jan. 5: Death of Edward the Confessor
		(Nov.) Harold masterminds overthrow of his brother Tostig as earl of Northumbria and his replacement by Morcar	Jan. 6: Coronation of Harold II
			May: Failed landings by Tostig on south and east coasts of England
			July: Major Saxon forces and fleet readied to withstand expected Norman landing

Harold himself took charge of those in the south, where the threat posed by William was judged the more imminent. Morcar was given responsibility for the north. Their strength seemed amply demonstrated by the ease with which Harold, then Morcar, withstood attempted landings by Tostig, who, with support from the Low Countries, had assembled a fleet of sorts. Rebuffed, Tostig continued north, to Scotland.

By early September, with no sign of either William or Hardrada, Harold was forced to stand down his defences and allow his men to return home. On the 19th, he learned that Tostig and Hardrada had mounted a joint invasion and were laying waste the north. In an epic of improvised organization and fortitude, Harold hastily regathered as many of his troops as he could and set out for Northumbria.

There, outside York, he annihilated Tostig and Hardrada. Three days later, 250 miles to the south, William's fleet landed. Harold set off on a further exhausting whirlwind march back the way he had come. Rather than re-group and pick off the Normans during the winter, Harold threw his depleted forces into action immediately.

The battle, fought near Hastings on October 14th, lasted all day. By evening, his army was overwhelmed and the Godwine family wiped out: Harold and his two remaining brothers, Gyrth and Leofwine, were among the dead. The Anglo-Saxon supremacy established by Alfred had been definitively ended. A decisive new chapter in the history of England and its kings had begun.

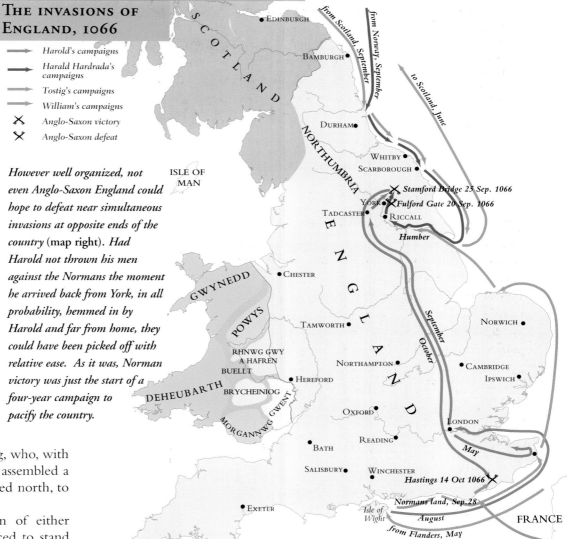

The invasions of England, 1066

→ Harold's campaigns
→ Harald Hardrada's campaigns
→ Tostig's campaigns
→ William's campaigns
✕ Anglo-Saxon victory
✕ Anglo-Saxon defeat

However well organized, not even Anglo-Saxon England could hope to defeat near simultaneous invasions at opposite ends of the country (map right). Had Harold not thrown his men against the Normans the moment he arrived back from York, in all probability, hemmed in by Harold and far from home, they could have been picked off with relative ease. As it was, Norman victory was just the start of a four-year campaign to pacify the country.

SCOTLAND
EDINBURGH
BAMBURGH
DURHAM
WHITBY
SCARBOROUGH
ISLE OF MAN
NORTHUMBRIA
✕ Stamford Bridge 23 Sep. 1066
YORK ✕ Fulford Gate 20 Sep. 1066
TADCASTER
RICCALL
Humber
ENGLAND
GWYNEDD
CHESTER
POWYS
TAMWORTH
NORWICH
RHNWG GWY A HAFREN
BUELLT
NORTHAMPTON
CAMBRIDGE
IPSWICH
DEHEUBARTH
BRYCHEINIOG
HEREFORD
MORGANNWG GWENT
OXFORD
LONDON
BATH
READING
May
SALISBURY
WINCHESTER
Hastings 14 Oct 1066 ✕
EXETER
Isle of Wight
Normans land, Sep. 28
August
FRANCE
from Flanders, May
ST VALERY
September
NORMANDY
from Scotland, September
from Norway, September
to Scotland, June
September
October

Harold, famously, was killed when he was shot in the eye towards the end of the Battle of Hastings (left). Despite their sapping 450-mile march to and from York, the Saxons had come close to holding off the Normans, whose repeated cavalry charges failed to break their defensive line. But a series of feigned Norman retreats then fatally drew elements of the Saxons away from their strong defensive position. Those that remained, Harold among them, became progressively more vulnerable to further Norman charges and the Normans' archers.

Early-Sept: Harold forced to disband most forces in southern England. Joint invasion of Northumbria by Harold Hardrada and Tostig
Sept. 12: Previously wind-bound Norman fleet sails for England; forced back by gales

Sept. 19: News of Hardrada and Tostig's invasion reaches Harold in London
Sept. 20: Hardrada and Tostig defeat Saxon army under Morcar at Fulford. Harold begins forced march north
Sept. 24: Harold reaches York

Sept. 25: Harold overwhelms Hardrada and Tostig at Stamford Bridge
Sept. 27: Normans make second attempt to cross Channel
Sept. 28: Norman invasion fleet lands at Pevensey

Early Oct: Harold begins second forced march (to London); arrives Oct. 6 or 7
Oct. 12: Harold leaves London to confront Normans in Sussex
Oct. 14: Battle of Hastings; death of Harold

ENGLAND: THE NORMANS 1066–1154

WILLIAM THE CONQUEROR 1066–87	*HENRY I 1100–35*
WILLIAM RUFUS 1087–1100	*STEPHEN 1135–54*

A SERIES OF INTERLOCKING THEMES DOMINATED ENGLAND IN THE AFTERMATH OF THE NORMAN CONQUEST IN 1066. BY FAR THE MOST OBVIOUS WAS THE WHOLESALE OVERTHROW OF ENGLAND'S ANGLO-SAXON RULING ELITE – NOT JUST ITS RULING FAMILY AND LEADING MAGNATES BUT PRACTICALLY EVERY LANDOWNER, LARGE AND SMALL, AS WELL AS ALMOST EVERY CHURCHMAN OF NOTE. ALL WERE REPLACED BY FOLLOWERS OF THE NEW KING, WILLIAM. THE MAJORITY OF THE NEWCOMERS WERE NORMAN BUT THERE WERE SUBSTANTIAL NUMBERS OF WILLIAM'S BRETON AND FLEMISH ALLIES AMONG THEM, TOO.

This displacement was begun and sustained by force. Along with significant areas of Scotland and Wales, England was placed under an occupying army that subjected it to a remorseless rule of conquest. All attempts at revolt were peremptorily crushed. The massive programme of castle-building begun by William was a permanent and visible mark of English subjection and Norman overlordship. The takeover of Anglo-Saxon England by the Normans was a root-and-branch operation. By any standard, it was hugely traumatic.

A number of consequences flowed from these central facts. One was that the position of the king himself was greatly strengthened. Having conquered and subdued England, in effect the country became William's personal property, to be disposed of as he thought fit. In practice this meant sharing the spoils among his French followers, whose principal motive for joining William's invasion had been precisely the prospect of enriching themselves in this way. But since it was directly to the king that they owed their new titles and huge estates – which could at any time revert to him – the king was placed at the heart of the burgeoning enterprise of conquest that was Norman England. Significantly, just a year before his death in 1087, William was able to insist that all his landholders, major and minor, swear an oath of personal loyalty to him. This was feudalism redrafted.

The king's position was further strengthened by continuing improvements in the efficiency of royal government. The Normans had a strong base on which to build. Anglo-Saxon government had been the most sophisticated in western Europe. When allied to the conquerors' own brand of absolute rule, it significantly expanded the reach of royal authority. The most celebrated example of this was the compilation of the Domesday Book, undertaken on the orders of William in 1086. Detailed information of this kind had simply never been available before. It is no exaggeration to claim that in the exercise of royal power Norman England saw something of a revolution-in-the-making.

Nonetheless, no king could rule without his leading subjects. If the most effective way to ensure their loyalty and support was by rewarding them lavishly, this also raised the risk that a coalition of disaffected magnates could muster sufficient strength to challenge the king. Needless to say, under strong rulers this was relatively less likely to happen. William himself and his two immediate successors, William Rufus and Henry I, were formidable personalities and practised manipulators of the subtle crudities of early medieval power politics.

By contrast, Stephen (Henry I's nephew), who came to the throne in 1135, found himself almost permanently at the mercy of these inherent instabilities. He was helped by the fact that the forces ranged against him, however powerful, were often as much at odds with each other as with him. Nonetheless, the pattern of baronial revolt and civil war that developed during his reign would become a recurring feature of English medieval history.

At stake of course was the crown itself. To a large extent, this was nothing new. Succession disputes and the ambitions of over-mighty subjects had been consistently destabilizing elements in Anglo-Saxon England. What was new now, however, was not just the shameless aggression the Normans brought to their family feuding but that their relentless struggles had acquired a wider, continental dimension. Put simply, the prize had been dramatically increased. Now, it was not merely the crown of England that was up for grabs but the dukedom of Normandy. The political fates of both had become inextricably intertwined.

A curious tension resulted, one that reflected the unusual imbalance in the status of England and Normandy. In part, this was the inevitable consequence of Normandy's geographical position. In an age of uncertain and slow communications, the effective exercise of cross-Channel power would test even the most dynamic of England's French kings. But the essential problem was more complicated still. By any objective measure, England was significantly more powerful than Normandy: it was substantially larger, very much richer, and considerably better governed. In short, it was a hugely valuable prize. In conquering England so unequivocally, William had achieved an extraordinary success. Furthermore, imbalance and tension were heightened by William's exceptional position: while he was only the duke of the conquering Normandy, he was the king of the subjugated England.

For William and his successors, Normandy remained the priority. This is partly explained by the natural inclination to give precedence to the mother-country over the colony: in most Normans' reckoning, Normandy would always count for more than England. More particularly, however, it was a reflection of the relative vulnerability of Normandy. In making Normandy the most powerful dukedom in France, William had made enemies of his neighbours. These included not just Brittany, Flanders and Anjou, but the kings of France, to whom William was at least nominally subject. But no French king could easily accept the presence of such a threateningly strong subject. Reducing the power of Normandy consequently became a central goal of French royal policy. The result, predictably, was near permanent conflict.

England in effect had not just become an offshoot of a much smaller power but a pawn in its native power struggles. In drawing it into the political orbit of France, William the Conqueror decisively and irreversibly altered the course of history.

William the Conqueror 1066–1087

BORN A BASTARD, AND INHERITING THE DUKEDOM OF NORMANDY AT ONLY SEVEN, THE ODDS AGAINST WILLIAM'S SURVIVAL IN THE VIOLENT WORLD OF 11TH-CENTURY FRANCE WERE LONG. YET IN LITTLE MORE THAN 30 YEARS HE NOT ONLY MADE NORMANDY THE STRONGEST DUKEDOM IN FRANCE BUT CONQUERED ANGLO-SAXON ENGLAND. BY ANY MEASURE, HIS ACHIEVEMENTS WERE EXCEPTIONAL.

1035	1047	1051	1062	1064	1066	1067	1068
Normandy inherited by William	William defeats his cousin Guy de Brionne to consolidate his hold on Normandy	William visits Edward the Confessor and is promised throne of England	William conquers County of Maine	Harold Godwine reputedly swears to uphold William's claim to English throne	Jan: Death of Edward the Confessor and accession of Harold Godwine (Harold II). summer: William assembles invasion fleet. Sept. 28: William lands at Pevensey. Oct. 14: Harold defeated at Battle of Hastings. Dec: London submits; William crowned	William returns to France (Feb.–Dec.): revolt by Welsh under Edric the Wild	Landings in southwest by Harold II's sons: William besieges and sacks Exeter. Revolts in Northumbria under Edwin and Morcar

O F THE 4,000 LAND-OWNING THEGNS (OR nobles) in England in 1066, only two were left by 1087. The whole of the rest of England had been divided among just 200 Norman and other French magnates. The Anglo-Saxon Church had been similarly purged. There was only one English bishop still in office when William died in 1087. As remarkable, this takeover of an England whose population approached two million had been achieved by no more than about 10,000 men.

Guillaume I le Bâtard, as the French know William, was among the most relentlessly single-minded and successful rulers of early medieval Europe. His conquest of England was not just daringly conceived but precisely planned and executed. Taking on a well-organized opponent fighting on home soil was a hugely ambitious undertaking. To have any chance of success, William needed the support not just of his nobles in Normandy but of a disparate collection of allies in Brittany and Flanders. Before he could assemble his forces, William was forced into a complex round of diplomatic manoeuvres, which included winning papal backing, that were hardly less demanding than the invasion itself.

Even so, had it not been for the simultaneous invasion of northern England by the Norwegians under Harold Hardrada, which left Harold II in

Castle Building

T he Norman Conquest was begun and maintained by force of arms. It was in every sense a military occupation by an alien power for whom war and conquest were central facts of life, justifications for almost any atrocity – provided they were successful. It was only appropriate that the most obvious visible expressions of this martial obsession were the castles the Normans built the length and breadth of the country. As the Bayeux Tapestry relates, almost the first thing William did on arriving in England was to build a castle, at Hastings itself (picture below). Thus established, the pattern of Norman occupation scarcely deviated. As they arrived in a new location, so they would throw up a castle which could later be rebuilt on a larger scale in stone. The practical use of these castles was obvious: a secure base from which to dominate the surrounding town or countryside. In time they evolved as much into administrative centres as purely military ones but their prime function as the focus of Norman power never changed.

KING WILLIAM I

BORN: 1028

ACCEDED: December 1066; crowned December 25 1066, Westminster Abbey

Duke of Normandy, Count of Maine, King of England

Unlike even Harold's most formidable professional soldiers, the huscarls, William's knights went into battle on horseback. The Normans are said to have brought up to 6,000 horses with them. At Hastings, their military superiority would eventually prove decisive. The illustration (below) from the Bayeux Tapestry shows William just before the battle.

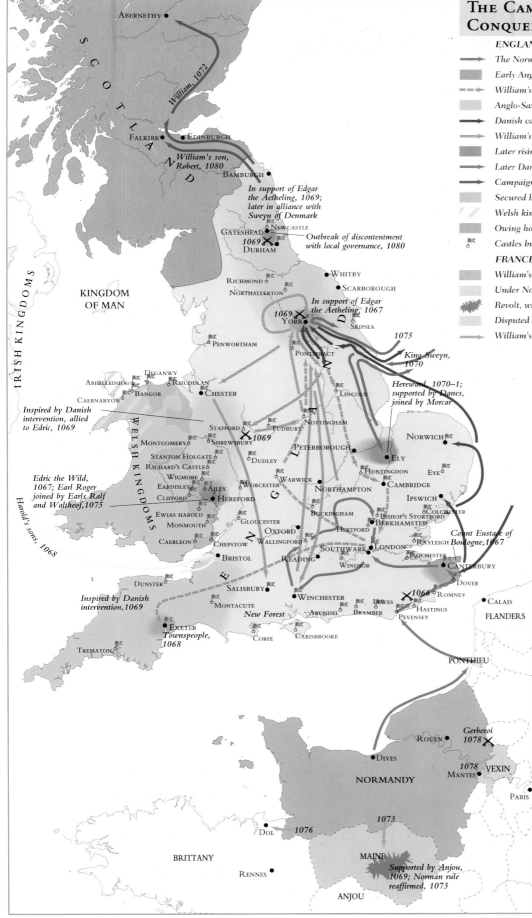

THE CAMPAIGNS OF WILLIAM THE CONQUEROR, 1066–1086

ENGLAND

- The Norman Conquest, to Dec. 1066
- Early Anglo-Saxon revolts, with details
- William's campaigns, 1068
- Anglo-Saxon revolts, 1069
- Danish campaign in alliance with Anglo-Saxon rebels, 1069
- William's campaigns, 1069
- Later risings, with details
- Later Danish interventions, with details
- Campaigns against Scotland, with details
- Secured by Normans in Wales by 1086
- Welsh kingdom, reduced to status of dependency
- Owing homage to William
- Castles built following the Norman conquest, to 1086

FRANCE

- William's holdings at the outset of his campaign to conquer England
- Under Norman rule, contested by Anjou
- Revolt, with details
- Disputed with king of France
- William's campaigns in France, with date

William the Conqueror's subjection of England was made in the face of numerous revolts, large and small, against his rule as well as further Danish attempts to seize the country (map left). It was a relentless and brutal process carried out with extraordinary single-mindedness and played out against the background of William's continuing campaigns to assert the position of Normandy in France.

Map labels

ABERNETHY — William, 1072 — SCOTLAND — FALKIRK — EDINBURGH — William's son, Robert, 1080 — BAMBURGH — In support of Edgar the Aetheling, 1069; later in alliance with Sweyn of Denmark — GATESHEAD 1069 — NEWCASTLE — DURHAM — Outbreak of discontentment with local governance, 1080 — WHITBY — RICHMOND — SCARBOROUGH — NORTHALLERTON — KINGDOM OF MAN — In support of Edgar the Aetheling, 1067 — 1069 YORK — SKIPSEA — 1075 — PENWORTHAM — PONTEFRACT — King Sweyn, 1070 — IRISH KINGDOMS — DEGANWY — RHUDDLAN — CHESTER — LINCOLN — Hereward, 1070–1; supported by Danes, joined by Morcar — ABERLLEINIOG — BANGOR — CAERNARVON — Inspired by Danish intervention, allied to Edric, 1069 — STAFFORD — 1069 SHREWSBURY — TUTBURY — NOTTINGHAM — NORWICH — WELSH KINGDOMS — MONTGOMERY — STANTON HOLGATE — PETERBOROUGH — ELY — HUNTINGDON — EYE — Edric the Wild, 1067; joined by Earls Ralf and Waltheof, 1075 — RICHARD'S CASTLE — WIGMORE — DUDLEY — WORCESTER — WARWICK — NORTHAMPTON — CAMBRIDGE — IPSWICH — EARDISLEY — AILEY — CLIFFORD — HEREFORD — BUCKINGHAM — BISHOP'S STORTFORD — COLCHESTER — Harold's sons, 1068 — EWIAS HAROLD — MONMOUTH — GLOUCESTER — OXFORD — HERTFORD — BERKHAMSTED — Count Eustace of Boulogne, 1067 — CAERLEON — CHEPSTOW — WALLINGFORD — SOUTHWARK — LONDON — RAYLEIGH — BRISTOL — READING — WINDSOR — ROCHESTER — CANTERBURY — DOVER — DUNSTER — Inspired by Danish intervention, 1069 — SALISBURY — WINCHESTER — LEWES — 1066 — ROMNEY — CALAIS — MONTACUTE — ARUNDEL — BRAMBER — HASTINGS — FLANDERS — New Forest — PEVENSEY — EXETER Townspeople, 1068 — CORFE — CARISBROOKE — TREMATON — ENGLAND — PONTHIEU — Gerberoi 1078 — ROUEN — DIVES — 1078 MANTES — VEXIN — PARIS — NORMANDY — 1073 — DOL 1076 — BRITTANY — MAINE — Supported by Anjou, 1069; Norman rule reaffirmed, 1073 — RENNES — ANJOU

The White Tower at the Tower of London (above) was just one of the 70 castles built by William the Conqueror in his vast kingdom.

Timeline

1069	1070	1071	1072	1078	1079	1080	1085	1086	1087
Revolt in Maine forces William to return to France. York captured by Edgar the Aetheling and Sweyn II of Denmark (Sept.), recaptured by William (Dec.); Northumbria laid waste by William (to 1070)	Norman-born Lanfranc of Bec appointed Archbishop of Canterbury	Uprising in East Anglia suppressed	Malcolm III of Scotland forced to submit to William at Abernethy	Tower of London begun. Robert, William's son, supported by Philip I of France, leads revolt in Normandy	Robert defeated at Battle of Gerberoi. New Forest made exclusive royal hunting preserve	Robert leads punitive campaign against Malcolm III	Threatened invasion of England by Cnut IV of Denmark. Domesday survey ordered	First draft of Domesday Book presented to William	William dies besieging Mantes

The Domesday Book

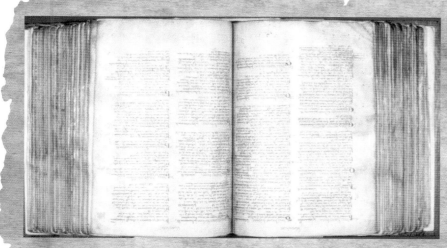

Domesday Book – so called because there was no appeal against it – was the most detailed land survey made in the whole of medieval Europe. It consisted of two immense volumes that not merely listed every landowner in England but gave a precise account of their worth. According to the 12th-century chronicler Orderic Vitalis, "... so very narrowly did he [William] have it investigated that there was no single hide [landholding] nor indeed was one ox or one cow or one pig left out that was not put down in his record." Even more remarkably, it also listed every pre-Conquest landowner, comparing the value of their properties before 1066 with those in 1086, when the survey was made. If it is clear that pre-Conquest Anglo-Saxon records were the basis on which the survey was compiled, Domesday Book thus also provides a vivid record of just how completely the Anglo-Saxon landowning class had been expunged by the Normans. William's motive in ordering the survey was to be able to tax his subjects more efficiently. If he knew in detail what they were worth, they would have no choice but to meet his demands. Ironically, though William was presented with a first draft on August 1 1086, he was personally able to make almost no use of it. Almost immediately, he returned to France, never to return to England.

England facing equally dangerous enemies at opposite ends of his kingdom, it is unlikely that William's cross-Channel assault would have succeeded. As it was, William was able to land unopposed in southern England before facing an English army that, in less than a month, had endured two forced marches of more than 200 miles each and a major battle.

With Harold defeated, William moved quickly to consolidate his victory. He marched his troops through southeast England in a formidable demonstration of his military superiority during which the key cities of Canterbury and Winchester both capitulated. Realizing the futility of continued resistance, the earls of East Anglia and Northumbria, Edwin and Morcar, submitted, as did Edgar the Atheling, grandson of Edmund Ironside, who had briefly been proclaimed king by the Witan. By December, William had taken London. On Christmas Day he was crowned at Westminster Abbey.

Within two months William was back in France. There is some evidence to suggest that he may have felt that England, having apparently been brought to heel, could now be left to take care of itself. If so, he was wrong. By the following December, when William returned, he was facing revolts on almost every side. Over the next four years, he systematically crushed them all. As important, William began the extension of Norman authority into Scotland and Wales. Neither was conquered but both were forced to acknowledge the reality of Norman power.

The challenges to his rule came from various quarters: there were spontaneous outbursts of local protest, notably in East Anglia and the north; more sustained attempts at his overthrow, chiefly by Harold's sons in the southwest; opportunistic Welsh and Scottish attempts to extend their rule into England; and a substantial Danish attempt at conquest of the whole of England by Sweyn II. That these challenges were piecemeal made their suppression relatively more easy. That they sprang up without warning across almost the whole country taxed even the implacable William.

His response was brutal and absolute. In 1068, revolts in the southwest were summarily put down. In the winter of 1069–70, huge areas of Northumbria, where Sweyn's invading Danes had been enthusiastically welcomed, were effectively obliterated. Villages and towns were destroyed in their hundreds; thousands of people were slaughtered. By the summer of 1071 the uprisings in East Anglia had been similarly eradicated. To contain the Welsh, William authorized the creation of the Marcher lordships along the borders of Wales where a handful of his most powerful supporters were effectively allowed to rule as they pleased, carving out huge territories for themselves. In 1072, Malcolm III of Scotland was forced to submit to William. Everywhere, Anglo-Saxon lands were expropriated and given to the king's French followers.

Almost everywhere castles were built, no less than 78 in William's reign. These were the focus of Norman rule, heavily garrisoned and easily defended strong points from which punitive military raiding parties could be sent almost at will. Simple earth-and-wood constructions at first, they were later rebuilt in stone as time and means allowed.

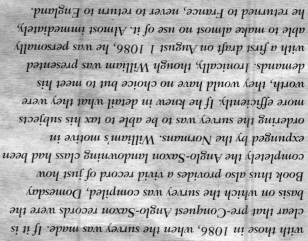

William's minting of coins followed a long-established pattern in stamping royal authority on his new kingdom. Interestingly, as with coins issued in the reign of his son William Rufus, he is named not as WILLIAM REX but PILLEM REX (above). The runic form of the letter W was P The Conqueror's Scandinavian roots had not been entirely forgotten.

Hunting: A Royal Pastime

Hunting was a central preoccupation of England's kings well before the Norman Conquest. But under the Normans it became royalty's pre-eminent leisure activity. William created no fewer than 22 hunting preserves, among them Cranborne Chase and Poorstock in Dorset. A typical example is the New Forest in Hampshire, so called because its "afforestation" in 1087 saw much of its ancient woodland removed in order to create a more favourable hunting ground. Some 22 Saxon villages were razed to create it. All hunting preserves were subject to what was known as the "Forest Laws", a new category of law introduced by the king and outside the Common Law. Under the Forest Laws, only the king or his nominees were allowed to hunt the "venison" – red and fallow deer, roe, and wild pig. The grazing of other animals was outlawed. Under his successor, William Rufus, the Forest Laws were made harsher still. Anyone found guilty of "disturbing" the deer would be blinded. Those found guilty of shooting deer would have their hands amputated. If convicted of killing a deer, the penalty was death. In the words of The Anglo-Saxon Chronicle, "The rich complained, the poor lamented; but he [William] was so hard he set their hate at naught."

Every major town and city had one, as did key strategic points such as Dover and Rochester in the south and the New Castle in the north.

Though Malcolm III continued to probe across the England's northern borders, notably in 1079, and the new king of Denmark, Cnut IV, had still not relinquished the Danish claim to the English throne, the Norman subjection of England was a fact by 1072.

During the last 15 years of William's rule, a pattern emerged that in various forms would characterize the reigns of most of England's French kings until into the 13th century. However important their position as kings of England, their real ambitions remained centred on France. England, once secured, tended to be seen largely as a means of financing further French campaigns. In William's case, these were directed not just against his neighbours – the counts of Anjou and Flanders and the French king, Philip I – but against his eldest son, Robert.

Since as early as 1066, Robert had been recognized – at least in Normandy – as his father's heir. Typically, however, William refused to allow him any real power and, by 1078, Robert was actively conspiring with the French king to overthrow his father. Though reconciled within two years – in 1080, William brought Robert with him to England, where he led a further campaign against Malcolm III – Robert's treachery began a round of dynastic infighting to secure the succession to William's second son, William Rufus.

William's final visit to England was in 1085, when he returned with a huge army intended to resist a Danish invasion under Cnut IV. Though the Danish threat petered out with the murder of Cnut, the difficulty of raising taxes in England to pay for his army persuaded William of the need for more accurate information on his English subjects and their holdings. The result was the compilation of the Domesday Book, the most extensive record of its kind in medieval Europe. Though it might have been made possible only as a result of the earlier Anglo-Saxon records on which it was partly based, it nonetheless remains a remarkable achievement wholly characteristic of the exceptional thoroughness of William's reign.

... For I did not attain that high honour by hereditary right but wrested it from the perjured King Harold in a desperate battle, with much effusion of blood, and it was by the slaughter and banishment of his adherents that I subjugated England to my rule. I have persecuted its native inhabitants beyond all reason. Whether noble or commons I have cruelly oppressed them: many I have unjustly disinherited ... Having therefore made my way to the throne of that kingdom by so many crimes I dare not leave it to anyone but God alone.

Deathbed confession of William the Conqueror according to Orderic Vitalis, from The Ecclesiastical History of England and Normandy, *early 12th century*

William died in Normandy in September 1087 while embarked upon yet another round of punitive campaigning against Philip I, who was again being supported by Robert. Almost at once, a damaging dynastic dispute broke out between William's sons for control of the Conqueror's Anglo-Norman legacy. It would prove to be no more than the forerunner of many such draining conflicts.

MONARCHY IN THE AGE OF FEUDALISM

FROM ABOUT 1000 ONWARDS, FEUDALISM WAS THE CORNERSTONE OF WEST EUROPEAN POLITICAL
ORGANIZATION, A KEY ELEMENT IN THE PRACTICAL AS WELL AS THEORETICAL EXERCISE OF ROYAL
AUTHORITY. DEVELOPED IN DIRECT RESPONSE TO THE DIFFICULTIES OF EXERCISING STRONG
CENTRAL GOVERNMENT IN AN AGE OF PERSISTENT TURBULENCE, IT SUBSTANTIALLY REINFORCED THE
REACH OF MEDIEVAL KINGSHIP.

THE BASIC PREMISE UNDERPINNING FEUDALISM WAS simple: a ruler would delegate authority over a given region (or "fief") to his followers (or "vassals") in return for a promise to support him politically, financially and, above all, militarily. The promise was sealed by a personal act of homage made by the vassal in which the vassal swore to bear "fealty" (or fidelity) to his lord. In turn, the lord promised to defend his vassal. This in effect was a contract that specified the rights and obligations of each party. Senior vassals were in turn expected to "subinfeudate" by extracting similar oaths of loyalty from their subjects, chiefly knights.

that the surrender of freedom implied in the act of homage could only be made by a freeman.

Feudalism first emerged, haphazardly, in France after the break-up of the Carolingian empire in the 9th century. The immediate impetus was to fend off incursions by the Vikings through military alliances, under the French crown, between otherwise rival French territories. With time, however, the leading French nobles, all of whom claimed descent from Charlemagne and thus considered themselves at least the equal of the king and certainly sovereign in their own lands, became progressively less willing to acknowledge the French kings as their full feudal lords. Most recognized the king as superior, or "suzerain", but refused to do homage or to render military service except when it was obviously in their own interests.

Nonetheless, it was essentially this French feudal system that William the Conqueror, himself a vassal of the French king, brought with him to England in 1066. Having crushed the native aristocracy, William also had the advantage of being able to impose feudalism wholesale. For a brief period, feudalism in post-Conquest England probably represented the purest form it ever attained. In essence, claiming that he held England "of no one but God", William was able to divide the country among his principal vassals, ecclesiastical as well as secular. As the king's men, these vassals then subdivided it among their own vassals and administered it on his behalf.

In constructing these chains of mutual self-interest – the nobles received substantial territories while the king was assured of valuable allies bound to him by a personal oath of loyalty – the scope of royal power was considerably extended. There were, however, significant risks for rulers. Providing military assistance in the form of men and arms may have been a fundamental requirement of vassals, but it also meant that the most powerful vassals possessed military assets that could rival or even outstrip the king's.

On the other hand, what the king had given he could also take away. Investing a vassal with a fief meant that the lord was in effect co-owner of the fief, not that he had relinquished his rights to it. In practice, however, the most powerful rebellious vassals could be dispossessed only by a major military action. In much the same way a coalition of vassals, when driven by common interest to act together, could challenge the authority of even the most powerful kings. In essence, it was precisely this kind of co-ordinated opposition by his barons that in 1215 obliged King John to agree, under Magna Carta, to their demands for greater feudal "liberties". Retaining the loyalty of their senior vassals was a prime preoccupation of all medieval kings.

John Balliol, king of Scotland paying homage to the English king, Edward I, in 1292 (above). Positioned at the top of the hierarchy as the king's vassal, Balliol would then be expected to extract similar oaths from his own subjects. That a king could submit himself as the vassal of another monarch was a distincive feature of the feudal system, but it inevitably caused tensions; when, in 1295, Balliol finally rebelled against the impositions of his feudal overlord, he was arrested and imprisoned in the Tower of London.

The result was a chain of relationships that descended vertically from the king and bound together all his leading subjects, the "feudal class". The feudal class consisted of nobles, knights, and monastic and secular clergy. It did not include women, children or the peasantry, all of whom were effectively the property of their lord and were in any case excluded on the ground

The position of ecclesiastical vassals was also a persistent source of difficulty. Since most senior churchmen were members of royal or noble families, and since the Church itself enjoyed such substantial feudal rights, the king's appointment of leading churchmen was every bit as politically sensitive as that of leading barons. But by the 12th century, senior Church figures were actively disputing that kings, anointed by God or not, could enforce feudal rights over the Church. At heart, this was a conflict between the temporal authority of the king and the spiritual authority of the Church. In general, the political strength or otherwise of individual rulers usually settled such disputes. But fundamentally this was an inherent conflict that was irreconcilable in feudal terms, one whose tensions ebbed and flowed throughout the Middle Ages.

Nonetheless, for the most part feudalism provided clear advantages for kings in financial as well as military terms. All vassals were obliged to provide their lord with financial help for particular projects, which in practice almost always meant financing wars. Similarly, though fiefs were normally hereditary, an heir could generally expect to inherit only on payment of a cash sum to his lord. This payment was known as a "relief" and was set at £5 for a knight, £100 for a baron. If the vassal died without an heir, the fief reverted permanently, or "escheated", to the king. By the same token, the widow of a vassal automatically found herself the king's property. If she was still marriageable, and the fief was valuable, the king gained an important asset to be bartered for the highest possible price.

Feudalism was a response to weak central authority; by the same token, strong central authority progressively rendered it redundant. With the emergence of powerful, territorially defined states by the 15th and 16th centuries, the system gradually withered. In England, it had effectively come to an end by Henry VIII's reign, although the notion of the contract that lay at its heart had by then been assimilated into English Common Law. Feudal tenures themselves were legally abolished in 1660.

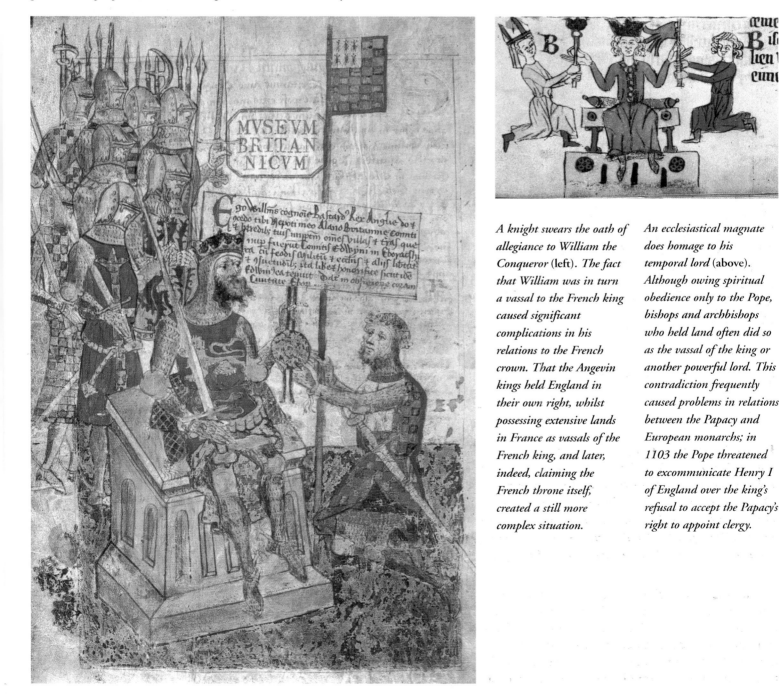

A knight swears the oath of allegiance to William the Conqueror (left). The fact that William was in turn a vassal to the French king caused significant complications in his relations to the French crown. That the Angevin kings held England in their own right, whilst possessing extensive lands in France as vassals of the French king, and later, indeed, claiming the French throne itself, created a still more complex situation.

An ecclesiastical magnate does homage to his temporal lord (above). Although owing spiritual obedience only to the Pope, bishops and archbishops who held land often did so as the vassal of the king or another powerful lord. This contradiction frequently caused problems in relations between the Papacy and European monarchs; in 1103 the Pope threatened to excommunicate Henry I of England over the king's refusal to accept the Papacy's right to appoint clergy.

WILLIAM II 1087–1100

BORN: *c.*1060
ACCEDED: September 9
1087; crowned
September 26 1087,
Westminster Abbey

King of England

William II from an early 13th-century manuscript by Matthew Paris (above). For early medieval monarchs to be depicted holding a church, as William is here, was a conventional recognition of their piety and support for the Church. William did, it is true, endow the abbey founded by his father at Battle in thanks for his victory over the Anglo-Saxons in 1066. But England can surely never have had a monarch more obviously out of sympathy with the Church than William II – nor one more cynical in his attempted manipulation of it.

THE SUCCESSION OF WILLIAM II IN 1087 SPARKED A DAMAGING SUCCESSION DISPUTE BETWEEN HIM AND HIS INDOLENT ELDER BROTHER, ROBERT, THE NEW DUKE OF NORMANDY, FOR THEIR FATHER'S ANGLO-NORMAN TERRITORIES. THE DIFFICULTIES OF UNITING ENGLAND AND NORMANDY UNDER ONE RULE WOULD DESTABILIZE THE ENGLISH MONARCHY UNTIL THE MIDDLE OF THE NEXT CENTURY.

WILLIAM II (OR "RUFUS", A REFERENCE to his red hair and ruddy complexion) has long been considered one of England's most unappealing kings, one whose coarse, brutal and dissolute reign threatened to undermine the new Anglo-Norman world and spark civil war. In many ways, the judgement is unfair, a reflection of the prejudices of contemporary ecclesiastical, chroniclers. There is no question that William was an unprepossessing figure or that he antagonized the Church. But that he was an effective ruler who consolidated Norman rule in England is equally plain.

William II came to the throne by the simple expedient of seizing it. The general assumption was that his elder brother, Robert, would inherit England as well as Normandy. But on William the Conqueror's death in Rouen in 1087, William Rufus made his way to England, secured the Treasury in Winchester, and persuaded the Archbishop of Canterbury, Lanfranc, to crown him. It is an episode that precisely illustrates the continuing uncertainties of royal succession even in an age when the monarchy itself was firmly established. With no automatic presumption of the right of the eldest son to succeed, the crown was always likely to go to the candidate at hand if only so as to avoid the damaging effects of a long drawn-out dispute.

The problem in this case was that England and Normandy now had two, mutually hostile rulers, which posed a near-insoluble dilemma for its leading subjects. Remaining loyal to one risked losing one's position under the other. With Normandy still very much the senior partner, most, led by Bishop Odo, preferred to throw in their lot with Robert. In 1088, William faced a serious revolt by his English magnates.

William dealt with the immediate problem in typical Norman style: he banished Odo and his supporters and confiscated their English estates. The fundamental difficulty remained, however, and there followed seven years of generally inconclusive campaigning, mostly by William in Normandy. This came to an

William and the Church

William had little time for the Church, barely bothering even with conventional pieties. For its part, the Church was shocked not just by William's licentious court but by his refusal to appoint new bishops and abbots so as to keep Church revenues for himself. When Anselm, who was to prove a persistent thorn in William's side, was appointed Archbishop of Canterbury by William in 1093, the see had been vacant for four years. But to this existing conflict was added a growing Europe-wide dispute over the primacy of monarchical authority in Church affairs. It had long been taken for granted that, as divinely anointed rulers, kings had supreme authority in spiritual as well as temporal matters. This was not only a religious matter. The Church was enormously rich: controlling its assets was a prime necessity for all rulers. Yet from the reforming papacy of Gregory VII in the mid-11th century, the view had grown that papal authority over the Church was absolute.

During William's reign, the issue was further clouded by the existence of two rival popes, the broadly pro-Gregorian Urban II in Rome and Clement III in Ravenna. Deciding which one to recognize was, for William, a simple matter of determining which was more likely to support him in his own struggles against the Church in England.

1088 In this year was the land much stirred, and filled with great treachery, so that the richest Frenchmen that were in this land would betray their lord the king, and would have his brother Robert king, who was early in Normandy ... When the king understood all these things, and what treachery they were employing against him, then was he in his mind much agitated.

The Anglo-Saxon Chronicle

1087	1088	1090	1091	1092	1093	1094
Accession of William	*William crushes uprising led by Bishop Odo, who with other anti-William magnates returns to Normandy*	*William leads inconclusive invasion of Normandy. Malcolm III of Scotland attempts to extend Scottish control over Northumbria*	*Degree of rapprochement reached between William and his brother Robert, duke of Normandy*	*William appoints Anselm Archbishop of Canterbury. Cumbria annexed by William; construction of Carlisle castle begun*	*Death of Malcolm III of Scotland; William engineers succession of pro-Norman Duncan*	*Attempt by William to conquer Wales is repulsed by Gruffydd ap Cynan; William authorizes further expansion of Marcher lordships*

The consolidation of Norman rule in England was vigorously continued by William Rufus (map right): The Marcher Lordships were expanded, Norman influence over its Scottish vassals reinforced. More damagingly, his reign also saw the first of a series of power-struggles – between the king and his leading magnates in England as well as between the king and his brother Robert in Normandy – that would destabilize much subsequent Norman kingship.

end in 1096, when Robert decided to join the First Crusade. To raise money for the venture, he pawned Normandy to his brother, who became regent of the duchy. Although this was clearly no more than a short-term solution – for it could be assumed that Robert would eventually return – it proved surprisingly effective for the remaining four years of William's reign. That Robert did return and, moreover, that William died childless, meant only that the succession problem had been postponed. It duly resurfaced on William's death, this time between Robert and his other brother, Henry.

The question of the succession took place against the background of two other far-reaching developments. One was William's dispute with the Church. The other was a further extension of Norman influence into Scotland and Wales. In Scotland, early disputes between William and Malcolm III of Scotland were decisively settled in William's favour in 1093 when, with Carlisle now in Norman hands, Malcolm was killed by a party of Norman knights. In the dynastic turmoil that followed, William played a leading role in the accession of Malcolm's sons, Duncan II and Edgar, both with strong Norman leanings. In Wales the Marcher lordships established by William the Conqueror were substantially expanded.

ENGLAND AND NORMANDY UNDER WILLIAM RUFUS 1087–1100

- Rebellions instigated by Odo de Bayeux on behalf of Robert in 1087, with leaders
- → William's campaigns, with dates
- Other revolts, with details
- Lost by Normans, recovered under William Rufus, 1097–9
- Annexed from Scotland, 1092
- Marcher Lordships, 1100
- Disputed with the King of France

The Death of William II

The apparently accidental death of William II on August 2 1100 in the New Forest has long given rise to suspicions that he was murdered. The most commonly accepted theory is that it was no more than mischance, that William was shot by a companion, Walter Tirel, entirely by accident. On the other hand, William's brother Henry, who had designs of his own on the English throne, was with the hunting party and thus conveniently placed no more than a few hours' ride from Winchester. In any case, when William died, Henry did what William himself had done on their father's death: he made straight for Winchester, secured the royal Treasury, and then headed for London where, three days later, he was crowned by the Archbishop of London. Crucially, he had forestalled the return of his brother Robert from the Holy Land by little more than a month. Had Robert returned in time, he would surely have been able to reunite Normandy and England under his sole rule. In the matter of William's death, the case against Henry – strong though it seems – remains entirely circumstantial. It is unlikely ever to be proved one way or the other.

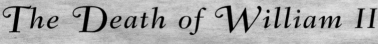

1095	1096	1097	1098	1099	1100
Further revolt against William by Norman magnates in Northumbria is crushed. Council of Rockingham meets to resolve disputes between Anselm and William and to decide between rival popes Urban II and Clement III	Robert pawns Normandy to William to finance his participation in First Crusade	Anselm flees to Normandy; William seizes his property	Attempted invasion of North Wales by Magnus "Barefoot", King of Norway, repulsed by marcher lords	Counties of Maine and Vexin in Normandy lost by Robert, retaken by William	Death of William in hunting accident in New Forest

HENRY I 1100–35

BORN: c.1068
ACCEDED: August 3
1100; crowned August 6
1100, Westminster
Abbey

*King of England, Duke
of Normandy (from
1106), Lord of Domfront
(from 1092)*

*Henry (picture above) was
an exceptionally able king,
well able to master the
seething, competing
ambitions of his barons
and rivals. He could also
be surprisingly generous.
He seems to have held
genuine affection for his
nephew and successor
Stephen, for example,
showering him with titles
and lands. Yet a streak of
cruelty bordering almost
on savagery ran through
him. In his youth, he is
said to have personally
thrown a rebellious
merchant in Rouen from
the castle battlements.
As king, he authorized
the blinding of two of
his grandchildren who
he was holding hostage.*

AFTER WILLIAM THE CONQUEROR, HENRY I WAS BY SOME WAY THE MOST SUCCESSFUL OF THE NORMAN KINGS OF ENGLAND. BY A RUTHLESS COMBINATION OF FORCE AND DIPLOMACY HE OUTMANOEUVRED ALL HIS ENEMIES TO MAKE HIMSELF ABSOLUTE RULER OF ENGLAND AND NORMANDY. YET ULTIMATELY HIS REIGN, TOO, WAS CLOUDED BY A SUCCESSION DISPUTE. HIS LEGACY WAS A WASTEFUL CIVIL WAR.

A S THE YOUNGEST SON OF WILLIAM THE Conqueror (and the only one born in England), Henry had had no realistic expectations of inheriting any of his father's lands. Instead, it was assumed that he would go into the Church. As a result Henry was the only one of William's sons to receive much in the way of an education and the only Norman king who was not illiterate – hence his nickname Beauclerc, or "good writer". That his own instincts led him in quite another direction was clear not just from an abortive bid for power against both his brothers in 1091 – with the result that each viewed him with equal mistrust – but from the decisive manner in which he grabbed the throne after the death of William Rufus in August 1100.

Robert, duke of Normandy, whose own hopes of becoming King of England had long been thwarted by William, had nonetheless agreed with William that each would inherit the other's territories if the other died first and without an heir. Arriving back in Normandy just a month after William's death, and hailed on all sides for his exploits in the Holy Land, Robert's hopes of taking England from Henry were high. Instead, he found himself comprehensively outmanoeuvred.

Henry's actions on coming to the throne set the tone for most of his reign. Within six days of his coronation, he married Edith, the daughter of Malcolm III of Scotland, whose mother was directly descended from the Anglo-Saxon rulers of England. At a stroke, he had simultaneously allied himself with Scotland and proclaimed his kinship with the dispossessed Anglo-Saxon majority. He also issued a series of proclamations promising to end William's oppressive practices while simultaneously courting his leading subjects by making extravagant promises of lands and titles in return for their support. Crucially, he capped his diplomatic offensive by striking alliances with both the King of France and Count of Flanders and repairing William's break in relations with the Church by inviting the exiled Anselm to return to his office as Archbishop of Canterbury.

Thus, when Robert launched his inevitable invasion of England the following June, he had neither the military nor the diplomatic advantage he might reasonably have expected. Humiliatingly – albeit in return for £2,000 a year, under a deal brokered by Anselm – he was forced to recognize Henry's right to the English throne and acknowledge him his heir in Normandy.

Henry was far from finished. First, he dispossessed all those Normans in England who had not supported him. Then he took the fight to Robert. In 1106 he invaded Normandy, defeated Robert and imprisoned him. Robert spent the remaining 27 years of his life as Henry's prisoner.

Despite being forced on to the back foot by the Church in 1107 when, threatened with excommunication, he was obliged to concede the Church's superior authority in "investing" new bishops and abbots, in almost every respect bar one, the rest of his reign as unchallenged ruler in Normandy and England was strikingly successful. His solitary failure was his inability to produce an heir. Henry had two legitimate sons, William and Richard, but they were both drowned when the *White Ship*,

1120 This year were reconciled the King of England and the King of France; and after their reconciliation all the King Henry's own men accorded with him in Normandy … And on this expedition were drowned the King's two sons William and Richard, and Richard, Earl of Chester, and Ottuel his brother, and very many of the King's household, stewards, and chamberlains, and butlers, and men of various abodes; and with them a countless multitude of very incomparable folk besides. Sore was their death to their friends in a twofold respect: one that they so suddenly lost this life; the other, that few of their bodies were found anywhere afterwards.

The Anglo-Saxon Chronicle

1100	1101	1103	1106	c. 1110	1114
Henry issues Charter of Liberties, promising good government and an end to William Rufus's oppressive practices. Anselm, Archbishop of Canterbury, recalled from exile	*Failed invasion of England by Henry's brother Robert, Duke of Normandy; Robert forced to recognize Henry's right to the English throne*	*Henry and Anselm clash over the king's right to "invest" bishops; Anselm returns to exile*	*Pope threatens to excommunicate Henry unless he accepts ecclesiastical supremacy in investiture of bishops. Henry invades Normandy and captures Robert at Tinchebrai; Henry becomes Duke of Normandy*	*Pipe Rolls – official Exchequer accounts – are introduced by Roger, Bishop of Salisbury*	*Henry's daughter Matilda married to Holy Roman Emperor, Henry V*

The White Ship

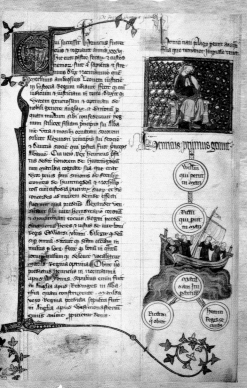

I t is one of the great ironies of English monarchical history that Henry I had no surviving legitimate male heirs at the end of his reign. Henry in fact fathered 29 children, more than any other king of England or Britain. Unfortunately all but four were illegitimate and of them only one, Matilda, survived into full adulthood. The deaths of the teenage William and Richard, Henry's two legitimate male heirs, in 1120 on the White Ship – which was run on to a rock outside Barfleur by its supposedly drunken crew – threw all Henry's careful plans for his succession into disarray. Though Henry made his barons accept Matilda as his heir in 1126, most did so with extreme reluctance. Her marriage in 1128 to the 14-year-old count Geoffrey of Anjou provoked further suspicion. Henry had meant to bind Anjou, a traditional enemy of Normandy, within his diplomatic web. But to many Normans, it looked like no more than an opportunity for Anjou to reassert its claims to Normandy. They were proved right. By 1135, Henry and Geoffrey were at war. It was a further irony that it was one of Henry's illegitimate sons, Robert Fitzroy, earl of Gloucester, who was the mainstay of Matilda's campaign to make herself queen after Henry's death, a campaign that produced a vicious and brutal 15-year civil war in the reign of Henry's eventual successor, his nephew Stephen of Blois.

ENGLAND AND NORMANDY UNDER HENRY I, 1100–1135

- → Robert Curthouse's abortive invasion, 1101
- ⚔ Strongholds of Robert de Bellême seized by Henry
- → Henry's campaign against Robert de Bellême, 1102
- ▭ Surrendered to Henry I by Robert Curthouse, 1104
- → Henry I's campaigns against Robert Curthouse, 1106
- Allied to Henry I, 1104-06
- Allies of the King of France, 1111–13, 1116–19
- Controlled by Anjou, periodically under Henry's influence
- Marcher Lordships, 1100
- New Marcher Lordships by 1100
- Brought under royal control by Henry I
- 🍂 Revolts, with details

Henry I's active brand of brutal kingship was strikingly successful in England and Normandy. Revolts in both countries were smartly suppressed (map right). As important, the threat posed by his elder brother, Robert, duke of Normandy, was put down equally effectively. Henry I did more than just consolidate the Norman hold on England: he actively redrafted the powers of medieval kingship.

taking them from Normandy to England, sank in November 1120. Henry's wife Edith (who had become known as Matilda) had died in 1118; in 1126, after a hurriedly arranged second marriage had failed to produce a new son, Henry designated his daughter, Matilda, his heir. In an age when female rights to any throne were viewed with deep suspicion, it was a move fraught with risk. When, in 1135, Henry famously died from a "surfeit of lampreys", a new round in England's long-running Norman succession crises was duly begun.

A saddened Henry I (left) after the death of his two sons in an accident in 1120 (see box). As Henry failed to produce another legitimate male heir, the accident represented the worst disaster of his reign.

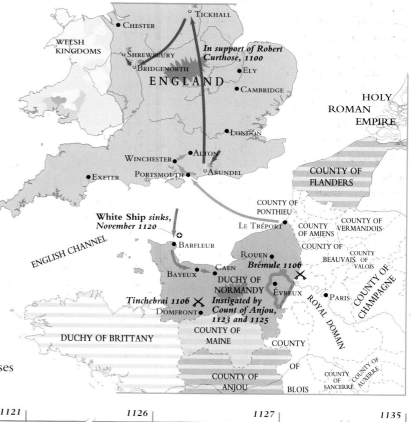

1119	1120	1121	1126	1127	1135
Louis VI of France forced to recognize Henry as duke of Normandy	Henry's two heirs, William and Richard, drowned on the White Ship	Henry remarries, to Adeliza, daughter of the count of Louvain	Henry nominates Matilda as his heir and forces his barons to swear an oath accepting her	Matilda remarries, to Geoffrey (count of Anjou from 1129)	Geoffrey and Henry at war over Normandy

SCOTLAND:
FROM DUNKELD TO
BRUCE 1034–1329

DUNCAN I 1034–40

MACBETH MACFINLAY 1040–57

LULACH 1057–58

MALCOLM III "CANMORE" 1058–93

DONALD III BÁN 1093–94
AND 1094–97

DUNCAN II 1094

EDGAR 1097–1107

ALEXANDER I 1107–24

DAVID I 1124–53

MALCOLM IV 1153–65

WILLIAM I THE LION 1165–1214

ALEXANDER II 1214–49

ALEXANDER III 1249–86

MARGARET 1286–90

JOHN BALLIOL 1292–96

ROBERT I THE BRUCE 1306–29

THE TERRITORIAL CORE OF A VIABLE SCOTLAND MAY HAVE BEEN ESTABLISHED AT THE DEATH OF MALCOLM II IN 1034, BUT IN REALITY MID-11TH-CENTURY SCOTLAND WAS JUST ONE AMONG A NUMBER OF COMPETING POLITIES IN THE REGION. THESE WERE TERRITORIES, ECONOMICALLY BACKWARD AND POLITICALLY IMMATURE, THAT EXISTED ON THE REMOTE MARGINS OF EUROPE. SCOTTISH KINGSHIP ITSELF WAS STILL AN ESSENTIALLY TRIBAL, OFTEN BRUTAL BUSINESS.

By 1290, however, though Scotland was still only in the second rank of western European polities, its independence and identity had been firmly established, its polit-ical institutions substantially strengthened and its territorial extent greatly increased. England aside, the chief threats to its continued existence – whether Irish, Norwegian or the disparate band of semi-independent barons and local rulers in the western isles – had all been forced to acknowledge Scottish supremacy. An independent Scottish kingdom had become a clear reality.

The key element in this transformation was Scottish kingship itself. By virtue both of the continuity provided by an unbroken line of royal succession between 1097 and 1290 and, from the 12th century, a deliberate if gradual extension of royal authority, Scotland's kings increasingly defined and shaped the emerging nation. To some extent, this was a matter of luck, above all in the appearance of a number of exceptionally able, long-lived rulers. Chiefly, however, it was a reflection of the transformation of medieval kingship occurring elsewhere in Europe. The rapid growth of feudal royal authority epitomized by Henry II in England found a ready echo in Scotland.

That said, the process was rarely clear-cut. Even during the reigns of the most dominant of these kings – David I and Malcolm IV in the 12th century, Alexander III in the 13th – there were clear limits to the reach of royal power. Rebellion on the part of disaffected barons was a recurrent problem, not least after the 12th-century influx of Anglo-Normans in the service of the crown that created serious disputes with the native aristocracy. Scotland's kings also had to contend with a shifting series of power bases, from which were mounted more or less serious challenges to their rule; these lay in the far north and west of the mainland as well as in the Norwegian-ruled Isle of Man and Western Isles.

Above all, Scotland was overshadowed by its stronger and often hostile neighbour, England. For substantial periods, Scotland was effectively no more than a client of England. Even after the border between Scotland and England had been more or less permanently fixed on the Solway-Tweed line in 1157, border clashes were a regular feature. And at the end of the 13th century, Edward I came close to ripping apart for good the still vulnerable Scottish polity.

It was precisely these aggressive Norman and Plantagenet kings, however, who provided the direct stimulus for the transformation of Scottish kingship. From the reign of Edgar onwards, Scotland's kings actively modelled themselves on their counterparts in England. In part, this emulation was almost a form of new Norman conquest. A number of Scottish kings, most notably David I, had been brought up in England under Norman protection. Importing the new style of French kingship was natural to them: it was a central element of a world they were intimately familiar with. But in part it was also a matter of necessity, a realization, however slow, that Scotland could only hope to keep England at bay by imitating the institutions that had made it strong.

The most obvious indication was the spread of feudalism, and through it the extension of royal power. By tying their nobles to them in direct chains of loyalty and service, Scottish kings in the 12th and 13th centuries substantially increased their own authority. The process was necessarily slow. Where William the Conqueror had been able to impose feudalism wholesale on England by the simple fact of conquest, in Scotland it could only be introduced piecemeal, often in the face of considerable resistance.

Alongside feudalism came the development of more effective forms of government, again on the Anglo-Norman model. David I was once more the key early figure. Not only was his court reorganized – with a steward, chamberlain, chancellor and constable – as an exact, if smaller version of Henry I's in England, he introduced Scotland's first counties, each with a sheriff to administer royal justice. The position of Scotland and its rulers was also significantly improved by the forging of closer links with the papacy, then at the height of its prestige.

As royal authority grew, so successive kings were able to extend their rule over larger areas. Moray, Caithness and Galloway were all brought under the actual rather than nominal rule of the crown. Crucially, in 1266 Norway was forced to surrender the western isles to Scotland.

The succession, in 1153, 1249 and 1286, of under-age rulers went undisputed, but in 1290 Scotland's dynastic luck ran out with the death of the uncrowned seven-year-old child-queen, Margaret, the "Maid of Norway". With no obvious successor left, the kingdom was suddenly vulnerable to the formidably rapacious Edward I of England. Whatever Scotland's new institutional stability, a new and bloodier chapter in Anglo-Scottish relations was begun.

1040	1054	1057	1058	1061	1066	1066	1068	1070	1072	1079	1091
Duncan I killed by Macbeth at Pitgaveny;	Macbeth defeated by Earl Siward of Northumbria and Duncan's son, Malcolm, at Dunsinnan in England	Macbeth killed by Malcolm at Lumphanan; accession of Malcolm III	Lulach killed, Lulach, his stepson, becomes king of Scots	Northumbria raided by Malcolm III	Malcolm and allies Harald of Norway and Tostig defeated by Harold II	Attempted conquest of England by Malcolm III	Edgar the Aetheling taken in by Malcolm III, who marries his sister Margaret	Malcolm III raids Northumbria	Malcolm III submits to William the Conqueror at Abernethy after Norman retaliatory action	Another invasion of Northumbria by Malcolm III provokes further Norman retaliatory action	Final invasion of Northumbria by Malcolm III leads to further Scottish submission to Norman king of England, William Rufus

The House of Dunkeld 1034–1153

THERE WERE SIX SUCCESSIONS TO THE THRONE OF SCOTLAND BETWEEN 1040 AND 1097. EVERY ONE OF THESE KINGS WAS EITHER MURDERED OR OVERTHROWN. BETWEEN 1097 AND 1290, BY CONTRAST, THE SUCCESSION OF NOT ONE OF THE COUNTRY'S SUBSEQUENT EIGHT RULERS WAS DISPUTED. THIS SIMPLE STATISTIC SPEAKS VOLUMES FOR THE GROWING POLITICAL MATURITY OF THE SCOTTISH MONARCHY.

T HE ACCESSION IN 1034 OF DUNCAN I, grandson of Malcolm II, brought the House of Dunkeld to the throne of Scotland. Its name came from Duncan's father, the Abbot of Dunkeld. Much of Duncan's six-year reign was spent campaigning against Thorfinn, earl of Orkney, and Macbeth Macbethad, mormaer (ruler) of Moray, a rival claimant as king of Scots. Such feuding was hardly unusual. There is no historical reason why Shakespeare should later have portrayed Duncan as particularly wronged and Macbeth as particularly scheming, even though in 1040 Macbeth overthrew Duncan, seized the crown, and drove Duncan's sons into exile in England. By the standards of the day, Macbeth's rule was not just stable; it was long-lived. And though it included considerable campaigning against the Norse in the north, Macbeth was secure enough to make a pilgrimage to Rome in 1050, evidence of Scotland's increasing integration with the wider European world. For the rest of the 11th century, Scotland's fate was closely bound with events in England. To begin with, two exiled sons, Malcolm and Donald Bán. In 1054, Edward the Confessor ordered a successful invasion

of Scotland in which Macbeth was overthrown. The following year, after a brief and confused rule by Lulach (Macbeth's stepson), Malcolm III "Canmore" ("big head") became king of Scots.

Though Malcolm's relations with Anglo-Saxon England were generally good, in 1066 he was nonetheless an eager participant in the failed invasion of England launched by the Norwegians and King Harold's disaffected brother, Tostig. The consequences for Scotland of the subsequent successful Norman takeover of England were momentous. That Malcolm was now also sheltering Edgar, the remaining Anglo-Saxon claimant to England's throne, made Norman aggression all the more likely. Yet at the same time Norman influence over the Scottish ruling house was rapidly growing. In 1072, not only was Malcolm forced to become William's vassal, his eldest son, Duncan, was given as a hostage to William. Brought up in a Norman court, Duncan became a keen proponent of Norman ways. The struggle between the pro- and anti-Norman factions within Scotland would become a dominant theme in the development of Scotland's monarchy well into the next century.

In 1093, the murder of Malcolm III himself by the Norman earl of Northumbria provoked a fierce anti-Norman backlash which brought Malcolm's brother, Donald III Bán, to the throne. Within a year, he had been ousted by a Norman-backed invasion led by the strongly pro-Norman Duncan. A year later, Donald Bán had taken the throne back. In 1097, a second Norman-sponsored invasion led by another of Malcolm's sons, Edgar, proved decisive. Donald Bán was captured and murdered. Edgar brought Scotland firmly within the Norman orbit, a process continued by his brothers and successors, Alexander I and David I. In part, this was a matter of the assertion of Norman and later Angevin overlordship. Equally important, however, it was a conscious attempt to remodel the Scottish monarchy on Anglo-French lines. Scotland could never hope to rival England, but by imitating its newly powerful kings it could go far towards assuring an independent and increasingly secure identity.

Duncan II's reign in 1094 may have been brief, but it dates the oldest surviving Scottish charter (above), a grant of land to the monks of Durham, then under Scottish rule. It is a distinct sign of the slowly growing sophistication of royal administration.

In becoming the first Scottish king to issue his own coins (above right), David initiated something of an economic revolution, one paralleled by his sponsorship of a number of trading communities, or "burghs", among them Berwick, Edinburgh, Stirling and Jedburgh. They not only transformed Scotland's economic life, opening valuable trading links across the North Sea, they were important sources of revenue for the king.

Double portrait of David I and his grandson, Malcolm IV (right), from the charter for Kelso Abbey, 1159. The biblical connotations in this rare portrait, produced shortly after David's death, are obvious. It is clearly intended that the old king should be seen as a reincarnation of the Old Testament King David, his youthful successor as a second King Solomon. The figures sit within the initial letter "M" of the charter.

SCOTLAND, 1034–1153

By the death of David I in 1153, the reach of a Scottish kingship actively modelling itself on its Norman and Plantagenet neighbours in England had been greatly increased. The west coast may still not have been brought under Scotland's kings but their authority, as well as their relations with England, had been transformed (map below).

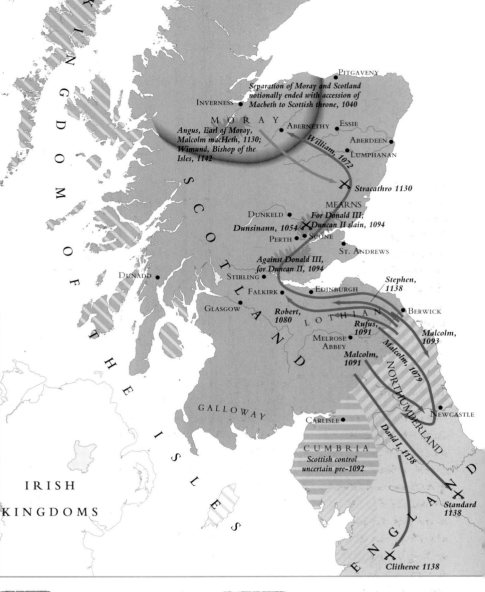

DUNCAN I 1034–40
(BORN c.1010) GRANDSON OF MALCOLM II

Last king of Strathclyde and first ruler of the House of Dunkeld. Attempts to extend his rule into the far north saw repeated clashes with Thorfinn, earl of Orkney, and Macbeth, ruler of Moray. Also unsuccessfully attempted to consolidate Scottish rule in Northumbria. Defeated and killed by Macbeth at Pitgaveny.

MACBETH MACFINLAY 1040–57
(BORN c.1005) Mormaer (RULER) OF MORAY FROM 1032

(Moray's rulers were longtime rivals of the Mac Alpin kings of Scotland). Though unable to subdue the Norse in Caithness and Sutherland, his rule was otherwise stable until, in 1054, Duncan's eldest son, Malcolm, supported by Siward, earl of Northumbria, defeated him at Dunsinnan. In 1057, he was killed by Malcolm at Lumphanan.

LULACH 1057–8
(BORN c.1032) STEPSON OF MACBETH

Last mormaer of Moray to become King of Scots, Macbeth ruled for less than a year before the future Malcolm III, already effective ruler of southern Scotland, killed him at Essie.

MALCOLM III "CANMORE" 1058–93
(BORN c.1031) SON OF DUNCAN I

Last of the fearsomely warlike warrior-kings of old. His first marriage, to Ingibiorg, daughter of the Earl of Orkney, cemented relations with the Norse and allowed him to concentrate on the attempted conquest of Northumbria, which he repeatedly raided. William the Conqueror and his son William Rufus permanently worsted him, however, extracting oaths of allegiance in 1072 and 1092 (when Cumbria was also lost).

DONALD III BÁN 1093–4 AND 1094–7
(BORN c.1032) SON OF DUNCAN I

Brother of Malcolm III. Came to the throne after Malcolm's murder by the Normans. Fierce opponent of the growing Norman influence in Scotland. Ousted by Malcolm's eldest son, Duncan, with the support of William Rufus. Within months, Duncan himself had been murdered and Donald restored. A second Norman-backed invasion in 1097, led by another of Malcolm's sons, Edgar, saw the final defeat of Donald.

DUNCAN II 1094
(BORN c.1060) SON OF MALCOLM III

Though initially a beneficiary of Norman support, he was obliged by fierce anti-Norman feeling within Scotland to dismiss all the Anglo-Normans from his court. Suddenly vulnerable, he was powerless to resist Donald III. His reign was chaotic and brief.

EDGAR 1097–1107
(BORN c.1074) SON OF MALCOLM III

Capable and competent; restored stability to the crown. Strongly subservient to Norman England, however, with whom relations were accordingly peaceful. The first Scottish king to imitate the English practice of sealed writs to enforce his will.

ALEXANDER I 1107–24
(BORN c.1077) SON OF MALCOLM III

Marriage to one of Henry I's many bastard daughters, Sybilla, cemented relations with England (as well as confirming Scotland's vassal status), allowing Alexander to launch successful campaigns against still strongly anti-Norman Moray, and to initiate basic reforms in government.

DAVID I 1124–53
(BORN c.1084) SON OF MALCOLM III

The dominant figure in Scottish 12th-century history, author of the "Davidian revolution". He almost single-handedly initiated the transformation of Scottish kingship, substantially increasing its authority and prestige, principally through the imposition of feudalism, a process supported by the introduction of large numbers of Anglo-Norman families. Successful subjugation of Moray from 1130 was matched by numerous administrative reforms and remarkable patronage of the Church. If unable to overcome Norman military superiority, he nonetheless helped to carve a distinctive and increasingly admired Scottish identity.

1093	1094	1097	1107	1124	1127	1128	1130	1136	1138	1149
Malcolm III murdered on orders of Robert de Mowbray, earl of Northumbria; his brother Donald Bán succeeds	Donald Bán briefly overthrown by Malcolm's son, Duncan II, then restored after death of Duncan	William Rufus sponsors invasion of Scotland by Malcolm III's son, Edgar; Donald Bán overthrown and Edgar accedes	Accession of Alexander I; initiates minor reforms	Accession of David; beginning of major programme of reforms	David I swears to uphold right of Henry I's daughter, Matilda, to throne of England (and again in 1133)	Holyrood Abbey founded by David I	Moray annexed for crown by David I	David I supports Matilda's claim to England after accession of Stephen (1135) by invading Cumbria.	Further invasion of Northumbria crushed by Stephen at Battle of the Standard	David I agrees to support claim of Matilda's son, Henry of Anjou, to English throne in return for right to retain Cumbria and Northumbria

- 1157 Henry II forces Malcolm IV to accept English control of Northumbria and Cumbria
- 1160-4 Galloway and Argyll subdued by Malcolm IV; rebellion by Somerled, Lord of Cumbria; Malcolm becomes Henry's vassal
- 1163 Malcolm IV forced to renew his homage to Henry II
- 1164 Argyll crushed
- 1174 William the Lion invades northern England, captured by Henry II and made his vassal (Treaty of Falaise)
- 1187 Revolts against William in Galloway put down
- 1189 The "Quitclaim of Canterbury": Richard I cancels the Treaty of Falaise
- 1196 Successful campaign by William against Norse earl of Orkney
- 1209-12 Invasions of Scotland by King John lead to restoration of English overlordship
- 1215 Alexander II supports Magna Carta and does homage to Prince Louis of France in attempt to aid the overthrow of John

THE HOUSE OF DUNKELD 1153–1296

THE NORMANIZING POLICIES OF DAVID I WERE CONTINUED BY HIS SUCCESSORS IN THE 12TH AND 13TH CENTURIES, CONSIDERABLY INCREASING SCOTTISH ROYAL AUTHORITY AS WELL AS THE TERRITORY UNDER ITS CONTROL. YET THROUGHOUT THE PERIOD SCOTLAND'S KINGS ALSO HAD TO CONTEND WITH A SERIES OF VERY MUCH MORE POWERFUL ENGLISH KINGS. SCOTTISH AMBITIONS ALWAYS HAD TO CONFRONT THE REALITY OF SUPERIOR ENGLISH ARMS.

T HE UNDISPUTED ACCESSION OF THE 11-year-old Malcolm IV, David I's grandson, in 1153 may have demonstrated a new political stability in Scotland but it also left the country vulnerable. The most obvious threat came from Henry II, King of England from 1154. Despite having promised David I in 1149 that he would allow Scotland to retain Northumbria and Cumbria if David would support his claim to the English throne, in 1157 Henry imperiously informed Malcolm that he was taking them back. Though the Anglo-Scottish border would not be formally fixed on the line of the Tweed and Solway until the Treaty of York in 1237, Malcolm and his immediate successors would make repeated attempts to regain northern England, in effect Scotland's southern limit had been permanently established.

The other danger came from those magnates, above all in the still strongly Gaelic and Norse west and north – Ross, Argyll, Moray and Galloway – who were alarmed at the continuing influx of Anglo-Normans into Scotland, and at David's determination to extend feudalism. Resistance centred on Somerled, so-called king of the Isles, who in the name of the king of Norway ruled a large, if vaguely defined area embracing much of western Scotland. Somerled's unsuccessful attempt to unseat Malcolm in 1164 led not just to his own death but brought Argyll and Galloway under increasing royal control.

The twin themes of conflict with England and the extension of royal authority, in the face of baronial and Norwegian resistance, into the north and west of Scotland persisted through the long reigns of Malcolm's successors, William the Lion and Alexander II. In 1174, with Henry II preoccupied with the attempt by his sons to overthrow him, William attempted to retake Northumbria. It was a humiliating fiasco. Under the subsequent Treaty of Falaise, William was forced to become Henry's vassal. English troops were garrisoned in Scotland (at Scottish expense), and the Church of Scotland was made subject to that of England.

Though Richard the Lionheart reversed the treaty in 1189 in return for a payment of 10,000 marks, his successor, John, was determined to reassert English overlordship. In 1212, in a further humiliating setback for the now ageing William, the Scottish king was obliged to confirm John as his lord and surrender his daughters for John to marry off (the elder in theory to John's heir). Hardly surprisingly, William's son, Alexander, who acceded in 1214, enthusiastically supported the English barons who forced Magna Carta on John in 1215. In a similar spirit of rebellion, Alexander also threw his weight behind the French claimant to the English throne, Prince Louis.

John's sudden death in 1216 and the accession of Henry III transformed Anglo-Scottish relations. The mood of co-operation, symbolized by Alexander's marriage in 1221 to Henry III's sister, Joan, allowed him and his son, Alexander III, to devote themselves to the extension of royal authority over western Scotland, a process which climaxed in 1266 with the Treaty of Perth, under which Norway surrendered the western isles to Scotland.

Through a mixture of pragmatism and military success, Alexander III had brought renewed stability to Scotland. However, the death in 1290 of his successor, his seven-year-old Norwegian-born grand-daughter, Margaret, en route to Scotland, opened the way for Edward I to reassert English overlordship. In 1292, he in effect appointed a new king, John Balliol, whom he lost no time in humiliating. In 1296, in flat contradiction of earlier promises, Edward began the conquest of Scotland.

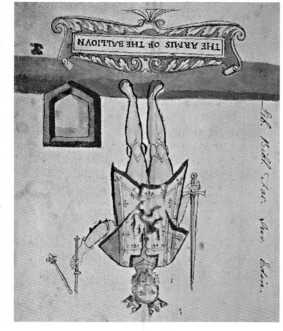

THE ARMS OF THE BALLIOL

Alexander II's imperial self-projection as ruler of a largely peaceful united Scotland is underlined in his image on his seal (right), majestically enthroned, sword and sceptre in hand. Though no less determined to increase his prestige than his predecessors, he was adept at balancing the competing ambitions of his nobles, Anglo-Norman and native alike.

John Balliol (below), his crown and sceptre symbolically broken. As has rightly been said, the humiliation of Balliol by Edward I was "a calculated exercise in demoralization". In 1293, summoned to Westminster by Edward I, John was treated almost as an object of ridicule by the English king. Disowned by his Scottish magnates and systematically abused and then overthrown by Edward, his eventual imprisonment in the Tower must have come almost as a relief to him.

Whatever the vicissitudes of its relations with Henry II and John, by the death of Alexander III in 1286 the authority of the Scottish crown had been extended well into the far north and west and a series of challenges to its rule dealt with (map below). In much the same way, the Anglo-Scottish border had also been more or less permanently fixed, albeit it very much in the former's favour.

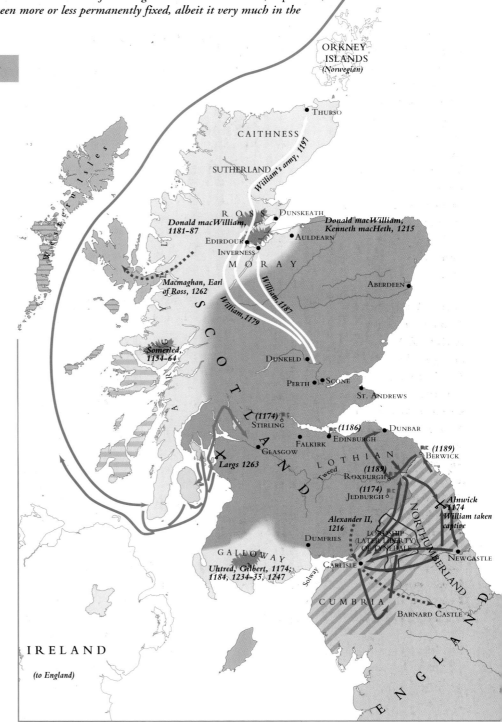

SCOTLAND 1153–1286

- Scottish control, 1153
- Effective Scottish control established by c.1164
- to England, 1157
- Personally held by Scottish kings, 1150-1296
- Taken by Somerled, Lord of Argyll, by 1158
- Other areas possibly controlled by Somerled, by 1158
- Acquired by Scotland in 2nd half of 12th century
- Towns occupied by English garrisons, 1174 (with dates of return to Scottish control)
- To Scotland under Treaty of Perth, 1266
- Campaigns to secure the north
- → William's campaign, 1174
- ┈➤ Other Scottish campaigns
- → Campaign of King John of England, 1216
- → Campaign of King Haakon IV of Norway, 1263
- Revolts
- Frontier, 1237

MALCOLM IV (BORN 1142)
1153–65
GRANDSON OF DAVID I
Consistently outflanked by Henry II, whose vassal he became, Malcolm was nonetheless successful in extending his authority into much of the west. The high point of his reign was the defeat of Somerled's rebellion in 1164. He was an ardent feudalizer and generous patron of the Church.

WILLIAM I THE LION (BORN 1143)
1153–1214
GRANDSON OF DAVID I
Longest-reigning king of medieval Scotland. Continued the extension of royal authority into western Scotland, successfully putting down a number of challenges to his rule; launched many administrative initiatives. Thwarted by Henry II, however, whose overlordship of Scotland was complete, and by his son, John, who treated William with close to contempt.

ALEXANDER II (BORN 1198)
1214–49
SON OF WILLIAM I
Early years of his reign dominated by attempts to regain Northumbria, which involved marching a Scottish army as far as Dover to do homage to Prince Louis of France. Thereafter reached a new accord with England, which included the new permanent southern border of Scotland on the Solway–Tweed line in 1237. Also made further progress in extending royal authority to the west.

ALEXANDER III (BORN 1241)
1249–86
SON OF ALEXANDER II
Despite inevitable difficulties in his early years – he was only eight when he came to the throne – Alexander's reign was solidly prosperous. Good relations with England allowed

him to push forward the conquest of the western isles, which, under the Treaty of Perth, became Scottish in 1266. His death in a riding accident plunged Scotland into crisis

MARGARET (BORN 1283)
1286–90
GRANDDAUGHTER OF ALEXANDER III
The Maid of Norway never set foot in her kingdom: daughter of the king of Norway, she died in the Orkneys, at only seven, on her way to Scotland. Her death, at just seven years old, allowed Edward I – who had welcomed her accession, proposing a marriage with his son – to stake his claim on Scotland.

JOHN BALLIOL (BORN c.1250)
1292–6
One among several possible candidates for the throne after Margaret's death, Balliol rapidly became no more than a pawn of Edward I, whose vassal he was. Captured by Edward in 1296, "Toom Tabard" as he was known, meaning "empty coat", possibly a reference to Edward's symbolic removal of his royal arms from his surcoat, was sent to the Tower of London. In 1299 he was released, under papal protection, and ended his days in France, where he died in 1313. His son, Edward, later bid for the Scottish throne, backed by Edward III of England.

1221	1237	1249	1251	1263	1266	1286	1290	1291	1296
Anglo-Scottish relations stabilized with marriage of Alexander II to sister of Henry III	Anglo-Scottish border fixed on Solway–Tweed line under Treaty of York	Death of Alexander II on further campaign against Western Isles	Marriage of Alexander III to Margaret, daughter of Henry III	Attempt by King Haakon of Norway to reassert Norwegian supremacy over Western Isles	Western Isles ceded to Scotland by Norway under Treaty of Perth	Death of Alexander III; three-year-old Margaret becomes queen	Edward I guarantees independence of Scotland under Treaty of Birgham. Death of Margaret	Edward I asserts overlordship of Scotland and approves choice of John Balliol as new king (1292)	John Balliol deposed by Edward I; conquest of Scotland launched

ROBERT I THE BRUCE 1306–29

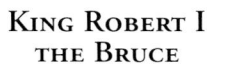

EDWARD I'S SYSTEMATIC ATTEMPTS TO BRING SCOTLAND PERMANENTLY UNDER ENGLISH RULE CAME CLOSE TO EXTERMINATING THE KINGDOM PAINSTAKINGLY ESTABLISHED BY DAVID I AND HIS SUCCESSORS. YET BY 1328, ENGLAND WAS FORCED TO RECOGNIZE SCOTLAND'S INDEPENDENT EXISTENCE UNDER A SINGLE RULER, ROBERT I, THE BRUCE. ROBERT REINVIGORATED A SCOTTISH SENSE OF IDENTITY THAT ENDURES TODAY.

BORN: July 11 1274, Turberry
ACCEDED: March 25 1306; crowned March 27 1306, Scone Abbey

King of Scotland

The achievements of Robert (above), not just in resisting the Plantagenets but in rekindling Scottish independence, were remarkable. That Scotland survived as an independent kingdom was almost entirely thanks to him.

THE INTERMITTENT CONFLICT BETWEEN England and Scotland was raised to new heights of savagery by Edward I's remorseless campaigns to subdue Scotland after 1296. In the face of Edward's overwhelming military superiority, Scotland's nobles had been forced to acknowledge a new English overlordship by 1304, under the "king's peace". The very public execution the following year of William Wallace, whose guerrilla campaigns had briefly threatened English supremacy, underlined Edward's apparently complete triumph.

Hopes of a Scottish revival were made all the more distant by infighting between the nobles. Prominent among the competing factions were the Comyns, consistent opponents of the English, and the Bruces, who had been prime candidates for the Scottish crown eventually awarded to John Balliol in 1292. In 1306, Robert Bruce, Earl of Carrick, brutally murdered his rival, John Comyn, in Greyfriars Abbey, Dumfries, and had himself crowned king. Yet the prospect of Robert posing any serious threat to English control of Scotland seemed remote at best. Almost immediately, he was defeated by an English army at Methven and forced into exile in the Western Isles.

The problems facing Robert were twofold: to triumph in what had effectively become a Scottish civil war; and only then, as he gathered strength, to overthrow the English. A long and brutal campaign of attrition and raiding followed, in which further Scottish rivals were eliminated and English strongholds in Scotland, as well as in northern England, were attacked. By 1314, Robert who was ably supported by his brother Edward, had established his control over all but southeast Scotland.

The death of Edward I in 1307 may not have reduced the scale of the Plantagenet war machine, but his successor, the impetuous and pleasure-loving Edward II, had none of his father's remorseless genius in deploying it. In 1314, with Robert threatening the great English fortress at Stirling, Edward II, determined to destroy him for good, led a massive army into Scotland. It was ignominiously routed at Bannockburn outside Stirling.

English defeat at Bannockburn may have confirmed Robert's position as king of Scotland, but it did nothing to lessen Anglo-Scottish hostility. The following years saw repeated cross-border attacks

The English defeat at Bannockburn (right) may partly have been the result of complacent generalship, but it was nonetheless a startling overturn of what had been a consistently superior English army. The Plantagenets were far from finished, but they could no longer count on automatic Scottish military inferiority.

1304	1305	1306	1307	1314	1315	1320	1324
The "king's peace": Scottish nobles submit to Edward I at Strathmore	Execution of William Wallace	Robert Bruce seizure of the Scottish crown after murdering John Comyn is swiftly followed by defeat, forcing Robert's exile	Death of Edward I allows Robert to begin the consolidation of his rule in Scotland	Battle of Bannockburn results in overwhelming Scottish victory	Attempted "liberation" of Ireland launched under Edward Bruce	Declaration of Arbroath	Papacy recognizes Robert as king of Scotland

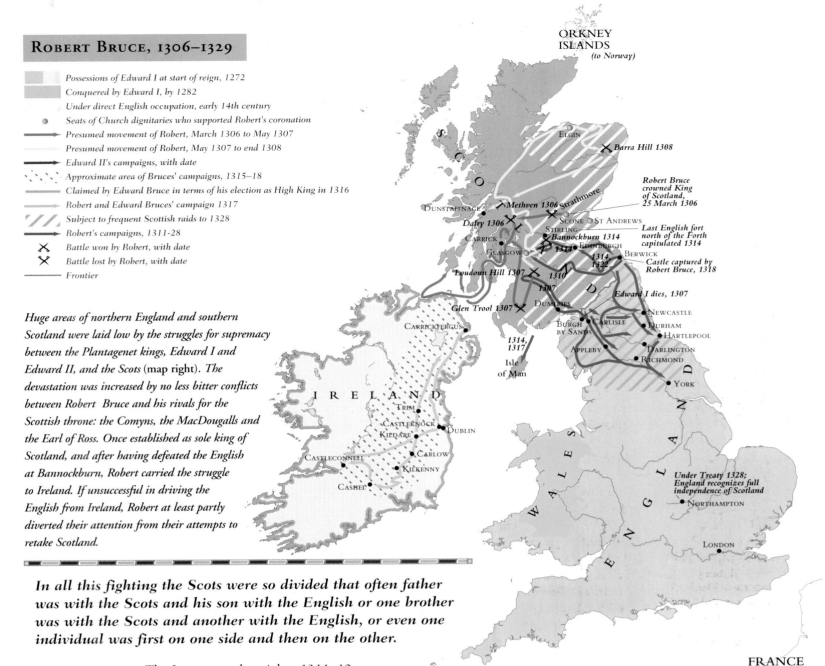

ROBERT BRUCE, 1306–1329

- Possessions of Edward I at start of reign, 1272
- Conquered by Edward I, by 1282
- Under direct English occupation, early 14th century
- Seats of Church dignitaries who supported Robert's coronation
- Presumed movement of Robert, March 1306 to May 1307
- Presumed movement of Robert, May 1307 to end 1308
- Edward II's campaigns, with date
- Approximate area of Bruces' campaigns, 1315–18
- Claimed by Edward Bruce in terms of his election as High King in 1316
- Robert and Edward Bruces' campaign 1317
- Subject to frequent Scottish raids to 1328
- Robert's campaigns, 1311-28
- ✗ Battle won by Robert, with date
- ✗ Battle lost by Robert, with date
- Frontier

Huge areas of northern England and southern Scotland were laid low by the struggles for supremacy between the Plantagenet kings, Edward I and Edward II, and the Scots (map right). The devastation was increased by no less bitter conflicts between Robert Bruce and his rivals for the Scottish throne: the Comyns, the MacDougalls and the Earl of Ross. Once established as sole king of Scotland, and after having defeated the English at Bannockburn, Robert carried the struggle to Ireland. If unsuccessful in driving the English from Ireland, Robert at least partly diverted their attention from their attempts to retake Scotland.

In all this fighting the Scots were so divided that often father was with the Scots and his son with the English or one brother was with the Scots and another with the English, or even one individual was first on one side and then on the other.

The Lancercost chronicler, 1311–12

ORKNEY ISLANDS *(to Norway)*

Barra Hill 1308

Robert Bruce crowned King of Scotland, 25 March 1306

Last English fort north of the Forth capitulated 1314

Castle captured by Robert Bruce, 1318

Edward I dies, 1307

Under Treaty 1328; England recognizes full independence of Scotland

---

by both sides devastating large areas of northern England and southern Scotland alike. Bannockburn also prompted an ambitious attempt by Robert in 1315 to outflank the English by making common cause with the Irish. The campaign, mostly led by Edward Bruce, was a failure, provoking only a bitter and futile three-year civil war and bringing misery to large areas of Ireland.

Much more significant, however, was what came to be called the Declaration of Arbroath, signed by Scotland's leading nobles in 1320, with the apparent encouragement of Robert, and amounting, in effect, to a potent assertion of Scotland's right to independent nationhood. Crucially, it made provision for the legal overthrow of Robert if ever he should surrender Scotland to the English. Scottish self-identity has rarely been more convincingly stated.

In 1328, following the deposition of Edward II, England finally renounced all claims to Scotland under the Treaty of Edinburgh. It was to prove no more than a temporary lull. The death of Robert the following year from leprosy, and accession to the English throne of the vastly more able Edward III the year after opened another, bitter chapter in Anglo-Scottish hostility.

The Declaration of Arbroath, 1320

[If Robert] should give up what he has begun and agree to make us and our kingdom subject to the king of England or the English we should exert ourselves at once to drive him out as our enemy and a subverter of his own rights as well as ours, and make some other man who was well able to defend us our king; for as long as but a hundred of us remain alive never will we, on any condition, be brought under English rule. It is in truth not for glory nor riches nor honour that we are fighting but for freedom – and for that alone which no honest man gives up but with life itself.

1327	1328	1329
Edward II deposed	Treaty of Edinburgh and Northampton England recognizes Scottish independence	Death of Robert the Bruce

The Auld Alliance, 1295–1560

BY THE END OF THE 13TH CENTURY, THE INTERMITTENT CONFLICT BETWEEN THE KINGS OF FRANCE AND ENGLAND WAS JOINED BY A NEW STRUGGLE, BETWEEN ENGLAND AND SCOTLAND. THE NET RESULT WAS THE FORGING OF THE SO-CALLED "AULD ALLIANCE" BETWEEN SCOTLAND AND FRANCE AGAINST THEIR COMMON AND, IN TIME, TRADITIONAL ENEMY, ENGLAND. IT PROVED EXCEPTIONALLY ENDURING, LASTING FULLY 265 YEARS.

THE DYNASTIC TURMOIL CAUSED BY THE DEATH OF THE seven-year-old Scottish queen, Margaret, presented Edward I of England with an all-but-irresistible opportunity to assert his overlordship. By 1295, it was clear that Edward was set on the total subjection of Scotland.

In response, the Council of Twelve, a self-appointed group of nobles and leading churchmen who effectively took over the government of Scotland, looked for allies wherever they could find them. With France and England themselves close to war after the French king, Philippe IV, had declared the English province of Gascony forfeit in 1293, alliance with France carried clear benefits. In October 1295, a Scottish embassy to Philippe agreed the Treaty of Paris.

As with most subsequent renewals of what became the Auld Alliance, the treaty was more favourable to the French than to the Scots. The French were required to do no more than continue their existing struggles with Edward in Gascony, while the burden of any outright military conflict between England and Scotland was to be borne entirely by the Scots. Nonetheless, Scotland, remote and impoverished as it was, was now formally allied to the greatest power in continental Europe. Even if more symbolic than actual, the benefits inherent in the alliance mattered.

In the short term, however, the treaty proved no protection against Edward I, whose whirlwind four-month invasion of 1296 all but exterminated Scotland as an independent kingdom. Worse still, peace between England and France in 1299, followed in 1303 by a treaty "of perpetual peace and friendship", allowed Edward to devote even more of his formidable military energies against the Scots. Scotland owed its eventual survival to Robert the Bruce and the military blundering of Edward II rather than to its French alliance.

When Robert the Bruce and Charles IV of France renewed the alliance in 1326, the motive was more precautionary than immediate: neither seemed to have much to fear from the English. But this changed rapidly after 1330, when Edward III set out to complete the conquest of Scotland and to reassert his authority in France. For the first time the Franco-Scottish alliance had been given real urgency. The prospects for both kingdoms were far from promising, however.

In 1346, Edward overwhelmed the French at Crécy. Two months later, David II of Scotland was captured in an abortive Scottish invasion of northern England. Not only did his enforced 11-year absence as Edward's prisoner increase the already bitter internal power struggles in Scotland, it led David to attempt to reach an accommodation with Edward III as the price of his freedom. Even after his release in 1357, David spent much of the remainder of his reign actively seeking ways to further English interests in Scotland.

Even with the accession in 1371 of the actively pro-French Robert II, who set in motion an immediate renewal of the alliance, the benefits to Scotland were mixed. In 1385, for example, plans for a simultaneous Franco-Scottish invasion of England – including the despatch, for the first time, of a small French force to Scotland – ended farcically when the French invasion failed to materialize. The tone of the deteriorating Franco-Scottish relations was summed up by the French chronicler Jean Froissart, who "wished the king of France would make a truce with the English for two or three years and then the march to Scotland and utterly destroy it".

Mutual regard, however, had never been the impetus behind the Auld Alliance. It was necessity that had driven France and Scotland together, just as it was necessity – specifically the imperative of resisting the aggressive new Lancastrian kings of England – that kept it alive in the early 15th century, in important respects the high point of the Auld Alliance.

Just as much as Scotland, early 15th-century France was gripped by dynastic dispute. Weakened by internal division and

A double portrait of James V and his French wife, Mary of Guise (above). The couple married in 1538, after the death of James's first wife Madeleine, daughter of François I of France. Although in the 1530s, relations between England and France were reasonably stable, by 1542 they had worsened again and Scotland was inexorably drawn into the conflict. A rout of the Scottish army at Solway Moss in November ensued and soon after James died.

confronting a palpably superior opponent in Henry V, France came close to total surrender to the English. In 1418, the Dauphin (later Charles VII) called on his Scottish allies for help. Between 1419 and 1424, perhaps as many as 15,000 Scottish troops were sent to France.

This was a formidable force. It was not uniformly successful, however. A major victory over the English at Baugé in 1421 was followed by equally disastrous defeats at Cravant in 1423 – prompting the Dauphin to comment: "only Scots, Spaniards and other foreigners … and who are no great loss [were killed]" – and Verneuil in 1424. But if it was the death of Henry V in 1422 and the improbable apparition of Joan of Arc to rally the French armies in 1428 that were ultimately the keys to revived French success, the importance of these Scottish "armées de mer" as evi-

dence of Scottish commitment to its French ally was indubitable.

Through the rest of the 15th century, though the alliance was formally renewed four times, the eventual French triumph in the Hundred Years War, combined with the dynastic turmoil within England sparked by the Wars of the Roses, greatly reduced the English threat, rendering the Auld Alliance increasingly obsolete. The marriage in 1502 of Henry VIII's sister Margaret to James IV of Scotland, and the signing of a Treaty of Perpetual Peace between England and Scotland seemed finally to have ended the Franco-Scottish alliance for good.

Its dramatic revival in 1512, when it was formally renewed (as it was again in 1517 and 1548), was the result chiefly of Henry VIII's extravagant attempts to conquer France and Scotland. Both soon fizzled out, but Scotland nonetheless suffered most, when James IV, along with most of his nobles, was killed at Flodden in 1513. Yet again dynastic turmoil loomed.

Periodic Anglo-French and Anglo-Scottish conflict continued throughout Henry VIII's reign, but the certainties that had driven the Auld Alliance were disappearing. With the rise of the Hapsburg Empire, the balance of power in Europe as a whole was changing: in essence; Scotland was becoming more marginal. At the same time, the Reformation was adding a religious dimension to European conflicts. To begin with, the survival of Catholicism in Scotland tended to reinforce its links with Catholic France. But as Protestantism gained ground in Scotland, so a growing body of Scottish opinion favoured closer links with Protestant England.

With the exile of Mary, Queen of Scots, to England in 1568, the political and dynastic prospects for Scotland and its new king, James VI, were transformed. James was heir to the Protestant English throne as well as king of Scotland, and both his own and Scotland's best interests were clearly served by forging new and stronger links with England. Anglo-Scottish distrust might endure but the Auld Alliance itself had clearly outlived its usefulness.

The siege of Berwick in 1333 (left). Edward III of England invaded Scotland in 1333 in support of Edward Balliol (the son of John Balliol). After a comprehensive defeat of the Scottish forces at Halidon Hill, David II was forced to flee to France, where he spent the next eight years, even though he was formally restored to the Scottish throne in 1336. Despite his sojourn at the French court, David became a resolutely pro-English king – a fact perhaps not unrelated to the huge sum of 100,000 marks he had to pay to Edward III under the Treaty of Berwick (1357).

ENGLAND: THE ANGEVINS AND PLANTAGENETS 1154–1399

HENRY II 1154–89	EDWARD I 1272–1307
RICHARD I 1189–99	EDWARD II 1307–27
JOHN 1199–1216	EDWARD III 1327–77
HENRY III 1216–72	RICHARD II 1377–99

IN THE 12TH AND 13TH CENTURIES, KINGSHIP ACROSS MUCH OF WESTERN EUROPE WENT THROUGH A PROCESS OF CONSOLIDATION AMOUNTING ALMOST TO A REVOLUTION. THIS WAS THE HIGH POINT OF MEDIEVAL ROYAL RULE. MONARCHICAL AUTHORITY IN A NUMBER OF COUNTRIES — SPAIN, FRANCE AND ENGLAND PRE-EMINENTLY — WAS SUBSTANTIALLY EXPANDED. SO TOO, AT LEAST PARTLY BY EXTENSION, WERE THE MECHANISMS OF GOVERNMENT, WHICH BECAME MORE POWERFUL, BETTER INFORMED AND SIGNIFICANTLY MORE EFFICIENT.

As Europe recovered from the centuries of disruption following the collapse of Roman power and the Muslim, Magyar and Viking invasions of the 8th to 10th centuries, the reach of its rulers increased. But this development was also a reflection of increasingly sophisticated ideas about the nature of royal rule and the rule of law. Though never wholly reconciled, these drew on Roman, Germanic and Christian traditions to create a theoretical ideal which justified and sustained medieval kingship and which placed the king, from whom all authority flowed, at the absolute heart of government. In England one crucial development was the acceptance after 1216 of royal succession through the king's eldest male heir. The damaging succession disputes of the pre- and post-Conquest age largely became a thing of the past.

In reality, theory and practice were rarely complementary. All medieval kings had to contend with a variety of checks to their authority: the ambitions of their leading magnates, the successful control of whom was a permanent preoccupation of all rulers; conflicts with the Church over supremacy in spiritual authority; wars with rival rulers; and the inevitable vicissitudes of strict dynastic succession, in which strong kings were frequently followed by weak or under-age ones. Nonetheless, that royal authority was being strengthened was undeniable.

In England, this period coincided with the country's single most successful royal dynasty, the Plantagenets, whose 331-year rule remains by far the longest of any English ruling house. Plantagenet rule divides broadly into three phases. The first was that of the Angevins – so-called because they were originally counts of Anjou in France – which lasted from the accession of Henry II in 1154 to the death of his last son, John, in 1216. The second phase ran from the accession of John's nine-year-old son, Henry III, in 1216 to the deposition of Henry's great-great-great-great-grandson, Richard II, in 1399. The third, which if only by virtue of the longevity of the Plantagenets more properly belongs in another chapter (*see* p.98), lasted from the usurpation of Henry IV to the overthrow of Richard III by Henry Tudor in 1485.

But there is a further reason for separating the final phase of Plantagenet rule from the earlier two: whereas the Plantagenet rulers after 1399 can justifiably be considered the first actively English kings of England since 1066, those before 1399 were just as clearly French – in culture, in speech, and in their dynastic and political instincts. No less than the Normans (whom they ousted in France as well as in England), the Angevin kings were at least as concerned to maintain their French lands and titles as to hold onto England. Their persistent wars with the French crown make most sense not so much as a conflict between two rival national polities – England and France – but as a continuation of a domestic conflict between the kings of France and their leading subjects. The kings of England, by virtue of their French lands and titles, were merely one among a number of such subjects, albeit often the most powerful. It is a precise reflection of Angevin priorities that Henry spent about a third of his reign in England, while his son Richard I spent only six months of his ten-year reign there. Both were buried in France.

The catastrophic loss by John of the great majority of his French lands by 1214 naturally led to a greater focus on English affairs. By incurring the wrath of his heavily taxed barons, most of whose own lands in France were also lost, it also indirectly gave rise to two of the most far-reaching developments of the period: Magna Carta and the growth of Parliament. Paradoxically, these tended more to reinforce royal authority than to dilute it. Provided the king was seen to be acting legally, Parliament in particular effectively became a bastion of kingship, an additional layer of royal legitimacy. But if the notion that Parliament in itself could constitute a higher authority than the king would have to wait until the 17th century, its first development under the Plantagenets was nonetheless of central importance.

Denied access to their traditional homelands in France, the more aggressive of the Plantagenets turned their attentions to the conquest of their British neighbours. The creation of an English "empire" in Britain is among the most enduring Plantagenet legacies. Henry II began the process, above all in Ireland, the invasion of which he authorized in 1167. But the key figure was Edward I, whose overwhelming conquest of Wales at the end of the 13th century saw the Plantagenet war-machine deployed at its most merciless. His no less ambitious but ultimately unsuccessful assaults on Scotland, however, served largely only to ensure continued tension between England and Scotland as well as to cement the Auld Alliance between Scotland and France.

That France nevertheless remained a prime focus of Plantagenet ambitions was emphatically underlined in the 14th century by Edward III, who launched a sustained attempt to re-establish Plantagenet supremacy there, beginning what later came to be called the Hundred Years War. In 1340, Edward went so far as to claim the French crown. On purely hereditary grounds, his claim was at least as good as that of the reigning French king, Philippe VI.

Whatever the temporary successes of Edward III and his son, the Black Prince, in France, it was clear nonetheless that the Plantagenets were gradually losing their French identity. By the time of the deposition and murder of the absolutist Richard II by his cousin Henry Bolingbroke in 1399, they had become as fully English as their subjects.

HENRY II 1154–89

KING HENRY II
BORN: March 5 1133,
Le Mans
ACCEDED: October 25
1154; crowned
December 19 1154,
Westminster Abbey

*DUKE OF NORMANDY
(FROM 1150),
COUNT OF ANJOU,
TOURAINE AND MAINE
(FROM 1151),
DUKE OF AQUITAINE
(FROM 1152),
KING OF ENGLAND*

HENRY II TRANSFORMED KINGSHIP IN ENGLAND. FOR OVER 30 YEARS HE HELD TOGETHER THE LARGEST EMPIRE IN WESTERN EUROPE THROUGH SHEER FORCE OF PERSONALITY. MOST OF HIS FRENCH HOLDINGS MAY HAVE BEEN LOST WITHIN 15 YEARS OF HIS DEATH, BUT ENGLAND, REINFORCED BY THE ADMINISTRATIVE AND INSTITUTIONAL UNITY HE HELPED TO CREATE, ENDURED NOT JUST INTACT BUT GREATLY STRENGTHENED.

HENRY II'S HUGE TERRITORIAL HOLDINGS made him by far the most powerful and richest ruler in western Europe. Anjou, Maine, Touraine and Normandy were his by inheritance; the vast sweep of Aquitaine, the hereditary lands of his wife Eleanor, came to him by marriage. Brittany, his other major French holding, became Henry's by diplomatic conquest in 1166, Ireland was his by outright conquest after 1167.

Henry's claim to the throne of England was much less clear cut than his Norman predecessors', if scarcely worse. His mother, Matilda, may have been unable to wrest the throne from her cousin Stephen (*see* pp. 56–7), but she could claim at least partial vindication in 1153 when Stephen confirmed Henry as his successor after the 20-year-old had mounted what in effect was an invasion of England. Henry's accession the following year was the first undisputed succession to the English crown since Harold II's in 1066.

Henry's immediate priority in 1154 was not just to repair the civil strife of Stephen's reign but to create sufficient stability in England to allow him to turn his attentions to France. In doing so, his distinctive brand of energetic kingship became immediately clear, above all his determination to stamp his authority everywhere. Within two years, Henry had overseen the destruction of scores of unlicensed castles, ending almost at a stroke the numerous local tyrannies that had flourished in Stephen's reign. At the same time, he secured the homage of Malcolm IV of Scotland and Owain Gwynedd in Wales.

Henry also set in train legal reforms that would decisively reduce the influence of local, baronial courts in favour of royal courts presided over by his own

Henry and Eleanor

On the face of it, the marriage of Henry Plantagenet and Eleanor of Aquitaine in May 1152 was just another arranged diplomatic marriage, albeit one in which the stakes were higher – and the personalities very much larger – than most. Henry was 18, Eleanor was 30. Until eight weeks earlier, Eleanor had also been queen of France, married to Louis VII, who had divorced her on the ground that they were too closely related. In reality, the marriage had been ended for a much more prosaic reason: Eleanor had not produced an heir. Under the terms of the divorce, all Eleanor's hereditary lands in Aquitaine were returned to her and she was free to remarry – but only if she received the king's permission. This she signally failed to do.

With Aquitaine thus added to Henry's existing lands of Anjou, Maine and Normandy, Louis found himself confronting the kind of extended power base that the terms of the divorce had been expressly designed to avoid. As king, Louis might have been expected to set about the immediate reduction of his over-mighty vassal. In practice, he was powerless.

Against the odds, Eleanor and Henry seem to have been attracted to each other, perhaps as a result of the heady power they now disposed of. By about 1163, however, it was clear that they were drawing apart, with the ageing Eleanor never able to compete with Henry's string of much younger mistresses. Eleanor withdrew to her court in Poitiers, which she made the most glamorous chivalric centre in France. Here, more and more embittered by her estrangement from Henry, she raised her children and plotted his downfall.

In 1173 Eleanor actively encouraged the revolt against Henry by his sons Richard and Geoffrey, who were jealous of the preferential treatment handed out to their older brother, Henry. Henry II, now in his prime, easily crushed the rebellion. Eleanor was shipped to England, where she spent the next ten years under arrest. The young Henry's death (from dysentery) in 1183 brought about a rapprochement of sorts between the king and his queen. Eleanor was allowed to return to France, where she immediately began to encourage her remaining sons to mount a further revolt. She had her final, bitter revenge in 1189 when her favourite, Richard, allied to the new king of France, Philippe II, forced a humiliating defeat on her husband.

Eleanor died in 1204, aged 82, the wife of two kings and the mother of two more. She was buried next to Henry at Fontevrault on the Loire.

Fresco, reputedly showing Eleanor, from the Chapel of St Redegone, Chinon.

1142	1147	1149	1150	1151	1152	1153
First visit by Henry, as nine-year-old, to England	*Unsuccessfully attempts to continue the struggle of his mother, Matilda, against King Stephen*	*Third visit to England; knighted by David I of Scotland*	*Created duke of Normandy*	*Death of Geoffrey of Anjou; Henry becomes count of Anjou and Maine*	*Marries Eleanor of Aquitaine, more than ten years his senior; becomes duke of Aquitaine*	*Invades England (Jan.); Stephen forced to designate Henry his successor under Treaty of Wallingford (Dec.)*

It was no more than appropriate that Henry II's seal showed him on horseback (picture left). He was an indefatigable traveller. Louis VII remarked, perplexed: "Now in England, now in Normandy, he must fly rather than travel by horse or ship."

Our king is peaceable, victorious in war, glorious in peace… He considers whatever pertains to the peace of his people, in whatever he speaks, in whatever he does; so that his people may rest, he incessantly takes on troubled and enormous labours. It aims to the peace of his people that he calls councils, that he makes laws, that he makes friendships, that he brings low the proud, that he threatens battles, that he launches terror to the people… In walls, in ramparts, in fortifications, in ditches, in enclosures of wild beasts and fish, there is no one more subtle, and no one more magnificent to be found.

Peter of Blois, 1177

KINGDOM OF THE ISLES

KINGDOM OF (Norwegian)

SCOTLAND

1157, 1174

STIRLING

EDINBURGH

ROXBURGH
BERWICK
JEDBURGH

NORTHUMBERLAND

Taken from Scotland, 1157
CUMBRIA

IRISH

KINGDOMS

Nominally awarded to Henry II by papal grant, 1155

DUBLIN

1171/75

Under direct Plantagenet rule by c. 1180
(1171)

WEXFORD
WATERFORD

CORK

(1157)
CHESTER

(1165)

WELSH KINGDOMS
1157/71

(1163)

YORK

Inherited, as king 1154

ELY

HEREFORD
CAMBRIDGE

(1147, 1152)

OXFORD

BRISTOL
LONDON

CANTERBURY

E N G L A N D

SALISBURY
WINCHESTER

EXETER

English Channel

HOLY ROMAN EMPIRE

The cross-Channel Angevin empire of Henry II, acquired through a mixture of inheritance, marriage and conquest, was the largest and most powerful in Europe (map right). Henry was assiduous in adding to it – and equally adept in preserving it. In England especially, politically much more stable than the king's French lands, his reign saw a significant expansion of energetic royal justice.

ROUEN
VEXIN

NORMANDY
Inherited, 1150

PARIS

FRANCE

BRITTANY
(1166, 1167, 1168)

MAINE

ANJOU
TOURS

NANTES

ISSOUDUN

DEOLS

POITOU
LA MARCHE

SAINTONGE
ANGOULÊME
LIMOUSIN

AUVERGNE

Acquired by marriage, 1152

A Q U I T A I N E

BORDEAUX

HENRY II AND THE PLANTAGENET EMPIRE

- *Taken from his brother, 1156*
- *Acquired via son's marriage treaty of 1158/1160*
- *Inherited from his brother, Geoffrey 1158*
- *Secured militarily following son's marriage treaty, by 1171*
- *Marcher Lordships, c. 1180*
- *Vassal/paid homage, with date of acknowledging suzerainty*
- *French Royal domain*
- *Garrisoned by English forces, 1174*
- *(1173)* *Date of Henry's intervention to secure area*
- *Frontiers, 1180*

GASCONY

TOULOUSE
1173

(1159)

TOULOUSE

continued on next page

1154	1155–7	1158–63	1159	1160	1162	1164
Accession of Henry II; Pope confirms Henry's overlordship of Britain	*Unlicensed castles in England destroyed; Malcolm IV of Scotland and Welsh princes submit to Henry*	*Henry in France*	*Major (ultimately unsuccessful) campaign to take county of Toulouse, claimed by Henry to be rightly Eleanor's*	*Regains disputed territory of Vexin from Louis VII*	*Thomas Becket appointed Archbishop of Canterbury*	*Becket agrees to Constitutions of Clarendon, confirming monarch's authority over the Church, then immediately retracts agreement; flees to France*

THE EVOLUTION OF THE ROYAL COURT

THE MOST VIVID EARLY DESCRIPTION OF MEDIEVAL COURT LIFE IS THAT PROVIDED BY THE 8TH-CENTURY ANGLO-SAXON EPIC POEM, *Beowulf*. THOUGH THE SOCIETY IT DESCRIBES – OF AN "ILLUSTRIOUS PRINCE AND GIVER OF GOLD RINGS" FEASTING WITH HIS FOLLOWERS – WOULD CHANGE, MANY OF ITS ESSENTIAL FEATURES ENDURED WELL INTO THE 13TH CENTURY.

DURING THIS PERIOD, TWO CENTRAL FACTORS STAND out. One was the primacy of the king, and of his court or household, in the government of the realm. The other was that the king and his court were permanently on the move.

The household had a dual function. It was domestic, in the sense of providing the king with the necessities of daily life. And it was also administrative, the epicentre of government, the whole presided over by the monarch himself. The earliest surviving factual account of a medieval royal household, the *Constitutio domus regis*, describes Henry I's court in detail. It is probable that the households of the Anglo-Saxon kings as early as the 9th century were fundamentally the same, if smaller.

Henry I's core household was at least 100 strong. Senior officials, mostly drawn from leading magnates and churchmen, included the chamberlain and the treasurer. They were jointly responsible for the royal chamber, where the king slept and ate (other than on special occasions), and the Treasury, a part of which travelled with the court and was kept in the king's chamber. Some chamberlains were clerics; most were laymen. Until the 1340s, the treasurer was always a cleric. The same was true of the chancellor, who was head of the royal chapel as well as being in charge of the royal scribes, themselves clerics (or "clerks"). The chancellor was also responsible for the king's seal, used to authenticate documents issued by the king. It was usual for a chancellor to be rewarded with a bishopric at the end of his term of office.

Among the exclusively domestic staff, the most important were the "sewers" or stewards, also called "cupbearers", who supervised the king's hall and household staff. Among these were the cooks and the butler, who occupied an important ceremonial position as well as being responsible for the supply of wine. Lesser members of staff included grooms, carters, packhorse drivers, tent-keepers, the bearer of the king's bed and launderers.

Significantly, the largest single department was the hunting staff. It included hornblowers, keepers of greyhounds, keepers of the royal pack, a leader and a feeder of the hounds, huntsmen of the "trained pack", a keeper of small hounds, wolfhunters, a series of archers and 20 sergeants.

The court was also the centre of the king's army, which was administered by the constables and marshals and consisted of household knights and often large numbers of infantry, the "household men" or *familiares*. This was in effect a permanent standing army, available for immediate deployment at moments of crisis. It could be rapidly expanded to deal with longer-lasting conflicts.

To this more or less permanent household were added sundry hangers-on, petitioners, merchants, nobles, justices, sheriffs and foreign dignitaries, some visiting on official business, many simply anxious to garner royal favour.

There were a small number of permanent royal palaces. Those at Yeavering in Northumberland and Cheddar in Somerset, the latter still being used as late as the reign of King John, were Anglo-Saxon. Both bear a marked resemblance to Heorot, the great "mead hall" described in Beowulf. They were imposing wooden halls – that at Yeavering was 90 by 18 feet – with simple window openings and a central fire. Though "golden tapestries" were hung to mark important occasions, permanent furniture was sparse: plain tables and benches. It was here that most of the household slept. The later Norman palaces at Winchester, Windsor, Westminster and the Tower of London itself, though larger and built of stone, would scarcely have been more comfortable. As late as the 12th century, glass windows remained an

As demonstrations of knightly prowess, tournaments were popular throughout the Middle Ages (above). *Banned in the reign of Henry II, who feared the large numbers of knights who congregated to them, they were restored by Richard I. Tournaments continued to be popular into the 16th century.*

almost unimaginable luxury. Among the goods lost by King John in 1216, when a number of his baggage carts were lost during an attempted crossing of the Wash, was his set of portable glass windows.

Though Westminster began to emerge as a permanent centre of government during the reign of Henry I, what most distinguished the medieval court was its constant travelling. In an age of difficult communication, the effectiveness of any ruler depended on his being able to make his presence felt personally. And as the court revolved around the king, the court travelled, too.

From 1069, with large areas of England in open revolt, William the Conqueror found himself permanently on the move from one end of his realm to the other. The same was true of Stephen in his civil war against Matilda. Henry I, with an even larger cross-Channel realm to administer, was another incessant traveller. In 1170, for example, despite spending almost two months seriously ill in Normandy, he still covered more than

Windsor Castle (above) showing the Round Tower and Upper Ward. The evolution of Windsor from the purely military structure erected by William I c.1080 to a sophisticated palace complex with royal apartments began under Henry I with the modification of the Round Tower. By the 1350s the Upper Ward, too, had been reconstructed as a grand royal palace.

> *If the king has said he will remain in one place for a day, he is sure to upset all the arrangements by departing early in the morning. And you see the men dashing around as if they were mad, beating packhorses, running carts into another, in short giving a lively imitation of Hell … I hardly dare say it but I believe in truth he took delight in seeing what a fix we were in. After wandering some three or four miles in an unknown wood and often in the dark we thought ourselves lucky if we stumbled upon some filthy hovel.*
>
> Peter of Blois, on Henry II's court

2,000 miles. In the course of his reign, he crossed the Channel 28 times. As the sinking of the *White Ship* in 1120 and the loss of John's baggage carts almost 100 years later underlined, the risks could be considerable.

If the logistics involved in moving the court were formidable, the consequences for those on whom the court descended could be severe. A monk from Canterbury described the calamitous impact of William Rufus's itinerant court: "Those who attended his court made a practice of plundering and destroying everything; they laid waste all the territory through which they passed. Consequently, when it became known that the king was coming everyone fled to the woods." When it was announced that Edward I would spend Easter at Nottingham, the local people were assured that the king would leave as rapidly as he had arrived.

The Dukes of York, Gloucester and Ireland dine with Richard II (above) from the 15th-century Chronique d'Angleterre. *The importance of the king's inner circle of favourites was increased by the growing size and sophistication of the court; the Richard de Vere, Duke of Ireland, became so influential that Parliament dismissed him and the Lords Appellant seized power from Richard III.*

RICHARD I 1189–99

1173	1189	1190	1191
With his brother Geoffrey, Richard rebels against his father, Henry II	Allies with Philippe II of France to defeat Henry II. Makes first visit to England (Sept.–Dec.) for coronation and to raise finance for Crusade	Leaves France (July) and, with Philippe II, leads Third Crusade to Holy Land	Reaches Holy Land (June) and takes Acre. John illegally takes over government of England

Richard and the Third Crusade

M easured against its stated objective of liberating Jerusalem, which had been captured by Saladin in 1187, the Third Crusade, led jointly by Richard I and Philippe II of France, was a failure. Furthermore, Richard and Philippe fell out even before they got to the Holy Land. Wintering in Sicily, they argued over Richard's continuing refusal to honour his promise to marry Philippe's sister, Alice. When Eleanor arrived with an alternative bride, Berengaria of Navarre, Philippe took offence. In high dudgeon, he sailed ahead on his own.

En route to the Holy Land, Richard captured Cyprus after its Greek ruler had come close to seizing the ship carrying Alice and Berengaria. The island would prove a crucial advance base for later crusaders. Richard celebrated the victory by marrying Berengaria.

Richard and Philippe were partly reconciled once Richard had arrived in the Holy Land in June 1191. Together they took Acre, whose Christian besiegers had themselves become besieged by Saladin. Richard was in his element. When Saladin delayed his payment of the ransom for the 2,700 prisoners taken by Richard, Richard had them executed. The victory was somewhat marred by Philippe's decision to return home early and by a bitter squabble between Richard and Duke Leopold of Austria over the division of the spoils.

From Acre, Richard made his way south to Jaffa and from there inland towards Jerusalem. The city proved impregnable, however. In September, realizing the futility of continuing the effort, Richard and Saladin came to terms. Richard sailed for home.

The value or otherwise of the Crusades have long been questioned. Compared to some of the more obviously catastrophic of the Crusades, Richard's effort was a success. Certainly, it confirmed his reputation as a great Christian warrior. But for the king of England to spend so long away from his kingdom smacked of a reckless disregard for the realities of political power.

> War defined Richard. His departure for the Holy Land in 1190 was a crusade in every sense. But as a contemporary recorded: "As the earth shudders at the absence of the sun, so the face of the kingdom was changed by the departure of the king."

King Richard I

THE CHIVALRIC IMAGE OF RICHARD I "COEUR DE LION" (LIONHEART) AS THE JUST, CHRISTIAN WARRIOR-KING PAR EXCELLENCE HAS ALWAYS BEEN ALLURING. IN REALITY, WHATEVER HIS KNIGHTLY PROWESS AND MILITARY ABILITY, AS KING OF ENGLAND HE WAS A DISTANT FIGURE. IT IS TESTIMONY TO THE GOOD GOVERNMENT ESTABLISHED BY HENRY II THAT HIS PROLONGED ABSENCES HAD SUCH LITTLE EFFECT.

T HE RELATIVE INSIGNIFICANCE OF ENGLAND in the wider Angevin world was unambiguously underlined by the reign of Richard I. The new king regarded England, which was inherently more stable and much more easily defended than his French realms, chiefly as a means of financing his foreign ventures, above all his passionate determination to "take the Cross". He had been raised on a diet of knightly virtue by his mother, Eleanor, who had herself made the arduous journey to the Holy Land with her first husband, Louis VII; tall, flamboyant and blue-eyed, Richard had little difficulty in seeing himself as the *preux chevalier* personified. In July 1190, exactly a year after coming to the throne and having spent less than four months in England, he left France for the Holy Land on the Third Crusade.

Self-regarding he may have been, but Richard understood the realities of Angevin power politics. As his overthrow (in tandem with Philippe II of France) of his father Henry II in 1189 made clear, Richard's capacity for naked self-advancement was fully the equal of his military talents. He was under no illusion that his inevitably lengthy absence in the Holy Land placed his realms at risk.

His precautions proved inadequate. Rightly seeing his younger brother John as the chief threat to his rule in England, Richard extracted a promise from John, whom he lavishly rewarded with lands and titles, that he would stay out of England until Richard's planned return three years later. Meanwhile, the Bishop of Ely, William Longchamp, was entrusted with the realm's government. Neither scheme worked. Longchamp alienated many leading barons, who naturally gravi-

BORN: September 8 1157, Oxford

ACCEDED: July 6 1189; crowned September 2 1189, Westminster Abbey

DUKE OF NORMANDY AND DUKE OF AQUITAINE (FROM 1172), KING OF ENGLAND

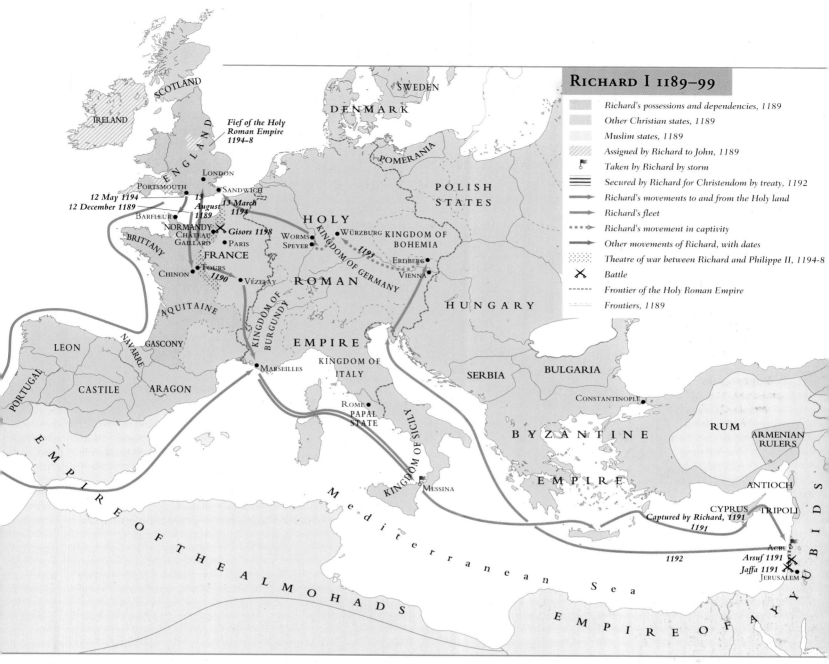

RICHARD I 1189–99

Richard's possessions and dependencies, 1189

Other Christian states, 1189

Muslim states, 1189

Assigned by Richard to John, 1189

Taken by Richard by storm

Secured by Richard for Christendom by treaty, 1192

Richard's movements to and from the Holy land

Richard's fleet

Richard's movement in captivity

Other movements of Richard, with dates

Theatre of war between Richard and Philippe II, 1194-8

Battle

Frontier of the Holy Roman Empire

Frontiers, 1189

SCOTLAND

IRELAND

SWEDEN

DENMARK

POMERANIA

POLISH STATES

Fief of the Holy Roman Empire 1194-8

ENGLAND

LONDON

PORTSMOUTH

SANDWICH

12 May 1194
12 December 1189

BARFLEUR

13 *August 1189*

13 March 1194

WÜRZBURG

KINGDOM OF BOHEMIA

HOLY

BRITTANY

NORMANDY
CHÂTEAU
GAILLARD

FRANCE

Gisors 1198

PARIS

WORMS

SPEYER

1193

ROMAN

ERDBERG

VIENNA

CHINON

TOURS
1190

VÉZELAY

KINGDOM OF GERMANY

KINGDOM OF BURGUNDY

EMPIRE

HUNGARY

AQUITAINE

LEON

NAVARRE

GASCONY

PORTUGAL

CASTILE

ARAGON

MARSEILLES

KINGDOM OF ITALY

SERBIA

BULGARIA

CONSTANTINOPLE

ROME
PAPAL
STATE

BYZANTINE

RUM

ARMENIAN RULERS

E M P I R E   O F   T H E   A L M O H A D S

KINGDOM OF SICILY

MESSINA

M e d i t e r r a n e a n   S e a

E M P I R E

ANTIOCH

CYPRUS

TRIPOLI

Captured by Richard, 1191
1191

ACRE

1192

Arsuf 1191

Jaffa 1191

JERUSALEM

E M P I R E   O F   A Y Y U B I D S

tated to John as a rival source of authority. For his part, John rapidly broke his word, made his way to England, and set himself up as king in all but name. Longchamp fled to Normandy.

Richard fared little better in France. Though his chief and most obvious French rival, Philippe II, had accompanied Richard to the Holy Land, the two quarrelled when Richard – who may have been homosexual – prevaricated over his marriage to Philippe's sister, Alice, to whom he had been engaged for 20 years. Returning early, Philippe launched a major assault against Normandy.

On his way home in 1192, Richard was captured by another former ally in the Holy Land, Duke Leopold of Austria, and ransomed for 150,000 marks (the equivalent of 34 tonnes of gold). By now, a much more able administrator, the new Chief Justiciar, Hubert Walter, had replaced Longchamp. It was Walter who was mainly responsible for raising the enormous ransom – almost the only direct impact Richard had on his kingdom. All his

subjects had to pay. Among the drastic measures was the requisitioning of the entire Cistercian wool crop. Once freed, in 1194 Richard paid his second (and last) visit to England, spending a mere two months there.

The remaining five years of Richard's reign were spent in France, campaigning to regain the territories lost to Philippe II. With the help of John, magnanimously pardoned for his attempted take-over of England, Richard repeatedly demonstrated his military ability. By the time he died, shot in the shoulder besieging the castle of Chalus in the Limousin, he had restored and strengthened all his French inheritance.

As a king, warfare was Richard I's only real talent. The niceties of administration bored him. Even more seriously, he failed in the elementary precaution of leaving an heir. In consequence, it was the unscrupulous John who inherited his throne. The great Angevin inheritance so painstakingly preserved by Henry II would not endure for long.

Whatever King John's difficulties with his barons in England, his reign was dominated by his catastrophic loss of the vast majority of Henry II's Plantagenet empire in France (map above). Disastrous in itself, it also enormously strengthened the hitherto much weaker kings of France, making its recapture all the harder. The contrast with Henry II's subtle stewardship could hardly have been greater.

1192	1193	1194	1194–99	1196
Two attempts to take Jerusalem (Jan. and June) rebuffed by Saladin; Richard and Saladin conclude truce (Sept.); while returning home, captured by Duke Leopold of Austria (Dec.)	*Hubert Walter appointed Archbishop of Canterbury and Chief Justiciar in place of William Longchamp*	*Richard ransomed and freed; makes second visit to England (Mar.–May)*	*French territories lost to Philippe II reconquered*	*Château Gaillard, Richard's most imposing fortress, built overlooking Seine*

KING JOHN

BORN: December 24
1167, Oxford

ACCEDED: April 6 1199;
crowned May 27 1199,
Westminster Abbey

*LORD OF IRELAND
(FROM 1177), COUNT OF
MORTAIN (FROM 1189),
DUKE OF NORMANDY
(1199–1203), KING OF
ENGLAND*

JOHN 1199–1216

THE RUTHLESS DYNASTIC SELF-SEEKING OF HENRY II'S SONS REACHED ITS APOGEE IN JOHN. THE REIGN OF THIS SUSPICIOUS, VIOLENT AND UNPRINCIPLED MAN WAS DOMINATED BY SHORT-TERM ATTEMPTS TO GAIN WHATEVER IMMEDIATE ADVANTAGE SEEMED MOST OBVIOUSLY AT HAND. THE RESULT WAS THE LOSS OF ALMOST ALL THE ANGEVIN LANDS IN FRANCE, AND, IN ENGLAND, BARONIAL REVOLT THAT CULMINATED IN MAGNA CARTA.

MOST OF JOHN'S LIFE WAS SPENT IN A fevered pursuit of power. The start was unpromising. As the youngest son, John was not due to inherit any of the immense Angevin realms, hence his nickname "Lackland". Richard's subsequent refusal to transfer his original inheritance, Aquitaine, to John when he, Richard, became heir to England, Normandy and Anjou in 1183 sparked the first armed clash between the brothers. Two years later, Henry sent John to rule in Ireland. John's four-month visit, in which he alienated almost everyone, was a disaster from first to last. Typically, he repaid his father by joining the revolt by Richard and Philippe II against the ageing king in 1189.

John's prospects immediately improved. To keep his brother out of England during his absence in the Holy Land, Richard, now king, gave John a series of vast estates in England and France. He also allowed him to marry the daughter of the Earl of Gloucester. John, however, wanted more.

Breaking his word, he set himself up in England and fomented resistance to Richard's nominee as ruler in his absence, William Longchamp. When Richard, at long range, managed to force him out again, John joined forces with Philippe II of France to plot Richard's overthrow. The conspirators were given added impetus in 1192 with the news of Richard's imprisonment in Austria. Normandy was invaded and John declared himself king of England.

Even in the context of Plantagenet family politics, Richard's subsequent pardon of John after his release seems surprising. However, John now rejoined forces with his brother against his former ally, and over the next five years he proved a more than competent military commander as together they retook all the lands lost to Philippe. John's reward was his designation as heir to all Richard's realm.

Within five years of his accession, John had lost almost all his French inheritance. John's problem was not just Philippe II but his nephew, Arthur, Duke of Brittany, whose claim to Richard's French territories was at least as good as his own. Arthur formed a natural rallying point for those French barons reluctant to accept John as their lord. In 1202, John compounded their resentment by capturing and murdering the 12-year-old Arthur, whose body

Magna Carta

Magna Carta, or "Great Charter", signed by a reluctant John in June 1215, has traditionally been seen as the cornerstone of English liberty, the first step in the development of English constitutional government. The actual impetus behind it was very different. After the defeat at Bouvines the year before, England's magnates were determined to assert themselves by rolling back the feudal privileges that the Angevins had been assiduously amassing. Nonetheless, by placing the king within a legal framework – by saying in effect that the law existed independently of the king and was more than whatever he declared it to be – the issuing of the Charter represented a key moment. For his part, John agreed to it simply to buy time. He had no intention of implementing the Charter. But when he died the following year, his heir, Henry III, was only nine. Immediately on his accession, the Charter was re-issued, as it was again in 1217 and 1225. In 1297, even as powerful a king as Edward I was forced to agree to a further confirmation of the Charter. Although the position of the king within the state was still absolute, Magna Carta had begun – however tentatively – the process by which the rule of law was to become supreme.

1177	1183	1185	1191	1193	1194	1200	1202	1203
John made Lord of Ireland by Henry II	Richard's refusal to transfer Aquitaine to John leads to armed conflict between the brothers	Visits Ireland (for four months), earning deep distrust on all sides	Journeys to England and conspires against Richard's regent, William Longchamp	Conspires with Philippe II to overthrow the imprisoned Richard; declares himself king of England	Pardoned by Richard, whom he joins in combating Philippe II in France	Divorces Isabella of Gloucester; marries Isabella of Angoulême, incurring wrath of her fiancé, Hugh de Lusignan	Refuses to pay homage to Philippe II, who formally dispossesses John of his French territories; war ensues	Murders his nephew, Arthur, duke of Brittany, in Normandy; retreats to England (Dec.)

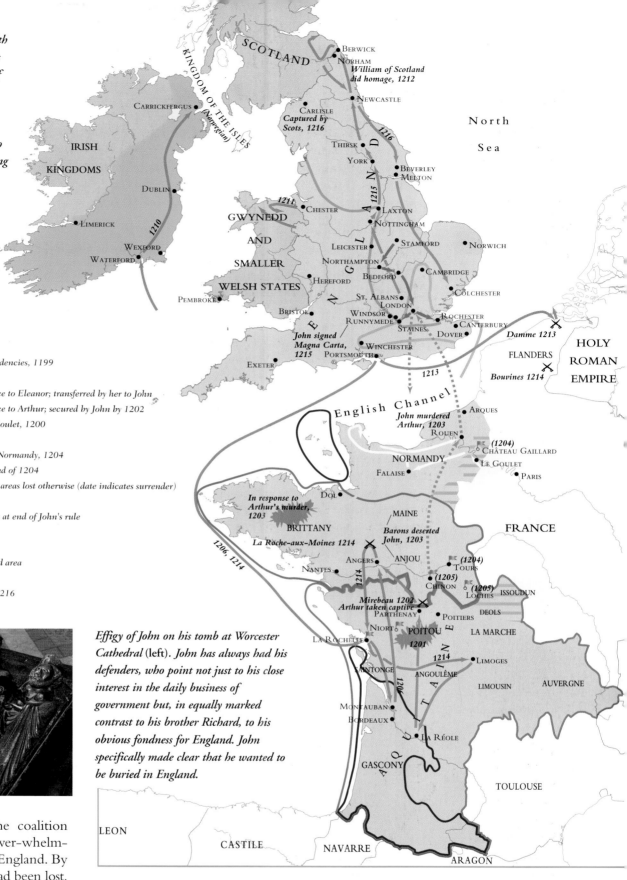

Whatever King John's difficulties with his barons in England, his reign was dominated by his catastrophic loss of the vast majority of Henry II's Plantagenet empire in France (map right). Disastrous in itself, it also enormously strengthened the hitherto much weaker kings of France, making its recapture all the harder. The contrast with Henry II's subtle stewardship could hardly have been greater.

SCOTLAND

KINGDOM OF THE ISLES (Norwegian)

BERWICK
NORHAM
William of Scotland did homage, 1212
NEWCASTLE

North Sea

CARLISLE
Captured by Scots, 1216

IRISH KINGDOMS

CARRICKFERGUS

THIRSK
YORK
BEVERLEY
MELTON

DUBLIN

1211
CHESTER
LAXTON
NOTTINGHAM

GWYNEDD AND SMALLER WELSH STATES

LEICESTER
STAMFORD
NORWICH

LIMERICK

1210

WEXFORD
WATERFORD

NORTHAMPTON
BEDFORD
CAMBRIDGE

ENGLAND

HEREFORD
ST. ALBANS
LONDON
COLCHESTER

PEMBROKE

BRISTOL
WINDSOR
RUNNYMEDE
STAINES
ROCHESTER
CANTERBURY

John signed Magna Carta, 1215
WINCHESTER
DOVER
Damme 1213

EXETER
PORTSMOUTH

1213

FLANDERS

HOLY ROMAN EMPIRE

Bouvines 1214

English Channel

ARQUES

John murdered Arthur, 1203
ROUEN

(1204)
CHÂTEAU GAILLARD
LE GOULET
PARIS

NORMANDY
FALAISE

DOL

In response to Arthur's murder, 1203

MAINE

BRITTANY
La Roche-aux-Moines 1214

Barons deserted John, 1203

FRANCE

ANGERS
ANJOU
(1204)
TOURS
(1205)
CHINON
(1205)
LOCHES
ISSOUDUN

NANTES

1214

Mirebeau 1202 Arthur taken captive
PARTHENAY
POITIERS
DEOLS
DEOLS

NIORT
POITOU
LA MARCHE
1201

LA ROCHELLE
1214
LIMOGES
ANGOULÊME

SAINTONGE

LIMOUSIN
AUVERGNE

MONTAUBAN
BORDEAUX

1202

AQUITAINE

LA RÉOLE

GASCONY

TOULOUSE

LEON

CASTILE
NAVARRE

ARAGON

JOHN 1189–1216

- Plantagenet possessions and dependencies, 1199
- John's movements, 1199
- Area where Barons swore allegiance to Eleanor; transferred by her to John
- Area where Barons swore allegiance to Arthur; secured by John by 1202
- English losses under treaty of Le Goulet, 1200
- Revolts against John in France
- French and Breton campaigns in Normandy, 1204
- Remained English in France by end of 1204
- Remaining English strongholds in areas lost otherwise (date indicates surrender)
- John's campaigns, with date
- English-held in Ireland and Wales at end of John's rule
- English vassals, 1216
- Campaign of rebel barons, 1215
- Southern limit of largely rebel-held area
- Prince Louis's landing, 1216
- Area of Prince Louis's activity in 1216
- ✕ Battles

Effigy of John on his tomb at Worcester Cathedral (left). John has always had his defenders, who point not just to his close interest in the daily business of government but, in equally marked contrast to his brother Richard, to his obvious fondness for England. John specifically made clear that he wanted to be buried in England.

he flung into the Seine. The coalition raised against John proved over-whelming. In 1203, he retreated to England. By 1205, Normandy and Anjou had been lost.

John's overriding priority was to retake his French lands. But only a massive and hugely expensive military operation could achieve this. Given the vastly increased level of taxation needed to sustain it, almost all of which fell on his English subjects, it was clear that John's English barons would support him only as long as he was successful in France. When the defeat at Bouvines in July 1214 signalled the final collapse of John's French hopes, it inevitably prompted a baronial revolt. John had not just lost his French lands, he was on the verge of losing England.

His agreement to Magna Carta (*see* box) in 1215 eased the immediate pressure, but the underlying problems were as acute as ever. His sudden death 16 months later in the midst of near full-scale civil war was about the best way out he could hope for.

1206	1207	1211	1212	1213	1214	1215	1216
All Angevin territories north of the Loire lost to Philippe II	John refuses to appoint Langton Archbishop of Canterbury. Papal interdict of England (1208) and John's excommunication (1209) follow	Successful Welsh campaign against Llywelyn the Great	Pope declares John no longer legal king of England	Restores relations with papacy by making England a papal fief; renews campaign to regain French realms	Final Angevin defeat in France by Philippe II at Bouvines (July)	John forced to agree to Magna Carta	Rebel barons declare Louis king of England; Louis invades and takes Tower of London (May); John loses crown jewels crossing the Wash (Oct.)

HENRY III 1216–72

HENRY III'S REIGN WAS A PARADOXICAL ONE. GENERALLY REGARDED AS ONE OF ENGLAND'S MOST INEFFECTUAL KINGS, HE REMAINS ITS LONGEST-REIGNING MONARCH. THOUGH NO LESS AUTOCRATIC THAN HIS PREDECESSORS, HIS REIGN SAW CRUCIAL DEVELOPMENTS IN WHAT WOULD BECOME EVENTUALLY DEVELOP INTO PARLIAMENT. ESSENTIALLY PACIFIC IN OUTLOOK, HE NONETHELESS PROVOKED A CIVIL WAR THAT THREATENED TO OVERTURN THE PLANTAGENETS.

KING HENRY III

BORN: October 1 1207, Winchester
ACCEDED: October 18 1216; crowned Gloucester October 28 1216, (and again Westminster Abbey, May 17 1220)

DUKE OF NORMANDY (UNTIL 1259), AND AQUITAINE, KING OF ENGLAND

Henry III has enduring claims to be regarded as one of the few English monarchs with a genuine interest in the arts. He sparked a wide-ranging artistic revolution in England, above all in Gothic church architecture. His greatest project was the rebuilding of Westminster Abbey, a 36-year undertaking that cost the huge sum of £46,000. The first portrait of an English monarch shows Henry directing the building of another new cathedral at St Albans (below).

HENRY'S REIGN BEGAN IN CRISIS. THE NEW king was only nine. In addition, many of his barons still supported the claims of Louis, son of Philippe II, to the English Crown. There was also the continuing problem of how to regain the huge French territories lost in John's reign. That these immediate crises were successfully overcome was largely due to what, for the period, was the unusually untroubled regency of Henry's early reign, competently presided over first by William Marshall, latterly by Hubert de Burgh.

Rapid victories by Marshall over Louis in 1217 summarily ended the lingering civil war. Though relations with some barons remained tense, for the immediate future they rarely spilled over into outright opposition – even if the relative weakness of Henry's position obliged him to approve two reissues of Magna Carta, in 1217 and 1225. More serious was the swift conquest of Poitou in 1224 by Louis, now king of France. Of the once-vast Angevin French lands, only Gascony was left.

Nonetheless by the time the 19-year-old Henry assumed personal control of England in 1227 his kingdom was largely stable, its mechanisms of royal government secure and efficient.

Henry's personal qualities – good and bad – were evident from the start. Though every bit as certain of the absolute nature of monarchy as his Plantagenet forebears, he had none of their relentless, martial energy. To the extent that his sedentary, self-indulgent kingship encouraged the development of more centralized government, above all at Westminster, Henry was in tune with his times. At the same time, however, it made him a singularly ineffective military leader. All his attempts at conquest, whether in Wales (in 1228, 1231 and 1232) or in France (in 1228, 1230 and 1242), ended in failure. Eventually, under the Treaty of Paris of 1259, and in return for confirmation of the Plantagenet rule in Gascony, Henry was forced to renounce all his claims to Normandy, Anjou and Poitou.

But Henry's most obvious failing, as with many medieval kings, was an inability to control his leading subjects. Simmering resentments over Henry's extravagant building projects were increased by Henry's high-handed promotion of his wife's Provençal relations and his own French-born stepbrothers over the interests of native-born magnates. They came to a climax in 1254 when, without consulting his barons, Henry agreed to finance a hugely expensive papal campaign to conquer Sicily.

By any measure, it was an exceptionally ill-judged move. In 1258, cowed by his charismatic brother-in-law, Simon de Montfort (*see* box), Henry was forced to agree to the Provisions of Oxford. In effect, he surrendered control of his realm to a council of barons. In 13th-century Europe, this was a breathtakingly radical step. Even as half-hearted a ruler as

... [Henry] acknowledged the truth of the accusations ... and humbled himself declaring that he had too often been beguiled by evil counsel and ... made a solemn oath at the shrine of St Edward that he would fully and properly amend his old errors and show favour and kindness to his native-born subjects.

Matthew Paris Chronica Majora,
on Henry III's promise in 1258
to limit royal power

1217	1219	1224	1227	1229	1232	1234	1236	1238	1242
Treaty of Lambeth: French dauphin, Louis, renounces claims to England after defeats at Lincoln and Sandwich	Death of regent, William Marshall; Hubert de Burgh appointed regent	Poitou lost to Louis IX of France	Henry III begins personal rule	French-born Simon de Montfort arrives in England, claiming earldom of Leicester	Hubert de Burgh dismissed; Peter des Roches, appointed in his place, encourages Henry to ignore advice of his principal barons	Rebellion by Richard Marshall forces Henry to expel Peter des Roches and other Poitevins in England	Henry's marriage to Eleanor of Provence begins influx of position-seeking Provençals	de Montfort consolidates position in England by secret marriage to Eleanor, Henry's sister	Unsuccessful attempt to retake Poitou

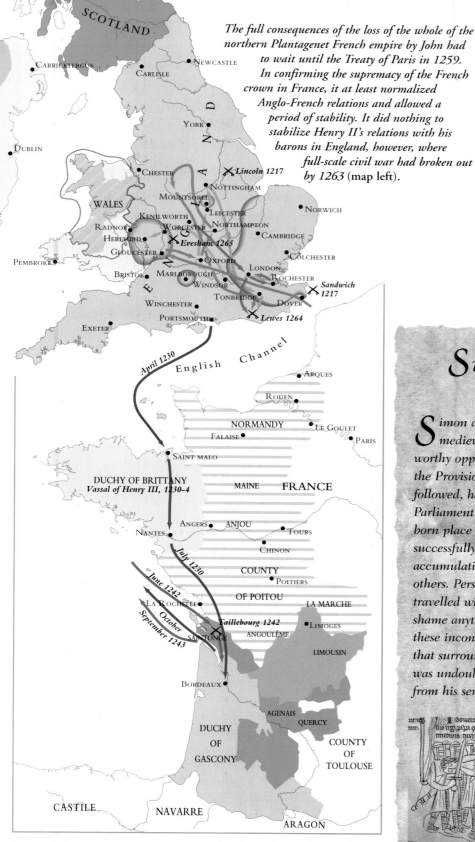

SCOTLAND

CARRICKFERGUS
CARLISLE
NEWCASTLE
DUBLIN
YORK
CHESTER
Lincoln 1217
NOTTINGHAM
MOUNTSOREL
WALES
LEICESTER
KENILWORTH
NORTHAMPTON
RADNOR
WORCESTER
NORWICH
HEREFORD
CAMBRIDGE
Evesham 1265
GLOUCESTER
COLCHESTER
PEMBROKE
OXFORD
ENGLAND
BRISTOL
LONDON
MARLBOROUGH
ROCHESTER
WINDSOR
Sandwich 1217
WINCHESTER
TONBRIDGE
DOVER
PORTSMOUTH
Lewes 1264
EXETER

The full consequences of the loss of the whole of the northern Plantagenet French empire by John had to wait until the Treaty of Paris in 1259. In confirming the supremacy of the French crown in France, it at least normalized Anglo-French relations and allowed a period of stability. It did nothing to stabilize Henry II's relations with his barons in England, however, where full-scale civil war had broken out by 1263 (map left).

English Channel

April 1230

ARQUES
ROUEN
NORMANDY
FALAISE
LE GOULET
PARIS
SAINT MALO
DUCHY OF BRITTANY
Vassal of Henry III, 1230–4
MAINE
FRANCE
ANGERS
ANJOU
NANTES
TOURS
July 1230
CHINON
COUNTY
June 1242
POITIERS
OF POITOU
LA MARCHE
LA ROCHELLE
October
September 1243
Taillebourg 1242
LIMOGES
SAINTONGE
ANGOULÊME
LIMOUSIN
BORDEAUX
AGENAIS
QUERCY
DUCHY
OF
GASCONY
COUNTY
OF
TOULOUSE

CASTILE
NAVARRE
ARAGON

Simon de Montfort 1208–65

Simon de Montfort is generally remembered as the greatest medieval champion of native-born English liberties, a worthy opponent of despotic royal power. As prime instigator of the Provisions of Oxford and the rowdy parliaments that followed, he is also celebrated as an early champion of Parliament itself. Yet not only was he just as much a foreign-born place seeker as those French favourites of Henry III he successfully expelled, his whole career was largely spent in the accumulation of the power and position he violently attacked in others. Personally abstemious and deeply pious, he nonetheless travelled with a retinue of lavishly attired knights that put to shame anything that Henry himself could muster. Yet whatever these inconsistencies and the hint of self-righteous fanaticism that surrounded him, his commitment to the pursuit of liberty was undoubtedly genuine — even if it can be hard to disentangle from his sense of his own self-worth and greater glory.

De Montfort was hacked to death at the Battle of Evesham. Afterwards, his hands and feet were cut off and his genitals draped on his face.

Henry III was stung to respond. Inevitably, civil war followed.

A crushing victory by de Montfort at Lewes in 1264 not only saw Henry and his heir, Edward, taken prisoner, but effectively confirmed the increasingly regal de Montfort as ruler of England. Henry became king in no more than name. That in the end the radicals were defeated, at the Battle of Evesham in 1265, owed little to Henry and almost everything to Edward, whose military prowess was in marked contrast to his father's petulant impotence.

Royal authority may have been re-established but ever-clearer limits to its scope had been set. Even as aggressive a king as Edward I would have to acknowledge the growing importance of Parliament.

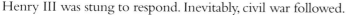

1245	1248	1252	1254	1258	1259	1261	1263	1264	1265
Reconstruction of Westminster Abbey begun by Henry	de Montfort appointed governor of Gascony	de Montfort arraigned for alleged misrule in Gascony; provokes early feud with Henry	Henry agrees to finance papal campaign to conquer Sicily; provokes widespread baronial resentment	The Provisions of Oxford: Henry forced to agree to appointment of magnate-dominated council to co-rule England	Treaty of Paris confirms Plantagenet loss of Normandy, Anjou and Poitou	Backed by pope, Henry renounces Provisions of Oxford	Armed campaign begun by de Montfort against Henry	de Montfort triumphs at Battle of Lewes: Henry and his heir, Edward, are captured	de Montfort overthrown and killed at Battle of Evesham; royal authority restored

*Though never more than conventionally pious, the briskly efficient Edward enjoyed generally harmonious relations with his leading churchmen, as he did with the majority of his leading subjects. Here (**above**), sword in hand, he consults with bishops.*

In a swift and exceptionally well-organized campaign, Edward's huge army cut off Llywelyn's forces. In view of what was to follow, the subsequent settlement was relatively mild. Though Llywelyn, who in 1278 finally performed homage to Edward, lost most of his southern territories, he was allowed to continue as Prince of Wales over Gwynedd.

When five years later Llywelyn's brother, Daffydd, led an uprising against the marches, Edward's response was savagely different. This time, his goal was nothing less than the annexation of Wales. Though the campaign dragged on into 1283, Llywelyn's death in November 1282 effectively signalled the end of Welsh resistance. Daffydd himself was captured and gruesomely executed as a traitor.

The subjection of Wales, brutal even by the standards of the time, was achieved and sustained by a massive occupying army based in the grimly imposing fortresses that Edward constructed across Wales. Under the Statute of Wales of 1284, it was also given legal force. Wales was divided into new shires on the English model with English officials brought in to administer them. Welsh humiliation was made complete the same year when Llywelyn's title, Prince of Wales, was appropriated by the king and bestowed on Edward's son, the future Edward II.

The expression of Edward's ambitions in Scotland were, to begin with, restricted to diplomacy. The accession of the three-year-old Margaret, the "Maid of Norway", to the Scottish throne after the sudden death of Alexander III in 1286 prompted Edward to propose marriage between his heir, Edward, and Margaret. However reluctantly accepted by the Scots, the eventual union of the Scottish and English crowns would then naturally have followed. Margaret's death in 1290 not only put paid to such dynastic ambitions but sparked a further succession crisis in Scotland. Even now, however, Edward, though asserting his overlordship of Scotland, acted as no more than arbiter in the choice of the new sovereign, John Balliol, in 1292.

The Eleanor Crosses

Edward's image as a ruthless warmonger is entirely belied by his relationship with his first wife, Eleanor, the Infanta of Castile (whose name, corrupted in English to "Elephant and Castle", is commemorated in the London district and many inns of the same name). Their marriage, in 1254, was conventionally diplomatic, intended to secure an important ally on the southern border of Gascony. Edward was 15, Eleanor 13. They had 15 children, nine of whom died. Remarkably, rather than the mutual loathing such marriages normally produced, Eleanor and Edward seem to have been genuinely fond of one another.

On her death, Edward wrote: "My harp is turned to mourning, in life I loved her dearly, nor can I cease to love her in death." As remarkable were the 12 stone crosses that were erected by Edward to mark the stopping points of her funeral cortège from Harby in Nottinghamshire, where she died, to Westminster Abbey, where she was buried. Three survive today, at Hardingstone and Geddington (right) in Northamptonshire and at Waltham Cross in Essex (far right). The most famous, at Charing Cross, is not the original cross but a replica put up in 1863.

Almost as surprising was that Edward's second marriage, in 1299, to Margaret, sister of Philippe IV of France, which was again arranged to cement a diplomatic alliance, was equally happy. Edward was 60, Margaret 20.

continued from previous page

1290	1292	1293	1294	1295
Death of first wife, Eleanor. Expulsion of Jews. Treaty of Birgham agrees marriage of Edward's son to new child queen of Scotland, Margaret; Edward agrees to respect "rights and liberties" of Scotland.	John Balliol confirmed by Edward as new king of Scotland	Escalating tensions with Philippe IV of France leads Philippe to declare Gascony forfeit	Revolt in Wales delays Edward's plans for French campaign	Scotland and France formally ally against England

It is an exceptional testimony to the sense of nation-hood fostered by Scotland's kings from the 12th century onward that, however overwhelming the forces directed against it by Edward I, the war-like Plantagenet was never able to conquer the country (map right). He would, however, guarantee contin-ued Anglo-Scottish hostility until well into the 16th century.

EDWARD I'S SCOTTISH CAMPAIGNS, 1296–1307

CAITHNESS

WESTERN ISLES

ROSS

ELGIN

INVERNESS

Andrew of Moray, 1297

ABERDEEN

SCOTLAND

MONCSA

DUNKELD

DUNDEE

PERTH

ST ANDREWS

Stirling 1297

Falkirk 1298

EDINBURGH

Dunbar 1297

GLASGOW

Roslin 1303

BERWICK

ROXBURGH

AYR

William Wallace, 1297

JEDBURGH

Robert Bruce, 1297

DUMFRIES

LIBERTY OF TYNEDALE
Held by Scottish kings to 1296

CARLISLE

ENGLAND

IRELAND

(to England)

ISLE OF MAN
Plantagenet-held from 1290

But now, buoyed by his success in Wales, it is clear that conquest rather than control was beginning to dominate Edward's ambitions. Though Balliol remained as defiant as his weakened circumstances allowed, by 1295 Edward had reduced him to scarcely more than a cipher. The Scottish response, to seek an alliance with France (*see* pp.66–7), was treated by Edward as tantamount to a decla-ration of war. In March 1296 he mustered an army of 25,000. Reaching Berwick, he slaughtered almost the whole population of 11,000. By July, the campaign was over. Edward declared himself king of Scotland and returned to England with the Stone of Destiny, the single most potent symbol of Scottish independence.

Ultimately, whatever his overwhelming military and financial superiority, Edward failed in Scotland, brought up short by the upsurge of patriotic leadership supplied first by William Wallace and more lastingly by Robert the Bruce (*see* pp.64–5). Further terrifying campaigns in 1298, 1300, 1301–2, 1303–4 and 1307, and the stationing of large permanent English garrisons across much of Scotland, highlight the extent of Edward's obsessional determination to subjugate his northern neighbours. But the bloodshed succeeded only in poisoning Anglo-Scottish relations for sev-eral centuries. Appropriately, Edward died near Carlisle leading another vengeful campaign against Scotland in 1307.

Like Henry II, Edward I imposed strong rule in an age that demanded it. But also like Henry, he was unable to guarantee it from beyond the grave. With-in years, his heir, Edward II, supine, vacillating and indolent, came close to bringing the whole mag-nificent edifice of Edwardian Plantagenet kingship crashing to the ground.

Though otherwise peaceful, relations between Edward and his French counterparts deteriorated after 1293. The following year, Edward renounced his homage to the French king. In 1295, parts of northern Gascony were overrun by the French. As his designs on Scotland took firmer shape, such cross-Channel distractions proved increasingly troublesome. Nonetheless, in 1297 Edward went to France where, with papal intervention, his lordship of Gascony was confirmed. In return, Edward renewed his homage to Philippe IV (left).

1296	1297	1298	1299	1300–7	1306
Edward invades Scotland; strips Balliol of crown and incarcerates him in Tower of London	*William Wallace leads Scottish resistance; defeats English at Stirling Bridge. Edward travels to France to secure Gascony from further French attacks*	*Wallace crushed by Edward at Battle of Falkirk*	*Peace treaty between England and France sealed by marriage between Edward and Margaret, sister of Philippe IV*	*Sustained efforts by Edward to conquer Scotland*	*Scottish resistance led by Robert Bruce, who is crowned King of Scotland*

1344	1345	1346	1348	1350	1355	1356	1358
Coinage reformed by Edward III	Sporadic campaigns in Flanders, Brittany and France	Major invasion of France: French victory at Crécy and seizure of Calais, David II captured at Neville's Cross	Black Death strikes France and England. Order of the Garter established	David attempts to secure release by proposing that Edward's heir inherits Scottish throne	Scots raid Berwick	Edward leads renewed campaign against Scotland. Black Prince captures Jean II at Poitiers	France disrupted by widespread rioting: the "Jacquerie"

continued from previous page

Though the younger Balliol's grip on Scotland was never more than tenuous and would in any case not last much beyond 1336, by 1334 he was nonetheless sufficiently well established to force the now nine-year-old David II to flee to France and to cede the whole of southern Scotland to Edward Balliol, doing homage to him for the rest.

But thereafter, though periodically sucked into the much larger Anglo-French conflict by virtue of the Auld Alliance, and despite a series of energetic Scottish campaigns by Edward in the mid-1330s, Scotland, beset by near-permanent dynastic unrest, became only a side-show in Edward's eyes. France was his real goal.

In essence, this new Anglo-French conflict, much later dubbed the Hundred Years War, was no more than a continuation of the much older one that began with the Norman Conquest. But it was given new urgency in 1328 with the death of the child-less Charles IV of France. As Edward was Charles's nephew, Edward could reasonably have expected to succeed to the French throne. But his claim, put forward by his mother, was rejected by the French Parlement. Instead it was Charles IV's cousin, Philippe VI, who was eventually chosen as the new king of France.

Simultaneously, the long-standing French resentment at the continued Plantagenet presence in Gascony, allied to Anglo-French rivalry in Flanders (by far England's most important Continental trading partner yet coveted by France), was increasing. The situation was temporarily improved in 1329 and in 1331 when Edward travelled to France to do homage to Philippe for Gascony, the last king of England to do so. But it deteriorated in 1334 when Philippe agreed to shelter the child-king of Scotland, David II. By 1336, Philippe was assembling a fleet for an invasion of England.

The following year, Edward dramatically upped the stakes by claiming the French throne. Philippe promptly declared Gascony forfeit and invaded it. In fact, skirmishing aside – a French raid on Southampton in 1338, an inconclusive invasion of France by Edward the same year – little of consequence happened until 1340. Edward needed time to put his finances on a firm footing and to secure allies elsewhere in Europe. In March 1340, Edward formally declared himself King of France, a title retained by every English and British monarch until 1801, and added the fleur-de-lys to his arms. In June, he wiped out the French fleet at Sluys. 16,000 French soldiers and sailors died.

A temporary truce in 1343 was followed in 1346 by Edward's first major invasion of France. It was stunningly successful. Not only was the much larger

The first major engagement of the Hundred Years War was fought in June 1340 at Sluys on the coast of Flanders, where Philippe IV had gathered a fleet of over 200 ships (above). The English victory was absolute. The numbers of French dead were such, it was claimed, that the fish could have learned French. Much more important, Sluys dissuaded the French from attempting any further large-scale invasion of England. Henceforth, the Hundred Years War would be fought in France.

The Most Noble Order of the Garter

E dward's love of ever-more elaborate chivalric ritual was epitomized by his foundation in August 1348 of the Most Noble Order of the Garter, the oldest and most prestigious chivalric order in Britain. As today, there were no more than 26 members, including Edward III himself and his eldest son. They became in effect King Arthur's imagined knights of the Round Table reborn, the king's most valued "companions-in-arms." They met, and solemnized their proceedings, in the chapel at Windsor Castle, which was rebuilt and dedicated to England's new patron saint, St George, whose heroic 3rd-century exploits had inspired English knights in the crusades.

It says something for Edward III's easy camaraderie with his fellow knights that, whatever the higher aims of the Order, its name and motto came from a slightly smutty in-joke. At a dance, the king's mistress, the countess of Salisbury, lost her garter. Gallantly, the king retrieved it with the words: "Honi soit qui mal y pense" – colloquially, "Keep your dirty thoughts to yourselves."

The distinctive star of the Order, with motto and garter surrounding the red cross of St George.

Both the beginning and the end of Richard II's reign were marked by rebellion (map right): the Peasants' Revolt in 1391, expertly defused by the youthful king; and Henry Bolingbroke's invasion in 1399, which led to the swift overthrow of the still-youthful Richard II. The king's attempts to subdue Scotland may have been inconclusive but in Ireland, which he visited twice, he was notably more successful in restoring Plantagenet hegemony.

RICHARD II

	English-held in Ireland at start of Richard's reign, 1377
	Irish vassals of Richard II
O'NEILL	Irish chieftains knighted by Richard and accepting vassal status, 1395
	Wat Tyler's revolt, 1381
	Maximum extent of Peasants' Revolt, 1381
→	John of Gaunt's campaign, 1384
→	Richard II's campaigns,
→	Scottish campaigns, 1388
	Revolts, 1393
⇢	Route of Richard in captivity
→	Henry of Bolingbroke's march on London, 1399

(Map showing Scotland, Ireland, England, Wales and France with locations: Edinburgh, Newbattle, Melrose, Berwick, Otterburn 1388, Newcastle, Carlisle, Durham, Pickering, Knaresborough, York, Ravenspur, Pontefract, Doncaster, O'Neill, Dundalk, O'Connor, Dublin, Conway, Flint, Chester, Nottingham, Norwich, Leicester, Cambridge, O'Brian, Mac Murrogh, Limerick, Kilkenny, Ireland, Waterford, Wales, Radnor, Hereford, Worcester, Northampton, Colchester, Mac Carthy, Haverfordwest, Gloucester, Oxford, London, Radcot Bridge 1387, Bristol, Windsor, Rochester, Tonbridge, Dover, Winchester, Calais, Portsmouth, Boulogne, Exeter, English Channel, France. Dates 1385, 1394, 1399.)

demanded their dismissal. Famously, Richard replied that he would not dismiss so much as a kitchen maid at its insistence. The next year, he was comprehensively outmanoeuvred. Led by a group of five senior magnates, the "Lords Appellants", Richard's inner circle was ruthlessly purged. Power passed to a "Council of Government" answerable to Parliament, itself now controlled by the Lords Appellants.

Even after Richard had declared his majority in 1389, and despite his abrasive conviction that he was "the deputy elected by the Lord", the king was still effectively circumscribed by the Lords Appellants. His response suggests a shrewdness at odds with his later image as power-mad tyrant. Richard bided his time, waiting for the moment of inevitable revenge. He also achieved two notable triumphs: in 1394 he restored at least a measure of order to an increasingly lawless Ireland; and in 1396 he negotiated a 30-year truce with France. That it lasted only 19 years was no fault of Richard's.

Richard struck against the Lords Appellants in 1397. Gloucester was murdered, Arundel executed, Warwick and Nottingham exiled for life, and Bolingbroke, John of Gaunt's son, was exiled for ten years. For the remaining two years of his reign, Richard's rule grew increasingly arbitrary and cruel. With the death of the ageing John of Gaunt in February 1399, Bolingbroke's exile was increased to life and his estates seized

It was a fatal mistake. Not even the most cowed of Richard's subjects could now feel anything but threatened. When in May Richard returned to Ireland, the way was clear for Bolingbroke's return. By September, Richard had been forced to abdicate. By October, Bolingbroke was king (Henry IV). Three months later, Richard was murdered.

Richard's self-projection as divinely sanctioned monarch is portrayed in the Wilton Diptych, painted in the 1390s (below). It seems likely that the painting was Richard's own travelling altarpiece. Though variously interpreted, its central message of the king's closeness to God is unmistakable.

> **You wretches, detestable on land and sea; you who seek equality with lords are unworthy to live. Rustics you were and rustics you still are: you will remain in bondage not as before but incomparably harsher. For as long as we live we will strive to suppress you, and your misery will be an example in the eyes of posterity.**
>
> *Richard II to the remaining leaders of the Peasants' Revolt, June 1381.*

1389	1394	1396	1397–8	1399	1400
Richard declares majority	English authority reimposed in Ireland after Richard visits it. Death of Richard's queen, Anne of Bohemia	Thirty-year truce negotiated with France	Richard breaks power of Lords Appellants	Death of John of Gaunt (Feb.); Richard increases sentence against his heir, Bolingbroke, and seizes his estates. Richard leaves for Ireland (May); Bolingbroke lands in Yorkshire (June) and raises revolt against Richard, who abdicates (Sept.)	Richard dies, almost certainly murdered by the new king, Henry IV

Projections of Royalty: One

FROM THE 12TH CENTURY ONWARDS, INCREASING PROSPERITY, THE GROWING SOPHISTICATION OF THE MACHINERY OF GOVERNMENT WITH THE KING FIRMLY AT ITS HEAD, AND THE EVOLUTION OF CHIVALRIC CODES CREATED THE CONDITIONS IN WHICH MONARCHY ITSELF BECAME NOT JUST GRANDER BUT ANXIOUS TO STRESS ITS GRANDEUR. PROJECTING ITS INCREASINGLY MAJESTIC NATURE WOULD BECOME A CENTRAL PREOCCUPATION OF KINGSHIP.

KINGSHIP AS A DIVINELY SANCTIONED office had been a commonplace of medieval theories of monarchy at least since the coronation of the Frankish emperor Charlemagne in Rome by the Pope on Christmas Day 800. In the case of Anglo-Saxon England, the double coronation of Alfred's great-grandson Edgar in 959 (*see* p. 33) reinforced the idea that the king, ruling by the authority of God, was as much priest as king. He may have been mortal, but he was not as other men. As the intermediary of God, his will was in effect God's will and, as such, law.

But it was the monarch's patronage of the arts that had the most lasting impact on the projection of royal authority. This took the form of increasingly sumptuous court buildings – the most startling and impressive example being the great hammer-beam roof constructed over Westminster Hall – and portraiture. The portrait of Richard II in Westminster Abbey, painted perhaps in 1395, epitomizes Richard's self-image: austere and absolute, staring hieratically amid a shimmer of gold leaf. As a symbol of royal authority, it was without equal in medieval England. Its importance also rests in its being almost the first known portrait of an English king – for all that it is as much icon as likeness.

That the actual person of the king was majestic – remote, mysterious and powerful, a presence demanding rigid and elaborate ceremony – was a development that occurred only later. The key figure was Richard II at the end of the 14th century. His self-absorbed personality, steeped in chivalric codes, took naturally to the notion that the mystique of his royal authority could be bolstered by – indeed demanded – the trappings of power and obeisance: in essence, an ever-more rigid courtly ritual centred on himself as king. It was no coincidence that Richard II was the first English king to style himself "highness". During his minority, even the most noble of his increasingly resentful subjects were allowed access to him only via his inner circle of pampered royal favourites. Later, as his belief in his own majestic person intensified, he built an immense throne from which he could look imperiously on his subjects below. If your eye ever caught his, you were obliged to look away.

Similarly overwhelming projections of royal authority would not reoccur until the 16th century. When they did, it was to even more striking effect. Both Henry VIII and Elizabeth I recognized almost instinctively that their own power – and by extension that of the state – could be enhanced by

Richard II, portrait in Westminster Abbey, c. 1390 (above).

Henry VIII by Hans Holbein the Younger, c.*1536* (far left)

Elizabeth I, Armada Portrait (left).

Charles I on Horseback *by Sir Anthony Van Dyck* c.*1637* (below).

projecting themselves as figures of absolute regal authority, and that royal propaganda of this kind was an essential tool in reinforcing their rule.

In part, this was no more than a reflection of developments elsewhere. Courtly ritual everywhere in Europe was becoming more elaborate and formal. Fashions, too, had grown more ornate and extravagant. But few European monarchs embraced the trend with the uninhibited gusto of the Tudors. Holbein's 1536 portrait of Henry is of the commanding Renaissance prince par excellence, legs apart, hands on hips, regally bestriding his kingdom and his subjects alike. His daughter Elizabeth's long and exultant reign was marked by innumerable portraits of the queen, all no less concerned to bolster her royal status. The *Armada Portrait*, painted to celebrate the defeat of the Spanish Armada in 1588, is as much religious icon as triumphant state portrait: the all-seeing, all-wise Regina, a chalky-white, mask-like face surmounting a halo of lace over a pearl-strewn silk dress. Behind her, the victorious English fleet basks in placid sunshine while the galleons of the impious Spaniards are dashed against a rocky coast. The queen's right hand, meanwhile, brushes a globe, her attenuated fingers resting on the New World colony named in her honour, Virginia. The message is clear: through their growing command of the seas, England and its virgin queen were becoming a world power.

If royal portraiture had become an established means of boosting royal ideology, it nonetheless still required artists of exceptional talent to do it full justice; competition among Europe's monarchs to attract leading painters could be intense. In the 17th century, Charles I (whose taste in art was a lot more sure than his political touch) was able to retain the services of the great Flemish portraitist Anthony Van Dyck only by knighting him and giving him a generous pension. Of the many paintings Van Dyck produced of Charles and his family, his *Charles I on Horseback,* painted probably in 1637, comes closest to Charles's view of himself as an ideal, omniscient ruler. Horse and rider alike deliberately echo the 2nd-century Roman equestrian statue of the Emperor Marcus Aurelius. The stammering, five-foot-four Charles has been transformed into a commanding Christian warrior-emperor, victoriously horsed and clad in glinting armour, his boots tipped with gold spurs. Behind him is a shield bearing the inscription: *Carolus Rex Magnae Britanniae.* But if art as the servant of kingship had reached its apogee, its limitations were clear. Not even the genius of Van Dyck could preserve Charles from the executioner's block.

ENGLAND: LANCASTER AND YORK 1399–1485

HENRY IV 1399–1413	*EDWARD IV 1461–70/1471–83*
HENRY V 1413–22	*EDWARD V 1483*
HENRY VI 1422–61/1470–71	*RICHARD III 1483–85*

THE ACCESSION OF THE TEN-YEAR-OLD HENRY III IN 1216 APPEARED TO HAVE SETTLED FOR GOOD THE DAMAGING DYNASTIC DISPUTES THAT HAD DISRUPTED THE NORMAN AND ANGEVIN KINGS. HENCEFORWARD, THE PRINCIPLE WAS ESTABLISHED THAT THE SUCCESSION AUTOMATICALLY PASSED TO THE KING'S ELDEST SON, REGARDLESS OF AGE. HERITABLE MONARCHY, WITH THE LEGITIMACY AND STABILITY THIS IMPLIED, HAD BECOME A FIXED POINT OF ROYAL GOVERNMENT.

Even the overthrow of Edward II in 1327 by his wife, Isabella, and her lover, Roger Mortimer, tended to reinforce the principle: however dubious the legality of Edward II's deposition, he was at least succeeded by his son, Edward III, for all that the boy-king's mother and Mortimer retained actual control of the government. That Edward III at 17 then subjugated Isabella and Mortimer seemed only to justify the principle of heritable kingship. The rightful king was ruling in every sense.

The overthrow of Richard II in 1399 by the new duke of Lancaster, Henry Bolingbroke, was a very different matter. The issue was not Richard's abuse of his office, albeit that even by the standards of late-medieval England Richard II had passed well beyond mere delusions of grandeur in the last two years of his reign. Rather, the problem was how Bolingbroke, now Henry IV, could justify his kingship when he was so far from being in the direct line of succession.

In effect, he could not. His was a usurpation in everything but name. A variety of mostly specious claims were put forward by Henry and his supporters. Parliamentary acclamation for the new king was also cited. But at bottom, justified or not, Bolingbroke had seized the throne and everyone knew it. That he was a vastly more just and able ruler than Richard II was not the point. The principle of hereditary monarchy underpinning the government of England had been overturned. The natural order had been set on its head.

The new king paid a heavy price. Ultimately, so would England. Lingering doubts about the legitimacy of his rule and intermittent baronial discontent punctuated his reign. He may have successfully founded a new dynasty, in the process restoring the kind of efficient government last seen in Edward III's reign, but for Henry personally the fruits of kingship were bitter.

With the accession of his son, Henry V, in 1413 all such anxieties were swept away in a blast of martial vigour when the war with France was begun again. A series of startling victories over the French (Agincourt in 1415 among them) not only dramatically increased the French territories under English control but forced the French – in the throes of a civil war of their own and ruled by the palpably insane Charles VI – to accept Henry V as heir to the French throne.

Whether Henry V's slender resources would have allowed him to rule both England and France is open to doubt. As Edward III had discovered, conquest was one thing, the establishment of stable government over the conquered territories another. But what is not in dispute is that Henry's early death from dysentery in 1422 brought not just another child-king to the throne, the nine-month-old Henry VI, but one who, in adulthood, demonstrated the disadvantages of a very different sort of hereditary principle.

Like his cousin Charles VI, Henry VI, saintly and well intentioned, suffered from a form of madness. In an age when effective government was almost entirely dependent on the personality of the king, it was a catastrophic disadvantage. Precisely as in France under Charles VI, Henry VI duly became the tool of his competing magnates. That his father's spectacular gains in France were now being lost almost as rapidly as they had been won only increased the stakes. His overthrow became a matter of time.

England itself may have become richer and more powerful but its government, personified in the feeble person of the king, was becoming scarcely more stable than during the unruly aftermath of William the Conqueror's reign.

Dynastic certainty was giving way to a naked struggle for power. This was the true legacy of Bolingbroke's *coup d'état*. It climaxed in 1461 and 1485, when England found itself in the grip of a protracted dynastic civil war. On the one hand there were the Lancastrians, supporters of Henry VI, himself a descendant of Edward III's youngest son, John of Gaunt, the duke of Lancaster. On the other were the Yorkists, descendants of Edward III's third son, the duke of York. Its poetic name, the Wars of the Roses, derives from each side's respective heraldic badge: a red rose for the Lancastrians, a white one for the Yorkists.

As with any family quarrel, logic had little to do with it. Both sides shared the same view of kingship yet believed their innate right to rule was unchallengeable. Neither was prepared to compromise. Inevitably, retaining the support of a fickle aristocracy whose own calculations were dominated by short-term advantage was a central pre-occupation. Treachery, betrayal and revenge became common currency.

The result was predictably vicious. In 1461, supported by the formidably unprincipled earl of Warwick "the kingmaker", Richard II's great-nephew, the duke of York, seized the throne as Edward IV. In 1470, he was ousted by an improbable alliance between Warwick, Henry's VI's endlessly scheming wife Margaret, and the king of France, Louis XI. The following year he triumphantly regained his throne.

His death in 1483 sparked a further round of dynastic turmoil. His heir, the 12-year-old Edward V, was abducted and probably murdered by Edward IV's brother, the duke of Gloucester, who had already declared himself Richard III. Within two years, Richard III himself was ousted by a new part-Welsh Lancastrian pretender, the obscure Henry Tudor, who became King Henry VII.

Richard III's death signalled more than just the end of the Wars of the Roses. After 331 years, Plantagenet rule in England had been brought to an end. Yet, though Tudor rule might elevate English kingship to new heights of "imperial" pretension, it, too, would prove no less vulnerable to the uncertainties of personal rule.

HENRY IV 1399–1413

KING HENRY IV

BORN: April 3 1367, Bolingbroke Castle
ACCEDED: September 30 1399; crowned October 13 1399, Westminster Abbey

Earl of Derby (from 1377), Earl of Northampton and Hereford (from 1384), Duke of Lancaster, Earl of Leicester and Earl of Lincoln (from 1399), King of England and France, Lord of Ireland

FROM THE START OF HIS REIGN, HENRY'S OVERRIDING CONCERNS WERE TO LEGITIMIZE HIS SEIZURE OF RICHARD II'S THRONE AND TO NEUTRALIZE THE INEVITABLE BARONIAL REVOLTS THAT THE USURPATION PROVOKED. HE WAS UNAMBIGUOUSLY SUCCESSFUL WITH THE LATTER. THE FORMER, HOWEVER, REMAINED TANTALIZINGLY ELUSIVE. IN THE END, THE STRAIN OF KINGSHIP DRAINED AND EXHAUSTED HIM.

HENRY IV HAD ALL THE ATTRIBUTES of a successful medieval king – decisiveness, high political intelligence and martial ardour. Dealing with mutinous barons was, if not a workaday matter, at least relatively straightforward. But squaring his conscience was altogether different. A contradiction remained at the heart of Henry's kingship, one that he could never forget: that it claimed to be hereditary when it had been acquired by force.

It did not, however, inhibit the new king from pursuing those magnates who, favoured by Richard II, had most to gain from Henry's downfall. In December 1399, a plot by the earls of Huntingdon, Kent and Salisbury was easily foiled. Their execution and those of 30 other rebel barons swiftly followed. At the same time, Henry had Richard II, now plain Richard of Bordeaux, a prisoner in Pontefract Castle, murdered. The corpse of the former monarch, who seems to have been starved to death, was displayed in London

The threat to Henry remained, however. It took

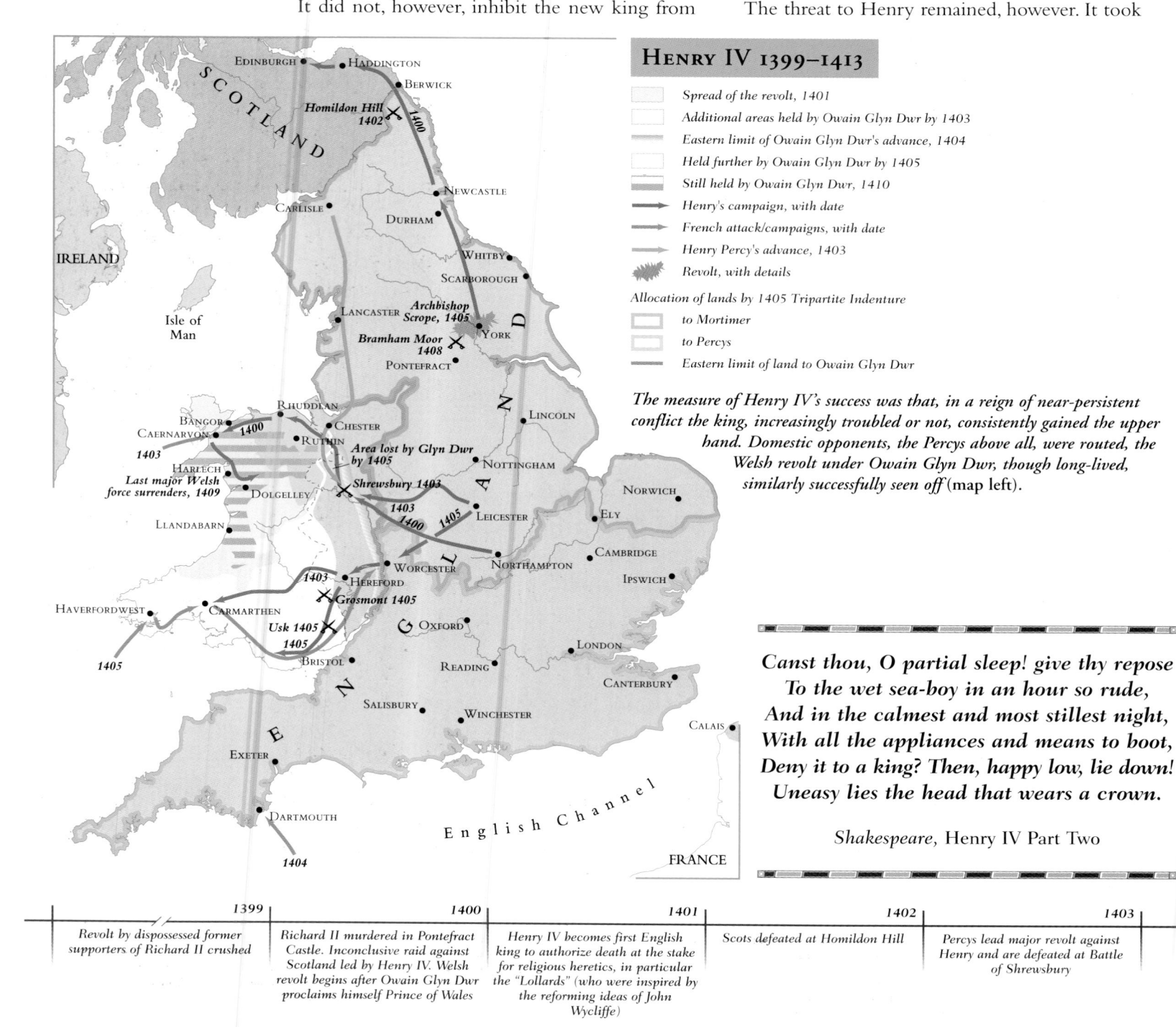

HENRY IV 1399–1413

Spread of the revolt, 1401
Additional areas held by Owain Glyn Dwr by 1403
Eastern limit of Owain Glyn Dwr's advance, 1404
Held further by Owain Glyn Dwr by 1405
Still held by Owain Glyn Dwr, 1410
Henry's campaign, with date
French attack/campaigns, with date
Henry Percy's advance, 1403
Revolt, with details

Allocation of lands by 1405 Tripartite Indenture
to Mortimer
to Percys
Eastern limit of land to Owain Glyn Dwr

The measure of Henry IV's success was that, in a reign of near-persistent conflict the king, increasingly troubled or not, consistently gained the upper hand. Domestic opponents, the Percys above all, were routed, the Welsh revolt under Owain Glyn Dwr, though long-lived, similarly successfully seen off (map left).

*Canst thou, O partial sleep! give thy repose
To the wet sea-boy in an hour so rude,
And in the calmest and most stillest night,
With all the appliances and means to boot,
Deny it to a king? Then, happy low, lie down!
Uneasy lies the head that wears a crown.*

Shakespeare, Henry IV Part Two

1399	1400	1401	1402	1403
Revolt by dispossessed former supporters of Richard II crushed	*Richard II murdered in Pontefract Castle. Inconclusive raid against Scotland led by Henry IV. Welsh revolt begins after Owain Glyn Dwr proclaims himself Prince of Wales*	*Henry IV becomes first English king to authorize death at the stake for religious heretics, in particular the "Lollards" (who were inspired by the reforming ideas of John Wycliffe)*	*Scots defeated at Homildon Hill*	*Percys lead major revolt against Henry and are defeated at Battle of Shrewsbury*

The young Henry (right) was exceptionally accomplished. He was vigorous and athletic, and a keen patron of the arts. He spoke English, French and Latin fluently and was very much more than usually devout. By the standards of the time, he was also remarkably well travelled. In 1390, he went to Lithuania, where he fought with the Teutonic Knights. In 1392, he journeyed to Jerusalem, meeting many of Europe's leading nobles and rulers en route.

The contrast between the vigorous young Henry and the care-worn, prematurely aged king is remarkable (left). His rule was decisive, fair-minded and just. Yet at only 40, he seemed a broken man, prey to a variety of possibly psychosomatic diseases. In his will, dated 1408, he wrote: "I Henry, sinful wretch, ask my lords and true people forgiveness if I have mistreated them in any wise."

two forms. First, a widespread and long-lasting popular uprising in Wales under the leadership of Owain Glyn Dwr, who in 1400 proclaimed himself Prince of Wales (see box). Second, a concerted effort to unseat Henry by his former supporters, the ambitious and disgruntled Percy family – the earl of Northumberland, his brother the earl of Worcester, and Northumberland's son Henry (or Hotspur).

In 1403, against the background of spreading revolt in Wales, Henry defeated Hotspur and his uncle in a savage battle at Shrewsbury. Hotspur was killed, Worcester was executed. Northumberland, however, was spared, though his castles and most of his honours were stripped from him. By 1405, he had joined forces with Glyn Dwr and the disaffected Marcher Lord, Edmund Mortimer. With the support of the Archbishop of York, Richard Scrope, they concocted an ambitious plan to overthrow Henry and divide England and Wales between them. Henry had his revenge. Though Northumberland escaped to Scotland and Mortimer fled to Wales, all the other conspirators, including the archbishop, were rounded up and executed. With Northumberland's death three years later in an abortive raid on England, domestic opposition to Henry was crushed.

Henry enjoyed notable successes in other fields. His relations with Parliament were generally good. Scotland, too, posed little threat after 1402 when a major border raid, the last such until 1513, was wiped out at Homildon Hill. Then, in 1406, the 12-year-old king of Scotland, James I, en route to sanctuary in France, was captured. He remained an English prisoner for 18 years. The campaign against Wales, if expensive, was also increasingly being won. By 1409, though Glyn Dwr himself remained at large, most Welsh resistance had been broken.

Yet Henry IV's last years were ones of obvious decline compounded by persistent ill-health. To some extent, this may have been provoked by his worsening relations with his son, the future Henry V. In 1411, the king reacted angrily to suggestions that

Owain Glyn Dwr
c.1359–c.1415

Owain Glyn Dwr, better known in English as Owen Glendower, was an unlikely rebel. Solidly prosperous and with substantial estates in northeast Wales, he appeared a natural supporter of the English cause in Wales. As a follower of the Earl of Arundel, he had fought in Richard II's 1385 campaign against Scotland. But in 1400, a minor property dispute with a neighbour escalated violently. Almost at once, it ballooned into open rebellion, with Glyn Dwr – self-proclaimed Prince of Wales in September 1400 – at its head. The decade or more of guerrilla warfare that followed presented Henry IV with his most testing problem. Substantial armies, as many as 4,000 strong, had to be mustered at equally substantial expense.

Glyn Dwr's plans for Wales were nothing if not ambitious. He didn't just aim to throw out the English but, with the Percys and Mortimer, to take over England itself. Wales would be extended to the Trent and the Mersey. The Welsh Church was to take over no less than five English bishoprics. Two Welsh universities were also to be founded, one in the north, one in the south. He recruited allies in Scotland and France. He had plans to transfer allegiance from the Pope in Rome to the Pope in Avignon. Crucially, he also established a Welsh Parliament.

In the end, as so often before, the English slowly crushed the life out of the Welsh rebellion. With the fall of Harlech Castle in 1409, it was as good as over. Glyn Dwr, now a fugitive on the run and taking refuge in caves, refused to surrender. In 1415 he turned down a pardon from Henry V. No one knows where or how he died.

he abdicate in favour of him. The following year, it was put about that the young Henry was actively trying to overthrow his father, an accusation angrily denied. But more than anything, Henry seems simply to have wasted away, tormented by the memory of his overthrow and murder of a legitimate king.

1404	1405	1406	1408	1409	1411
Owain Glyn Dwr calls first Welsh Parliament	Revolt following pact between Northumberland, Mortimer and Owain Glyn Dwr put down; Archbishop of York executed. French troops sent to Wales to support Owain Glyn Dwr	James I of Scotland captured during attempted escape to France	Northumberland killed in attempted invasion of England from Scotland	Rebel Welsh forces in Harlech Castle, including Edmund Mortimer, starved into submission – signals gradual end to Welsh revolt	Split between Henry and his son over suggestions that the king should abdicate in his favour

HENRY V 1413–22

THOUGH HE HAD THE SHORTEST REIGN OF ANY ENGLISH MONARCH SINCE HAROLD IN 1066, HENRY V IS WIDELY CELEBRATED AS ENGLAND'S MOST COMPELLINGLY HEROIC KING: A VALIANT CHAMPION OF HIS COUNTRY, A BRILLIANT POLITICAL MANAGER AND AN EVEN BETTER MILITARY STRATEGIST WHOSE CONQUESTS TOOK HIM WITHIN REACH OF THE FRENCH THRONE.

DESPITE THE 30-YEAR TRUCE AGREED WITH France by Richard II in 1396, the conflict had resumed by 1411. Unlike the now secure Henry IV, the hapless French king, Charles VI, ruled over an increasingly faction-ridden country that from 1407 had fallen into a state of near civil war. For the English, it was too tempting a prospect to resist. But in expeditions in 1411 and 1412, Henry IV could afford to commit only relatively modest forces. Henry V, however, was determined from the start on a much larger invasion. But to mount it, he needed finance, which meant Parliamentary approval. It is a remarkable feature of Henry V's reign that he not only secured this but, in part by extension, gained the trust and support of practically every one of his magnates. For the first time, a general sense not just of England but of Englishness was being created. Brilliantly stage-managed by the young king, it united the

Henry V has had a consistently good press. It is no accident that Shakespeare's Henry V is the centrepiece of his history cycle. Just, a devout patron of the Church, a keen enthusiast for the spread of English, a shrewd politician, a brilliant propagandist and, above all a great conqueror, there seemed almost no limits to his attainments. This portrait (above), painted in about 1600, remains the best-known image of him.

Prince of Wales,
Duke of Cornwall, Earl of Chester,
Duke of Lancaster and Duke of Aquitaine (from 1399),
King of England,
King of France and Lord of Ireland

BORN: September 16 1387
ACCEDED: March 20 1413: crowned April 9 1413, Westminster Abbey

whole country in a growing blaze of patriotic fervour. Henry's Norman, Angevin and earlier Plantagenet predecessors had been French kings of England struggling to hold on to or expand their traditional lands in France against their feudal superior, the king of France. Henry V, however, whatever his French origins, was indisputably an English king leading an English army against France in an outright war of conquest. It was a crucially important difference. In the spring of 1415, Henry formally revived the claim to the French throne first put forward by Edward III. In addition, he demanded the return of all former Plantagenet lands in France. In August, having successfully put down the only baronial revolt he faced, he sailed for France with an army of 10,000. Within three months of his departure, Henry was making a triumphal return to London: in September he had stormed Harfleur; a month later, at Agincourt, he had annihilated a French army three times larger than his own.

Having seized the initiative, Henry did not intend to let it go. In August 1417, he was back in France. This time, there would be no lightning victories;

The Battle of Agincourt, 1415

By any measure, Agincourt was an exceptional victory. Henry V's original plan had been to march on Paris but, with the season so far advanced and Harfleur already in English hands, the king judged it more prudent to make for Calais. Exhausted and bedraggled, the English struggled across the Somme only to be confronted by a French army outnumbering them three to one.

Henry V's generalship has never been questioned but there is no doubt that the French made his victory simpler by sending their heavy cavalry on a narrow front straight at the English bowmen, much as they had at Crécy 70 years before. The result was little more than a slaughter – 6,000 Frenchmen were killed while English losses amounted to only about 400. Henry's chaplain recorded: "No king of England ever achieved so much in so short a time and returned home with so great and glorious a triumph."

The battle may have confirmed England's military superiority but the French did not make the same mistake again. In all subsequent campaigns they prudently refused to be drawn into large set-pieces battles. Fighting on home soil inevitably gave them the advantage in the grim, attritional struggle that followed. Had Henry lived, it is possible he could have continued his triumphs. But after 1429, the English were increasingly on the defensive. The prospect of total victory, opened up by Agincourt, proved an illusion.

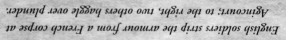

English soldiers strip the armour from a French corpse at Agincourt; to the right, two others haggle over plunder.

1414 — Lollard rising put down. Henry accepts principle that king can accept or reject bills put forward to Parliament but not amend them

1415 — Henry breaks off negotiations with the French and demands throne (June). Revolt by earls of March and Cambridge suppressed. Sails for France (Aug.); takes Harfleur (Sept.); defeats main French army at Agincourt (Oct.); returns to London (Nov.)

1416 — Treaty of Canterbury agrees alliance with Holy Roman Empire. English naval victory at Harfleur

1417 — Henry's mother Joan of Navarre imprisoned on suspicion of witchcraft. Minor Scottish raids against Berwick and Roxburgh. Henry resumes Norman campaign

English possessions in France, 1415

→ Henry's campaign, 1415

→ Henry's campaign, 1417–19

→ Henry's campaign, 1421–2

Under English control by 1422

⚑ Dauphinist outposts surrendering, 1422–6

Burgundian-held, 1428

Dauphinist-held, 1428

English arms had never been more consistently successful than under Henry V (map below). To his victory at Agincourt in 1415 was added a series of attritional campaigns that by 1420 had confirmed not just the Plantagenet stranglehold over northern France and Henry's recognition as heir to the French throne but a significant expansion of English territory in the southwest.

The Treaty of Troyes, signed in May 1420, was the climax of English ambitions in France that dated back to the Norman Conquest. Here, Henry kneels before Charles VI (below). That summer, Henry took the witless French monarch with him on campaign, as he also took the king of Scotland, James I, an English prisoner since 1406. It was a startling vindication of superior English arms.

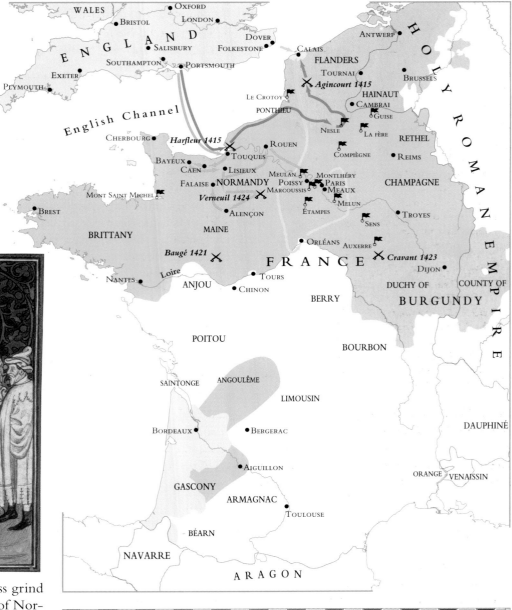

instead there would be the slow, remorseless grind of siege warfare. But with the capitulation of Normandy in 1419, Henry was in a position to dictate terms to the French. Under the Treaty of Troyes of May 1420, Henry was recognized as Regent of France and heir to Charles VI. The agreement was sealed with his marriage to Charles's daughter, Catherine. In return, Henry agreed to carry the fight to Charles's now formally disinherited son and heir, the Dauphin. In early 1421, Henry returned to England with Catherine for her coronation. Thereafter, acclaimed on all sides, the king took his queen on a royal progress around her new kingdom. It was his apotheosis.

By June, Henry had returned to France. For once, the news was less than good. In March, in a major skirmish at Baugé near the Loire, an English force under the king's brother, the duke of Clarence, had been routed by the Dauphin. Henry himself, however, pressed on.

Our mother tongue, to wit, the English tongue, hath in modern days begun to be honourably enlarged and adorned ... and our most excellent lord, King Henry V, hath procured the common idiom to be commended by the exercise of writing and [the] greater part of the Lords and Commons have begun to make their matters noted down in their mother tongue.

The London Company of Brewers

His last victory, the surrender of Meaux, came in May 1422. By now, the king was already ill, probably with dysentery. By the end of August, he was dead. His triumphs, real though they were, would prove shortlived.

HENRY VI 1422–61/1470–1

IT IS DOUBTFUL IF ANY ENGLISH KING WAS LESS QUALIFIED FOR HIS ROLE THAN THE PIOUS, SIMPLE-MINDED HENRY VI. IN STARK CONTRAST TO HIS FATHER, HE WAS ALWAYS THE VICTIM, NEVER THE MASTER, OF EVENTS. THE RESULT WAS RAPID DESCENT INTO ANARCHY LEADING TO HIS OVERTHROW, AN UNLIKELY RESTORATION AND FINALLY HIS MURDER.

BORN: December 6 1421
ACCEDED: September 1 1422; crowned November 6 1429, Westminster Abbey, and December 16 1431, Notre Dame de Paris
DEPOSED: March 4 1461; RESTORED: October 3 1470; DEPOSED: April 11 1471

Duke of Cornwall, King of England, King of France, and Lord of Ireland

THE ACCESSION OF HENRY VI AT THE AGE OF nine months – he was the youngest-ever king of England – carried with it the inevitable risk of instability. In fact, his minority under a council headed by his uncle, the duke of Gloucester, was reasonably stable; and as he grew older, Henry himself appeared intelligent and dutiful. There seemed no reason for him not to become a capable monarch.

At much the same time, however, the initiative in the war in France was beginning to slip towards the French. In 1431, in a panicky move to shore up crumbling English rule, the ten-year-old Henry was shipped to France for his coronation as Henri II. It was an empty gesture. Power in France was rapidly passing to Charles VI's son, who had in any case been crowned Charles VII in 1429.

English hopes of clinging on in France were ended in 1435 when its key ally, Burgundy, defected, and the inspirational English commander in France, the Duke of Bedford, died. The following year Paris fell to Charles VII. Though it took another 18 years for the final English defeat in France, the story thereafter was one of accelerating French military success.

It was against this background of mounting crisis

Henry VI's (above) misfortune was to be a man of peace in an era of perpetual war. In fact, in the face of a resurgent France, even the most active ruler might have found it difficult to hold on to England's French territories. Henry VI was simply overwhelmed by them. Nonetheless his greatest failing was his inability to exercise even the smallest degree of control over his magnates. The king was trapped between their competing ambitions and his wife's equally fierce determination to do them down.

THE HUNDRED YEARS WAR: THE FINAL PHASE, 1429–53

→ Joan of Arc's campaigns, 1429-30
----▶ Joan of Arc's movements in captivity, 1430
━▶ Other French campaigns, with details
  English losses, (including lands no longer recognizing Henry as King of France), by 1453
  Held by Charles VII, 1453
  Burgundian-held, 1453
  English possessions, 1453
  Revolt, with details

The loss of the final English lands in France may have been played out only slowly (map right). Nonetheless, from the mid-1430s, inspired by Joan of Arc's improbable heroics in 1429, French gains became inexorable. With the final French victory at Castillon in 1453, English territory in France had been reduced to Calais and its immediate hinterland.

WALES
OXFORD
LONDON
BRISTOL
ENGLAND
Cade, 1450
DOVER
SALISBURY
FOLKESTONE
ANTWERP
H O L Y R O M A N E M P I R E
CALAIS
SOUTHAMPTON
PORTSMOUTH
FLANDERS
TOURNAI
EXETER
ARRAS
BRUSSELS
PLYMOUTH
HAINAUT
CAMBRAI
LE CROTOY
PONTHIEU
NESLE
LA FÈRE
RETHEL
CHERBOURG
HARFLEUR
ROUEN
COMPIÈGNE
REIMS
BAYEUX
TOUQUES
CAEN
LISIEUX
MEULAN
PARIS
CHAMPAGNE
VAUCOULEUR
FALAISE
NORMANDY
POISSY
MARCOUSSIS
MONTLHÉRY
MONT SAINT MICHEL
ALENÇON
MELUN
DOMREMY
ÉTAMPES
TROYES
BREST
Duke of Brittany, 1448
MAINE
SENS
Patay 1429
ORLÉANS
AUXERRE
BRITTANY
Charles VII, 1449
GIEN
NANTES
ANJOU
TOURS
F R A N C E
DIJON
CHINON
BOURGES
BERRY
DUCHY OF
COUNTY OF
BURGUNDY
POITOU
BOURBON
ANGOULÊME
SAINTONGE
COGNAC
LIMOUSIN
Jean Bureau, 1451
Blanquefort 1451
BORDEAUX
Castillon 1453
DAUPHINÉ
AIGUILLON
ORANGE
VENAISSIN
GASCONY
ARMAGNAC
TOULOUSE
BÉARN
CASTILLE
NAVARRE

1429	1431	1435	1436	1437	1440	1441	1444	1447
Siege of Orléans lifted by Joan of Arc	Henry VI crowned King of France in Paris. Joan of Arc executed	Burgundians ally with Charles VII. Death of English commander in France, the duke of Bedford	Paris recaptured by Charles VII	Henry VI reaches his majority	Eton College founded by Henry VI	King's College, Cambridge, founded by Henry VI	Treaty of Tours signed with Charles VI; Henry VI marries Charles's niece, Margaret of Anjou	Maine returned to French control; Duke of Gloucester, arrested and executed on charges of conspiring to overthrow the king

Eton and King's College

Henry's most admirable qualities were his generosity, his meekness, and his dislike of violence, none of them attributes that would serve a late-medieval king well. He was also passionately attached to the ideal of Christian education. His greatest memorials are Eton College (the King's College of Our Lady of Eton beside Windsor), and King's College, Cambridge (the College Royal of Our Lady and St Nicholas). The former was founded in 1440, when Henry was only 18, the latter in 1441.

The two were intended as interconnected institutions. The 70 scholars at Eton, all of them educated for free, were expected to go on to King's College. Indeed, until the 18th century, King's accepted only Etonians. Both institutions were lavishly funded – King's College had an annual grant of £1,000 – and were intended to be magnificent. In 1448, Henry ordered that the chapel at Eton, still unfinished, be demolished to make way for a larger one.

King's College Chapel, Cambridge

that in 1437 Henry VI achieved his majority. He showed alarming political naivety from the start, turning over his government to a narrow circle of magnates, chief among them the earl of Suffolk. They in turn excluded all those other magnates who might reasonably have expected a share of power. The seeds of future conflict were being sown.

The five-year truce negotiated with France in 1444, under which Henry married Margaret, daughter of the duke of Anjou, caused further splits: between those determined to continue the war and those seeking peace. Henry's response was hand-

We say our sovereign lord may understand that his [Suffolk's] false council has lost his law, his merchandise is lost, his common people is destroyed, the sea is lost, France is lost, the king himself is so set that he may not pay for his meat nor drink, and he owes more than ever any King of England ought, for daily his traitors [are] about him where anything should come to him by his laws, and they take it from him.

Jack Cade's Proclamation of Grievances against the misrule of the earl of Suffolk, 1450

Joan of Arc's impact on the Wars of the Roses was brief but spectacular and played a key role in inspiring the Valois comeback under Charles VI. In 1430, the year after she had broken the English siege of Orléans (left), she was captured by the Burgundians who sold her to the English, who in turn tried her for heresy. She was burned at the stake in Rouen in May 1431.

wringing anguish. Margaret herself proved a further source of friction when she persuaded Henry to hand over Maine to the French crown. The decision not only provoked crisis in England, it did nothing to placate the French. By 1450, the French had retaken Normandy.

Henry's reign effectively disintegrated. Three years later, Gascony was overrun, ending its 300-year rule by England's kings. The loss provoked Henry's first bout of madness. For 18 months, he was plunged into silent melancholia, apparently unaware of his surroundings. In the inevitable power struggle that followed, control see-sawed between the dukes of Somerset and York, both with claims to the throne as descendants of Edward III. By 1455, armed conflict – the Wars of the Roses – had begun (see pp.106–7).

By 1461, Henry, little more than a bemused spectator, had lost his throne to the duke of York's son, Edward IV. He spent the next four years partly in Scotland, latterly wandering aimlessly around northern England until, in 1465, he was captured and imprisoned in the Tower of London. To his evident surprise, in October 1470 he was briefly restored after a falling-out between Edward IV and the Earl of Warwick (hitherto Edward's most important supporter).

Henry's "Readeption" lasted the seven months it took Edward IV to regroup and, in short succession, overwhelm Warwick and Margaret. In May 1471, a prisoner of Edward once more, Henry VI was stabbed to death in the Tower of London.

1449	1450	1451	1453	1461	1463	1465	1470	1471
Rouen recaptured by French	Normandy recaptured by French; earl of Suffolk impeached and executed; rebel Jack Cade leads popular revolt	Guyenne recaptured by French	Battle of Castillon: Henry suffers mental collapse (Aug.); son, Prince Edward, born (Oct.)	Edward (son of duke of York), proclaimed King Edward IV. Defeats royalist army at Towton	Margaret flees to France with Prince Edward	Henry VI captured and imprisoned	Henry VI restored; Edward IV flees to Burgundy	Edward IV restored; Henry VI re-imprisoned and executed

THE WARS OF THE ROSES PLUNGED ENGLAND INTO A LONG ROUND OF DAMAGING DYNASTIC DISPUTES. KINGSHIP BECAME A MATTER OF ARMED FORCE RATHER THAN OF LEGITIMACY, AS WELL AS DISTURBINGLY DEPENDENT ON THE FICKLE LOYALTIES OF A RAPACIOUS, OFTEN VENGEFUL ARISTOCRACY. AT INTERVALS OVER 30 YEARS, ORDERLY GOVERNMENT CAME CLOSE TO COLLAPSE.

THE WARS OF THE ROSES STEMMED FROM Henry IV's seizure of Richard II's throne in 1399. The problem was not just that a legitimate king, however tyrannical, had been deposed but that his designated heir, the earl of March, had also been bypassed. In purely pragmatic terms, there was much to support Henry IV's action, not least that the earl of March was only seven. In contrast to the inevitable threat of instability that a minority would bring, the worldly, experienced Henry Bolingbroke could at least promise firm, capable government.

In the event, whatever the baronial disturbances of the early part of his reign, Henry's usurpation came to seem increasingly justified. Stability was restored, the more unruly magnates brought under control. The new order was then emphatically consolidated by the dazzling success of his son, Henry V, after 1415. The overthrow of Richard II was beginning to look more like a blip rather than a rupture in English hereditary kingship

Two factors conspired to undermine the new order: the unravelling of English rule in France in the face of a resurgent Valois dynasty; and the personality of Henry V's heir, Henry VI, who even before his majority at the age of 15 in 1437 was showing himself almost uniquely ill-equipped for late-medieval kingship. More specifically, with power concentrated in the hands of a narrow clique of magnates, first the duke of Suffolk, then the duke of Somerset – both actively supported by Henry VI's wife, the fearsomely aggressive Margaret of Anjou – those excluded from government became increasingly embittered

Foremost among them was the duke of York, nephew of the Earl of March whose claims to the throne had been ignored by Henry IV. From 1450, a state only just short of outright warfare existed between York and Somerset, each already with an eye on the throne following Henry and set. Margaret's failure to produce an heir. In 1452, York went so far as to lead an army against London, though his revolt fizzled out rapidly.

In 1453, however, events swung decisively York's way. The loss of Gascony not only tainted Somerset's government, it tipped the ailing king into madness. York was able to step into the power vacuum and declare himself Protector. From his point of view,

the only drawback was the surprising birth of an heir to Henry and Margaret the previous autumn. There were many, then and now, who doubted the child was Henry's.

The king's partial recovery of his sanity in the spring of 1455 led to York's overthrow and Somerset's restoration. It also made a final trial of strength between them all but inevitable. This duly followed in May when the two clashed at St Albans. Despite the presence of Henry VI at the battle, it was more a matter of two private armies meeting than of a king of England reasserting his authority over a rebellious magnate. As with the whole sorry

Edmund, Duke of Somerset, is executed at the Battle of Tewkesbury, 1471 (above). With the death of the Beaufort Duke of Somerset in 1455, his heir, Edmund, had taken every opportunity to destabilize the Yorkists. His motive, first and last, had been revenge. For his part, Edward IV, finally victorious at Tewkesbury, was equally swift to order the execution of Somerset.

1452	1454	1455	1458	1459
Duke of York attempts armed overthrow of duke of Somerset	*Duke of York appointed Protector; arrests duke of Somerset*	*York dismissed, Somerset restored (Feb.). York and Somerset clash at St Albans (May); Somerset killed, York restored as Protector*	*Henry attempts reconciliation of warring parties*	*Margaret defeats York at Ludlow, forcing him to flee to Ireland*

conflict until his death in 1471, Henry VI had become no more than a spectator.

St Albans signalled the formal start of the Wars of the Roses. If more skirmish than battle, it nonetheless saw the death of Somerset and the capture of Henry. Yet though York was afterwards clearly in the ascendant, there was still no question of his overthrowing the king. Few wanted another dynastic upheaval. By the same token, the majority of the previously excluded magnates were content for Henry to remain king now that they were able to share in the fruits of government. It had been the overthrow of Somerset they wanted, not that of the king.

That the war continued – in fact became ever more savage – was partly the result of something approaching a Mafia-style blood-feud that developed between losers and winners after St Albans, and partly the result of the queen's implacable desire to do down York. In 1459, with the support of the Percy earls of Northumberland, Margaret all but destroyed the Yorkists at Ludlow. York fled to Ireland; his son, the earl of March, and the earl of Salisbury with his son, the earl of Warwick, fled to Calais.

The war now entered its most confused and improbable phase, with each side gaining and then losing an apparently decisive advantage in the space of less than a year. In late summer 1460, at Northampton, the Yorkists won an overwhelming victory in which Henry was captured. Though York succeeded in being named Henry's heir, his bid for the throne was rejected by Parliament.

Margaret meanwhile had regrouped at Wakefield. In December, her army destroyed the Yorkists. The duke of York himself was killed. On Margaret's orders, his severed head, wearing a paper crown, was displayed on the gates of York. Hurrying south to press home her advantage, Margaret swept aside a small force under the earl of Warwick at St Albans, recapturing the king at the same time. She got no further, however. London had already welcomed the new duke of York, who had declared himself Edward IV at the beginning of March. Turning north again, she was pursued by Edward and the remnants of Warwick's army. They met at Towton in Yorkshire. Here, Edward wiped out her army.

Whatever the firmness of Edward's rule, the degree of instability engendered by this first phase of the Wars of the Roses – combined with the apparently impregnable position that the Earl of Warwick, the self-styled "kingmaker", had engineered for himself – would always make a renewal of conflict likely. That Margaret herself, now in France and actively supported by Louis XI, was thirsting for revenge almost guaranteed it.

In 1470, the conflict duly began again. Edward IV was forced to flee to Burgundy. Warwick meanwhile declared the witless Henry VI king again. For all that this second phase of the war saw equally extreme swings in each side's fortunes, this time it was swiftly resolved. Supported by the Burgundians, Edward returned to England in March 1471 and in rapid succession inflicted victories over Warwick (who was killed) at Barnet, and over Margaret at Tewkesbury, where Henry VI's son, Prince Edward, was killed.

The final Yorkist victory proved a false dawn. Within 12 years, the dynastic unrest began all over again when Edward IV's brother, Richard, seized the throne, in the process doing to death Edward's sons, Edward V and his brother Richard. Within scarcely more than two years, Richard II himself had been killed by the last of the Lancastrian claimants, Henry Tudor. Even then, there were risks of renewed rebellion.

The years of actual conflict may not have been that many, but the dynastic turmoil that climaxed in the Wars of the Roses destabilized England and its monarchy for close to a century.

Richard Neville, the Earl of Warwick dies at the Battle of Barnet, 1471 (above). The earl epitomized the power-hungry manoeuvrings of England's senior magnates in the Wars of the Roses. The man who more than anyone was responsible for putting Edward IV on the throne had no hesitation in turning against the king when Edward asserted his authority.

1460	1461	1470	1471	1483	1485
Royalist army defeated by York at Northampton; Margaret and Henry flee to Scotland; York attempts to persuade Parliament to declare him king (Oct.). Royalist army defeat and kill York at Wakefield (Dec.)	Royalist army defeats earl of Warwick at St Albans but is refused entry to London. New duke of York proclaimed Edward IV (Mar.). Royalist army defeated at Towton	Warwick allies with Margaret, Louis XI and Edward IV's brother; Edward IV flees to Continent; Henry VI restored	Edward IV allies with Burgundians; defeats Warwick at Barnet and Margaret at Tewkesbury, where Prince Edward is killed. Edward IV restored	Death of Edward IV; Richard, duke of Gloucester, seizes throne as Richard III; Edward V and brother, Richard, murdered in Tower of London	Richard III killed by Lancastrian claimant, Henry Tudor, at Bosworth. Henry assumes throne as Henry VII; unites Lancastrians and Yorkists with marriage to daughter of Edward IV, Elizabeth of York

Richard III 1483–85

King Richard III

BORN: October 2 1452
ACCEDED: June 26 1483; crowned July 6 1483, Westminster Abbey

Duke of Gloucester, King of England and Lord of Ireland

Richard III's (above) *reputation suffered so badly at the hands of the Tudors – whose systematic blackening of his name was a crude attempt to justify their rule – that even today it is generally assumed that the king had a body as warped as his mind was said to have been. The widespread belief that he was a hunchback is without any foundation. In fact, though he was smaller than Edward IV, at five-foot-eight Richard III was considerably taller than average for the time.*

In ousting Edward IV's heir, the 12-year-old Edward V, and secretly murdering him and his brother, Richard III earned himself an enduring reputation as uniquely evil. In reality, his actions were always rational and, by the standards of the time, not notably treacherous. His tragedy was to be the victim himself of a further coup two years later.

Before his seizure of the throne in 1483, Richard III, then Duke of Gloucester, had consistently shown himself to be his brother Edward IV's most reliable supporter. His devotion to the Yorkist cause was absolute. While their brother, the Duke of Clarence, was conspiring with the Earl of Warwick to overthrow Edward IV in 1470, Richard remained steadfastly loyal, accompanying Edward in his brief Burgundian exile and thereafter serving with distinction at the battles of Barnet and Tewkesbury that regained him his throne.

Richard's reward was marriage to the younger of Warwick's daughters, Anne, automatically making him one of the greatest landowners in England, and giving him responsibility for the administration of northern England. It was a task he carried out with tact, energy and intelligence. In effect, as "Lord of the North" he became king of the whole region in all but name, dispensing "good and impartial justice to all who sought it, were they rich or poor, gentle or simple". Richard's successful, if expensive, campaign against Scotland in 1482 was typical of his all-round competence.

For Richard, service in the north had the added advantage of distancing him from the intrigues of Edward's increasingly dissolute court. He could not completely escape it, however, and it is clear that Richard shared the general Yorkist distrust of Edward's queen, Elizabeth, and her many Woodville relations. Certainly, he seems to have held the queen largely responsible for pressurizing Edward to order Clarence's execution for treason in 1478.

Richard's suspicions of the Woodvilles were justified. Though Richard had been appointed Protector in Edward IV's will during Edward V's minority, the Woodvilles swiftly succeeded in overturning the decision and setting up a Regency Council under their control. For Richard, increasingly convinced that the true Yorkist inheritance was safe only with him, the choice was straightforward: to await an inevitable Woodville-inspired charge of treason or seize the throne himself.

The manner of his usurpation was characteristically decisive. The new king, Edward V, was intercepted

Richard III, 1483–5

Rebellion
Buckingham's advance, 1483
Area reinforced against expected landing by Henry Tudor
Henry Tudor's campaign, August 1485
Frontiers, 1485

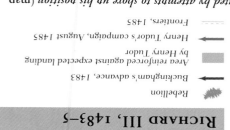

SCOTLAND
IRELAND
Isle of Man
DUBLIN
NEWCASTLE
CARLISLE
YORK
CHESTER
NOTTINGHAM
Richard's move to counter Henry
SHREWSBURY
MACHYNLLETH
WALES
Bosworth 1485
LEICESTER
NORWICH
Buckingham, 1483
WORCESTER
NORTHAMPTON
CAMBRIDGE
CARDIGAN
BRECON
HEREFORD
GLOUCESTER
HARWICH
HAVERFORDWEST
OXFORD
BRISTOL
WINDSOR
LONDON
Gravesend 1483
TONBRIDGE
DOVER
Buckingham, 1483
WINCHESTER
PORTSMOUTH
POOLE
EXETER
CALAIS
Henry Tudor's aborted landing, 1483
E N G L A N D
English Channel
HARFLEUR
FRANCE

Richard III's reign was dominated by attempts to shore up his position (map right). *The revolt by his former ally, the duke of Buckingham, in 1483 was relatively easily contained, in the process thwarting the attempted landing by the last Lancastrian pretender, Henry Tudor. Within less than two years, however, Henry Tudor mounted a new invasion. Deserted by key allies, Richard III was killed by Henry Tudor in August 1485 at Bosworth.*

1469	1470–71	1472	1478	1482
Richard suppresses Welsh rebellion on behalf of Edward IV	*Accompanies Edward IV to Burgundy before assisting in his restoration*	*Charged with responsibility for north of England by Edward IV*	*Duke of Clarence executed for treason*	*Richard leads successful invasion of Scotland; storms Edinburgh and takes Berwick*

> From this day, these dukes [Gloucester and Buckingham] acted no longer in secret, but openly manifested their intentions. For, having summoned armed men, in fearful and unheard-of numbers, from the north, Wales and all other parts then subject to them, the said Protector Richard assumed the government of the kingdom, with the title King, on the twentieth day of the aforesaid month of June; on the same day, at the Great Hall of Westminster [he] obtruded himself into the marble chair.
>
> The Croyland Chronicle

Edward V was king for two months and 17 days. It was the shortest reign of any king of England. The young Prince Edward was brought up by his uncle, Lord Rivers, at Ludlow. It was while he was being brought from there to London in April 1483 for his coronation, due to take place on June 24, that Richard, professing his loyalty to his new king, effectively arrested him and sent him to the Tower of London. A month later, Edward was joined by his younger brother, the Duke of York, who on Richard's orders had been removed by force from Westminster Abbey where he and his mother had taken sanctuary. There are reports of both children playing in the gardens of the Tower but "day by day [they] began to be seen more rarely behind the bars and windows until at length they ceased to appear altogether."

Though the precise fate of the children has never been established, there can be little doubt that it was Richard III who had them murdered. That said, it is true that their deaths were equally in the interests of Henry Tudor, who was accordingly keen to blame Richard. In 1674, two skeletons, presumed to be those of the princes, were discovered in the Tower. They were reburied in Westminster Abbey. In 1993, tests established they were of approximately the right ages to have been the princes but no definitive identification was possible.

Edward V, as Prince of Wales, with Edward IV and Elizabeth Woodville

en route to London for his coronation and placed in the Tower of London with his younger brother, Richard, duke of York. The queen's brother, Lord Rivers, was summarily executed, as was Richard's former ally, Lord Hastings, who had objected to Richard's plans to oust the new king. However flimsy Richard's legal justification for assuming the throne – that both Edward IV's sons were illegitimate – it was nonetheless accepted by Parliament on June 25. The next day Richard was proclaimed king. The two princes were last seen alive the following month.

Richard's motive in ordering the deaths of his nephews was the obvious one of removing a potential focus of rebellion against him. But with the death of his own son the following year, it also meant that only Richard now stood between Henry Tudor – the sole remaining Lancastrian claimant – and the crown. Once Henry, already supported by Charles VIII of France, allied himself to the Woodvilles, it was clear he would mount a bid for the throne. In August 1485 Henry Tudor defeated Richard at Market Bosworth and became Henry VII.

In attempting to assert the legitimacy of Yorkist rule, Richard III had managed only to perpetuate the lawlessness and treachery generated by the dynastic disputes of the 15th century. Richard III, the last English king to die in battle, was also the last victim of the Wars of the Roses.

What evidence there is suggests that Richard III and his queen, Anne Neville (right), "his most dearly beloved consort", were unusually close. In very striking contrast to Edward IV, Richard seems to have had no mistresses after his marriage, though he had fathered several children before it. Ironically, given the fate of his young nephews, when Richard and Anne's sole child, Prince Edward, died in 1485 at only eight, it was reported that: "You might have seen his father and mother in a state almost bordering on madness by reason of their sudden grief."

1483	1484	1485
Mar: Death of Edward IV, accession of Edward V; Richard is Protector; Apr: With duke of Buckingham, Richard intercepts Edward V en route to London; executes queen's brother, Lord Rivers; May: Edward V installed in Tower of London; June: Edward's brother, the duke of York, removed from sanctuary in Westminster Abbey and joins Edward in Tower; Richard proclaimed king; Sept: Presumed death of Edward V and brother in Tower; Oct: Revolt by duke of Buckingham (intended to coincide with attempted invasion from Brittany by Henry Tudor), crushed; Buckingham executed; Henry turns back	Death of Richard III's only son, Prince Edward. Henry Tudor flees to France after Richard attempts to seize him in Brittany. Three-year truce agreed with Scotland	Mar: Death of Richard's wife, Anne Neville; Aug: Henry Tudor successfully lands in Wales; defeats and kills Richard at Battle of Market Bosworth

SCOTLAND: FROM BRUCE TO STUART 1329–1625

DAVID II 1329–33/1336–71

EDWARD BALLIOL
1332/1333–34/1335–36

ROBERT II 1371–90

ROBERT III 1390–1406

JAMES I 1406–37

JAMES II 1437–60

JAMES III 1460–88

JAMES IV 1488–1513

JAMES V 1513–42

MARY, QUEEN OF SCOTS 1542–67

JAMES VI 1567–1625

WHATEVER THE SUCCESSES OF ROBERT THE BRUCE (SEE PP.64–5) IN WITHSTANDING THE ATTEMPTED PLANTAGENET CONQUEST OF SCOTLAND AND IN REINVIGORATING SCOTTISH KINGSHIP, HE WAS FOLLOWED BY A SERIES OF INEPT AND WEAK KINGS. BETWEEN THEM, THEY PRESIDED OVER A SCOTLAND THAT, WHEN NOT BEING FURTHER THREATENED BY ENGLAND, WAS TORN APART BY DYNASTIC INSTABILITY, THE AMBITIONS OF ITS LEADING MAGNATES, CIVIL STRIFE AND ECONOMIC BACKWARDNESS. THOSE RULERS WHO SUCCEEDED IN IMPOSING A DEGREE OF CENTRAL CONTROL ALMOST ALWAYS FELL FOUL OF THEIR DISGRUNTLED LEADING SUBJECTS. MOST, HOWEVER, FOUND THEMSELVES NEAR-PERMANENTLY AT THE MERCY OF EVENTS.

Of the 10 Scottish monarchs who followed Robert the Bruce, eight were minors at their accession, including all seven in succession from James I to James VI. Of the remaining two, both came to the throne in their 50s already exhausted. One, Robert II, had become so incapacitated he was widely known as "Auld Blearie". His son, Robert III, who became little more than an invalid after being kicked by a horse, composed his own memorable epitaph: "Here lies the worst of kings and the most miserable of men". He asked to be buried in a dungheap.

Two kings, David II and James I, were imprisoned by the English for 11 and 18 years respectively. David II was also forced to spend most of his childhood and youth in France, Scotland's only reliable ally in the period (see The Auld Alliance, pp.66–7). The long periods of regency government such enforced absences imposed only added to the near endemic instability. In both cases, the enormous ransoms demanded for their release also proved an intolerable burden on the country's slim economic means.

Exposure to the much more sophisticated mechanisms of royal government in England at least had the virtue of demonstrating to David II and James I the kind of strong, centralized government that could be introduced in Scotland. In practise, though David II had some success in asserting his authority, like James II he, too, consistently had to contend with an unruly baronage that resisted all attempts to reduce their own powers. In James I's case this baronial resentment led to his assassination. As an indication of the continuing turbulence, 15 years later James I's successor, James II, personally stabbed to death his most rebellious subject, the Earl of Douglas. It was perhaps a mark of the ill-fortune that dogged Scotland in the period that at 30, having established a measure of control over Scotland, James II himself was killed when a cannon exploded at the siege of Roxburgh.

That said, from the mid-15th century onwards royal authority was very slowly being increased. The reign of James III, while disastrous at its end, saw the Orkneys and Hebrides ceded by Norway and brought under nominal Scottish control. With the exception of Berwick, lost permanently to England in 1482, Scotland had attained its current extent. His successor, James IV, further extended active Scottish rule in the Western and Northern Isles, in 1493 formally ending the 200-year-old semi-independent rule of the Lords of the Isles in the Hebrides. James III and James IV also began to bring Scotland into gradual contact with Renaissance ideals of learning and the arts.

Yet fundamentally it was relations with England that did most to destabilize Scotland and undermine its kings. Edward III, for example, actively attempted to exploit dynastic divisions within Scotland by sponsoring the attempts of John Balliol's son, Edward Balliol, to seize the Scottish throne after the death of Robert the Bruce in 1329. Having proclaimed himself king in 1332, Balliol was deposed three times and restored twice in the space of only three years. In much the same way, 150 years later Edward IV sponsored the efforts of the self-styled Alexander IV to oust his brother, James III.

Similarly, of the nine kings of England between Edward III and Henry VIII, only three did not launch invasions of Scotland. Even during the Wars of the Roses, when England itself was at its most vulnerable, Scotland, by formally allying itself with the losing Lancastrians, managed only to spark bitter internal divisions as well as to invite Yorkist reprisals. Even the most apparently successful and martial Scottish king of the period, James IV, decisively came unstuck against superior English arms, losing his life at the disastrous Battle of Flodden in 1513. The equally crushing English victory over Scotland at Solway Moss in 1542 was followed within a month by the death of the 30-year-old James III, apparently from cholera. As a result, it brought the youngest-ever British monarch to the throne, the week-old Mary, "Queen of Scots".

The catalogue of woe continued. After being ousted from her throne in 1567 at only 24 in yet another power-struggle, Mary spent the last 19 years of her life a prisoner of her English cousin, Elizabeth I. She remains the only Scottish monarch to be executed by the English.

Yet a paradox runs through this sorry tale. The succession of Robert II in 1371 had brought a new dynasty to the Scottish throne, the Stewarts (Mary, Queen of Scots, introduced the later, French spelling of Stuart). The marriage in 1503 of James IV to Henry VII's daughter Margaret under the short-lived Treaty of Perpetual Peace between England and Scotland gave rise to a dynastic alliance of unforeseen but momentous consequences. The failure of Henry VIII's three children to produce a single heir between them meant that with the death of Elizabeth I in 1603, the English crown passed to Margaret Tudor and James IV's great-grandson, James VI. However improbably, the king of Scotland had also legally inherited the throne of England.

DAVID II TO JAMES II 1371–1460

AFTER THE DEATH OF ROBERT THE BRUCE IN 1329, SCOTTISH KINGSHIP WAS PERSISTENTLY UNDERMINED BY DYNASTIC DISPUTES AND INTERNAL WEAKNESS, THE WHOLE AGAINST A BACKGROUND OF RECURRENT ENGLISH DESIGNS ON SCOTLAND. THE REIGNS OF EACH OF THE FIRST FIVE OF BRUCE'S SUCCESSORS WERE DISRUPTED, OFTEN CATASTROPHICALLY. THE SURVIVAL OF AN INDEPENDENT SCOTTISH KINGDOM WAS FREQUENTLY IN THE BALANCE.

I N 1328, AT THE AGE OF FOUR, ROBERT THE Bruce's son, David, was married to Edward II's seven-year-old daughter Joan. For Robert the Bruce, it marked the symbolic climax to the Treaty of Edinburgh: not only had England been forced to acknowledge the independence of Scotland but the two countries were now dynastically linked. David marked the occasion of his marriage with a different kind of symbolism that more accurately presaged the years to come. Suffering from diarrhoea, the four-year-old "David Drip-on-Altar" emptied his bowels during the ceremony.

Three years later, following the revoking of the papal interdict placed on his father, David II became the first Scottish king to be crowned and anointed. It may have been a mark of the growing status of Scottish kingship under Robert the Bruce, but it was no reflection of the reality of Scotland under the new boy-king. In less than a year, David was deposed by Edward Balliol. The resulting dynastic turmoil opened the way for Edward III, who, having reached his majority, lost little time in rejecting the Treaty of Edinburgh. Edward invaded Scotland, inflicting a shattering defeat on David's forces in July 1333. David was forced to France.

Though Edward Balliol effectively gave up his claim to Scotland in 1336, and the English king then turned his attentions to France, David did not feel secure enough to return to Scotland until 1341. Within five years, however, he was an English prisoner, captured at the Battle of Neville's Cross.

To all intents and purposes, Scotland remained subservient to England for the rest of David's reign. Even after his release in 1357, David suggested that Edward III's son Lionel should succeed as King of Scotland if he, David, died childless. In fact, though David never produced an heir, the throne passed to his sister's son, Robert Stewart, Robert II.

The reign of the first two Stewart kings, Robert II and Robert III, marked the low point of Scottish kingship. Both were ailing and infirm when they succeeded. Neither demonstrated any obvious talent for personal rule. Under Robert III, power effectively passed to his younger brother, the duke of Albany, who in 1401 arrested the heir to the throne, his nephew David, and starved him to death. Rousing himself for a final, feeble effort, in 1406 the king arranged for his remaining son and new heir, James, to be sent to France for safe-keeping from his uncle. En route, James, as he had now become, was captured and for the next 18 years kept prisoner in England. When he at last secured his release in 1424, he returned to a country gripped by lawlessness and ruled by a series of factious magnates. Though his often successful efforts to assert his authority inevitably brought him into conflict with his barons, it was military failure against England that eventually accounted for him. In 1437, a disastrous attempt to take Roxburgh sparked his murder.

The baronial feuding, which was by now endemic, disfigured the minority of his successor, James II. But on reaching his majority in 1449 the new king seemed to have the measure of his subjects. In a campaign of exceptional ruthlessness, in which his most obvious rivals were systematically executed and their lands declared forfeit, he set about restoring his authority. James II himself killed the earl of Douglas, stabbing him in the neck, though more in sudden rage than as a premeditated act. However, despite his own death in 1460 and the succession of yet another child-king brought only a further round of instability.

The Declaration of Arbroath 1320

But if your Holiness puts too much faith in the tales the English tell and will not give sincere belief to all this, nor refrain from favouring them to our prejudice, then the slaughter of bodies, the perdition of souls, and all the other misfortunes that will follow, inflicted by them on us and by us on them, will, we believe, be surely laid by the Most High to your charge

James II (above), the only survivor of twins, was disfigured by a prominent scarlet birthmark which covered the left side of his face, giving rise to his nickname 'James of the Fiery Face'. He proved a vigorous ruler, more than able to control the magnates who had destabilized his minority.

The efficient administration implied by Robert II's issuing of his own coinage (right) is at odds with his reign itself. Though he had been an effective regent during his (younger) uncle David II's absences, his reign itself was chaotic and lawless. For the last six years of his rule he was largely senile.

1331	1332	1333	1334	1336	1341	1346	1357	1371	1384	1385	1390
Coronation of David II	Edward Balliol claims throne of Scotland	Edward III crushes Scots at Halidon Hill; restores Edward Balliol	David II forced into exile in France	David II renounces claim to Scotland; Robert Stewart (later Robert II) made regent	David II returns from France	Scots crushed at Neville's Cross, David II prisoner of English; Robert Stewart reassumes regency	David II released, returns to Scotland. Accession of David II	Accession of Robert II, first Stewart king	Effective administration of Robert II, passes to Robert II's son John, the earl of Carrick	Scotland raided by Richard II	Accession of Robert III, government passes to his brother, the duke of Albany

By the accession of Robert II, the first Stewart king, in 1371, the country was being destabilised not just by England but by the rival ambitions of a series of Scottish magnates (map left). Foremost among them were the lords of the Isles and the earls of Douglas, both effectively beyond the reach of the enfeebled Scottish crown.

SCOTLAND UNDER THE STEWARTS 1371–1460

→ Scottish campaigns, with date

→ English campaigns, with date

⬚ Semi-autonomous lordship of the Isles and earldom of Ross, c. 1410

Donald's campaign, 1411

⚑ Held by the Livingstones and allies, 1449

LINDSAY Controlled by earl of Douglas and allies c.1452, (with names of allied families)

⚑ Held by Scottish crown during civil war

▨ Lordships and earldoms annexed to the Crown, 1455

(map labels: Western Isles, ROSS, ELGIN, INVERNESS, LOCHINDORB, Harlaw 1411, KILDRUMMY, RUTHVEN, ABERDEEN, MACDONALD, SCOTLAND, DOUGLAS, LINDSAY, Brechin 1452, DUNDEE, SCONE, PERTH, ST ANDREWS, STIRLING, Carron 1455, KINGHORN, DUNOON, DUMBARTON, LINLITHGOW, EDINBURGH, 1384, 1400, Nesbit Muir 1402, BERWICK, Scarborough, 1378, Bute 1452, Inverkip 1452, HAMILTON, MELROSE, ROXBURGH, JEDBURGH, Homildon Hill 1402, Cumbrae 1452, Brodick 1452, BRODICK, DOUGLAS, AYR, CUMNOCK, Otterburn 1388, 1388, DUMFRIES, Arkinholm 1455, 1388, NEWCASTLE, CARLISLE, DURHAM, IRELAND, DOUGLAS, ENGLAND, 1400, 1385, 1384, Isle of Man)

Following his capture at Neville's Cross in 1346, David II became a firm friend of his English gaoler, Edward III (above). He was particularly taken by the chivalric atmosphere of the English court.

DAVID II JUNE 1329–AUG. 1332 (DEPOSED), DEC. 1332–MAR. 1333 (DEPOSED), 1336–FEB. 1371
BORN 1324 SON OF ROBERT THE BRUCE

Aged only five at accession, his minority rule was repeatedly challenged by Edward Balliol, bringing a return of the Balliol–Bruce rivalry that disfigured Scotland in the 1290s. He was exiled in France between 1336 and 1341. Led Scottish army to defeat by England in 1346 at Neville's Cross, where he was captured and held prisoner in England until ransomed in 1357. Thereafter, attempts to raise huge annual ransoms provoked repeated baronial rebellions.

EDWARD BALLIOL AUG. 1332–DEC. 1332 (DEPOSED); MAR. 1333–1334 (DEPOSED); 1335–1336; FORMALLY RESIGNED CLAIM TO THRONE 1357
BORN c.1290

Effectively no more than a tool of Edward III, who successfully used him to destabilize Scotland. In theory Balliol ceded the whole of southern Scotland to Edward III. If only a footnote in Scottish history, Balliol still contributed to the dynastic and baronial turmoil that damaged his country so persistently.

ROBERT II FEB. 1371–APR. 1390
BORN c.1316

First of the Stewart kings. For long periods, he was an effective and efficient regent of Scotland during David II's absences. But when he came to the throne, he was a spent force and largely delegated control to his son John, Earl of Carrick (later Robert III) and then to his corrupt younger son Robert, Duke of Albany.

ROBERT III APR. 1390–APR. 1406
BORN c.1337

A pawn in his brother Robert's hands almost from the start of his reign. In 1398, his much more alert wife, Annabella, attempted to make their son, David, ruler as Lieutenant of the Realm. He, too, was unable to resist his uncle, who in 1401 had David killed. Robert III presided over a period of lawlessness and dissolution of royal authority.

JAMES I APR. 1406–FEB. 1437
BORN 1394

Effectively raised in England, where he had been held prisoner since the age of 12. In 1424, at the age of 30, he returned to Scotland determined to reassert royal authority, but he succeeded only in antagonizing his leading magnates. He was murdered by Sir Robert Graham after a failed attempt to retake Roxburgh.

JAMES II FEB. 1437–AUG. 1460
BORN 1430

Acceded at only seven and spent much of his minority the prisoner of warring magnate factions within Scotland. On his majority, he proved forcefully aggressive and could possibly have made an effective king had he not been killed by an exploding cannon during yet another siege of Roxburgh.

1393	1398	1400	1401	1402	1406	1424	1428	1437	1449	1452	1460
Brief attempt by Robert III to regain control of Scottish government	Robert III's heir, David, made Lieutenant of the Realm	Scotland invaded by Henry IV	David murdered by his uncle, the duke of Albany	Scots defeated at Homildon Hill	Duke of Albany Governor of Scotland after capture of James I	Release and coronation of James I	Rebellious clan leaders in Highlands suppressed by James I	James I murdered after failure of siege of Roxburgh; accession of James II	Majority of James II	Earl of Douglas murdered by James II as king gains firmer control of Scotland	Accidental death of James II at siege of Roxburgh; accession of James III

ENGLAND AND WALES: THE TUDORS 1485–1603

HENRY VII 1485–1509

HENRY VIII 1509–47

EDWARD VI 1547–53

MARY I 1553–58

ELIZABETH I 1558–1603

ON THE FACE OF IT, HENRY VII'S SEIZURE OF THE THRONE IN 1485 WAS NO MORE THAN ANOTHER ROUND IN THE DYNASTIC TURMOIL THAT PLAGUED 15TH-CENTURY ENGLAND. FOUR KINGS HAD BEEN OVERTURNED (ONE OF THEM TWICE) AND MURDERED. THREE SEPARATE DYNASTIES HAD FORCIBLY INSTALLED THEMSELVES ON THE THRONE. YET HENRY TUDOR'S TAKE-OVER OF POWER NOT ONLY PROVED ENDURING BUT, AT ANY RATE IN RETROSPECT, IT CAN BE SEEN TO HAVE MARKED THE BEGINNING OF A NEW ERA NOT JUST OF ENGLISH, AND LATER BRITISH, MONARCHY BUT, BY EXTENSION, OF ENGLISH AND BRITISH HISTORY AS A WHOLE.

In part, this was a matter of a return to strong, stable government in place of the chaos of the middle years of the century. This was not something that Henry VII can claim sole credit for. The process was already well underway in Edward IV's reign, though it is certainly true that Henry VII's very much more active style of kingship accelerated it. But as important was a parallel growth in the power of the state itself. This was a largely new development, one of lasting importance.

In essence, England, in common with a number of other west European states, France and Spain pre-eminently, saw a rapid growth in the mechanisms and efficiency of its government. Expanding economies and growing populations meant that larger resources became available to the crown – provided that taxes could be collected efficiently and law and order maintained. The creation of a stable, centralized, bureaucratic government accordingly became a priority.

Henry VII, though otherwise inexperienced in kingship, proved to have precisely the kind of meticulous, calculating mind that made the concentration of this kind of power possible. The crucial consequence, however slowly it unfolded, was that the monarchy's dependence on its leading subjects was reduced. Medieval kings would certainly not have claimed to have enjoyed any less authority than their Tudor counterparts, but their ability to deploy it and to exercise power effectively was unquestionably less. To take only one obvious example, medieval armies had to be raised by the leading magnates, whose troops in effect they were and thus potentially able to be turned against the monarch. From the 16th century onwards, armies and later navies, raised and paid for by the state, were answerable directly to the monarch. In an era of almost perpetual warfare, it was a vitally important difference.

Though Henry VIII had none of his father's administrative talents, he more than made up for it by his eager embrace of the quasi-imperial nature of this new monarchy. However unpredictable and extravagant, he instinctively understood that his power had to be projected absolutely. It was further reinforced after 1534 when, breaking with Rome, Henry made himself Supreme Head of the new Church of England. By any measure the monarchy's personal standing had been enhanced. As a spin-off, with the existing administrative structures unable to cope with the regulation of the Church, new councils and boards had to be created, strengthening central authority further.

In reality, the acquisition of greater royal authority was never a straightforward business. For one thing, the avaricious Henry VII aside, the Tudor monarchs were permanently hedged in by a lack of resources. Growing it may have been but 16th-century England was never as rich as France let alone Spain, the super-power of the age. One obvious consequence was that England's capacity to wage wars was always limited. Henry VII, pragmatic to the last, scarcely even tried to. Henry VIII, by contrast, made repeated efforts. Yet even against Scotland he made patchy progress at best. Only against Wales was he unequivocally successful. Against France, he consistently came off worst. Elizabeth I, by nature highly cautious, adopted an exclusively defensive posture.

But as important, with onset of the Reformation, the Tudors also had to contend with religious conflict. This was a wholly new, even more destabilizing phenomenon, one that transformed the political map of Europe, plunging it into a seemingly endless round of divisive wars. The huge problems it created were complex and multi-layered, giving long-standing international rivalries a new twist. Put most simply, for Spain, France and the Papacy, whatever their own rivalries, the overthrow of Protestant, heretic England became not just a matter of conventional conquest so much as an absolute crusade. In precisely the same way, as the Protestant nature of England took firmer shape, so resisting the Papists, bent as they were on their ungodly subjection of England, became just as much of a necessity.

The manner in which wider European political and religious issues had become so thoroughly intertwined and could spark such bitterness found a ready and inevitably dangerous parallel in England itself. For many, especially in the north, giving up Catholicism was unthinkable. Well into the 17th century, England would be destabilized by religious conflict. The Tudors themselves encapsulated these conflicts. For Henry VIII the adoption of Anglicanism was a matter of state, not of religious conviction: Henry remained a devout Catholic to the end of his life. His heir, Edward, by contrast, espoused a very much more ardent, not to say fanatical Protestantism. His successor, Mary, was an equally committed Catholic, determined to restore the Roman church. In the space of no more than a year, England was wrenched from one religious pole to the other.

It was the particular genius of Elizabeth I to calm these passions. Though England under Elizabeth became unequivocally Protestant, its identity all the more strongly felt, it avoided the worst excesses of religious conflict that disfigured so much of the rest of Europe. However much on the defensive, Elizabethan England saw the birth of an English identity that persists even today.

In the end, the Tudors, for all that they presided over the transformation of English kingship, were the victims of a permanent threat to all dynasties: their failure to provide sufficient heirs. With the death of Elizabeth, the virgin queen, in 1603, the throne passed to the Stuarts. That their realm had been immeasurably strengthened, however, is undoubted.

HENRY VII 1485–1509

KING HENRY VII

HENRY VII'S CLAIM TO THE THRONE WAS THE WEAKEST OF ANY KING OF ENGLAND SINCE WILLIAM THE CONQUEROR. YET HE NOT ONLY ESTABLISHED A NEW DYNASTY, HE LAID THE FOUNDATIONS FOR WHAT WOULD PROVE A NEAR REVOLUTION IN ROYAL GOVERNMENT. ENGLAND UNDER HENRY VII BEGAN THE PROCESS THAT WOULD LEAD A NEW ERA OF ABSOLUTIST MONARCHY.

BORN: January 28 1457
ACCEDED: August 22 1485: crowned Westminster Abbey, October 30 1485
Earl of Richmond (from 1457), King of England and Lord of Ireland

It is doubtful if England has ever had a more naturally astute – or tough-minded – king than Henry VII (above). Yet for all his reputation for avarice, he was a generous patron of the church and of the arts. Yet "serious, sad and full of thoughts", his life, like his court, became increasingly sombre.

THE DEATH OF RICHARD III AT THE BATTLE of Bosworth in August 1485, along with all rivals to the new king, Henry VII. It was a significant advantage, no less than had been the murders of the Princes in the Tower by Richard III two years earlier. Of equal importance, Henry now added all the former Yorkist lands to his existing Lancastrian lands. As by far the richest individual in the kingdom, Henry was not only removed from dependence on any one faction, the crown itself was elevated above dynastic squabbling, allowing the restoration of impartial, royal authority. Henry's claim to the throne may have been tenuous but it was effectively unchallenged from the start.

That said, he was consistently at pains to emphasize his legitimacy. His marriage in 1486 to Edward IV's daughter, Elizabeth, just as much as his personal device, the Tudor rose, which combined the red and white roses of York and Lancaster, was deliberately intended to underline the new union of the dynasties. He also permanently stressed his Welsh and thus "British" blood, ensuring for example that his eldest son, symbolically named Arthur, was born at the Anglo-Saxon capital, Winchester. In the event, the die-hard Yorkist challenges that did emerge were relatively easily contained, including those of the two improbable pretenders Lambert Simnel and Perkin Warbeck (see box).

Perhaps as a result of the insecurity of his upbringing, 14 years of it as a Lancastrian exile in Brittany, Henry remained highly cautious, not to say suspicious, to the end of his reign. Equally, there is no question but that the particular cast of his mind – methodical, painstaking and shrewd – allowed him to reinforce royal authority to an unprecedented degree. His preferred means were as "the best businessman ever to sit on the throne of England" – and the concentration of government in the hands of a small group of trusted advisors, with Henry unambiguously as its head. This, the King's Council, meeting in the Star Chamber, effectively by-passed Parliament, whose importance in approving new taxation was in any case greatly lessened by Henry's parsimoniousness. At the same, Henry developed a new means of taming his magnates by levying often huge fines for alleged misdemeanours. The king also authorized no less than 138 Acts of Attainder under which the property of those convicted of treason passed to the crown.

The Yorkist Pretenders

Uncertainty over the fate of Edward IV's two young sons, Edward V and Richard, duke of York, both in fact murdered by Richard III, gave rise to bizarre attempts by Yorkist supporters to pass off two transparent impostors as the real heirs to the throne.

The first, Lambert Simnel, son of an Oxford joiner, was recruited by the earl of Lincoln, Edward IV's nephew. He claimed variously that Lambert was the younger of Edward IV's sons then that he was another of Edward IV's nephews, the earl of Warwick. (To Henry VII's evident amusement, the real earl of Warwick, meanwhile, was a prisoner in the Tower.) In 1486, the earl of Lincoln took Lambert to Ireland. There, in May 1487, he was crowned Edward VI. The next month, Lincoln invaded England and was almost immediately defeated. Henry VII took pity on Simnel and gave him a job in the royal kitchens.

Perkin Warbeck's challenge was more sustained but no less absurd. He was a Fleming who spoke no English. Nonetheless, in Ireland after 1491 he claimed first to be the earl of Warwick, then an illegitimate son of Richard III and finally the duke of York. With the support of Edward IV's sister, Margaret of Burgundy, and the Holy Roman Emperor Maximilian I, who saw him as a means to destabilize Henry VII, in October 1494 he was proclaimed Richard IV. He also won the support of James IV of Scotland.

By the time Warbeck had assembled an army of sorts, his insistent, self-important demands had already alienated most of his supporters. Warbeck pressed on, however, landing in Cornwall in 1497 and raising a small army among those already protesting at Henry VII's punitive levels of taxation. Within a month he had been captured. When he tried to escape, he was placed in the Tower with the real earl of Warwick. When, inevitably, they plotted to overthrow Henry VII, the king had them executed.

1471	1483	1485	1486	1487	1492
Henry Tudor forced into exile in Brittany	Attempted invasion of England, in tandem with duke of Buckingham, thwarted. Henry vows to marry Elizabeth of York if he wins crown of England.	Successful landing at Milford Haven followed by defeat of Richard III at Bosworth (Aug.); Henry VII's legitimacy recognized by Parliamentary statute (Oct.); King's Council (Star Chamber) formed	Marriage of Henry VII to Elizabeth of York; birth of Prince Arthur. Papal recognition of Henry VII's legitimacy granted	Lambert Simnel and Yorkist supporters routed at Stoke	Brief invasion of northern France

For he began to treat his people with more harshness and severity than had been his custom, in order (as he himself asserted) to ensure that they remained thoroughly and entirely in obedience to him. The people themselves had another explanation for his action, for they considered they were suffering not on account of their own sins but on account of the greed of their monarch. It is not indeed clear whether at the start it was greed; but afterward greed did become apparent.

Polydore Vergil, Anglicae Historia, 1534

Rebellion, with date

Route of Lambert Simnel's Yorkists supporters

Lambert Simnel's campaign, following his Dublin crowning as Edward VI

Resisted Simnel's pretence, 1487

Perkin Warbeck's movements, with details

Supported Perkin Warbeck, 1495, with name

Campaign in support of Perkin Warbeck, 1495

Rebel campaign, 1497

Henry's campaigns, with date

Other English campaigns, with date

Whatever the attempts by the remaining Yorkists, chiefly based in Ireland, to oust Henry VII, in reality Henry's throne was secure (map below). Both the Yorkist pretenders, Lambert Simnel and Perkin Warbeck, the latter half-heartedly supported by James IV of Scotland, could mount only token attempts on Henry's throne. The king's foreign relations were similarly stable. Prudence was the consistent theme of his reign.

For all that theirs was a dynastically arranged marriage, Henry VII and Elizabeth of York developed what seems a genuine affection. When she died, in 1503, Henry "privily departed to a solitary place and would no man should resort unto him". They were buried side by side in the magnificent chapel Henry built at Westminster Abbey. Their tomb effigy (below), by the Florentine sculptor Pietro Torrigiano, is one of the earliest Renaissance works in England.

STIRLING
EDINBURGH
SCOTLAND
Attack jointly with king of Scotland, 1496
CASTLEROE
NEWCASTLE
North Sea
DUNDALK
Isle of Man
1486
YORK
GALWAY
THE PALE
DUBLIN
IRELAND
Loosely controlled by England
CHESTER
NEWARK
NOTTINGHAM
Stoke 1487
LIMERICK
KILKENNY
LEICESTER
DESMOND
CLONMELL
WATERFORD
WEXFORD
WALES
KENILWORTH
1486
NORTHAMPTON
CORK
CAMBRIDGE
KINSALE
Escape, 1495
OXFORD
RICHMOND
LONDON
Aborted landing, 1495
BRISTOL
Deptford Bridge 1497
DEAL
1492
SLUYS
1495 action harmonized with Desmond
Landing, 1495
TAUNTON
SALISBURY
DOVER
1492
1489
NIEUPORT
SOUTHAMPTON
WINCHESTER
CALAIS
DIXMUNDE
Landing, 1497
Earl of Lincoln, Lowell, 1487
1497
EXETER
BEAULIEU
PORTSMOUTH
BOULOGNE
ARRAS
HOLY ROMAN EMPIRE
PLYMOUTH
1488
ÉTAPLES
CAMBRAI
English Channel
1489
FRANCE
MORLAIX
ST MALO
BREST
GUINGAMP
St Aubin du Cormier 1488
CONCARNEAU
BRITTANY

The same instinctive caution was evident in Henry's foreign policy. Though he conducted one invasion of France, in 1492, it lasted only a day and ended with a handsome pay-off from the French king, Charles VIII. A one-day invasion of Scotland in 1496 was followed the next year by a week-long invasion.

Even more typical were the marriage alliances with Aragon and Castile in 1501, under which Prince Arthur married Catherine of Aragon, and with Scotland in 1502, under which, the following year, Henry's eldest daughter married James IV. In both cases, Henry's aim was to secure important allies against the traditional enemy, France.

Henry VII's secretive, close nature may never have made him a likeable figure. But he was unquestionably among the most effective of England's kings. English kingship was turning a crucial corner.

1496	1497	1499	1501	1502	1503	1508
Brief invasion of Scotland after James IV supports Perkin Warbeck	Further invasion of France. Cornish rising, protesting at high levels of taxation, suppressed. Perkin Warbeck captured after landing in Cornwall	Execution of Perkin Warbeck and earl of Warwick. Richmond Palace begun	Revolt by duke of Suffolk suppressed. Marriage of Prince Arthur to Catherine of Aragon	Treaty of Perpetual Peace between England and Scotland. Death of Prince Arthur	Marriage of Margaret Tudor to James IV of Scotland. Chapel to Henry VI (later Henry VII's chapel), Westminster Abbey, begun	Execution of duke of Suffolk, last Yorkist claimant

HENRY VIII 1509–47

KING HENRY VIII

THE 17-YEAR-OLD HENRY VIII CAME TO THE THRONE AS RULER OF AN INCREASINGLY WEALTHY CATHOLIC COUNTRY. HE DIED THE RULER OF A NEAR-BANKRUPT PROTESTANT COUNTRY WHOSE DECISIVE SPLIT FROM ROME SPARKED RELIGIOUS CONFLICTS THAT PERSISTED FOR DECADES. WHATEVER ITS SUPERFICIAL GLAMOUR, IN THE SHORT TERM AT LEAST HIS REIGN SPAWNED ONLY DIVISION AND ECONOMIC DISLOCATION.

G LAMOROUS AND ACCOMPLISHED, BURSTING with youthful vigour, the new King Henry seemed destined to consolidate his father, HenryVII's, achievements. England was poised to become a power of European repute under a ruler whose dazzling potency would put even the Holy Roman Emperor in the shade. As the Venetian ambassador reported in 1515: "His Majesty is the handsomest potentate I have ever set eyes upon... he is in every respect a most accomplished prince". Yet the fundamental shallowness of Henry's character was clear from the start. Within a year of his accession, he had executed his father's two principal tax collectors in an attempt to curry popularity. Of more lasting significance, in the same year he also married Catherine of Aragon, who had previously been married to Henry's elder brother, Arthur, who had died in 1502.

Two themes dominated Henry's reign, both intended to reinforce what the king increasingly came to see as his "imperial" status. The first was foreign conquest, the second church reform. If the latter was essentially a reaction to events, the former was a conscious act of policy from the start.

Casting himself as a reborn Henry V, in 1513 Henry mounted a costly invasion of France, the net result of which was the capture of two towns, Tournai and Thérouanne, and the so-called Battle of the Spurs, in reality little more than a skirmish. Similarly inconclusive campaigns were launched against France in 1522 and 1523 and again in 1542.

But if Henry's fantasies of continental conquest came to nothing, he came much closer to success in Scotland, even if in the end he could no more make himself master of Scotland than could Edward I. In 1513, attempting to exploit Henry's absence in France, James IV of Scotland invaded England. His army was peremptorily annihilated on the Anglo-Scottish border at Flodden by an English force under Thomas Howard, the earl of Surrey. Among the victims, his corpse hauled from under a pile of dead Scots, was James himself.

Encouraged, Henry spent much of his reign attempting to unite the English and Scottish crowns. His efforts climaxed in the 1540s when, after a further crushing defeat of the Scots at Solway Moss in 1542, Henry began what he called his "Rough Wooing", a series of invasions of Scotland in 1544 and 1545 in which Henry attempted to force the Scots to accept his young son, Edward, as the husband-to-be of Mary.

BORN: June 28 1491
ACCEDED: April 21 1509; Westminster Abbey June 24 1509.

Duke of York, Duke of Cornwall, Prince of Wales, Earl of Chester, King of England and Ireland

By the last years of Henry VIII's reign, the lithe and handsome youth had become bloated ruin, scarcely able even to walk: he had to be pushed around Hampton Court in a specially built cart. Not even Holbein could hide the reality of "a gross and selfish tyrant" (above).

The Field of the Cloth of Gold

Henry VIII's early attempts to reconquer France may have ended in failure but, in 1520, they gave rise to one of the most remarkable spectacles of the period: the Field of the Cloth of Gold. Ostensibly called to confirm peace between England and France, the meeting outside Calais between the 29-year-old Henry and the new king of France, Francis I, was an opportunity for each to demonstrate to the other as much as to the world, their imposing power. Effectively the whole of England's nobility, probably in excess of 5,000 earls, churchmen and knights, were transported to France. Francis brought even more men. A small city of gaudily decorated tents was erected. As a sign of their fellowship, Henry and Francis hunted, feasted and wrestled together. The promise of England and France alike as world powers in the making had never appeared more convincing. The emptiness at the heart of the spectacle was exposed less than two years later when war between England and France was resumed.

1512	1513	1520	1522	1529	1533	1534
First invasion of France	Second invasion of France; Scots defeated at Flodden by the Earl of Surrey – James IV of Scotland killed	Field of the Cloth of Gold confirms peace with France	War with France and Scotland renewed	Cardinal Wolsey dismissed (died 1530); Thomas More made Chancellor	Catherine of Aragon divorced	Act of Supremacy establishes Church of England

Henry's Wives

CATHERINE OF ARAGON (1485–1536)
MARRIED: Arthur, Prince of Wales, 1501;
Henry VIII, June 1509 (marriage annulled May 1533)
SURVIVING CHILDREN: Mary, b. 1516

ANNE BOLEYN (1501–1536)
MARRIED: Henry VIII, January 1533
(executed May 1536)
SURVIVING CHILDREN: Elizabeth, b. 1536

JANE SEYMOUR (1509–1537)
MARRIED: Henry VIII, May 1536
SURVIVING CHILDREN: Edward, b. 1537

ANNE OF CLEVES (1519–1557)
MARRIED: Henry VIII, January 1540
(marriage annulled June 1540)
SURVIVING CHILDREN: none

CATHERINE HOWARD (1520–1542)
MARRIED: Henry VIII, July 1540
(executed February 1542)
SURVIVING CHILDREN: none

CATHERINE PARR (1512–1548)
MARRIED: Sir Edward Burgh, 1529;
John, Lord Latimer, 1533; Henry VIII, July 1543;
Thomas Seymour, 1547
SURVIVING CHILDREN: none

Henry VIII's Continental ambitions consistently outstripped his means to put them into practise (map right). Early invasions of France achieved almost other than prodigious expenditure. The king's naval campaigns were no more successful. His attempts to subdue Scotland met with similar lack of success. Only in Wales, incorporated with England in 1536, could Henry claim to have to achieved his ambitions.

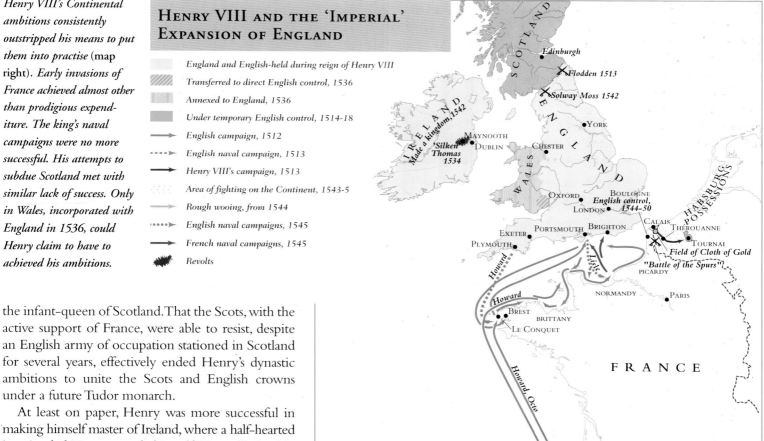

HENRY VIII AND THE 'IMPERIAL' EXPANSION OF ENGLAND

- England and English-held during reign of Henry VIII
- Transferred to direct English control, 1536
- Annexed to England, 1536
- Under temporary English control, 1514-18
- → English campaign, 1512
- ----> English naval campaign, 1513
- → Henry VIII's campaign, 1513
- Area of fighting on the Continent, 1543-5
- Rough wooing, from 1544
- •••••> English naval campaigns, 1545
- → French naval campaigns, 1545
- Revolts

the infant-queen of Scotland. That the Scots, with the active support of France, were able to resist, despite an English army of occupation stationed in Scotland for several years, effectively ended Henry's dynastic ambitions to unite the Scots and English crowns under a future Tudor monarch.

At least on paper, Henry was more successful in making himself master of Ireland, where a half-hearted invasion led Henry to style himself King of Ireland in 1541. In reality, English rule was restricted to the Pale, the area immediately around Dublin. Only in Wales, which was united with England in 1536, was Henry unequivocally successful (see box).

1535	1536	1539	1540	1541	1542	1543
Execution of Thomas More. Dissolution of monasteries launched	*Pilgrimage of Grace. Act of Union integrates Wales with England*	*Act of Six Articles reaffirms primacy of Catholic orthodoxy. English-language Great Bible published*	*Cromwell executed*	*Henry declared "king" of Ireland*	*Scots defeated at Solway Moss*	*Renewed invasion of France; Boulogne captured*

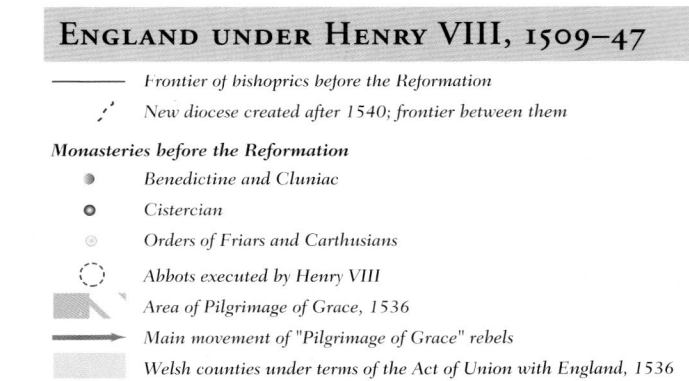

———	Frontier of bishoprics before the Reformation
⟋	New diocese created after 1540; frontier between them
Monasteries before the Reformation	
●	Benedictine and Cluniac
◉	Cistercian
○	Orders of Friars and Carthusians
⭕	Abbots executed by Henry VIII
	Area of Pilgrimage of Grace, 1536
→	Main movement of "Pilgrimage of Grace" rebels
	Welsh counties under terms of the Act of Union with England, 1536
	Transferred to England from Wales under the terms of the Act of Union
	Jurisdiction of the Council in the Marches under the terms of the Act of Union
	Jurisdiction of the Council in the North from 1537
NORWICH	Cathedral town

Other than the absorption of Wales in 1536, by far the most striking act of Henry VIII's reign in England was his break from Rome and subsequent take over of the country's monastic foundations (map left). It would lead directly to widespread anti-Reformation movements, notably the Pilgrimage of Grace in the still strongly Catholic north.

By 1527, Henry had convinced himself that Catherine's failure to produce a son was a punishment from God for having married his brother's wife (though she had six children, only one, a girl, Mary, survived). In fact Henry, now in his late 30s, was not merely neurotically anxious to secure an heir but had fallen obsessively in love with the much-younger Anne Boleyn. He instructed his Lord Chancellor, the otherwise supremely able Cardinal Thomas Wolsey, to persuade the pope to approve a divorce.

Even for Wolsey, this was a royal command too far. Infuriated by his Chancellor's failure to give him what he wanted, 1529 Henry stripped Wolsey of his office and condemned him to death.

By 1534, prompted by a new and equally capable Chancellor, Thomas Cromwell, and a new Archbishop of Canterbury, Thomas Cranmer, both enthusiastic supporters of the Reformed church, the necessary legislation that would give birth to the Church of England, with Henry at its Supreme Head, was put in train.

The logical consequence was that the church's properties in England should now also belong to the monarch. From 1536, Cromwell began the "dissolution" of England's monasteries. It was a campaign of systematic vindictiveness in which, in less than four years, charges of laxity and corruption were used to justify the forced dismemberment of every single one of the country's monasteries. 560 were suppressed, yielding the crown more than £200,000. Over 15,000 monks and nuns were displaced.

*This gold medal (above) showing Henry as Supreme Head of the new Church of England, bears the words **Fidei Defensor** (Defender of the Faith). Ironically, the title was awarded by Pope Leo X to Henry VIII in 1521 for a pamphlet written in 1519 in which Henry defended the Catholic church against Protestant attacks.*

Henry's church reforms, by contrast, were successful from the start, at any rate in his terms. By establishing the Church of England under the 1534 Act of Supremacy, with the monarch its Supreme Head, Henry not only engineered a complete split from papal authority but placed Britain firmly in the north European Protestant camp. As elsewhere in Europe, the religious divide thus created would lead to prolonged and bitter struggles. The consequences were momentous.

Henry's motive was never religious reform. He remained a devout Catholic to the end of his life, profoundly opposed to all attempts to reform Catholic religious practice. Rather, his goal was short-term and expedient: to secure a divorce from his ageing queen, Catherine of Aragon. His solution – that he could exploit religious reforms elsewhere in Europe to make himself his own pope able to authorize his own divorce – was an idea that seems to have dawned only slowly.

In becoming head of the church and acquiring the enormous riches of the country's monastic foundations, Henry had theoretically greatly increased the power of the monarchy. In practice, almost the opposite was the case. To give his claims against the monasteries legitimacy, Henry had been forced to co-opt parliament. The long-term result was that it was parliament's influence that was strengthened rather than the king's. At the same time, Henry's permanent need for money obliged him to sell off most monasteries almost as soon as he acquired them, prompting the greatest change in land ownership since the Norman Conquest. Henry squandered the wealth of the church in a matter of years.

Characteristically, Henry's infatuation with Anne proved short-lived, not least as the only child she had produced was a girl, Elizabeth. In 1536, his queen was beheaded on charges of adultery. (As sign of his clemency, Henry agreed she could be decapitated with a sword

The Pilgrimage of Grace

*T*he execution of Anne Boleyn in 1536 sparked the most serious civil uprisings since the Peasants Revolt in 1381, the Pilgrimage of Grace. It was not the actual beheading of Anne that caused the protests but the assumption that, with her death, Henry's split with Rome was now no longer necessary and could be reversed. Vast crowds assembled, above all in the Catholic strongholds of the north, demanding the restoration of papal authority. Faced with popular protest on this scale, Henry had no option but to give way. Once the immediate threat was over, however, he exacted a fearsome revenge, instructing the Duke of Norfolk that "you shall cause such dreadful execution to be done upon a good number of every town village and hamlet that have offended as they may be a fearful spectacle to all others hereafter that would practise any like matter". His deception – and cruelty – was entirely in character.

Whilst Henry VII had begun the building of warships, it was under Henry VIII that a large-scale expansion of the navy began, the largest such programme since the time of Alfred the Great. Pictured (right) is the Henri Grace à Dieu, *the largest ship in the fleet. It weighed over 1,000 tons and had 72 guns.*

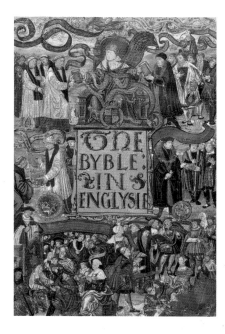

rather than an axe.) Two weeks later, Henry married Jane Seymour. Though the rigours of childbirth killed her, she was at least able to give the king a son, Edward.

Three further wives followed. The first was Anne of Cleves, in 1540. Young and apparently beautiful, as the sister of the German duke of Cleves she would also provide Henry with an important Protestant ally. But having only seen Holbein's ravishing portrait of his bride-to-be, Henry was appalled to meet a fleshy young woman of, at best, lumbering charm. Their unconsummated marriage ended in divorce after six months. Within three weeks, Henry married the teenage Catherine Howard, who briefly put a spring into his gouty step. Two years later, Henry had her executed for infidelity. His sixth and final wife, the matronly Catherine Parr, the only one of his wives to survive her despotic husband, seems finally to have brought a degree of serenity to his premature old age.

Henry may have owned 55 palaces by his death, but his reign ended as a gross parody of the promise with which it had begun. His wars against Ireland, Scotland and France were effectively bankrupting the kingdom. Simultaneously, a total of only three surviving legitimate children, one boy and two girls, left the succession worryingly uncertain. Above all, the country was wracked by religious turmoil. The legacy of the "most accomplished prince" was chaos and misery.

The title page of the Great Bible (right), which was published, in English, in 1539 under the auspices of Thomas Cromwell. Henry distributes the new bible to Cranmer (to the king's right) and Cromwell (to his left) who in turn hand copies to clergy and laity alike.

The Act of Union with Wales

*I*n 1536, simply by asserting it as fact – His Highness therefore… established that this said country… of Wales… shall be… incorporated, united and annexed to and with this realm of England… – Henry presided over the absorption of Wales into what became the renamed Kingdom of England and Wales. A series of reforms were enacted, of which the most important was the banning of the Welsh language for all official business and the reorganization of Wales into 13 counties, five of them new. All the counties had the right to be represented by Members of Parliament at the English Parliament in Westminster. At the same time, the border between England and Wales was precisely fixed for the first time and the privileges of the Marcher lords, introduced by William the Conqueror, were ended. Though inevitably the cause of resentment among many Welsh, the Act, at any rate in English terms, achieved exactly what it was intended to: the first step in the creation of an English "empire" in Britain.

Edward VI 1547–53

KING
Edward VI

BORN: October 12 1537
ACCEDED: January 28 1547; crowned Westminster Abbey February 20 1547
Duke of Cornwall, King of England and Ireland

EDWARD VI'S SIX-YEAR REIGN WAS DOMINATED BY RELIGIOUS CONTROVERSY. HENRY VIII'S BREAK FROM ROME HAD PRESERVED THE FORMS OF CATHOLIC WORSHIP INTACT. UNDER EDWARD, HOWEVER, CHILD THOUGH HE WAS, AN IMPLACABLE PROTESTANTISM WAS EMBRACED. COMBINED WITH ECONOMIC DISLOCATION AND CONTINUING CONFLICT WITH SCOTLAND AND FRANCE, THE RESULTS WERE RARELY LESS THAN TRAUMATIC.

THE PERILS OF A MINORITY WERE EPITOMIZED by Edward VI's reign. However carefully prepared for kingship, including a demanding education that saw him learning Latin and Greek at five, and however specific Henry VIII's provisions for a Council of Regents to prevent power falling into the hands of an individual behind the throne, within weeks of Henry VIII's death, Edward's uncle, the Earl of Hertford, had effectively seized power. Hertford disbanded the Council of Regents, declared himself Lord Protector and persuaded the young king to make him duke of Somerset.

Precocious or not, the nine-year-old Edward immediately found himself a tool in Somerset's hands. The Protector's goals were twofold: the continuation of Henry VIII's ruinously expensive

Child or not, Edward VI's embrace of Protestantism, though clearly manipulated by Somerset, Cranmer and Warwick, was quite genuine. At 10, he called the Pope 'the true son of the Devil, an anti-Christ and an abominable tyrant'. His enthusiasm thereafter for the imposition of Protestantism never wavered. Fanaticism of this order in a child was chilling. This portrait (above left) was painted shortly after he became king.

Lady Jane Grey

Though endorsed by Edward VI shortly before his death – indeed, possibly originated by the king – the attempt to proclaim the 15-year-old Lady Jane Grey his legitimate heir was so transparent a ruse that it is hard to see how Edward or Northumberland ever imagined it could work. As Henry VIII's great niece, her claim to the throne was genuine if distant. Nonetheless, both Edward's sisters, Mary and Elizabeth, had clear priority as had been spelled out in Henry VIII's will. Moreover, by marrying his son to her a matter of weeks earlier, Somerset's own motives were almost laughably obvious.

On July 10, three days after Edward's death, Lady Jane Grey was declared queen by the Council. On July 19, she was deposed. In the meantime, support had rapidly grown for Mary, effectively exiled in Hertfordshire. Within days, an army up to 15,000 strong had rallied to her. In the circumstances, there was no hope either for Lady Jane Grey or for her father-in-law, Northumberland, who was almost immediately executed. Lady Jane Grey and her husband were sent to the Tower where, in February 1554, they, too, were executed.

1547	1548	1549
Earl of Hertford abolishes Council of Regents, declares himself Lord Protector and is made Duke of Somerset. Scots defeated at Battle of Pinkie (September), pushing them closer to French. Henry VIII's Act of Six Articles repealed.	Henri II declares war against England, sending 6,000 troops to Scotland and laying siege to Boulogne	Act of Uniformity outlaws all Catholic practices. Cranmer's English-language Book of Common Prayer published. Uprising in West Country and East Anglia (Kett's Rebellion). Somerset overthrown.

Tudor propaganda such as this allegory of Edward VI's succession (left), painted by an unknown artist two years after he became king, leaves little room for doubt as to the legitimacy not just of Edward's succession but of his victory over a corrupt papacy. Edward's own right to rule is confirmed by Henry VIII's deathbed gesture. The new king sits on his throne under the royal arms. The pope is hunched at his feet, crushed by the English text in the bible over his neck: "The word of the Lord endureth for ever". Two monks are sent from the room next to the legend: "feigned holiness". To Edward's left is Somerset, the Lord Protector; to Somerset's left, the Royal Council, Cranmer (in white) among them.

wars against France and Scotland, chiefly with the aim of implementing the Treaty of Greenwich, under which Edward was to marry Mary, Queen of Scots; and the establishment of an aggressively Protestant church. If the former was pursued with a characteristic combination of vacillation and inefficiency on Somerset's part, the later, relentlessly directed by the Archbishop of Canterbury, Thomas Cranmer, was implemented much more single-mindedly.

Victory over the Scots at the Battle of Pinkie in 1547 succeeded only in driving the Scots closer to France, despite the active Protestant minority within Scotland. By the summer of the following year, the French king had sent 6,000 troops to Scotland, declared war on England and laid siege to Boulogne. Agreement between the Scots and French the same year that Mary should marry the heir to the French throne effectively signalled the collapse of Somerset's foreign policy.

At the same time, Cranmer's reforms were taking shape. As early as July 1547 traditional Catholic forms of worship had been banned. Anything that suggested idolatry – stained glass windows, wall paintings, sculptures, even bell ringing – was outlawed. The measures were given legal force in 1549 with the Act of Uniformity, itself reinforced by the publication of Cranmer's *Book of Common Prayer*. Its use was compulsory.

Combined with a rapidly deteriorating economy, exacerbated by the expense of Somerset's ineffectual military campaigns, the net result was widespread unrest. Uprisings in the Catholic West Country in the summer of 1549 in protest against the *Book of Common Prayer*, which saw Exeter besieged, were paralleled by an even more serious rebellion in East Anglia against land enclosures.

In the resulting turmoil, Somerset, predictably, was overthrown. By 1550, the prime instigator of the coup, the earl of Warwick, had declared himself "Lord President of the Council". The following year he had himself created duke of Northumberland.

Northumberland, no less unprincipled than Somerset had been but considerably more pragmatic, successfully extricated England from its French and Scottish entanglements. He also turned his attention to the

The Lady Mary, my sister, came to me at Westminster where after salutations she was called of my Council into a chamber where it was declared how long I had suffered her [Catholic] mass. She answered that her soul was God's and her face she would not change nor would she dissemble with contrary doings.

Edward VI confronting his sister Mary's refusal to abandon Catholicism, 1549

succession. By 1552, it was clear that Edward, now 14, was dying. With no prospect of his producing an heir and with his legitimate successor, his sister Mary, as avowedly Catholic as Edward was Protestant, it became a matter of real urgency to ensure a Protestant succession. The cynical solution was the nomination of Edward's cousin, Lady Jane Grey, as heir (see box). Northumberland meanwhile took the precaution of marrying his son, Guildford Dudley, to her.

With Edward's death, Lady Jane Grey, like her father, was swept away on a tide of enthusiasm for Mary. It was premature. Her reversal of Edward's religious reforms plunged England into chaos.

1550	1551	1552	1553
Warwick made Lord President of the Council	*Warwick created duke of Northumberland*	*Somerset executed*	*Second edition of* Book of Common Prayer *published. Forty-two Articles of Religion establish theological principles of Protestant Church of England. Edward names Lady Jane Grey his heir*

MARY I 1553–58

MARY NOT ONLY REVERSED EDWARD VI's PROTESTANT REFORMS, IN RESTORING PAPAL SUPREMACY SHE REVERSED HER FATHER'S, TOO. FOR MARY, DOCTRINAL PURITY AND POLITICAL EXPEDIENCY HAD BECOME THE SAME. IN SUBSEQUENTLY MARRYING PHILIP II OF SPAIN, SHE CAME CLOSE TO MAKING ENGLAND A PAWN OF CATHOLIC SPAIN. ONLY HER EARLY DEATH SAVED ENGLAND FROM FURTHER RELIGIOUS DIVISION.

BORN: February 18 1516
ACCEDED: July 19 1553;
crowned Westminster
Abbey, October 1 1553

*Queen Consort of Spain
January 16 1556 to
November 17 1558,
Queen of England
and Ireland*

IN 1533, MARY, THE ONLY SURVIVING CHILD OF Henry VIII's first wife, Catherine of Aragon, was declared a bastard by Act of Parliament. Princess Mary became plain "The Lady Mary". Henry's divorce from Catherine of Aragon and marriage to Anne Boleyn necessitated wiping the slate clean in every sense. Much as would later happen to Elizabeth after her mother, Anne Boleyn, was executed, Mary became a non-person.

Not surprisingly, though subsequently reconciled with Henry at the prompting of his last wife, Catherine Parr – and, like Elizabeth, restored to her place in the succession – the memory of her mother's fate at Henry's hands remained the dominant motif of her life, confirming the ardent Catholicism under which she had been brought up. Even at the height of her brother, Edward VI's, imposition of militant Protestantism, Mary obstinately refused to tone down her

Any child of Henry VIII's might justifiably feel alienated. In Mary's case, not just excluded from the succession at 14 but legally proclaimed illegitimate, the result was predictable. With her mother shunned by the king and her own status threatened, it is hardly to be wondered at that she grew up suspicious and alarmed. Yet contemporaries consistently described an intelligent, dutiful child, always anxious to please. This portrait (far left) shows Mary at 13.

Catholic observance. She was her father's daughter in more ways than one.

Whatever Mary's clear espousal of the old religion in a country ever more obviously embracing Protestantism, her accession was nonetheless generally welcomed – and not just by those who had remained true to the Catholic church. It was widely assumed that Mary would reinstate Catholic forms of worship while confirming the primacy of the Church of England – in other words, that she would broadly restore the status quo under Henry VIII.

From the outset, Mary disabused them. Almost immediately it became clear that her goal was the full restoration of Catholic supremacy. A series of parliamentary measures were enacted repealing Edward's Protestant legislation. At the same time, Mary announced her intention to marry Philip, son of

> *When they send me orders forbidding me the Mass, I shall expect to suffer as I once suffered during my father's lifetime … I am like a little ignorant girl and I care neither for my goods nor for the World but only for God's service and my conscience.*
>
> Princess Mary, 1549

Foxe's Book of Martyrs

The publication in 1563 of John Foxe's Acts and Monuments, more generally known as The Book of Martyrs, confirmed Mary's reputation as a cruel, Catholic fanatic. Above all, it was the book's evocative and explicit woodcuts of Marian Protestant martyrs at the stake that damned her in the by now firmly Protestant national imagination. The book was clearly propaganda. Foxe double-counted some of the victims. He made no mention of the burnings under Henry VIII. Yet its impact was immense, above all that of the 1589 edition, published the year after the Spanish Armada.

The illustration shows the deaths in February 1556 of the Bishop of London, Nicholas Ridley, and the Bishop of Worcester, Hugh Latimer. "Be of good comfort, Master Ridley, and play the man," Latimer is reputed to have said. "We shall this day light such a candle by God's grace in England as I trust shall never be put out." Watching the scene on the right is the imprisoned Thomas Cranmer, chief architect of Edward VI's Protestant reforms and himself burned five months later.

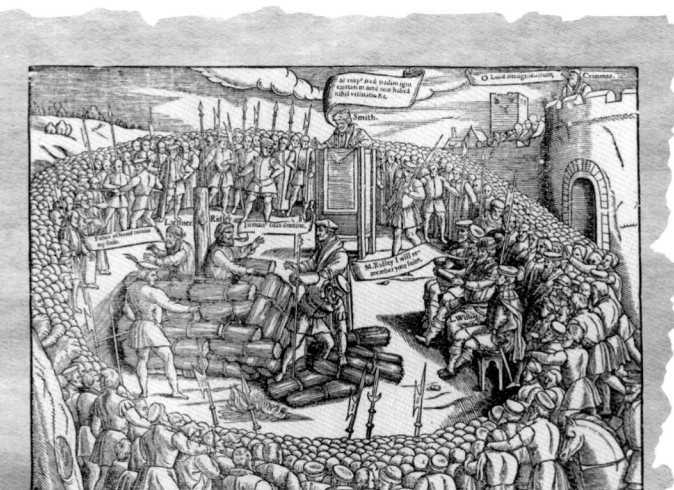

1533	1544	1553	1554
Mary declared illegitimate after marriage of Henry VIII and Catherine of Aragon declared void	*Mary partly reconciled with Henry VIII after intervention of his sixth wife, Catherine Parr*	*(Aug.) Triumphal entry of Mary to London as queen at head of army 15,000 strong; coronation of Mary (Oct.) makes her first regnant queen of England since Matilda in the 12th century*	*(Jan.) Thomas Wyatt's uprising in protest at Mary's planned marriage to Philip of Spain put down. (Feb.) execution of Lady Jane Grey. England officially reunited with church of Rome and return of Reginald Pole as papal legate (Nov.)*

Charles V of Spain. At 38, and with the succession paramount, the question of Mary's marriage necessarily loomed large. But for Mary to insist on marriage to the son of the most powerful and militantly Catholic ruler in Europe disturbed all but her most ardent supporters. That he was 11 years her junior was scarcely an issue.

Though a nervous compromise was reached whereby Philip would become king consort only – and be excluded from the succession if no heir was produced – resistance to the union was widespread. In January 1554, there was an armed uprising, led by Thomas Wyatt, against London. Though easily suppressed, it was symptomatic of the wider unease.

Mary subsequently not only aligned England with Spain in a disastrous war against France in which Calais, England's last foothold in France – and last link with its Norman, Angevin and Plantagenet kings – was lost, she also engineered the return of Reginald Pole, the papal legate, who in 1556 was appointed Archbishop of Canterbury.

It was under Pole's urging that in February 1555 Mary began what subsequently confirmed her status as the demonized enemy of Protestant England, "Bloody" Mary herself: the burning at the stake of Protestant martyrs. In fact, with heretics being done to death across Europe, there was little unusual in her actions. Nonetheless, the 287 Protestants executed on Mary's orders alarmed even Catholic opinion, fearful at the reaction it would provoke.

When Mary, to the horror of her advisors, decided to marry Philip of Spain (left), *the Spanish approached the projected match with a cynical mixture of pragmatism and contempt. A Spanish witness to the wedding wrote: "If she dressed in our fashions, she would not look so old and flabby. It will take a great God to drink this cup." For his part, Philip spent less than a year with his bride, leaving as soon as he decently could for the Netherlands and his mistresses. The tragedy for Mary, who just a year earlier had written to the Spanish ambassador saying that "[I] have never felt that which is called love, nor harboured thoughts of voluptuousness", is that she seems genuinely to have loved Philip. Two false pregnancies only confirmed her sense of loss.*

In the event, all came to nothing – except in later Protestant propaganda. Mary, increasingly ill, ever more convinced of her Catholic destiny, died childless and embittered only five years after coming to the throne. Her husband had all but abandoned her, her country was on the brink of full acceptance of the heretic Protestant religion. Her failure was painfully total.

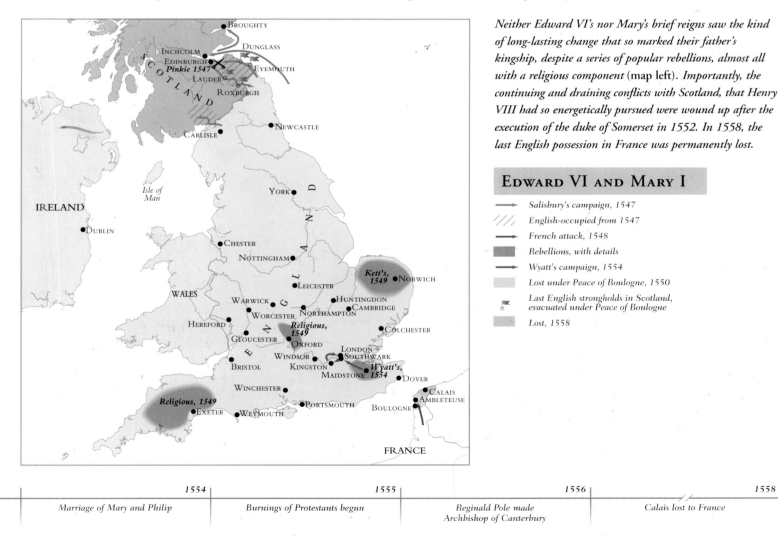

Neither Edward VI's nor Mary's brief reigns saw the kind of long-lasting change that so marked their father's kingship, despite a series of popular rebellions, almost all with a religious component (map left). *Importantly, the continuing and draining conflicts with Scotland, that Henry VIII had so energetically pursued were wound up after the execution of the duke of Somerset in 1552. In 1558, the last English possession in France was permanently lost.*

EDWARD VI AND MARY I

→	Salisbury's campaign, 1547
///	English-occupied from 1547
→	French attack, 1548
▮	Rebellions, with details
→	Wyatt's campaign, 1554
	Lost under Peace of Boulogne, 1550
⚑	Last English strongholds in Scotland, evacuated under Peace of Boulogne
	Lost, 1558

1554	1555	1556	1558
Marriage of Mary and Philip	Burnings of Protestants begun	Reginald Pole made Archbishop of Canterbury	Calais lost to France

Elizabeth I 1558–1603

BORN: **September 7 1533**
ACCEDED: **November 17 1558; crowned Westminster Abbey January 15 1559**

Queen of England and Ireland

Very unusually for the period, Elizabeth (above) was fearsomely well educated. It showed later when, as queen, she wrote all her own speeches, often producing several drafts in her exceptionally elegant handwriting. This portrait was painted at the request of her brother Edward VI when she was 13. She wrote to him: "For the face I might well blush to offer, but for the mind I shall never be ashamed to present".

ELIZABETH I'S REPUTATION BELIES THE UNCERTAINTIES OF HER EARLIER YEARS ON THE THRONE. YET ONCE ESTABLISHED SHE PRESIDED OVER AN INCREASINGLY SELF-CONFIDENT NATION WHOSE SENSE OF AN INEVITABLE PROTESTANT DESTINY BECAME EVER CLEARER. DESPITE HER FAILURE TO MARRY AND ENSURE HER SUCCESSION, SHE CAME TO PERSONIFY HER KINGDOM AS NO MONARCH BEFORE OR SINCE.

WHATEVER THE OUTBURST OF PATRIOTIC fervour that greeted the accession of the 25-year-old Elizabeth in 1558, she was confronted with an immediate political problem. The violent see-sawing between her brother, Edward VI's Protestantism, and her sister, Mary's, equally aggressive Catholicism, had polarized England. If there was a general acceptance that England's destiny was now broadly Protestant, encapsulating this in Parliamentary legislation that would not permanently alienate both extremes called for an unusual degree of tact.

This Elizabeth possessed in abundance. The hallmark of her reign, however occasionally infuriating she could be, was an ability to combine regal authority with an almost infinite capacity to prevaricate, all the while appearing wholly in sympathy with her subjects. That she also enjoyed the support of a number of exceptionally able ministers, William Cecil and Francis Walsingham in the early and middle parts of her reign, Robert Cecil, William's son, at the end of it, underlined a shrewd judgement backed by an intelligent willingness to delegate.

Elizabeth's childhood encapsulated the perils of Reformation England. At less than three, her mother, Anne Boleyn, was beheaded and Elizabeth declared a bastard by Act of Parliament, removing her from the succession. Until her reconciliation with her father, engineered by Catherine Parr in 1544, she was brought up an exile from the court. Her education, however, was exemplary. By her teens, she was fluent in French, Italian, Latin and Greek. "Her mind", wrote her tutor, Roger Ascham, "has no womanly weakness... her memory long keeps what it quickly picks up".

Even in the reign of her younger brother Edward VI, otherwise almost the only secure period of her youth, she was falsely suspected by the Duke of Somerset, the Lord Protector, of a plot to overthrow him. In the reign of her sister, Mary, she was not only re-declared a bastard, in 1554 she was sent to the Tower for two months on suspicion of involvement in Thomas Wyatt's uprising. Only on Mary's deathbed was Elizabeth reluctantly acknowledged heir by her sister.

Let Tyrants fear I ... have placed my chiefest strength and safeguard in the loyal hearts and goodwill of my subjects. ... I know I have the body of a weak and feeble woman, but I have the heart and stomach of a King and a King of England too and think it foul scorn that Parma or Spain or any Prince of Europe should dare to invade the borders of my realm ... I myself will be your General, Judge and Rewarder of every one of your virtues in the field. I know already for your forwardness you have deserved rewards and crowns; and we do assure you, on the word of a Prince, they shall be duly paid to you.

Elizabeth I, Tilbury, August 9 1588

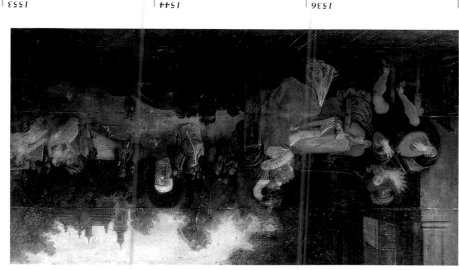

Virgin queen or not, there were many who were convinced that Elizabeth and Robert Dudley, the Earl of Leicester, must have been lovers. Elizabeth was to have a number of similar relationships later in her reign, including with Robert Devereux, the Earl of Essex, and the Duke of Alençon (who the queen called 'frog'). But none approached that with Leicester for intensity or duration. He was never a serious candidate as king, however. It was widely thought the death of his wife in 1560 after falling down stairs was more than coincidence. Here (left) the queen and Leicester are shown at Kenilworth.

1536	1544	1553	1554	1558
Elizabeth declared illegitimate and removed from succession after execution of Anne Boleyn	Elizabeth reinstated as royal heir and restored to Henry VIII's court	Re-declared illegitimate on succession of Mary	Sent to Tower on suspicion of involvement in Thomas Wyatt's uprising against Mary	Accession of Elizabeth

Elizabeth I's foreign policy was conceived in almost entirely defensive terms (map right). Whatever the threats posed by France, Scotland and militantly Catholic Spain, she consistently resisted entangling English forces in wider Continental conflicts, though she was happy to allow privateers such as Drake and Frobisher to mount raids of their own. The defeat of the Armada in 1588 was a triumphant vindication of her stance.

ELIZABETH I 1558–1603

🌿 Rebellion

→ Northern rebellion; campaign and retreat, 1569

⧄ Subject to English raids, 1570

IRELAND

▨ "Planted" under Elizabeth, with date

▨ Principal areas from where English settlers moved to Ireland

⧉ Limit of the Pale, 1596

→ O'Neill's campaign, 1601

→ Essex's campaign, 1588

→ Other English campaigns

→ Route of the Armada

┈┈▶ Other Spanish campaign, with date

⚑ "Cautionary towns" English held, from 1585

○ Other English occupied towns in the continent, with dates

▨ Spanish Habsburg possessions

⧄ Approximate extent of English activities in the Netherlands from 1586

⋯⋯ Frontiers, 1600

────── Frontier of the Holy Roman Empire, 1600

The Elizabethan period saw the beginnings of a golden age of English seafaring. Elizabethan England could scarcely claim yet to rule the waves, but the seeds of later British maritime domination were being sown. For Elizabeth herself, the advantages were less the country's burgeoning naval strength than the semi-private raiding ventures, mostly directed against Spain, carried out by the likes of Drake (below), Frobisher and Hawkins, pirates in all but name. Their ventures cost the country nothing but guaranteed it a share of the profits.

Map labels

SCOTLAND

North Sea

✕ Lough Swilly 1567

Earl of Tyrone (O'Neill), 1595–1603

1570

1591

BRANCEPETH   DURHAM
Westmoreland / Catholic earls, 1569   RICHMOND
LANCASHIRE   RIPON
SELBY

IRELAND

Essex, 1601

LIMERICK

James Fitzmaurice / Munster Confederacy, 1569–73
Munster rising, 1579–83

1586
1586   KINSALE

DUBLIN

WATERFORD

WALES   ENGLAND

CHESHIRE

LONDON

SOMERSET   DORSET

In revolt against Spanish rule from 1567
NETHERLANDS
AMSTERDAM
✕ Zutphen 1586
BRILL

FLUSHING   RAMMEKENS
✕ Ostend 1601
✕ Nieuport 1600
✕ Gravelines 1588
CALAIS

John Norrey, 1591
English Channel

1591
Frobisher, 1593

DIEPPE
LE HAVRE 1562–3
Willoughby, 1590
✕ Ivry 1590   PARIS

PAIMPOL
BREST
1593
CROZON

✕ Craon 1592

FRANCE

Religious wars, 1562–98

1601
Drake/Essex, 1589
Drake, 1587
1588

Bay of Biscay

BORDEAUX

CORUNNA

VIGO

PORTUGAL

SPAIN

PENICHE
John Norrey, 1589
LISBON

Drake, 1587
Essex, 1596
✕ CADIZ

1559	1560	1561	1562	1569	1570
Acts of Supremacy and Uniformity re-instate Protestantism; Elizabeth declared Supreme Governor (not Head) of Church of England	Temporary peace with Scotland (Treaty of Berwick) and France (Treaty of Edinburgh). Irish Act of Uniformity attempts to impose religious settlement on Ireland, in rebellion to 1573	Mary, Queen of Scots, returns to Scotland	Armed assistance unsuccessfully given to French Huguenots	Renewed peace with France (Treaty of Cateau-Cambrésis). Catholic uprising in north of England under earls of Westmoreland and Northumberland	Elizabeth excommunicated by Pope Pius V

continued on next page

JAMES I 1603-25

JAMES I WAS AMONG THE MOST PARADOXICAL OF KINGS. CONVINCED OF HIS ABSOLUTE RIGHT TO RULE, HE WAS FORCED INTO ACCOMMODATIONS WITH PARLIAMENT THAT SAW THE MAJORITY OF HIS INITIATIVES THWARTED. THE MOST INTELLECTUAL OF ENGLAND'S KINGS, HE WAS ALSO AMONG ITS MOST DISSOLUTE. YET HIS REIGN WAS GENERALLY STABLE, HIS INTENTIONS NEARLY ALWAYS HONOURABLE.

WHEN JAMES STUART BECAME KING OF England in 1603, as James VI he had already been King of Scotland for 36 years. Only in the last ten of them had he been able to impose himself on his kingdom. His mother, Mary, Queen of Scots, was forced off her throne when James was only one, shortly after the murder of his father, Lord Darnley. His 16-year minority, which saw the violent deaths of all four Scottish regents against a background of political infighting and religious controversy, was hardly less unstable. In addition, after the execution of Mary in 1587, James's subsequent reign was dogged by uncertainty as to whether he would, as he fervently hoped, succeed the childless Queen Elizabeth in England. Even as Elizabeth was dying in the spring of 1603, he could not be sure of the succession.

As James I of England and Ireland, his prospects were transformed. His new kingdom was substantially richer, his own powers, especially over the church, more extensive. Furthermore, James himself had not just had wide experience of the uncertainties of 16th- and 17th-century monarchy; he was a man of impressive learning with a natural grasp of the imperatives of political moderation, above all in the sensitive matter of religion. Set against this were English suspicions of a

When God hath conjoined then, let no man separate. I am the Husband, and all the whole Isle is my lawful Wife; I am the Head, and it is my Body; I am the Shepherd, and it is my flock: I hope therefore no man will be so unreasonable as to think that I that am a Christian King under the Gospel, should be a Polygamist and husband to two wives; that I being the Head, should have a divided and monstrous Body; or that being the Shepherd to so fair a flock should have my flock parted in two.

James I addressing Parliament on the proposed union of England and Scotland, 1604

James I's combination of high intelligence, learning, vanity and occasional sloth make him the most unusual of England's kings. His published works, above all The True Law of Free Monarchies *(1598) and* Basilikon Doron *("The Prince's Gift", 1599), make him the only English king with claims to literary stature. Similarly, his attempts to unite England and Scotland were far-sighted, reflecting his "wish above all things … to leave one worship to God: one kingdom, entirely govern-ed: one uniformity of laws".* This portrait (above), by Nicholas Hilliard, was painted just after he came to the English throne in 1603.

Duke of Rothesay, Duke of Albany, Earl of Ross and Baron Ardmannoch, King of Scotland, England and Ireland

BORN: June 19 1566
ACCEDED IN SCOTLAND:
July 24 1567; crowned
July 29 1567; Stirling
ACCEDED IN ENGLAND
AND IRELAND: March 24
1603; crowned July 25
1603, Westminster
Abbey

James's "sweete boyes"

JAMES I's homosexuality manifested itself in a number of infatuations with younger men. In the early part of his English reign, his favourite was a Scot, Robert Carr, made viscount Rochester in 1611, then earl of Somerset in 1613. Carr's fall two years later was spectacular. His wife, Frances Howard, "that base women", was discovered to have murdered her principal critic, Sir Thomas Overbury, by arranging for a poisoned enema to be administered to him.

George Villiers's (above) hold on the king's affections was even more remarkable. In rapid succession he was made viscount Villiers (1616), earl of Bucking-ham (1617), marquess of Buckingham (1618) and duke of Buckingham (1623), by which point "Steenie", as James I called him, had become almost an equal partner with the king. Buckingham's outrageous flattery of the king, his "deare dad" was equally extreme. He was stabbed by a madman in 1628.

Scottish King of England, and Scottish suspicions that James would abandon his native land for England. In addition, there was the inescapable matter of James's personal oddities. Bulging eyes, a tendency to drool, indolence and drunkenness hardly suggested the dig-nified absolute monarch James professed to be. His extravagance and an obvious homosexuality allied to

1582	1583	1586	1587	1589	1591	1592	1596	1599	1600	1603	1604
The "Ruthven Raid": James seized by Lord Gowrie	Majority of James VI	Treaty of Berwick names James as successor to Elizabeth I in England	Execution of Mary, Queen of Scots, prompts only faint protest from James VI	Marries Anne of Denmark	Attempted kidnap of James by earl of Bothwell (and 1592)	Presbyterianism established as official religion in Scotland	James establishes firmer church control over religion in Scotland	Treatise on kingship, Basilikon Doron, published by James	Attempted kidnap of James by Lord Gowrie	James I named as successor to Elizabeth	Hampton Court Conference attempts religious settlement with Puritans and Catholics leads to

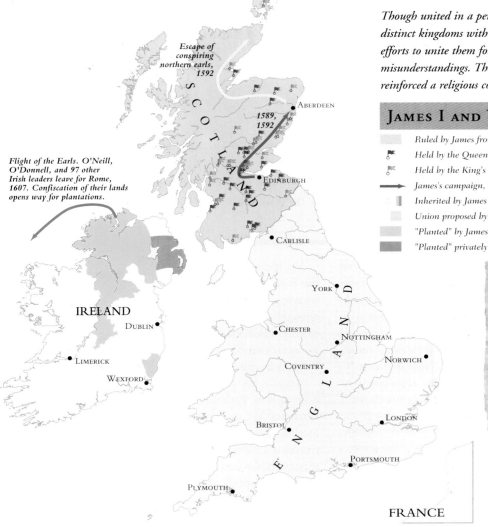

Escape of conspiring northern earls, 1592

SCOTLAND

ABERDEEN

1589, 1592

Flight of the Earls. O'Neill, O'Donnell, and 97 other Irish leaders leave for Rome, 1607. Confiscation of their lands opens way for plantations.

EDINBURGH

CARLISLE

IRELAND

DUBLIN

LIMERICK

WEXFORD

YORK

ENGLAND

CHESTER

NOTTINGHAM

NORWICH

COVENTRY

BRISTOL

LONDON

PORTSMOUTH

PLYMOUTH

FRANCE

Though united in a personal union under James, Scotland and England remained distinct kingdoms with their own quite different laws (map left). The king's visionary efforts to unite them foundered on persistent Anglo-Scottish jealousies and misunderstandings. The Plantation of Ireland by Protestant Scots, begun in 1611, reinforced a religious conflict that survives today.

JAMES I AND VI 1603–25

- Ruled by James from 1567
- Held by the Queen's men during civil war, 1567–73
- Held by the King's men during civil war, 1567–73
- → James's campaign, with dates
- Inherited by James I, 1603
- Union proposed by James to parliament, 1606–07 (Plan abandoned)
- "Planted" by James
- "Planted" privately during James's rule

The Gunpowder Plot

Writing to Robert Cecil in March 1603, just before he became king of England, James asserted that he would: "never allow in my conscience that the blood of any man be shed for diversity of opinions in religion". Unfortunately, in the over-heated religious climate of early 17th-century England, this moderation found few supporters.

Anti-Catholic prejudice was raised to new heights in November 1605 with the discovery of the Gunpowder Plot, an attempt to blow up both the Houses of Parliament along with the king and the Prince of Wales. Whether the plot had been encouraged by James's chief minister, Robert Cecil, in the hope of allowing the conspirators to incriminate themselves, or was discovered only at the last minute, remains unknown.

Either way, the predictable effects of the plot's discovery was to scupper all hopes of extending tolerance to Catholics prepared to practise their faith discreetly, and to create an even more rabidly anti-Catholic mood. It also provided a huge boost to James's popularity. Parliament declared November 5 a national holiday, in the process praising James as: "… the most great learned and religious king that ever reigned".

Towards the end of his life, James I had become a shambling, gout-ridden, semi-senile figure (right), made all the more improbable by self-regarding pomposity. Yet his reign was far from a failure. He bequeathed his heir, Charles, a stable and secure if indebted throne. This portrait, by Daniel Mytens, was painted in 1621.

shameless promotion of court favourites, above all George Villiers (made duke of Buckingham in 1623), created great resentment.

Of more lasting importance was a political tactlessness, most obvious when James was haranguing his Parliament even when accepting its right to refuse him new taxes or to pass his laws. This inability to gauge the political temperature was responsible for the failure of James's most cherished project: the union of Scotland and England. After several years of increasingly strained relations with Parliament, all James achieved, by 1607, was the repeal of mutually hostile laws between England and Scotland, and the adoption of a new Anglo-Scots flag for all ships, the "Great Union", or "Union Jack" as it was known after the king's preference for the French form of his own name, Jacques.

If at the end of his reign James found himself reluctantly sucked into the wider European religious conflict that would become the Thirty Years War, for the most part he managed to keep England clear of costly foreign wars. He was also successful after 1611, in beginning the Ulster "Plantation", the settlement of mostly Scottish Presbyterians in Ulster, the most Catholic province of Ireland, in order to stamp on potential Catholic uprisings. Successful in its own terms, it would blight Ireland itself for centuries.

James I scarcely deserved his description, in the memorable phrase of the French king, Henri IV, as "the wisest fool in Christendom". Yet it contains a kernel of truth about a likeable, well-intentioned but faintly absurd figure.

1605	1606	1607	1610	1611	1612	1613	1616	1619	1623
commissioning of English-language King James Bible (1611). Peace reached with Spain	Catholic attempt to blow up James and Parliament – the Gunpowder Plot – foiled	Union Jack introduced	Union of Scotland and England – Instrument of Union – rejected	The "Great Contract", an attempt to reform royal finances rejected by Parliament	Ulster Plantation begun	Death of James's elder son Henry, Prince of Wales	Marriage of James's daughter Elizabeth and Frederick, Elector Palatine	Rise of new court favourite, George Villiers, begins	Palatine Elector accepts throne of Bohemia, provoking war with Spain	Villiers and Charles, Prince of Wales, make disastrous secret visit to Spain attempting to secure new Anglo-Spanish alliance by marriage of Charles to the Infanta

1639	1640	1641	1642	1644
First Bishops' War: Charles's weak army easily defeated by Scots	"Short" Parliament dismissed after less than a month. Second Bishops' War (Aug.): Scots occupy Newcastle. "Long" Parliament (meets until 1660) called and insists on dismissal of Laud and execution of Strafford; Ship Money rescinded	Catholic uprising in Ireland. Parliamentary grievances in form of Grand Remonstrance presented to Charles (Dec.)	Attempted arrest of parliamentary critics (Jan.) by Charles turns into embarrassing fiasco. Formal declaration of hostilities by Charles at Nottingham (Aug.); first major battle, at Edgehill (Oct.), inconclusive	Parliamentary victory at Marston Moor, Yorkshire

...vociferous Puritan critics, was little better than papism.

Though the political opposition and religious protest provoked by Charles were separate, the two overlapped in crucial respects. Certainly, when the Civil War began, it was the case that there were few Puritans on the king's side just as there were few Laudians, let along Catholics, on the Parliamentary side. But what most united opposition to the king was not just his overbearing sense of divinely appointed self-righteousness – his refusal, once his mind was made up, ever to change it – so much as his use of any means, however low, to put his will into practice. Trust, like compromise, was not an option that Charles I entertained.

At least in retrospect, his reign began its sudden unravelling in 1637, when Laud instructed the Scottish Kirk to use the *Book of Common Prayer*. Within a year, virulent Scottish opposition had hardened in the form of a massive popular protest and petition – the Great Covenant. The following year, a Scottish "Covenanter" army invaded England. Charles's response – to invade Scotland in turn – immediately fell foul of his inability to raise the necessary taxes to finance an army. In April 1640 he was humiliatingly forced to summon a new Parliament in London.

The following 18 months would prove the most remarkable and unpredictable in English kingship. Amid a mood of mounting and apparently unstoppable crisis, the certainties of Tudor and early Stuart monarchy evaporated. Scarcely more than two years later, a bitterly divisive civil war had begun.

The immediate cause was partly parliamentary resentment at the king's abrupt dismissal of his new Parliament less than a month after he had summoned it, partly growing anxiety that, if he could not raise an English army, Charles planned to exploit a Catholic uprising in Ireland to raise a Catholic Irish army, potentially supported by Spain, to repress the

Scots. Even so, when Parliament had to be recalled the following November, the vast majority of its members favoured an accommodation with the king. What they sought was a reaffirmation of Parliament's established place in the government of the country, not the overthrow of the monarchy.

Backtracking rapidly, Charles appeared, in February 1641, to have come to an accommodation with his Parliament, agreeing to a series of measures that significantly reduced his royal prerogative. The king, however, was doing no more than play for time. Precisely like King John when he signed Magna Carta in 1215, Charles had no intention of honouring his commitments. By the following August he was in Scotland attempting to persuade the

continued from previous page

The legality of Charles's trial had been as it had been ordered by the "Rump" of the Long Parliament, troubled many. In the event, the judges, though hand-picked, divided almost exactly, 68 to 67 – a majority in favour of the king's death of just one. His guilt as a "tyrant, traitor and murderer, a public and implacable enemy to the Commonwealth of England" was announced on January 28. This painting (right) by Edward Bower of Charles at the trial shows the king haggard and drawn but dignified to the last.

The Irish Dimension

By 1640, something like 100,000 Protestant settlers had been introduced into Ireland, the majority of them Scottish Presbyterians, most of whom settled in Ulster. The Catholic Irish – whether the "Old English" descendants of the original Norman settlers or the native Gaels – were dispossessed or forced to the less fertile western extremities of Ireland. The policy sought to prevent a recurrence of the Catholic Irish revolts of the later 16th and early 17th centuries by fusing Ireland culturally with Scotland and England. Especially with the appointment of the hard-nosed Thomas Wentworth, earl of Strafford, as Lord Deputy of Ireland in 1633, it was a success.

Strafford, however, was as tough on the native Protestant "New English" and the Scots Presbyterians as he was on the native "Old English". When Parliament engineered his execution in 1641, on the ground that he had been an "evil counseller" to the king, the Catholic Irish lost what small protection they had enjoyed. The success of the Scots "Covenanter" armies was another cause of Irish Catholic fear, and in October 1641 an uprising began, ostensibly to aid Charles I in his struggle against Parliament and the Covenanters alike.

Much of the planned rebellion never even started, but in Portadown more than 2,000 Protestants were killed. In the heightened political climate of the day, evidence of a renewed popish uprising of this kind was electrifying. Rumours of further massacres abounded. Charles himself was said to have masterminded the revolts and was seeking Spanish help to train an Irish Catholic army to invade England – as usual – was Ireland's, the political fallout for the king was scarcely less great, and further reinforced Puritan parliamentary opinion to oust him.

the Scots to mount a further invasion of England to quell his troublesome English Parliament for good.

His actions had the inevitable result of hardening parliamentary opposition to him in England. In December 1641 he was presented with a "Grand Remonstrance". For the first time, the notion was made explicit that Parliament could dismiss a king who was held to have broken his trust with his people. Charles responded by a botched attempt to arrest the ringleaders, arriving at the House of Commons with an armed troop. By now, almost every convention governing relations between monarch and Parliament had collapsed. The war, when it came, appeared inevitable.

In ways unparalleled before or since, the Civil War divided communities and opinions across England. There were few clear-cut loyalties. Support for the king only rarely meant the same as opposition to Parliament. Likewise, support for Parliament was rarely the same as opposition to the king. For all but the Puritans, convinced of their role as the agents of a benevolently vengeful God, the resulting bloodshed and suffering were all the more unbearably arbitrary.

Charles proved a resilient general, resisting the growing strength – and professionalism – of the parliamentary armies for almost five years. Even after his capture in 1646, he was able to exploit the continuing atmosphere of division and uncertainty dogging the country. Unlike his earlier attempts to control Parliament, Charles now revealed a near masterly talent for playing off one side against another – although always with his own restoration in mind.

That Parliament decided on the king's execution was mainly the result of an enforced takeover of Parliament by the only force that now really counted: the parliamentary "New Model Army", godly, forthright and, above all, victorious. Dominating it was a man who would repudiate completely Charles I's failed brand of absolute monarchy, Oliver Cromwell.

In January 1649 Charles was tried, found guilty and executed. Ironically, it was Parliament, purged of its royalist members, that now seemed to have become the tyrant. In death Charles I found the dignity that his duplicitous kingship had so obviously lacked.

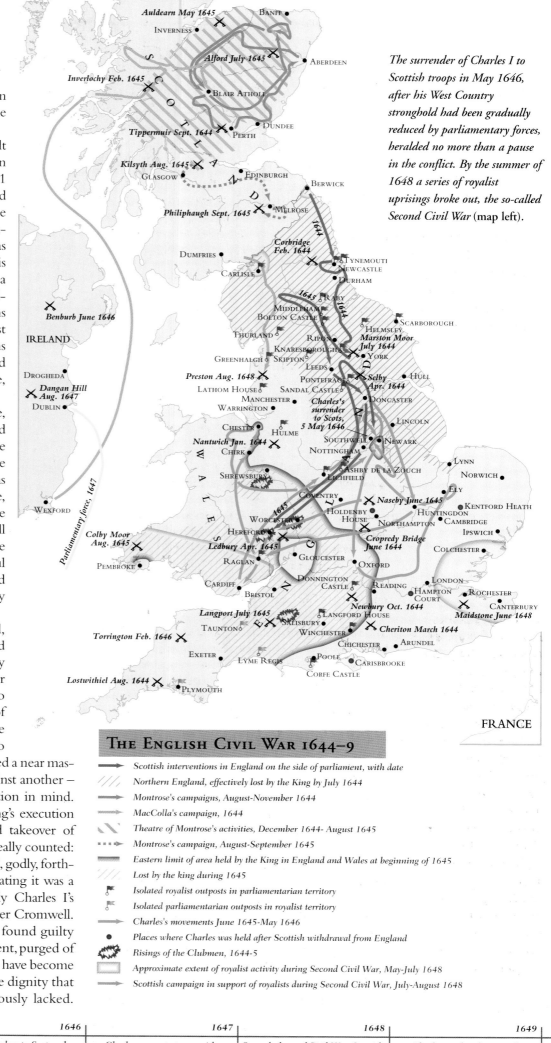

The surrender of Charles I to Scottish troops in May 1646, after his West Country stronghold had been gradually reduced by parliamentary forces, heralded no more than a pause in the conflict. By the summer of 1648 a series of royalist uprisings broke out, the so-called Second Civil War (map left).

THE ENGLISH CIVIL WAR 1644–9

→ Scottish interventions in England on the side of parliament, with date

/// Northern England, effectively lost by the King by July 1644

→ Montrose's campaigns, August–November 1644

→ MacColla's campaign, 1644

/// Theatre of Montrose's activities, December 1644– August 1645

⋯► Montrose's campaign, August–September 1645

━ Eastern limit of area held by the King in England and Wales at beginning of 1645

/// Lost by the king during 1645

⚑ Isolated royalist outposts in parliamentarian territory

⚑ Isolated parliamentarian outposts in royalist territory

→ Charles's movements June 1645–May 1646

● Places where Charles was held after Scottish withdrawal from England

※ Risings of the Clubmen, 1644-5

▨ Approximate extent of royalist activity during Second Civil War, May–July 1648

→ Scottish campaign in support of royalists during Second Civil War, July–August 1648

1645	1646	1647	1648	1649
Parliamentary New Model Army formed; royalists routed at Naseby. Laud executed	Charles surrenders to Scots, who come to terms with English parliamentarians; Charles handed over to parliamentarians	Charles comes to terms with Scots, promising to impose Presbyterianism on England	Second phase of Civil War: Scottish invasion of England defeated by Cromwell; remaining royalist resistance crushed. New Model Army purges Parliament of members seeking accommodation with Charles (Dec.), leading to "Rump" Parliament	Charles tried and executed in London (Jan.)

THE COMMONWEALTH 1649–60

THE EXECUTION OF CHARLES I IN 1649 LAUNCHED ENGLAND ON AN EXPERIMENT IN NON-MONARCHICAL GOVERNMENT WITHOUT PARALLEL IN EUROPE. IT WAS DOMINATED BY THE FORBIDDING FIGURE OF OLIVER CROMWELL. IN THE EVENT, EVEN HE WAS UNABLE TO DEVISE A STABLE FORM OF GOVERNMENT THAT RECONCILED PURITAN DEMANDS WITH LIBERTY UNDER THE LAW. BY 1660, THE MONARCHY HAD BEEN RESTORED.

I N MAY 1649, FOUR MONTHS AFTER THE EXECUTION OF Charles I, the Rump Parliament declared the existence of the Commonwealth and Free State of England. The supreme authority of Parliament was confirmed, as was the abolition of the monarchy. The House of Lords was similarly ended along with the Anglican Church and its bishops.

It was under this new and radical constitutional arrangement that, in September, Oliver Cromwell was sent to Ireland at the head of a parliamentary army to suppress the remaining Irish Catholic royalist elements, at least in part as revenge for the massacres of Protestants in 1641, and to bring the country firmly under parliamentary control. His brutal victories, at Drogheda and Wexford, were as complete as those he subsequently inflicted over the Scots at Dunbar in September 1650 and over Charles I's son, the future Charles II, at Worcester the following summer. Whatever royalist discontent still existed, an English Republic, which now in effect extended over the whole of Britain, had become a fact.

Yet despite these successes, soon to be matched by victory over the Dutch in the first of three wars over commercial supremacy (itself the herald of a new age of English commercial and colonial expansion), a lasting political settlement remained elusive. Cromwell's appointment as Commander-in-Chief of the parliamentary army in 1651 confirmed what had been evident even before the death of Charles I: that Cromwell, the outstanding parliamentary general in the Civil War and a man of unflinching Calvinist rectitude – part country squire, part reborn Moses – had become the dominant figure of the age. Now, as leader of the only really coherent political body in the country, the army, his pre-eminence was absolute

Cromwell was practical, decisive and competent, but he was also, first and last, a man of God, wholly certain that any attempt at the "healing and settling" of the nation had to be based on a government guided by religious principle. Indeed, at least since the 1630s religion and politics for Cromwell had become inseparable. "Religion was not first the thing contended for [in the Civil War] but God brought it to that issue at last and at last it proved to be what was most dear to us," he ringingly declared

The Rump Parliament by contrast, at least for Cromwell, had degenerated into a self-serving, worldly body, more interested in lining its own pockets than in dispensing justice. Certainly it was no vehicle for God's will. In April 1653, in a fury of Old Testament rage, Cromwell abolished it, mounting in effect an armed coup, striding up and down the chamber shouting: "You are no parliament. I say you are no parliament…. In the name of God, go."

His motive was honourable. Cromwell genuinely intended to establish a new Parliament, as indeed he did within a matter of months. But his means called into question the very principles for which the Civil War had been fought: the protection of parliamentary independence in the face of Stuart tyranny. In the event, the new Godly assembly, the so-called "Barebones" Parliament, appointed rather than elected, lasted a matter of months before dissolving itself and handing power back to Cromwell.

In December 1653, a new constitution was adopted, the

By 1658, Cromwell was king in all but name. Here, as the "Embleme of England's Distractions" (above) *he is shown at his most regal, a just Christian warrior and bringer of peace to all the countries of Britain, crushing underfoot the serpent of error and the whore of Babylon.*

Oh, I lived in and loved darkness, and hated the light. I was a chief, the chief of sinners. This is true; I hated godliness, yet God had mercy on me. O the riches of His mercy!

Oliver Cromwell, 1638, on his Christian reawakening

"Instrument of Government". Under it, Cromwell was made Lord Protector, and a Council of State was formed to take on the daily business of government. Parliament, even though now to be elected every three years, would not be allowed to challenge the "fundamentals" of the new constitution, which was extended to include Ireland and Scotland.

It was to prove no more successful a solution than its predecessors. When the new Parliament met, in September 1654, it immediately insisted on its own supremacy. Predictably, Cromwell dissolved it, replacing it in July 1655 with a wholly new system under which the country was divided into 12 regions, each ruled by a major general. If in many ways the high point of righteous Puritan rule – a Swearing and Cursing Act was passed; the penalty for adultery was death – in practice the system proved unworkable. Elections the following year revealed its unpopularity. Puritan representation in the new House of Commons all but disappeared.

By the summer of 1657, yet another constitution had been adopted, the "Humble Petition and Advice". Under an "Ordinance of Union", originally issued by the Council of State in 1654, Ireland and Scotland were formally united with England. At the same time, the House of Lords was revived. The resulting arrangement was so similar to the reformed monarchy the Long Parliament had tried to persuade Charles I to accept in 1641 and in 1647, that the revival of the monarchy itself seemed logical and inevitable. All but the most fervent Puritans had come to realize that stable government under the law and sanctioned by parliamentary authority was impossible without the central figure of a monarch to unite it.

Cromwell declined repeated requests to become that king himself, despite the fact that he was already styled "Your Highness" and had been given Whitehall Palace to live in. This was the result of his unshakeable religious conviction. Cromwell took it as fact that the monarchy could only have been overthrown because God had wanted it. Unless given equally incontrovertible evidence of a divine change of heart, Cromwell was unprepared to disobey his God.

Yet that Cromwell had become king in all but name was clear not just by his naming his son, Richard, to succeed him as Lord Protector, but also by his dissolution of yet another Parliament in the spring of 1658. This came just months after he had extolled it with the assertion: "If there be any higher work which mortals

The most serious charge to be levelled against Cromwell was not that he was a dour, irascible Puritan bigot – in fact he was remarkably liberal in matters of religion – so much as that he was an increasingly despotic figure whose often arbitrary exercise of power was very much more damaging than anything Charles I did. His dissolution of the Rump Parliament in April 1653 (above), a clear violation of Parliament's legally sanctioned independence, was undertaken for no better reason than that Cromwell lost his temper.

Despite its military successes, The Commonwealth struggled to find a lasting political settlement (map below). Crushing victories by Cromwell in Ireland and Scotland were followed in summer 1651 by the defeat of Charles II, accepted as king of Scotland in 1650. Devising a workable form of non-monarchical government, however, was beyond even Cromwell.

THE COMMONWEALTH 1649–60

- Ruled by Charles II as King, 1649: formally incorporated into Commonwealth, 1657–60
- Cromwell's campaigns
- Land reserved for the government or provided for parliamentary army
- Land assigned to the Irish
- Montrose's campaign, 1649–50
- Charles II's campaigns, 1651
- Other movements of Charles II
- Engagement in First Dutch War
- Revolts
- Frontier of administrative units of 1655, with name of Major General
- Monck's advance, 1660

can attain unto in this world, I acknowledge my ignorance of it." In the end, Cromwell's visions of parliamentary liberty and religious zeal proved incompatible.

After his death in September 1658, the unstable British Republic gently collapsed. Richard Cromwell, with none of his father's messianic potency, resigned as Lord Protector after just eight months. By October, chaos threatened. That it was avoided was thanks to George Monck, commander of the parliamentary army in Scotland. Marching his men to London early in 1660, he restored the Long Parliament, which in turn dissolved itself and called for new elections. To no one's surprise, this new "Convention" Parliament immediately voted to restore the monarchy. The wheel had come full circle.

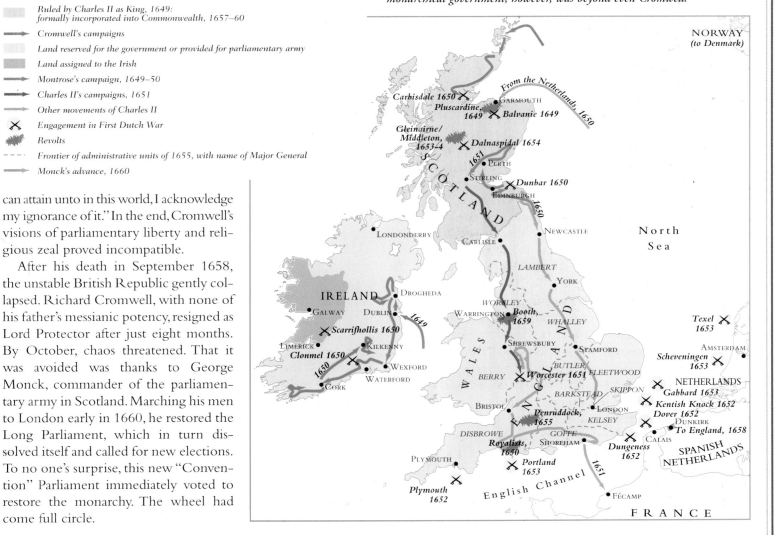

CHARLES II 1660–85

CHARLES II WAS THE MOST SUCCESSFUL STUART KING OF ENGLAND. NOT ONLY WAS HIS RESTORATION A TRIUMPHANT VINDICATION OF THE REVIVED PRINCIPLES OF HEREDITARY MONARCHY, HE MANAGED THE FALLOUT FROM THE TUMULTUOUS REPUBLICAN EXPERIMENT WITH EXCEPTIONAL SKILL. NONETHELESS, THE UNDERLYING TENSIONS BETWEEN PARLIAMENTARY AND ROYAL AUTHORITY RESURFACED WITH THE ACCESSION OF CHARLES'S BROTHER, JAMES II, IN 1685.

KING CHARLES II

BORN: May 29 1630
ACCEDED IN SCOTLAND: June 11 1650; crowned January 1 1651, Scone Abbey; deposed September 3 1651; restored May 29 1660
ACCEDED IN ENGLAND AND IRELAND: May 29 1660; crowned April 23 1661, Westminster Abbey

Duke of Cornwall and Rothesay, King of Scotland, England and Ireland

THE DEFT POLITICAL TOUCH OF CHARLES II was amply demonstrated by his Declaration of Breda in April 1660. With England desperate for a return to legitimate royal government after the inconclusive republican experiments headed by Cromwell, Charles, exiled in Holland, decisively reinforced his position, promising to honour parliamentary liberties and religious freedoms. It

Inconclusive in themselves, the three Anglo-Dutch wars were nonetheless important in the longer term in reinforcing England's emerging naval prowess (map below). The first, fought between 1652 and 1653, was prosecuted with characteristic vigour by Oliver Cromwell. Under Charles II, the conflict flared up twice more, in 1665 to 1667 and in 1672 to 1674. In fact, Anglo-Dutch rivalry was already nearing its end: a shared Protestant destiny would prove more important than mercantile rivalry.

was all that was needed by an England clamouring for a return to legitimate royal rule. In May 1660, both Houses of Parliament voted overwhelmingly for Charles's restoration. He arrived in London on May 29 1660, his 30th birthday, to a triumphant welcome.

The ambiguously worded Declaration of Breda aside, Charles had had to make few compromises to regain his crown. In almost every important sense, he was restored to a throne that was as absolute as his father's. The Godly republican experiments of Cromwell might never have been. That said, in ways that would have seemed unimaginable to Charles I,

The worst that can be said of Charles II (above) is not just that he allowed a sense of drift to settle over his government, reacting to events rather than guiding them, but that his concern to preserve the monarchy led him to align himself too closely with Catholic France, where monarchy and Catholicism seemed to have reached their apogee in Louis XIV. In a country where virulent anti-Catholic feeling was always close to the surface, it would not always prove a prudent course.

CHARLES II 1660–85

✗	*Engagement in Second Dutch War, with details*
	Nominal foe in Second Dutch War
///	*Temporary ally in Second Dutch War*
	Overrun temporarily by Münster during Second Dutch War
🦪	*Revolt, with details*
///	*Walcheren, to become English under secret Treaty of Dover, 1672*
✗	*Engagement in Third Dutch War, with details*
	Ally in Third Dutch War
→	*French attack on Holland, 1672*
	Frontiers, 1664

Attack on Dutch convoy results in Demark declaring war on the side of the Dutch, 1665

BERGEN ✗

NORWAY (to Denmark)

SCOTLAND

PERTH
Bothwell Brig rebellion, 1679
EDINBURGH
Pentland rising, 1666
NEWCASTLE
CARLISLE

IRELAND

DUBLIN

ENGLAND

YORK

WALES

SHREWSBURY

HODDESDON

BRISTOL

LONDON

PORTSMOUTH

PLYMOUTH

Thames Estuary 1667

Landing at Terschelling 'Holmes's Bonfire' 1666

Naval blockade, 1666

Texel 1673

Lowestoft 1665
AMSTERDAM

✗ *Southwold Bay 1672*

NETHERLANDS

B. OF MÜNSTER

✗ *'St James's' 1666*

✗ *'Four Day's' 1666*

DUNKIRK *Sold to France, 1662*

SMALL STATES

SPANISH NETHERLANDS

FRANCE

1646	1648	1649	1650	1651	1658	1660	1661	1665
Escapes into exile in France after first collapse of royalist cause	*Briefly commands royalist naval forces during Second Civil War*	*Execution of Charles I; monarchy overthrown in England*	*Charles arrives in Scotland (June) to take up his throne there in return for support for Presb-yterianism; Scots defeated Dunbar (Sept.)*	*Crowned King of Scotland (Jan.); defeated at Worcester by Cromwell (Sept.) and forced into further exile*	*Death of Cromwell followed by breakdown of Protectorate*	*Declaration of Breda (Apr.) followed by Restoration of Stuart monarchy (May). Supremacy of Church of England restored. Royal Society established*	*Election of "Cavalier" Parliament; sits until 1679. Marriage of Charles II to Catherine of Braganza*	*Second Anglo-Dutch War (to 1667). Recurrence of plague*

his son recognized from the start the need to reach an accommodation with Parliament.

Worldly, cynical and shrewd, even if his belief in absolute monarchy was at least the equal of his father's, Charles was always prepared to compromise for the sake of his throne. Also, unlike his unbending father, he had the common touch. For easy charm, Charles II was rivalled only by Edward IV. Like his Plantagenet forebear, Charles was a notorious womanizer, his court a byword for sophisticated and extravagant dalliance.

If his attempts to secure religious freedoms for all his subjects, Presbyterian as much as Catholic, were thwarted by an intolerant Parliament, Charles's inclusive early administrations went far to heal the divisions of the Civil War. Puritans, parliamentarians and royalists alike were drafted in. The wounds of the previous 20 years were successfully bandaged.

Charles's relaxed kingship may have helped set the tone for an increasingly expansive, confident and prosperous Protestant nation, but unresolved issues remained. Religion, inseparable from the question of parliamentary liberty, remained the core issue — as almost always in 17th-century England. Charles's own instincts were clearly in favour of the Catholicism of an increasingly powerful France. In 1670, he agreed a secret treaty with the Catholic Louis XIV of France, promising to help Louis in his wars against the Protestant Dutch in return for a handsome pension. His hands are reported to have shaken visibly when he denied the existence of the treaty to Parliament.

Even more destabilizing to his regime was the attempt, masterminded by the earl of Shaftesbury from 1679, to exclude his brother James, a Catholic, from the succession. Charles saw off the threat with characteristic insouciance and nerve. If nothing else, he could later console himself at his death in 1685 that the principle of hereditary monarchy had been defended. In fact by the time the "Exclusion" crisis had been settled in the king's favour in 1681, a booming economy, leading to increased customs revenues, which accrued to the crown without the

The Great Fire of London

The euphoria of Charles II's restoration was undermined by three calamitous events in the mid-1660s. In 1665, the Great Plague returned to London, carrying off fully one-sixth of its population. In 1667, the Dutch humiliatingly raided the Medway, less than 50 miles from the capital.

Sandwiched between them was an even more terrifying disaster, the Great Fire of London, which broke out early in the morning of September 2 1666, in a baker's shop. The fire burned uncontrolled for four days, destroying 13,000 houses and making 100,000 people homeless. Eighty-eight churches were burned down, including St Paul's Cathedral. "Oh the miserable and calamitous spectacle," wrote John Evelyn. "… all the skie were of a fiery aspect, like the top of a burning Oven, and the light seen above 40 miles round about for many nights." "It made me weep to see it," Samuel Pepys reported. "The churches, houses and all on fire and flaming at once, and a horrid noise the flames made, and the cracking of the houses at their ruin."

Although work on rebuilding the city began almost at once, and the Rebuilding Act of 1667 enacted — for the time — strict building regulations to prevent a similar disaster, the sense that this was a punishment was widespread. For many, it seriously suggested divine wrath that England had turned its back on its Puritan heritage.

need for parliamentary approval, had made the king financially secure. In the last four years of his reign, Charles II was able to govern without once summoning Parliament. However, with no legitimate heir, Charles's throne was poised to pass to James. His reign may have shown that England could not be governed without a monarch, but the exact relationship between monarch and an increasingly assertive Parliament was about to be finally decided.

Essentially an indolent man, Charles II (right) raised pleasure seeking almost to an art form. He took a real and deep interest in the theatre. He established the racecourse at Newmarket. He was the first monarch to have his own yacht, the Royal Escape. *His string of mistresses was legendary. As Charles put it, he did not believe "God would damn a man for a little irregular pleasure". Not all his subjects were inclined to take such an indulgent view. The diarist John Evelyn saw the excesses of Charles's court as little short of scandalous, finding in it "a sense of utmost vanity".*

1666	1667	1670	1672	1673	1678	1679	1681	1683
Great Fire of London	Dutch naval raid on the Medway	Secret Treaty of Dover with Louis XIV of France: Charles joins anti-Dutch French coalition	Charles issues Declaration of Indulgence guaranteeing religious freedoms. Declares war against Dutch	Charles obliged to withdraw Declaration of Indulgence and assent to Test Act, under which Catholics disqualified from public office	False rumours of popish plot to assassinate Charles spread by Titus Oates, creating renewed anti-Catholic fervour; Earl of Danby, Charles's chief minister, impeached	Earl of Shaftesbury attempts to pass Exclusion Act banning Duke of York from succession; Charles dissolves Parliament three times (to 1681)	Exclusion crisis resolved; Shaftesbury forced into exile	"Rye House Plot" to assassinate Charles and Duke of York in favour of Charles's illegitimate son, the Duke of Monmouth, foiled

WILLIAM III AND MARY II 1689–1702

King William III OF ENGLAND AND IRELAND, WILLIAM II OF SCOTLAND

*Ruled jointly with
Mary II until
December 28 1694*
BORN: November 4 1650
ACCEDED: February 13
1689; crowned April
11 1689, Westminster
Abbey
*Prince of Orange
and Count of
Nassau-Dillenburg, King
of England, Scotland
and Ireland*

QUEEN MARY II

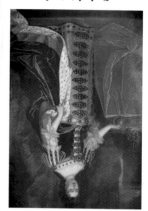

*Ruled jointly
with William III*
BORN: April 30 1662
ACCEDED: February 13
1689; crowned April 11
1689, Westminster
Abbey
*Queen of England,
Scotland and Ireland*

THE PROCLAMATION OF WILLIAM AND MARY AS JOINT MONARCHS OF ENGLAND MAY HAVE REPRESENTED A TRIUMPH FOR PROTESTANT PARLIAMENTARY SUPREMACY, BUT IT HAD NOT SEEN OFF THE CLAIMS OF JAMES II. FURTHER, THE EXPANSIONIST AIMS OF JAMES'S CHIEF SUPPORTER, LOUIS XIV, REMAINED A PERSISTENT THREAT. CONTENDING WITH BOTH WOULD PROVE THE DOMINANT THEME OF THE JOINT MONARCHY.

ALTHOUGH WILLIAM AND MARY WERE proclaimed joint monarchs in 1688, in reality ''the sole and full exercise of regal power'' was vested in William. It was an arrangement that suited both parties. Mary had little interest in government, though she agreed to act as regent during her husband's many absences abroad. For his part, even if his long-term – indeed overriding – interest was the defeat of Louis XIV's aggressively expansionist France, in the short term it was the consolidation of his Scottish and Irish thrones that was William's immediate priority.

Strictly speaking, James VII was still King of Scotland. In practice, however, the Scottish Parliament accepted the new sovereigns with only token objections, deposing James with a Claim Act that was broadly similar to England's Bill of Rights. Resistance remained, however, especially in the Catholic, pro-Stuart Highlands. In July 1689, a small force under Viscount Dundee at Killiecrankie inflicted what might have been a decisive victory over the Williamite troops, had not Dundee himself been killed in the fighting. Without his leadership, the Jacobite cause temporarily collapsed. William still insisted on extracting oaths of loyalty from the clan leaders, a policy that largely backfired with the notorious Glencoe Massacre in February 1692. When the Chief of Glencoe, Alasdair Macdonald, failed to take his oath, it was officially decided to put the Macdonalds to the sword. The resulting scandals severely dented William's popularity.

Ireland saw bloodshed on a far wider scale. As early as March 1689, James II had arrived there with 20,000 French troops. Huge numbers of Catholic Irish joined him. In May, the Irish Parliament formally declared their support for him. In December, the siege of Protestant Londonderry was begun. Six

William (left) *was never a popular figure. To some extent this was the result of inevitable English distrust of a foreigner – and of the Dutchmen he brought with him to England; as late as 1699, Parliament demanded that he expel his Dutch Blue Guards, a request the king agreed to only reluctantly. But William himself was an unprepossessing figure, short, stooped, withdrawn, and a chronic asthmatic. He had few personal interests other than hunting and gardening, his life was dominated by his single-minded determination to do down Louis XIV.*

Sweet-natured, elegant and charming, Mary (below left)*, five inches (12cm) taller than her husband, was hugely popular and much admired for her efforts to raise the moral tone of the court. Her marriage to William, arranged in the face of her father's bitter opposition, was purely a matter of state dictated by the need for Charles II to strengthen the anti-French alliance. Mary herself reacted unenthusiastically, ''weeping all afternoon and the following day''. Yet on the whole, though their marriage produced only three stillborn children, William and the dutiful Mary seem to have been well suited. She was only 32 when she died from smallpox in December 1694.*

The Tory-dominated House of Lords in particular would have preferred to make Mary sole ruler and preserve the sanctity of the divine right of succession. However, Mary herself refused, partly from guilt at having abandoned her father, James II, and not wishing to appear to have usurped his throne. William, perfectly aware of his unique opportunity to strengthen the anti-French Protestant alliance, was simply adamant that he would accept nothing less than the crown itself, asserting that he would not be ''his wife's lackey''. The picture (above) shows them on their way to the Banqueting House in February 1689 to accept their joint crowns.

1670 — *William of Orange makes first visit to England*

1672 — *Restoration of William of Orange in Holland*

1677 — *Marriage of William of Orange and Mary, daughter of the Duke of York*

1685 — *Anglo-Dutch treaty renewed*

1688 — *William signals his agreement to invade England in response to invitation by disaffected ''Immortal Seven'' (Sept.): invasion army lands at Torbay (Nov.)*

1689 — *William and Mary accept English throne as joint rulers under the Declaration of Rights. Act of Toleration allows limited religious toleration. Jacobite uprising in Scotland collapses despite victory at Killiecrankie (July). Troops sent to confront James II in Ireland (Aug.). Grand Coalition formed to confront France (Sept.): King William's War begins (to 1697)*

Forty years on from Cromwell's brutal reinforcement of Protestantism in his Irish campaign of 1649–50, William III's routing of the Catholic Irish and French army assembled by James II in Ireland just as crucially hardened the religious divide in Ireland. James II and his French allies were hardly likely to prove indulgent toward the Protestants in Ireland, as their 105-day siege of Londonderry (left) from December 1689 proved. Equally, William's defeat of James II at the Battle of the Boyne created a myth of Protestant supremacy that endures today.

WILLIAM AND MARY 1689–1702

- Accepted William as head of state by February 1689
- Accepted William as head of state by 1690
- Religious riots in Scotland, 1688
- Retained James as ruler; subdued by William's forces, 1690-1
- James II's campaigns
- Protestant strongholds successfully resisting siege by James's forces
- William's campaigns
- Other English campaigns
- French fleet from the Mediterranean, 1690
- Jacobite stronghold successfully resisting siege by William
- Conquered by William's forces, 1691
- Clans largely supporting James
- Area of William's military activities 1692-4
- Frontiers, 1689

William and Mary's joint monarchy provoked widespread conflict in Scotland and Ireland (map left). If Scottish opposition to the joint monarchs was relatively easily contained, in Ireland it gave rise to bitter fighting. William's resounding defeat of James II at the Battle of the Boyne did nothing to reduce Catholic Irish opposition to the Protestant monarchs.

months later, William himself was in Ireland with an army of Danes, Germans, Dutch and English. At the Battle of the Boyne, he led them to a resounding victory. Within three days, James had fled back to France.

Whatever the scale of his Irish victories, for William they were essentially sideshows compared with his real struggle with Louis XIV. By September 1689, the king had formed a Grand Coalition, headed by the Dutch and the English, against Louis. King William's War, as it became known, was inconclusive. The Treaty of Ryswick, which ended it in 1697, really signalled no more than a pause in the hostilities, which duly restarted in 1702. But its consequences for England were substantial. For the first time since Elizabeth I's reign, England was involved in a full-scale Continental conflict. From being a spectator of Continental wars, England was poised to become a major player. Almost as important was the foundation in 1694 of the Bank of England, intended chiefly to facilitate the financing of the war. Its long-term impact on England's burgeoning commerce would be difficult to overstate. Scarcely less important, William's long absences meant that power became further concentrated in Parliament.

William's relationship with Parliament was rarely smooth. He may have owed his position to it but he still resented the limitations it placed on him. Nevertheless, crucially, he always submitted to it – however grudgingly. More than ever it was Parliament in which ultimate authority was vested, something unmistakably underlined in 1701 with the Act of Settlement. Under this, the wholly obscure but reliably Protestant German Hanoverians were named successors to Queen Anne, William's own successor.

1690	1692	1693	1694	1696	1697	1700	1701
James II defeated by William at Battle of the Boyne	Glencoe Massacre. Naval victory over French at La Hogue	French victory over Dutch and English at Neerwinden	Foundation of the Bank of England. Jacobite plot against William foiled. Death of Mary	Further Jacobite plot foiled	Civil List Act strengthens parliamentary control over royal finances	Death of Duke of Gloucester, son of Mary's sister Anne, prompts renewed succession fears	Act of Settlement nominates Hanoverians as legal successors

ANNE 1702–14

QUEEN ANNE

PORTLY, SOMEWHAT DOUR, BUT ALWAYS CONSCIENTIOUS, ANNE PRESIDED OVER A NATION EXPANDING MILITARILY AND COMMERCIALLY. HER REIGN ALSO SAW THE GROWTH OF PARTY POLITICS OF A RECOGNIZABLY MODERN KIND. AS IMPORTANT, IN 1707 IT WITNESSED THE FORMAL UNION OF ENGLAND AND SCOTLAND. ANNE WAS THE FIRST MONARCH OF GREAT BRITAIN.

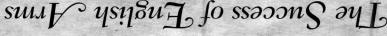

1683	1688	1692	1701	1702	1704
Marriage of Anne to George, Prince of Denmark.	Anne lends her support to invasion and subsequent succession of William and Mary, against her father, James II.	Rift between Anne and Mary over Anne's continued friendship with Sarah Churchill after temporary disgrace of Sarah's husband, John to Anne.	Act of Settlement names Dowager Duchess of Hanover as successor to Anne.	War of Spanish Succession begins.	Gibraltar captured; Churchill victorious at Battle of Blenheim. Introduction of Queen Anne's Bounty: Anne agrees to surrender traditional income from Church to support impoverished clergy.

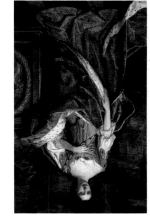

BORN: February 6 1665
ACCEDED: March 8 1702, crowned April 23 1702, Westminster Abbey
Queen of England, Scotland and Ireland; from 1707, Queen of Great Britain and Ireland

An inescapable sense of tragedy surrounds Anne (above). She was haunted by a sense of having betrayed her father, James II, however much she opposed his religious stance. In 1692, she fell out with her sister, Mary, over her continued friendship with Sarah Churchill. Her relations with William, "that Dutch monster", were hardly more cordial. Her celebrated friendship with Sarah Churchill also ended in recrimination. "I believe nobody was ever so used by a friend as I have been since coming to the Crown," wrote Anne in 1710. For her part, Sarah asserted that, "She [Anne] meant well and was no fool, but nobody can maintain that she was wise, nor entertaining in conversation."

As the younger daughter of James II, Anne had never had much realistic expectation of becoming queen. Even after the deposition of her father, it was reasonable to assume her sister, Queen Mary, would produce children. It was only the refusal of William to remarry after the death of the childless Mary in 1694 that confirmed Anne as heir. Anne herself would prove no more able to secure her succession. Though marriage to her dull-witted but amiable husband, George, Prince of Denmark, produced 18 pregnancies (one with twins), only one child, William, Duke of Gloucester, survived infancy. His death at the age of 11, reopening the possibility of a Catholic Stuart succession, provoked the Act of Settlement of 1701, which named the elderly Sophia, Dowager Duchess of Hanover, as heir to the English throne.

Scotland, where pro-Stuart sentiments still ran strong, was another matter. In 1703, the Scottish Parliament asserted its obvious right as an independent kingdom to choose its own monarch. With England now fully committed to a major European struggle against Louis XIV, the prospect of a restored Catholic Stuart King of Scotland allying himself with France in a renewed Auld Alliance became alarmingly real. The solution, a formal union of England and Scotland, may not have been popular in Scotland – backed by implied English threats of something very much less advantageous and accompanied by a huge one-off payment to Scotland – amid considerable Scottish rancour, in 1707 the Kingdom of Great Britain was born.

For England, it was just one part of a rapid consolidation as a major European power. The War of Spanish Succession, which began in 1702 and saw England in another Grand Alliance against France, produced a series of startling English victories over the French, most famously John Churchill's victory at Blenheim in 1704. Furthermore, when the war ended in 1713, Britain had acquired a string of new colonial possessions, Gibraltar among them.

If Anne's reign is generally viewed as a triumphant period of English and then British conquest and imperial expansion, it was also one of tur-

The Success of English Arms

As late as the reign of James II, England – let alone Scotland – was dismissed as scarcely even a second-rate military power in the wider European world. It was seen as effectively no more than a pensioner of Louis XIV, propped up by the French king's regular handouts to Charles II and James II. Even under William III, when England found itself re-engaged in Continental warfare, its military impact was less than formidable. But the remarkable victories enjoyed by the English in the War of Spanish Succession, above all under the generalship of John Churchill, created Duke of Marlborough in 1702, were of a kind and scale that had not been known since the reign of Henry V in the early 15th century.

The war may have turned into one of colonial conquest, but for England it began principally as a means to prevent Louis XIV's renewed sponsorship of James II's son, James Stuart, the "Old Pretender." But from at least 1708 onwards, there was a growing tide of Tory opinion in England against the war as a result of its prodigious cost, which by its end in 1713 was £150 million. Nonetheless, Britain's growing military and naval prowess was being unmistakably established.

The Battle of Malplaquet, 1709.

The emergence of England, after 1707 of Great Britain, as a major European power was clearly signalled in Anne's reign (map right). The union of England and Scotland was in itself a significant step, one which would transform Scotland's hitherto secondary position. As important was the startling success of English and British arms in Europe.

ANNE 1702–14

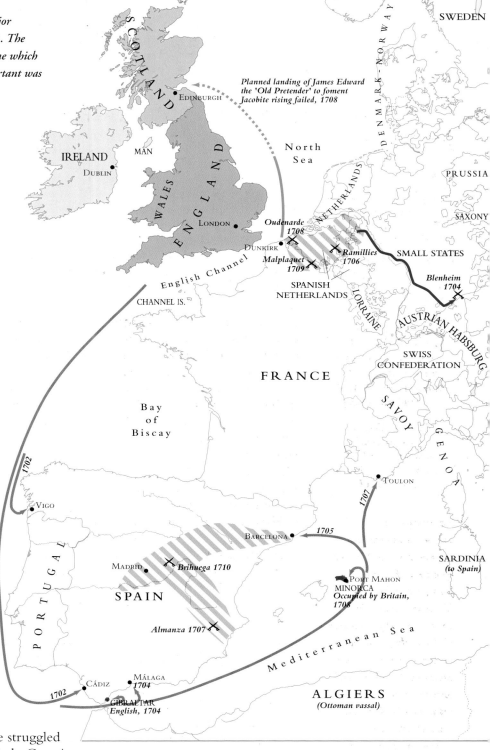

Great Britain from 1707

English, later British, dependencies

English/British naval activities during the Spanish War of Succession

Marlborough's campaign 1704

Other theatres of English/British campaigns

Awarded to Britain under Treaty of Utrecht, 1713

Frontiers, 1702

Charles II memorably said of Anne's husband, George (below), Prince of Denmark: "I have tried him drunk and I have tried him sober, and there is nothing in him." To most only a dolt, to Anne he was "an inestimable treasure". Their greatest sadness was their failure to produce healthy children. Anne had 13 stillborn children and at least one miscarriage. With the death in 1710 of their only surviving child, William, the Protestant Stuart succession ended.

bulent political division, something with which Anne struggled to come to terms. In many ways it was hardly her fault. Constitutional monarchy of the kind that was rapidly evolving was quite new. The rules could only be made up as everyone went along. If the queen's initial public preference was for a government drawn from all shades of political opinion, her natural instinct was to favour the Tories, still the party of a strong monarchy. However, she was rapidly forced to confront the reality of aggressive Whig political power, which pushed not only for a continuation of what was proving an extremely expensive war, but also for further limits on the Crown prerogatives. In the end, anti-war sentiments in the country at large saw a return in 1710 to a Tory administration, headed by Robert Harley and Henry St John. It was they who secured the Treaty of Utrecht in 1713, which for the time being ended the long struggle against France.

The final years of Anne's reign were blighted by ill-health. The queen was not only in permanent pain, her corpulence was such she could scarcely walk and often had to be moved with pulleys. At her death, her doctor touchingly wrote: "I believe sleep was never more welcome to a weary traveller than death was to her."

Her Majesty was labouring under a fit of the gout, and in extreme pain and agony ... Her face, which was red and spotted, was rendered something frightful by her negligent dress, and the foot affected was tied up with a poultice and some nasty bandages ... Nature seems inverted when a poor infirm woman becomes one of the rulers of the world.

Sir John Clerk on Queen Anne in 1707

1705	1707	1708	1710	1711	1713
Moderate Whig government elected. Former royal manor at Woodstock granted to John Churchill; Anne persuades Parliament to approve £240,000 for building of a palace there	Act of Union: England and Scotland formally united to create Kingdom of Great Britain	General Election confirms Whig dominance. Death of Anne's husband, George	Tory government elected on wave of anti-war feeling	Rift with Sarah Churchill confirmed with her dismissal from royal duties	Treaty of Utrecht ends war with France and confirms British colonial gains

GREAT BRITAIN AND IRELAND: THE HANOVERIANS 1714–1917

GEORGE I 1714–27

GEORGE II 1727–60

GEORGE III 1760–1820

GEORGE IV 1820–30

WILLIAM IV 1830–37

VICTORIA 1837–1901

EDWARD VII 1901–10

IN DECLARING "THE MOST EXCELLENT PRINCESS SOPHIA, ELECTRESS AND DOWAGER DUCHESS OF HANOVER" THE LEGAL HEIR TO THE THRONE OF ENGLAND UNDER THE *ACT OF SETTLEMENT* IN 1701, PARLIAMENT SET ASIDE NO FEWER THAN 57 STUARTS WITH BETTER HEREDITARY CLAIMS. AS A GRANDDAUGHTER OF JAMES I, SOPHIA COULD LAY AT LEAST SOME CLAIM TO THE LINE OF SUCCESSION. BUT THAT AN OTHERWISE OBSCURE GERMAN PRINCESS SHOULD BE SO DRAMATICALLY ACCELERATED TO THE HEAD OF THE QUEUE EMPHATICALLY UNDERLINED, EVEN MORE THAN IN 1689, THAT THE CHOICE OF MONARCH WAS NOW THE GIFT OF PARLIAMENT RATHER THAN A MATTER OF DIVINE-RIGHT HEREDITARY SUCCESSION.

The selection of Sophia as the successor to Queen Anne had been dictated by an absolute imperative in Protestant England: that of preventing a Catholic Stuart succession. Put simply, however far removed from the main line of succession, Sophia and her family were the closest decently Protestant heirs available. Further, unlike many of the Stuarts proper, they were prolific. Sophia herself had six sons.

Barring calamities, the Protestant succession looked guaranteed.

Even the Hanoverians' most obvious drawback – that they were foreigners speaking not a word of English – could be turned to advantage, as it made them dependent on English advisors and thus unlikely to meddle in the affairs of Parliament. It may not be true that under the new arrangement the accession of "a deaf-mute would not have been entirely amiss": the power of the Crown remained formidable. But there is no question that the Hanoverian succession was a decisive step towards a limited constitutional monarchy.

In fact Sophia died first (at the age of 83), albeit only two months before Anne herself. Parliament, however, had already prudently taken care to make Sophia's eldest son, Georg Augustus, an English subject in 1705. Thus with the death of Queen Anne on August 1 1714, the British throne passed to the man immediately proclaimed "George I, King of Great Britain, France and Ireland". However improbably, Britain found itself ruled by a native German dynasty, the Hanoverians. An enforced change of family name aside (under George V in 1917), it persists today. As a mark of this profound German influence, and even as the Hanoverians themselves became more obviously English, every single Hanoverian monarch until Edward VII in 1901 was married to a German.

That said, historically it makes little sense to treat the British monarchy from 1714 to the present as an unbroken whole. The changes in Britain between the accession of George I in 1714 and that of Victoria in 1837 – a period in which Britain was raised from first among equals in Europe to being the world's leading power – were necessarily reflected in the status of its monarchy. For, over this period, the monarchy was transformed from a semi-divinely ordained office, albeit increasingly answerable to Parliament, to a constitutional monarchy of an ever more limited kind.

In much the same way, as Britain became definitively the world's leading power in the long reign of Victoria, so its monarchy underwent a further transformation. As royal prerogative was forced to give way to final parliamentary supremacy – with Victoria, however reluctantly, stepping across the invisible but real line between ruling and reigning – so the monarchy, whatever its importance as symbol of the world's premier state, was increasingly boxed in. To all intents and purposes, by Victoria's death in 1901 constitutional monarchy on a recognizably modern model had come into being.

All of this was very different from the world of the early Hanoverians. George I, irascible, vain and dull, may have been little more than a bad-tempered link between the last of the Stuarts and the emergence of a new, aggressively colonizing Britain. But like his heir, George II, he nonetheless had to contend not just with the reality of a monarchy increasingly answerable to parliamentary party politics but with the after-shocks of the overthrow of James II in 1689. Although they were the most serious, the Jacobite risings in 1715 and 1745 were not the only manifestations of a long-standing Stuart threat to the security of Protestant Hanoverian Britain, albeit one effectively ended with the failure of the 1745 uprising.

If George II could subsequently console himself with having presided over a massive extension of British colonial rule, his successor, George III, who could at least speak English without a German accent, had to confront the equally unmistakable and very much less palatable reality of the loss of Britain's American colonies. It is a measure of Britain's growing standing in the 18th-century world that the monarchy itself, whatever George III's unsuccessful attempts to dictate the composition of his governments, emerged largely unscathed from the American disaster. Ultimately, however, his reign would be blighted by madness, the king reduced to a slobbering ruin, at the mercy of misguided doctors inflicting a series of pointless and humiliating cures.

Even with the Regency and subsequent reign of George IV, unquestionably Britain's most dissolute monarch as well as, when sober, the most talented and artistically minded of the Hanoverians, the monarchy prospered. Britain by now, as confirmed by its defeat of Napoleon, was so clearly a world power that its throne could scarcely fail to reflect its extravagant glory.

Yet a profound change was in the offing. Unwilling or not, Victoria, 18 when she came to the throne in 1837, 81 when she died in 1901, presided over a fundamental redefinition of monarchy. As her actual powers were surrendered and with them any suggestion of an active political role, so her symbolic importance as personification – and hence ultimate guarantor – of the legitimacy and stability of the British state and its empire grew. Accident or not, an entirely new concept of monarch as constitutional symbol had been created.

GEORGE I 1714–27

GEORGE I WAS NEVER A POPULAR KING. BAD-TEMPERED, UNCOUTH AND SPEAKING ONLY THE MOST LIMITED ENGLISH, TO HIS SUBJECTS HE WAS THE BOORISH FOREIGNER PERSONIFIED. HIS ATTEMPTS TO INVOLVE BRITAIN IN HANOVERIAN INTERESTS ALSO DID LITTLE TO ENDEAR HIM TO HIS BRITISH SUBJECTS. BUT HIS BRIEF REIGN SAW THE SUCCESSFUL CONSOLIDATION OF THE PROTESTANT HANOVERIANS AND THE FURTHER REINFORCEMENT OF PARLIAMENTARY GOVERNMENT.

King George I

Duke and Elector of Hanover, King of Great Britain and Ireland

BORN: June 7 1660, Hanover
ACCEDED: August 1 1714; crowned October 20 1714, Westminster Abbey

ALMOST THE FIRST ACT OF GEORGE I ON becoming King of Britain in early August 1714 was to declare himself, on his own authority, King of Hanover, a title that would not be recognized elsewhere until 100 years later. He then set off on a leisurely and triumphant progress through Germany, arriving in England only at the very end of September. At 54, he was the oldest ever successor to the English throne.

From the start, he struggled with his new kingdom, finding its customs and habits almost as irksome as the limitations that were imposed on his royal pre-rogative by Parliament. Whereas in Hanover he had

enjoyed almost unlimited power – all expenditure over £13 had to be personally approved by him – in England he found himself constantly thwarted by Parliament. In truth, almost anyone might have struggled to find their feet in the confused, often venomous political climate of early 18th-century Britain. Party politics on the British model were unknown elsewhere. As a non-English speaker, reliant on his son George to translate for him or otherwise forced to speak to his ministers in French, occasionally in Latin, it is hardly to be wondered at if the impatient George I was often out of his depth.

The king's own preference was firmly for the Whigs, a view that helped push a number of Tories into the Jacobite camp, in the process guaranteeing their continued political exclusion, especially with the failure of the Jacobite Rebellion of 1715 (see pp. 160-1). That said, relations between the king and the Whigs were rarely harmonious. Nonetheless, by 1717 George had managed to engineer a more pliant administration – evidence of the still formidable prerogative of the throne – in the process driving the most ambitious and able of the Whigs, Robert Walpole, into the orbit of the Prince of Wales, whose relations with his father, never good, had now broken down almost entirely.

This stand-off was transformed in September 1720 with the spectacular collapse of the South Sea Company, a private venture set up nine years earlier to take over the spiralling National Debt. In 1718 the king had been made governor of the company, so it was with more than just suspicion that the court and government were directly implicated in the greed-driven scandal. Thousands saw their entire investments lost, and the resulting crisis – unquestionably the most serious of George I's reign and actively inflamed by the Jacobites – threatened to bring the Hanoverian dynasty to a sudden end.

George I (above) at least had the virtue of consistency. His most serious failing was his bad temper. In 1694, he discovered his wife, Sophia Dorothea, then 28, was having an affair with a Swedish soldier, Philip von Königsmark. The Swede disappeared, reputedly after George had him hacked to death. For her part, Sophia Dorothea was divorced and incarcerated for life in the Castle of Ahlden. She remained there, forbidden to see her children, until her death 32 years later. It was this treatment of his mother, which shocked Europe, that led to the life-long rift between George and his son, the future George II. At the same time, the king had two publicly acknowledged mistresses. One, Sophia Charlotte, was widely rumoured to be the king's half-sister; in later life she became extremely fat, so much so that she and the king were known as the Elephant and Castle. The other, whom the king was believed to have married in secret, was Ehrengard Melusine von Schulenburg, as thin as her rival was fat. They were described, memorably, as, "old, ugly trulls, such as would not find entertainment in the most hospitable hundreds of old Drury."

The "South Sea Bubble" in September 1720 came close to bringing down the Hanoverians. Though the scheme was not fraudulent when launched, the need to gain political backing for the scheme, essentially by offering stock at artificially low prices to politicians and members of the court, subsequently took it perilously close to illegality. The crisis itself was caused by huge paper profits that rapidly led to a feeding frenzy as others demanded to be let in. Prices were pushed sky high until, as suddenly, they disintegrated, leaving a handful of lucky investors sitting on large fortunes but the vast majority all but wiped out. Hardly surprisingly, there was a widespread demand that someone should be punished, a demand that the more Jacobite Tories were only too keen to encourage. The court's obvious involvement with the scheme made it a natural target. This engraving (right) caricatures the transformation of the "Great South Sea Caterpillar" into a butterfly.

The great South Sea Caterpillar Transformed into a Bath Butterfly

1682	1698	1714	1715	1716
Marriage of Georg Augustus to Sophia Dorothea of Celle	Georg Augustus becomes Elector of Hanover	Georg Augustus accedes to British throne as George I. Arrives in London (Sept.)	Jacobite Rebellion (Sept.) suppressed. Discredited Tory administration gives way to Whigs	Tory hopes of rapid return to government thwarted by Septennial Act, under which elections are to be held only every seven years

Hanover, ruled by George since 1697

Great Britain and dependencies, 1714

Added to Hanover, 1715

Frontiers, 1714

------ Frontier of the Holy Roman Empire, 1714

The accession of the otherwise obscure elector of Hanover as king of Great Britain and Ireland in 1714 was the clearest possible evidence that it was Parliament who made and unmade monarchs now. It was a crucial moment in the history of British kingship (map right).

Sir Robert Walpole (above) was the first recognizably modern politician, a master of patronage and a brilliant manipulator of party political advantage. If George I initially resented him for his Whig sympathies, he as soon came to value him for his crisis management after the South Sea Company collapse. George I can hardly be said to have wittingly encouraged the development of party political government, but his willingness to allow Walpole his head after 1720 was crucial to the further consolidation of parliamentary supremacy.

An honest, dull German gentleman, as unfit as unwilling to act the part of a king ... lazy and inactive, even in his pleasures, which were therefore lowly sensual ... England was too big for him.

Lord Chesterfield on George I

An honest blockhead ... our customs and laws were all mysteries to him, which he neither tried to understand, nor was capable of understanding.

Lady Mary Wortley Montagu on George I

Walpole's supreme ability as a political fixer not only calmed the panic, in the process reconciling him with the king (who thereafter came to regard him as indispensable), it also cemented his position as the dominant political figure of the age. With his appointment as First Lord of the Treasury in 1721, he emerged, in effect, as the country's first Prime Minister. A long period of Whig hegemony was begun.

Thoroughly alarmed by the crisis and with Walpole so obviously capable, the king went to ground politically. The last years of his reign were given over to the modest pleasures of his placid court: gardening (at Hampton Court and Kensington Palace preeminently), card playing, horses, and his mistresses. Whenever possible, he also visited Hanover, where it is clear he was most at home and where, in June 1727, he died and was buried.

1717	1720	1721	1722
Near permanent rift between George I and Prince of Wales. Walpole ousted; Tories under Lord Stanhope clear way for George I's anti-Russian alliance with France and Holland	Collapse of South Sea Company – the "South Sea Bubble" – implicates king and court. George I forced into reconciliation with Walpole and Prince of Wales. Royal Academy of Music established under patronage of George I	Walpole made First Lord of the Treasury, effectively Prime Minister	Jacobite "Atterbury Plot" foiled

The Jacobite Uprisings 1689–1745

WHATEVER THE GROWING POWER OF PROTESTANT BRITAIN, IT WAS PERSISTENTLY THREATENED BY EFFORTS TO ENGINEER A STUART RESTORATION. UNTIL THE MIDDLE OF THE 18TH CENTURY, THERE WERE REPEATED STUART ATTEMPTS, CHIEFLY AIDED BY FRANCE, TO REGAIN WHAT THEY CONSIDERED THEIR LEGITIMATE THRONES IN ENGLAND, SCOTLAND AND IRELAND. THE TWO MOST SUSTAINED CHALLENGES WERE MOUNTED IN 1715 AND 1745.

HE YEARS BETWEEN THE ACCESSION OF WILLIAM III AND Mary II in 1689 and the Hanoverian succession in 1714 were an aggressive statement of intent about the future of Protestant parliamentary government in England. But if England had decisively turned its back on Stuart Catholic abso-lutism, the Stuarts were no less determined to regain their thrones and to overthrow a constitutional settlement that was considered by the exiled James II to be ''contrary to the law of God, nature and the nation''. After 1689, the Jacobite cause – from the Latin Jacobus, meaning James – became one of the most persistent and important features of European politics as well as the most serious danger to post-1688 order in England.

Stuart efforts centred on three figures: James II, the ousted king of England and Scotland; then, after James's death in 1701, his son, the ''Old Pretender'', also called James; and in turn, his son, Charles, the ''Young Pretender''. Their motives were straightforward and consistent: to return to a throne usurped in 1689. Their supporters, on the other hand, always acted for a more mixed variety of reasons. Consistently the most important, and the major source of funds and men to the Jacobites, was the France of Louis XIV and his successor, Louis XV. Certainly, defending the legitimacy of fellow absolutist Catholic monarchs was a factor that weighed heavily with the French crown. But more important in French eyes was the potential of the Jacobites to destabilize England, which by the early 18th century had emerged as its major European rival. Catholic Spain was a similar if less consistent supporter of the Jacobites: Franco-Spanish rivalry ruled out sustained Spanish support.

In Ireland, other than in the now Protestant north, and in Scotland, above all in the still largely Catholic Highlands, Jacobite support was widespread. If the survival of Catholicism in these areas was the prime factor, anti-English feeling and, for the Scots, loyalty to what was originally a native Scottish dynasty were similarly significant. Indeed by the early 18th century, resentment against England would make Scotland the overwhelming focus of the Jacobite cause. Such resentment was reinforced by the Act of Union in 1707, bitterly objected to by most Scots, and by the Hanoverian succession of George I, ''the wee, German laddie'', in 1714.

Hardly surprisingly, English Jacobites were much thinner on the ground, though even here growing dislike of the ''foreign'' dynasties of William and Mary and of the Hanoverians, particularly their pursuit of Continental wars at English expense, gave rise to a growing Jacobite camp. With the Hanoverian succession, the Tories in par-ticular, who had always harboured doubts about the legitimacy of the settlement in 1689, came to see a Stuart restoration as increasingly desirable, if only to offset George I's obvious anti-Tory prejudice.

The first attempts at a Stuart restoration – in Ireland in 1689 and

massively underwritten by Louis XIV – were crushingly defeated by William III at the Battle of the Boyne in 1690 (see pp.153). Remaining Irish resistance was mopped up by John Churchill the following year at Aughrim. The subsequent Treaty of Limerick effectively ended Jacobite ambitions in Ireland, though it also allowed an Irish army – the ''Wild Geese'', aptly described as a ''Jacobite army-in-waiting'' – to leave for France. It was this ''Irish Brigade'' that formed the nucleus of two further French-sponsored attempt-ed Jacobite invasions of England in 1692 and in 1696. Neither came to anything, despite the numbers involved. The former collapsed when the Royal Navy destroyed the French ships assembled for the invasion at La Hogue. The latter, scuppered by a falling out between Louis XIV and English Jacobites, never got further than Calais. Louis was far from finished. On the death of James II, he provocatively recognized James's son as James III of England and

James Stuart (left), the soi-disant James III and VIII, was an uninspiring figure, dour, gloomy and dutiful. His loyalty to the Jacobite cause, like his Catholicism, was unquestioned, his capacity to inspire it all but non-existent. During his sole, depressing visit to Scotland in the abortive uprising at the end of 1715, a Jacobite reported: ''Our men asked if he could speak.'' With the failure of the rebellion, he abandoned further attempts to regain his thrones, living in Rome in a state of ''pious melancholy''. The poet Thomas Gray said of him in 1740 that he ''... the air and look of an idiot, particularly when he laughs or prays. The first he does not often, the latter continually.''

James VIII of Scotland. In 1708, he sent 18,000 troops to Scotland under the nominal command of James where they were intended to join forces with a Scottish Jacobite army 30,000 strong. In the end, the Scottish Jacobites never materialized while the French, meeting an English fleet, turned back in sight of the Scottish coast. In December 1715, by contrast, the Old Pretender at least made it on to Scottish soil. It was already too late, however. A planned invasion of the West Country in September had been abandoned almost as soon as it began while a simultaneous Jacobite uprising in northern England was similarly ineffective. Undeterred, the Earl of Mar pressed ahead with the main revolt in Scotland, seizing a series of towns before narrowly avoiding defeat by a much smaller Hanoverian force at Sheriffmuir in November. Thereafter, despite

1689	1690	1691	1692	1696	1697	1701	1702	1707
Scottish Jacobite army under Viscount Dundee defeated by Williamite forces at Killiecrankie	Franco-Irish Jacobite army under James II defeated by William III in Ireland after the Battle of Boyne	Williamite victory over Irish Jacobites at Aughrim followed by Irish political settlement under Treaty of Limerick	Glencoe Massacre. French-sponsored Jacobite invasion halted after English naval victory at La Hogue	Further French-sponsored Jacobite invasion fails to leave France	Treaty of Ryswick signals temporary Anglo-French rapprochement	Death of James II in France; successor recognized by Louis XIV as James III and VIII	War of Spanish Succession: renewed Anglo-French conflict (to 1713) increases Jacobite tension	Act of Union between England and Scots fuels anti-English Scottish Jacobite sentiments

Though lavishly supported by the French, the Jacobite uprising of 1715 (map right) was a complete failure. James Stuart himself, the "Old Pretender", proved a dour, uninspiring figure, incapable of generating either loyalty or enthusiasm for the Stuart cause. His brief stay in Scotland only confirmed the paucity of his military talents.

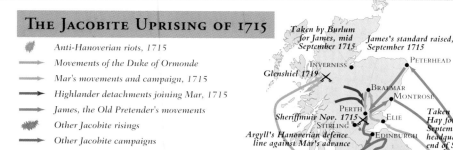

THE JACOBITE UPRISING OF 1715

- Anti-Hanoverian riots, 1715
- Movements of the Duke of Ormonde
- Mar's movements and campaign, 1715
- Highlander detachments joining Mar, 1715
- James, the Old Pretender's movements
- Other Jacobite risings
- Other Jacobite campaigns

Taken by Burlum for James, mid September 1715
James's standard raised, September 1715
PETERHEAD
INVERNESS
Glenshiel 1719 ✕
BRAEMAR
MONTROSE
Taken by Colonel Hay for James, mid September; Mar's headquarters from end of September 1715
PERTH
Sheriffmuir Nov. 1715 ✕
STIRLING ELIE
EDINBURGH
Argyll's Hanoverian defence line against Mar's advance
Burlum's advance, October 1715
Thomas Forster M.P., October 1715
Viscount Kenmure, September 1715
CARLISLE NEWCASTLE
February 1716
GREAT
IRELAND
York
DUBLIN
Preston November 1715 ✕
CHESTER
BRITAIN
NORWICH
COVENTRY NORTHAMPTON
OXFORD
CARDIFF BRISTOL LONDON
1719
EXETER
August 1715
Landing attempts failed, October and December 1715
From Lorraine
FRANCE
December 1715

the belated arrival of James, who spent six increasingly gloomy weeks in Scotland, the uprising fizzled into nothing. But if it was easily suppressed in the end, it had nonetheless caused considerable alarm in England. The reprisals, fully supported by George I, were relentless, just as they would be after 1745.

The Jacobites had suffered a simultaneous set back in 1715 with the death of Louis XIV, for so long the mainstay of the Stuart cause. French championship of the Jacobites increasingly became a matter of lip service. The Stuart court in France, 3,000 strong and maintained entirely at French expense, was turning into an expensive embarrassment to its hosts.

The Spanish subsequently took up the running, in 1719 launching a substantial fleet with weapons for 30,000 Scots Jacobites. It made it only as far as Coruña in northern Spain before being forced back by a gale. Thereafter, despite a minor Jacobite

Where his father was pedestrian, Charles Stuart (shown here, right, at only 12), at least when leading the 1745 Jacobite Rebellion, was dashing and heroic. But if his capacity to inspire loyalty was undoubted, his political and military talents were slim at best, the product of a naivety and optimism that led, in 1746, to the extermination of his army at Culloden. His life thereafter degenerated into indolence and sloth. He was, it was said, "never quite sober".

By the time the Young Pretender had led his hastily raised army south to Derby, the Stuart cause suddenly looked as though it might after all succeed (map right). In the event, isolated and uncertain, the Scots turned back to what, in the spring of 1746, would prove a crushing defeat.

uprising in England in 1722 – the Atterbury Plot – the Jacobite cause languished before reviving briefly and, for a moment gloriously, in 1745. It was the final and, in the end, futile Jacobite flourish.

The 1745 Jacobite Rebellion was led by the youthful, charismatic Young Pretender – Bonnie Prince Charlie – who landed in Scotland in July 1745 with just seven men. Charles's rallying of the clans and subsequent march into England promised much. Panic in London aside, it delivered nothing. By the time Derby had been reached, it was clear that far from outflanking the pursuing Hanoverians Charles had merely isolated himself in enemy territory. Dispirited and increasingly bedraggled, the remnants of his army returned to Scotland. The following year, it was annihilated at Culloden. Five months later, Charles escaped to France.

The Jacobites would not finally abandon their claim to their thrones until the death of Charles's younger brother, the titular Henry IX, in 1807. But after 1745 their cause had become little more than an exercise in nostalgia.

Culloden April 1746
INVERNESS
Cope, Aug. 1745
Cumberland, April 1746
Eriskay
ABERDEEN
GLENFINNAN
James's standard raised, August 1745
MONTROSE
HIGHLAND
PERTH
STIRLING EDINBURGH
Falkirk June 1746
GLASGOW DUNBAR
Gladsmuir (Prestonpans) Sept. 1745
DUMFRIES
GREAT
CARLISLE
NEWCASTLE
Cumberland, in pursuit of Charles Edward to Perth
French support to Charles Edward Jan. 1746
PRESTON
YORK
IRELAND
MANCHESTER
DUBLIN
Cumberland, December 1745
DERBY
LICHFIELD
NORWICH
COVENTRY
NORTHAMPTON
Charles Edward, From Nantes, June 1745
BRITAIN
CARDIFF
LONDON
BRISTOL
French expedition to support planned Jacobite rising aborted due to bad weather, 1744
DUNKIRK
EXETER
THE JACOBITE UPRISING OF 1745
Elisabeth carrying troops and supplies as part of Charles Edward's campaign damaged in engagement with Captain Brett; forced to return, June 1745
FRANCE

- Campaigns from France in support of/by Jacobites, with details
- Charles Edward's advance
- Charles Edward's retreat from England and further campaigning in Scotland
- Area strongly supporting Charles Edward
- Hanoverian campaigns, with details

1708	1715	1719	1722	1745	1746	1766	1788
Attempted French-sponsored invasion reaches Scotland but is deterred by English fleet	Major Jacobite uprising in Scotland under Earl of Mar (Sept.); Old Pretender lands Scotland (Dec.) but returns to France after six weeks	Spanish-backed invasion turns back near Coruña	Jacobite Atterbury Plot in England foiled	Young Pretender lands in Scotland (July) and rallies clans; takes Edinburgh (Sept.); Derby reached (early Dec.)	Young Pretender defeated at Culloden (Apr.); escapes to France (Sept.)	Death of Old Pretender; Jacobites declare Charles III titular king of England and Scotland	Death of Young Pretender; succeeded by titular Henry IX (dies 1807)

Projections of Royalty: *Two*

THE CONSTITUTIONAL BASIS OF BRITAIN'S MONARCHY MAY HAVE BEEN TRANSFORMED BY THE HANOVERIAN SUCCESSION IN 1714, BUT OFFICIAL IMAGES OF ROYALTY SCARCELY CHANGED AT ALL. WINTERHALTER'S 19TH-CENTURY PORTRAITS OF VICTORIA ARE RECOGNIZABLY IN THE SAME TRADITION AS VAN DYCK'S 17TH-CENTURY PORTRAITS OF CHARLES I. BUT THE COURT ITSELF IN THE SAME PERIOD CHANGED DRAMATICALLY.

G IVEN THE RICHNESS OF VAN DYCK'S heroic images of Charles I, as influential elsewhere in Europe as in Britain, it is no surprise that well into the 19th century essentially the same 17th-century pictorial language was being used in official portraits of monarchs and their families. The talents of later court artists may not always have matched those of Van Dyck but their debt to his large-scale, dramatic, heavily idealized images was undoubted.

However, despite this enduring approach to royal portraiture, the public profile of the monarch and his court was changing. Where once the court, with the monarch at its heart, had formed the absolute centre of the nation's political and social being, after 1689 it increasingly became something of a side-show. To a considerable extent, this was a natural reflection of the changed political realities after 1689 and the diminishing of royal power in favour of Parliament. As a result, the court's place as the natural hub of political gossip, intrigue and advancement was gradually taken over: not just by Parliament but by the aristocratic houses in London and elsewhere and, from the early 18th century, the capital's coffee shops and clubs, each with its own political affiliation. The political centre of gravity was shifting irreversibly

The trend began with the accession of William III in 1689. Close, secretive and above all a foreigner, he had little taste for the high drama of court life. Partly, too, as a result of his asthma, which made London uncongenial to him, he was always more at home in the relatively modest surroundings of rural Kensington Palace, bought by him and Queen Mary in 1689. Even in the much grander Hampton Court, he and Mary occupied no more than a handful of rooms. But the public projection of the joint Protestant monarchs was a very different matter, nowhere more strikingly demonstrated than on the ceiling frescoes of the Great Hall at Christopher Wren's new Royal Naval Hospital at Greenwich. The visual language of building and ceiling alike is Baroque, pure and unadulterated. If this was a style that originally, in Rome and later in France, was associated with Catholicism and absolutism, above all at Louis XIV's Versailles, here it is just as emphatically pressed into service on behalf of the Protestant, parliamentary cause. In James Thornhill's great ceiling, William, resplendently enthroned, holds out the cap of liberty to Europe while

This noticeably lower public profile of the court also reflected the tastes and aspirations of the country's new monarchs, above all a marked preference for the domestic over the ceremonial. Where once the monarch had essentially lived in public, increasingly he began to live in private

Family of George III, by Johann Zoffany, c.1770

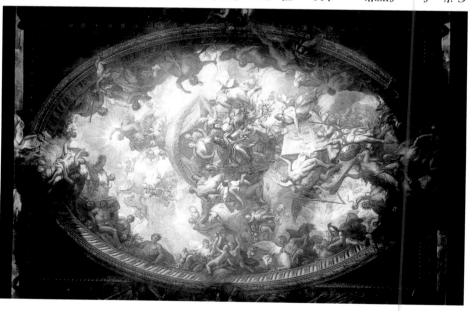

Ceiling fresco of William and Mary, The Painted Hall, Greenwich, by James Thornhill, 1700.

trampling tyranny, holding a broken sword, underfoot. The king is no less omniscient than his Stuart forebears but it is tolerance, freedom and prudence he now champions

Neither of the first two Georges made much effort to enhance the majesty of their office. Both took over their palaces if not reluctantly then at least rather like temporary tenants, doing little or nothing to extend or renovate them. Under George II in particular, whether at Windsor or Hampton Court, court life settled into a round of tedious decorum that Charles II for one would have found unrecognizable.

Perhaps not surprisingly under a monarch whose main interest was farming, George III's court was every bit as domestic, almost frugal. His new London home, Buckingham House, bought by him in 1762, was graceful, but it was no Versailles. It was only in the 19th century that most of the alterations that produced today's much grander palace were undertaken. In very much the same spirit, George III's queen, Charlotte, had a marked preference for the still smaller Kew Palace

Nonetheless, whatever their personal tastes, portraits of the king and queen continued to reflect the Baroque image of royalty established in the 17th century. Johann Zoffany, otherwise a brilliant exponent of a new domestic style of portraiture, went so far as to portray the royal family in full 17th-century garb. His portrait of George III, the queen and the first six of their children, painted in the 1770s, is conceived in terms almost indistinguishable from those of his 17th-century predecessors. This is a heroic vision of royalty that would not have disappointed Charles I.

The shining exception to this otherwise persistent Hanoverian preference for domesticity over public ceremony was provided by George IV. As portrayed by Thomas Lawrence in 1822, the king is the epitome of self-conscious, heroic monarchy. Given the painter's unpromising subject matter – an overweight and debauched middle-aged man – Lawrence's achievements in transforming the prince are unmatched. Yet it was even more as a patron of architecture that George IV excelled, both as prince and king. His

King George IV by Thomas Lawrence, 1822

lavish building projects, at Carlton House, Buckingham Palace, which he had extensively enlarged and rebuilt by John Nash, Windsor Castle, if anything even more substantially transformed, and above all at the Brighton Pavilion testify not just to an exceptional natural taste but to a relentless desire to transform the grandeur of the monarchy's setting. It was a remarkable and enduring legacy which by itself is enough to justify his otherwise indolent reign. Britain's constitutional monarchy may have lost its political power but its majesty was being incomparably enhanced.

To this extent at least the glamorous portraits of the young Victoria and her family by another German painter, Winterhalter, at least reflected a court setting that was now as grand as its official imagery. In fact, no one could mistake Winterhalter for Van Dyke. Just as much a virtuoso and no less concerned to emphasize the iconic status of the royal family, he was equally determined to give Victoria and her family a new human face. His great achievement was to reconcile these two apparent opposites. Winterhalter made Hanoverian domesticity majestic.

Family of Queen Victoria by Franz Xavier Winterhalter, 1840s

1867	1868	1871	1872	1874	1876
Second Reform Bill. Canada given independent dominion status	Disraeli's first Conservative administration; Gladstone's first Liberal administration (to 1874)	High point of Republican movement	Albert Memorial completed	Disraeli's second Conservative administration (to 1880)	Victoria created Empress of India

The expansion of empire under Victoria (map below) made Britain not just the world's pre-eminent industrial power, at least until the 1870s, but unquestionably its greatest colonial power. If it was in Africa that the greatest expansion of British colonial rule occurred, mostly after 1880, India, whose empress the queen became in 1876, remained the most important colonial possession.

single-handedly rewrote the rules governing it. From the self-indulgent shambles of George IV and William IV's reigns, Albert deliberately set out to re-create the British Crown as impartial, moral and above reproach, an arbitrator in the country's political life and a model of responsible behaviour for its people. This was monarchy redrafted on a hugely ambitious scale.

Albert's achievement was all the more remarkable given that Victoria, for all that her devotion to him knew no bounds, initially assumed he had to be kept in the background. So far as she was concerned, he may have been her husband but he was certainly not the monarch. Further, whatever her own German background, as a German himself Albert was necessarily somewhat adrift when he first arrived in England. That he should so successfully have won the confidence not just of the queen but of her ministers, in the process making himself king in all but name, was a triumph of startling proportions. When he died in 1861, aged only 42, the queen was inconsolable. Yet though she could not have known it, she was little more than a third of the way through her reign. There was nothing forced about the long years of Victoria's mourning for Albert. Her grief was never less than real. But for the queen to

No royal consort has been mourned with the single-minded devotion Victoria lavished on the memory of her husband. There was something almost sinister in the passionate intensity of Victoria's grief. It also became increasingly dangerous. What after all was the point of an expensive monarchy if it refused to show itself in public? Here (far right) she poses with her second daughter, Princess Alice, in front of a bust of Albert in a photograph taken in 1862.

Queen Victoria on the death of Prince Albert, December 14 1861

I took his dear left hand which was already cold ... and knelt down by him ... All, all was over; I stood up and kissed his dear heavenly forehead & called out in a bitter and agonizing cry, "Oh! My dear darling!" and then dropped on my knees in mute distracted despair, unable to utter a word or shed a tear! ... Then I laid down on the sofa in the Red Room, & all the gentleman came in and knelt down & kissed my hand, & I said a word to each.

BRITISH COLONIAL EXPANSION UNDER VICTORIA, 1837–1901

- British-held territory, 1837 that remained British by the end of Victoria's rule
- Territory/claim given up during Victoria's rule (with date)
- Added to British control during Victoria's rule
- Frontiers of British possessions, 1901

NEW ZEALAND
NORFOLK I.
TONGA
FIJI
SOLOMON IS.
ELLICE IS.
OCEAN I.
GILBERT IS.
AUSTRALIA Commonwealth, 1901
BRITISH NEW GUINEA
COCOS IS.
SINGAPORE
SARAWAK
BRUNEI
BR. NORTH BORNEO
MALAYA
NICOBAR IS.
CEYLON
MALDIVE IS.
SEYCHELLES
CHAGOS
MAURITIUS
ZANZIBAR
ANDAMAN IS.
LACCADIVE IS.
BRITISH SOMALILAND
SOCOTRA
HADHRAMAUT
MURIA IS.
KURIA
ADEN
OMAN
TRUCIAL OMAN
BAHRAIN
KUWAIT
BURMA
BHUTAN
BRITISH INDIA
INDIA Empire, 1876
WENANWEH
HONG KONG
UGANDA
BRITISH EAST AFRICA
NORTH EAST RHODESIA
SOUTHERN NIGERIA
NORTHERN NIGERIA
ANGLO-EGYPTIAN SUDAN
EGYPT
Ottoman dominions under British control
Ottoman dominions
GOLD COAST
SIERRA LEONE
GAMBIA
ASCENSION
ST. HELENA
WEST RHODESIA
NORTH RHODESIA
SOUTH RHODESIA
CENTRAL AFRICA
BECHUANALAND
WALVIS BAY
NATAL
CAPE COLONY
BASUTOLAND
GOUGH I.
TRISTAN DA CUNHA
FALKLAND IS.
BRITISH GUIANA
TRINIDAD (1860)
WINDWARD IS.
LEEWARD IS.
BARBADOS
MOSQUITO COAST (Claim abandoned, 1894)
BRITISH HONDURAS
JAMAICA
TURKS AND CAICOS IS.
BAHAMA IS.
BERMUDA
COOK IS.
PITCAIRN I.
OREGON (Claim abandoned, 1846)
NEWFOUNDLAND
CANADA Dominion, 1867
UNITED KINGDOM
HELIGOLAND (1890)
IONIAN IS. (1863)
MALTA
CYPRUS
GIBRALTAR

Osborne House and Balmoral

Both Victoria and Albert found the formality of Buckingham Palace and Windsor uncongenial. Soon after their marriage they wanted to buy a small, secluded house in the country. Their first choice was the Isle of Wight, remote but still easily reached from London. In 1845 they bought Osborne House, with an estate that eventually amounted to over 2,000 acres, overlooking the Solent near Cowes. The house was torn down and rebuilt as an Italianate villa, largely to the designs of the prince, who also remodelled the grounds. From the start, queen and prince were enchanted. The queen went swimming for the first time; Albert compared the Solent to the Bay of Naples. "Never do I enjoy myself more or more peacefully," wrote the queen. Not everyone was as impressed. The future Edward VII wrote: "Even as a child I was struck by the ugliness of the house." Lord Rosebery said he had never seen an uglier drawing room than at Osborne – until he saw the one at Balmoral. Edward VII gave the house to the nation shortly after coming to the throne.

The Queen and Prince Albert with all nine of their children at Osborne, 1857, the Prince stern, the Queen maternal, the children bored. Bertie, the future Edward VII, is at the extreme right.

Balmoral, "A pretty little Castle in the old Scotch style" in the words of the queen, was originally leased by Victoria and Albert in 1847. The following year, they bought the freehold of the 20,000-acre estate and set about rebuilding the castle, again to Albert's designs, this time in a more or less baronial style. As at Osborne, Albert was also responsible for the interiors, including the famous tartan chair covers, wall-papers, curtains and carpets. For the queen, the castle, like its setting, was "charming … delightful … everything perfection". Others were less taken with it. The most frequent complaint, other than its inaccessibility 700 miles from the capital, was how cold it was. Even when the queen could be prevailed upon to close the windows, the fires were meagre. Tsar Nicholas II said Balmoral was colder than Siberia.

mixture of flattery and guile, above all in agreeing in 1876 to her own pert suggestion that she be restyled Empress of India, Disraeli gradually coaxed the queen out of retirement.

That the queen had come to occupy a core place in the nation's affections was triumphantly underlined in 1887, her Golden Jubilee. Ten years later, they were even more emphatically underlined in her Diamond Jubilee celebrations. Frail and elderly though she was, she had become the central symbol of Britain and its worldwide empire. In ways that have never really changed since, the monarchy had not just found a new stability, it had found a new role.

remove herself so completely from the public gaze was to court disaster. In her own terms, she continued to attend to her responsibilities no less diligently, reading government papers, meeting her ministers, offering advice. Yet whether she realized it or not, her refusal to show herself in public amounted to a dereliction of duty. For her subjects at large it was her public face that mattered, not her private one.

That Victoria was eventually persuaded to return to public life was largely thanks to the second great influence on her life, Benjamin Disraeli. It was Disraeli, twice Victoria's prime minister, who understood better than anyone that, as the constitutional monarch of the world's leading power, the queen had a unique role as the symbol of her nation – but not if she hid herself away. Using an outrageous

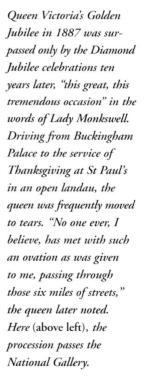

Queen Victoria's Golden Jubilee in 1887 was surpassed only by the Diamond Jubilee celebrations ten years later, "this great, this tremendous occasion" in the words of Lady Monkswell. Driving from Buckingham Palace to the service of Thanksgiving at St Paul's in an open landau, the queen was frequently moved to tears. "No one ever, I believe, has met with such an ovation as was given to me, passing through those six miles of streets," the queen later noted. Here (above left), the procession passes the National Gallery.

Despite a variety of increasing infirmities in her old age, above all trouble with her legs, the queen remained vivacious, almost sprightly, virtually to the end (left). But by the autumn of 1900 she was fading visibly, suffering from insomnia and loss of appetite. In the end, she simply faded away, dying at Osborne in January 1901. Not a single one of her subjects under 64 had known any other monarch.

1880	1884	1886	1887	1892	1897	1899
Gladstone's second Liberal administration (to 1885)	Third Reform Act	Gladstone's third Liberal administration	Victoria's Golden Jubilee	Gladstone's fourth Liberal administration (to 1894)	Victoria's Diamond Jubilee	Boer War (to 1902)

THE DEVELOPMENT OF CONSTITUTIONAL MONARCHY TO 1901

SINCE 1689, IT HAD BEEN CLEAR THAT THE AUTHORITY OF THE THRONE HAD BEEN — AND WAS CONTINUING TO BE — REDUCED IN FAVOUR OF PARLIAMENT. BUT IT WAS IN THE BRIEF REIGN OF WILLIAM IV THAT THE KEY MOMENT IN THE TRANSFORMATION THAT WOULD LEAD TO A FULLY CONSTITUTIONAL MONARCHY TOOK PLACE: THE REFORM ACT OF 1832

I N DECEMBER 1834, WILLIAM IV DISMISSED THE WHIG PRIME minister Lord Melbourne, appointing in his place the Conservative Lord Peel. The decision, the king asserted, was "his own immediate and exclusive Act. He removed Ministers whom he considered no longer capable of carrying on the business of the country … and he called to his councils others whom he considered deserving of his confidence." It turned out to be the last time any British monarch would dismiss a government.

In the subsequent general election, called to endorse the king's decision, the Conservatives emerged as the largest single party in the Commons. Still in an overall minority, however, they were effectively powerless, unable to carry the House with them. Nonetheless, Peel struggled on, reluctant to humiliate his sovereign by resigning. But in April 1835, after six defeats in the Commons in as many weeks, he bowed to the inevitable and stepped down. To the clear chagrin of the king, Melbourne was returned to office.

What William IV had discovered so painfully, and what would remain a central fact of life in the reigns of all his successors, was that the Reform Act, passed only two years earlier, had introduced a new and inescapable political reality. Effective power had slipped permanently from the king's grasp. The implications on the still-changing balance of power between the throne and Parliament are hard to overstate.

The Reform Act may have been much less far-reaching than many radicals had wanted but in expanding the franchise, however limited it remained, the Act had an unexpected consequence of huge significance: the development of organized, disciplined political parties. Put most simply, the abolition of rotten or pocket boroughs coupled with the introduction of a larger electorate meant that for the first time politicians had to make a much more coherent appeal to voters if they were to be elected. As was quickly discovered, the most effective way of doing this was through an organized political party. Within a matter of years after 1832, the House of Commons whose members had once been only loosely grouped in factions, themselves frequently fluid, had given way to one dominated by a handful of larger parties following clearly defined goals.

The consequences were twofold. One, the monarch could now no longer hope to strengthen his position by playing off one parliamentary faction against another in pursuit of his or her policies. Two, these new parties were themselves clearly answerable to the electorate rather than to the sovereign. In other words, even if not properly democratic in a modern sense, a fundamentally different political balance was being struck in which ultimate authority was passing to the electorate, restricted though it was.

A parallel development was the rise of what came to be called "responsible government" – that the government was "responsible" for policy in every sense, determining it, executing it and, should it fail, being held to account for it. Again the consequences were twofold. First, that the sovereign's influence on the formation of policy all but disappeared: the sovereign could seek to change government policy if he or she disagreed with it but in the final analysis would always have to bow to it. Second, that even though the government acted in the name of the sovereign, the sovereign could not be blamed for failures of government policy. This would come to be a crucial point.

Constitutional changes of this magnitude were played out very slowly, and many people – at the court and in government alike – had only the vaguest sense of what they actually meant; in extreme cases they were barely aware that they were happening at all. Certainly, when she came to the throne Queen Victoria assumed not just that she was head of state but head of the government, too. That none of these changes was codified – and has never been – added to the general uncertainty, even if this also allowed all sides vital flexibility in adjusting to changing circumstances.

But as Victoria would discover, her estimate of her own powers was quite wrong (though in her idiosyncratic way she frequently continued to insist on them). In effect, the power of the monarchy had now been reduced to no more than influence. But just how extensive this influence was and how it could be deployed best remained largely unknown. As in so many aspects of her reign, the crucial figure in resolving these conundrums was her husband, Prince Albert.

From the start, Albert accepted that the actual power of the throne had been heavily circumscribed. But as he also saw the monarchy as a deeply moral force, he believed that its influence should be as wide as possible. He fervently held that only the monarchy, by virtue of its permanence, could have the best interests of the nation at heart. "Is the sovereign not the natural guardian of the honour of the country?" as he put it. To make its presence felt as strongly as possible, he maintained that the monarchy should be dutiful, conscientious and above all politically neutral.

In fact, in pushing for the widest possible royal influence, neutral or not, Albert was already swimming against the tide. It has been suggested that his early death in 1861 may have prevented a possible later clash between the throne and the government. Within six years of the prince's death, the journalist Walter Bagehot, in his book *The English Constitution*, had produced what remains the classic definition of the constitutional monarchy's influence: the right to be consulted, the right to encourage, and the right to warn.

It can, of course, be objected, as it frequently was, that a throne whose influence had been so severely limited was at risk of becoming no more than a cipher, even that it might wither completely. That this did not happen was the result of an entirely unforeseen series of circumstances that took shape slowly from about 1870. Almost without anyone quite noticing it, what the monarchy had lost in power it gained in prestige.

In part, this was a result of the new respectability Albert had insisted on: the throne had rediscovered its dignity. No less important, it was also a reflection of the country's enhanced imperial status. Most important of all, the throne was increasingly invested with a new role as the essential source of the

country's political stability, the ultimate guarantor of the legitimacy and stability of its parliamentary government. As a symbol of Britain and its empire, this recast monarchy proved not just hugely popular but an active source of pride, a focus for the nation's emotions and aspirations. It was, as Gladstone put it in the 1890s, "a subtle, silent yet … almost entire transformation."

There is a significant irony here. At first sight parliamentary democracy and monarchy look incompatible, the one forward-looking and liberal, the other backward-looking and conservative. Yet whether intended or not it is a fact that parliamentary government as it evolved in 19th-century Britain succeeded in harnessing the ancient institution of hereditary monarchy to its own ends. In the process, it substantially strengthened not just itself but the monarchy. Impartial, benevolent and permanent, the monarchy had come to be seen as a natural partner of Parliament, the fundamental bedrock of the nation's liberties. Accidentally or not, an entirely new conception of monarchy had come into being.

The King [Edward VII] is no longer merely King of Great Britain and Ireland and of a few dependencies whose value consisted in ministering to the wealth and security of Great Britain and Ireland. He is now the greatest constitutional bond uniting together in a single Empire communities of free men separated by half the circumference of the Globe. All the patriotic sentiment which makes such an Empire possible centres in him or centres chiefly in him; and everything which emphasizes his personality to our kinsmen across the seas must be a gain to the Monarchy and the Empire.

Letter to Edward VII from A.J. Balfour, February 1901

GREAT BRITAIN: THE WINDSORS FROM 1917

GEORGE V 1910–36	*GEORGE VI 1936–52*
EDWARD VIII 1936	*ELIZABETH II 1952–*

IN 1917, QUEEN VICTORIA'S GRANDSON AND GEORGE V'S FIRST COUSIN, KAISER WILHELM II OF GERMANY, MADE A JOKE. TOLD THAT GEORGE V HAD CHANGED THE BRITISH ROYAL FAMILY'S NAME FROM SAXE-COBURG-GOTHA TO WINDSOR, HE REMARKED THAT HE WAS LOOKING FORWARD TO SEEING A PRODUCTION OF "THE MERRY WIVES OF SAXE-COBURG-GOTHA".

George V, king of Britain or not, came from a family that was entirely German. Victoria and Albert themselves almost always spoke German to each other and to their children. Both Queen Victoria (whose mother was German) and Edward VII spoke English with slight but unmistakable German accents. (Queen Victoria once complained that her eldest son, later Edward VII, only ever wrote to his then fiancée, Alexandra, in English.) Prince Albert himself was unambiguously German. Further, George V's aunt, the Princess Royal, mother of the Kaiser, had married the Crown Prince of Germany, Wilhelm I, in 1858. George V himself had a German wife, Princess Mary of Teck. However you looked at it, the German pedigree of the Saxe-Coburg-Gothas was impeccable.

Yet with the outbreak of the First World War, this German background, once a source of pride, was becoming more and more embarrassing. As early as October 1914, George's cousin, Prince Louis Battenburg had been forced to resign as First Sea Lord because of presumed German sympathies. As anti-German sentiments mounted during the war, the king bowed to the inevitable. On July 17 1917, it was announced that the family's name would be changed to Windsor. The name itself, suggested by Lord Stamfordham, the king's private secretary, was pure invention. But it was deemed to have a sufficiently British resonance to make it acceptable. At the same time, all the family's "other German degrees, styles, titles, dignatories, honours and appelations" were dropped.

In identifying himself with his people so publicly, George V was acting entirely in character: acknowledging that the German Hanoverians, 200 years after they gained the throne of Britain, were now definitively British; and setting a benchmark for his successors – that duty comes first. The nine-month reign in 1936 of the wayward Edward VIII apart, the hallmarks of the House of Windsor have been precisely the combination of patriotism and duty that George V so conspicuously espoused.

This has always been more than a matter of setting an example. Rather, it reflects that, as constitutional monarchs of a democratic country, the prime, in some senses only, justification for the monarchy has been that it should be above reproach. Only then, properly neutral politically, can it provide the stability that underpins and legitimizes the state.

Even the most hardened republican would be hard pressed to deny that George V and his successors have fulfilled this role with exemplary devotion, the inconvenient example of Edward VIII aside. Further, the stability of the Windsors has found a clear echo in the political stability of Britain as a whole over the same period.

By comparison, elsewhere in Europe the reign of George V alone saw the overthrow of "five emperors, eight kings and 18 more dynasties". The Windsors by contrast have successfully endured two world wars, a series of more or less serious constitutional crises, the shrinking of their realm (with Irish independence) and the almost complete loss of empire.

Further, however stodgy their image, they have proved unusually adaptable. The reign of Elizabeth II has seen changes as sweeping as any that occurred under Queen Victoria. As a result, though her sense of duty may be the equal of her father's and grandfather's (and her constitutional position unchanged), her style of monarchy has become quite different. In place of the "mystique" of George V's reign, which demanded that he be remote, distant and unapproachable, Elizabeth II, though scarcely a populist herself and attacked in the early part of her reign as tweedy and out of touch, has inevitably adopted a more low-key, human approach.

Such informality carries its own dangers. The more visible the monarchy – the more it mingles with the crowd in response to the demands of a less deferent age – the more it risks dissolving the indefinable barrier that separates royal from commoner. By far the most serious danger the throne has faced since about 1985 is that, seen in close-up, their royal "magic" put to one side, the Windsors have not always looked very appealing.

To some extent, this has been the result of an increasingly rampant, sensation-seeking press. Where once the press was fawning in its approach to the royal family, since at least 1990 its coverage of royal affairs has been relentlessly aggressive. If the queen herself has escaped their sights, remaining a model of rectitude and propriety, the rest of her family have come to be viewed as greedy, incompetent, vulgar, or merely eccentric.

They have not always helped their own cause. In stark contrast to the queen and her redoubtable mother – who was clearly the real force behind the potentially shaky throne of George VI – they have married badly. Three of the queen's four children, as well as her sister, Margaret, have been divorced, something that would have been unthinkable even for a minor member of the royal family before the Second World War.

General dissatisfaction with the royal family came to a dramatic head in 1997 with the death of the Princess of Wales, widely seen as the innocent victim of a sustained campaign by the cold-hearted Windsors. The extraordinary displays of public grief for her carried with them an implicit rebuke. In death, the princess had captured the nation's affections in ways the Windsors had not always managed. There was talk that this amounted to the most serious crisis to face the royal family since the abdication of Edward VIII.

But if the future necessarily remains unknowable, it may equally be the case that the relative unpopularity of the royal family after 1980s was little more than a blip. The mourning for the death of the venerable Queen Mother in 2002, followed by unforced national celebrations for the queen's Golden Jubilee celebrations in May 2002, as widespread as they were genuine, may in time come to be seen as much more properly representative of the real standing of the House of Windsor. Duty may yet turn out to be its own reward.

GEORGE V 1910–36

GEORGE V's IMAGE AS A BLUFF DISCIPLINARIAN IS AT ODDS WITH THE REALITY OF A SHY MAN WHO STRUGGLED TO COME TO TERMS WITH AN UNLOOKED-FOR ROLE AS KING. HOWEVER STILTED, HIS OBVIOUS DECENCY AND SENSE OF DUTY PRODUCED A REIGN THAT SAW HIS COUNTRY THROUGH A SERIES OF CRISES INCLUDING THE FIRST WORLD WAR.

1877	1890	1891	1892	1893
Enters Royal Naval College, Dartmouth	Given first command, HMS Thrush	Appointed commander in the Navy	Death of Prince Albert, George's elder brother; Prince George leaves Navy	Marriage of Prince George to Princess Mary of Teck

King George V
BORN: June 3 1865
ACCEDED: May 6 1910; crowned June 22 1911, Westminster Abbey

Duke of York, Earl of Inverness and Baron Killarney, Duke of Cornwall and Rothesay, Prince of Wales and Earl of Chester, King of the United Kingdom of Great Britain and Northern Ireland and the British Dominions beyond the Seas, Emperor of India

The Prince of Wales, the future George V, with his family in Scotland, 1906 (right). With five sons, the prince had done more than his bit to secure his succession. From left to right, the children are: Mary created the Princess Royal in 1932; Henry, subsequently duke of Gloucester; George, subsequently duke of Kent; John, subsequently Edward VIII; and Albert, subsequently George VI. John was an epileptic and died at only 13 in 1919. The Duke of Kent was killed in an air crash in 1942. Despite Edward VIII's later complaints of the unreasonable discipline imposed by his parents, by late-Victorian standards his parents were generous, almost indulgent.

s the second son of Edward VII, the future George V had never expected to become king. The death in 1892 of George's elder brother, the dissolute Prince Albert, Duke of Clarence, made George heir to his father, the new Prince of Wales. George didn't just inherit his place in the succession from his elder brother, he inherited his fiancée, too. In 1893 he married the formidably upright Princess Mary of Teck, who the year before had been engaged to marry Albert.

By now, George's life had undergone a near-complete transformation. George had been destined for the Navy, which he joined in 1877, aged only 12. Over the next 15 years, he served with considerable distinction. It was a period that decisively shaped his outlook and personality. At heart the prince would remain a conscientious and commonsensical naval officer all his life. His extensive travels across the globe also inculcated a fierce pride in Britain's empire, a considerable amount of which he saw at first hand. Forcibly retired from the Navy on the death of Prince Albert, George now began to be actively groomed for the throne. Established at St James's Palace in London and at York Cottage on the Sandringham estate, his life with Princess Mary rapidly settled into

George V (above, on the right) as Prince of Wales with his first cousin, the Tsar, at Cowes, 1904. The physical resemblance between the two is striking; the political difference immense. Where George would inherit a limited constitutional throne, Nicholas ruled Russia as an unabashed autocrat. As king, George never enjoyed the same close relationship with another first cousin, Kaiser Wilhelm II. George would later write, "I look upon him as the greatest criminal known for having plunged the world into this ghastly war." By 1918, the Tsar had been murdered, the Kaiser forced into exile.

> **I may be uninspiring but I'll be damned if I am an alien**
>
> *George V replying to H.G. Wells's claim that his court was "alien and uninspiring"*

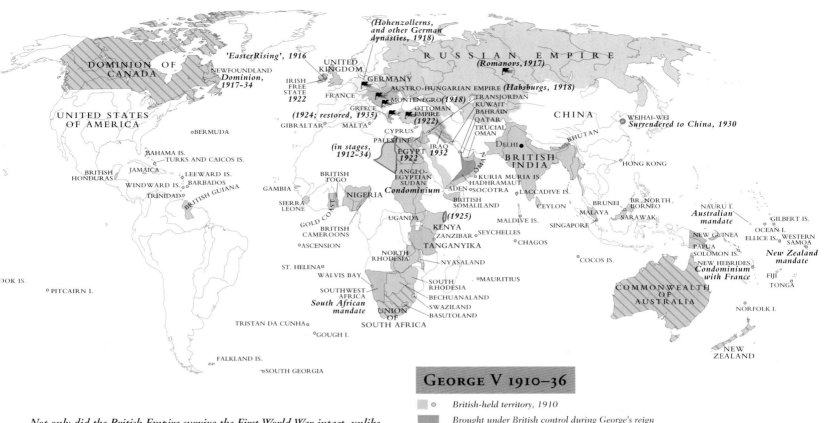

○   *British-held territory, 1910*

    Brought under British control during George's reign

    Acquired by Britain as League of Nations' Mandate after World War I

    Lost to another power during George's rule (with date)

    Gained independence, with date

    Dominion, with date, if achieved status during George's rule

    Dynasties overthrown in or after World War I

    Revolt with dates

    Frontier of British Empire possessions and dependencies, 1936

Not only did the British Empire survive the First World War intact, unlike those of Russia, Germany, Austria-Hungary and the Ottomans, it was substantially increased in extent (map above). With the take-over of the former German colony of Tanganyika, Cecil Rhodes's imperial vision of a belt of British territory from the Cape to Suez was briefly attained. The United Kingdom itself was reduced with Irish independence in 1922, Northern Ireland aside.

Despite last-minute efforts to mediate with the Kaiser on the eve of war, George V was in no doubt about the inevitability of war with Germany in August 1914. The king visited the Western Front seven times during the First World War. He also personally distributed 58,000 decorations. He made numerous visits to factories and hospitals in Britain itself. Throughout, his patriotism never flagged. Rightly, as it would be in 1945, it was Buckingham Palace that became the immediate focus of national euphoria with the ending of the war. Here (left), the king with Queen Mary and the Prince of Wales (back left) are seen at Abbeville, France, in 1917.

one of affectionate, domestic and orderly calm. As resolutely non-intellectual as his father, the prince was able to indulge his passion for sport – yachting, golf, and above all shooting (George was generally acknowledged as one of the best shots in the country) – and for his other great hobby, stamp collecting. By his death, his stamp collection was the largest in private hands in the world. Even more important, a clear mark of his level-headed sense of duty, George was consistently faithful to Mary. By the end of his

reign, he had become the first British king since Charles I to whom no hint of sexual scandal had been attached. It was in very marked contrast to his Hanoverian forebears.

In equally marked contrast to his father's experience as Prince of Wales, George was given a share in the king's responsibilities: when Edward VII came to the throne in 1901 he allowed the new Prince of Wales to see state papers and invited him to set up his desk beside his own at Buckingham Palace.

1894	1901	1910	1911	1914
Birth of Prince Edward (later Edward VIII)	*Death of Queen Victoria. New Prince and Princess of Wales make 231-day visit to Australia, New Zealand and Canada*	*George V agrees "hypothetical understanding" with Liberal government to end Conservative majority in House of Lords by creating Liberal peers*	*Coronation of George V followed by visit to India for installation as King-Emperor at Delhi Durbar*	*Inconclusive Round Table Conference at Buckingham Palace hosted by George V in attempt to resolve Irish Home Rule (July). Germany declares war against Britain (Aug.): the First World War*

Typically, though utterly opposed to the means employed by the Trades Unions in calling a General Strike in May 1926, the king was quick to urge Baldwin's government to adopt a conciliatory approach. In the end the government's firm line paid off: the strike was abandoned

after only nine days. But it was a foretaste of wider social and economic disruption in the years to come. Here (above), an armoured car patrols London.

Two Constitutional Crises

*I*n the early part of his reign, George V faced two serious crises that the rules of the still youthful constitutional monarchy struggled to accommodate. The first was his Liberal government's determination to pass a Parliament Bill restricting the right of the House of Lords to veto legislation passed in the House of Commons. The second was Irish Home Rule. In neither case was George helped by widespread Liberal suspicions of his strongly ingrained Conservative prejudices. In 1908, he had called H.H. Asquith, the Liberal prime minister, "not quite a gentleman". Lloyd George, the Liberal Chancellor of the Exchequer, was "that damned fellow".

In fact, George V was highly conscious of his constitutional responsibilities to be politically neutral and to act in accordance with his ministers' advice. Amid a welter of conflicting advice, in the autumn of 1910 he secretly agreed to create sufficient new Liberal peers, possibly several hundred, to vote through the Parliament Act in the event of a Liberal victory in the subsequent general election. In the event it proved unnecessary. The Lords backed down and passed the Parliament Act. But Asquith's announcement the following summer of the king's agreement provoked fury on George V's part, implying as it did that George could not have been trusted to do his constitutional duty. It was the "dirtiest thing ever done" in the king's view.

Home Rule, threatening outright civil war on the part of loyalist Unionists in Ulster who refused to join a new independent Irish state, proved more intractable still. The king's characteristic response was to act as a mediator, summoning a Round Table Conference at Buckingham Palace in July 1914 to allow all parties to resolve their differences. Good will would never be enough to find a way through a problem that has still not been settled. When eventual Irish independence was granted after the war, it was to the accompaniment of precisely the civil war the king had hoped to avoid. The king's instincts as a conciliator were never less than honourable, however.

When George V came to the throne in 1910, the monarchy had probably never been held in higher regard, a fact that the deliberate magnificence of the new king's coronation and his even more splendid investiture as Emperor of India at the Delhi Durbar the following year were deliberately intended to underline (see p.189). Hindsight has tended to present these years before the First World War as a kind of glorious high summer of certainty and calm. In reality, it was a period of considerable political and military turmoil. The danger was not merely the obvious aggression of Kaiser Wilhelm II's Germany, it was a new political climate that would immediately present the new George V with the two most serious constitutional crises of the 20th century (see box).

Serious as these constitutional threats were, however, they paled in the face of the outbreak of war with Germany and Austria-Hungary in August 1914, which shattered the long period of Victorian and Edwardian peace. The king's response was typical. "I cannot share your hardships," he declared to his soldiers, "but my heart is with you every hour of the day." There is no doubt he meant it. In a gesture of solidarity, he and the queen gave up alcohol for the duration of the conflict, "a great bore" in the king's words but a resolve he stuck to with characteristic phlegm.

The king made a series of visits to his troops on the Western Front as well as to the Grand Fleet. In October 1915, he broke his pelvis badly on the Western Front when he was thrown from a horse, an injury that caused him pain for the rest of life. Only once in the war was a question mark raised over his conduct when, in March 1917, he overruled Lloyd George's decision to allow the deposed Tsar of Russia and his family to come to England. The king's motive was sensible: fear of sparking revolutionary sentiments in Britain. But in effect he was condemning his cousin to death.

The world that emerged after 1918 had been ineradicably changed. British global pre-eminence had decisively given way to American superiority. And while the empire, at least in the short term, remained intact, other changes could not be resisted: the creation of the Irish Free State in 1922; the appointment of the first Labour prime minister, Ramsay MacDonald, in 1924; the social and economic unrest that led to the General Strike in 1926; the formation of a National Government in 1931 to confront the crisis created by the Great Depression. Throughout, the king acted precisely in accordance with his constitutional role, attempting to find common ground and appealing for calm whenever appropriate, never once seeking to go against the wishes of his governments.

1915	1916	1917	1918	1922	1924
George V breaks pelvis during visit to Western Front	Abortive Easter Rising by Irish nationalists, Dublin	George V refuses to allow Tsar Nicholas II and family to come to Britain	German surrender (Nov.): end of First World War	Creation of Irish Free State against background of continuing civil war	Formation of first (minority) Labour government

Ill-health undermined the king's last years. In November 1928 septicaemia had brought him close to death. In early 1936 he fell ill again, with bronchitis. It was now that Queen Mary reputedly suggested he convalesce at Bognor Regis (named in honour of the king after his earlier convalescence there), prompting the celebrated (but apocryphal) comment, "Bugger Bognor." The king and Queen Mary are seen here (left) being driven to church at Balmoral in 1930.

However, he could do nothing to prevent the gradual drift towards full independence of the country's dominions, Australia, New Zealand, Canada and South Africa. To all intents and purposes fully responsible for their own domestic affairs since at least 1914, in 1931 they gained control over their foreign affairs, too. Importantly, the king remained their head of state; indeed the prime relationship between the dominions and Britain became the monarchy rather than Westminster. But however close their remaining ties with Britain, the dominions were now independent. As important, in 1930 George V was forced, much against his better judgement, to agree to the appointment of the first non-British governor general in Australia. That independence would have to be conceded to other parts of the empire, India, above all, was becoming increasingly obvious.

George V's own status throughout the post-war years was unquestioned. Unbending and intimidating though he was, his hold on the affections of the nation was clear. The celebrations to mark the king's Silver Jubilee in 1935 made clear not just the high regard in which the king was held but his great personal popularity. He found it deeply affecting. That said, and declining health aside, his final years were clouded by growing worries over the fitness of his heir, the future Edward VIII, to inherit the throne. Popular and glamorous he may have been; dutiful he wasn't. "After I am dead, the boy will ruin himself in 12 months," said the king. It was an uncannily accurate prophecy.

George V was never a natural innovator but his radio broadcast to the empire at Christmas 1932 (right) began a tradition that endures today. The king may still have been an almost infinitely remote figure to the overwhelming majority of his subjects but never before had such direct contact between king and subjects been possible.

I will not have another war. I will not. The last one was none of my doing and if there is another one and we are threatened with being brought into it, I will go to Trafalgar Square myself and wave a red flag myself rather than allow this country to be brought in.

George V to Lloyd George, 1935

1926	1931	1932	1935
General Strike paralyses Britain (May). Imperial Conference redefines relationship between Britain and its dominions (formalized 1931 in Statute of Westminster creating British Commonwealth of Nations)	*Coalition National Government formed. Sir Isaac Isaacs becomes first Australian-born Governor General of Australia (the monarch's direct representative)*	*George V makes first Christmas radio broadcast to British Empire*	*Silver Jubilee of George V*

THE GROWTH OF ROYAL CEREMONY

THE PAGEANTRY SURROUNDING THE ROYAL FAMILY IS A RELATIVELY RECENT DEVELOPMENT. HOWEVER HISTORIC IT APPEARS, MUCH OF IT WAS DEVELOPED ONLY FROM THE LATE-VICTORIAN PERIOD AS THE NECESSITY OF INVESTING THE NEWLY CONSTITUTIONAL MONARCHY WITH A MUCH MORE VISIBLE PRESENCE AND GRANDEUR BECAME OBVIOUS. FROM THE START, IT HAD A CONSCIOUSLY IMPERIAL DIMENSION.

 RITING IN 1861, LORD SALISBURY COMPLAINED about the apparent British inability to contrive convincing royal spectacles: "Some nations have a gift for ceremonial … In England the case is exactly the reverse. We can afford to be more splendid than most nations; but some malignant spell broods over all our most solemn ceremonials, and inserts into them some feature which makes them all ridiculous."

Yet 50 years later, with the coronation of George V in 1911, the British monarchy and spectacle on the grandest of scales had become almost synonymous. No less than 60,000 troops were pressed into service to line the route from Westminster Abbey to Buckingham Palace for George's coronation. They represented not just every branch of Britain's armed forces but large numbers of its imperial forces. There were also special detachments from Germany and Austria as well as from Spain.

The royal families of Europe were present in impressive force. Every ruling European house was represented, as were the Emperor of Japan, the Ottoman Sultan and the Shah of Persia, "… come amongst us to see the descendent of Alfred crowned in the Temple of the Plantagenets" in the words of *The Times*.

The next day, the king journeyed to Portsmouth to review "… the most formidable fleet ever assembled. It was formed in seven columns, each nearly five miles long. The British warships present were 165 – eight Dreadnoughts, twenty-four earlier battleships, four Dreadnought cruisers, sixty-seven destroyers, twelve destroyers' depôt ships, twelve torpedo boats and eight

> *Once more we have to extend our horizon and to regard this ancient Monarchy as the mother of nations and the centre of a world-wide Empire, held together by no bonds of conquest and no assertive central authority, but by some force which none of us can properly name or define, impalpable and intangible as gravity, yet, like that mysterious force, maintaining the system intact while allowing for all the perturbations due to the minor interactions of several parts.*
>
> The Times, *on George V's coronation, June 1911*

Following his coronation in 1937, George VI (above), wife and daughters by his side, were rapturously greeted on the balcony of Buckingham Palace by a huge crowd.

submarines … His Majesty expressed his marked satisfaction with the review." It was hardly to be wondered at. The express purpose of the coronation had been to underline the might of Britain in all spheres, imperial above all.

The association with monarchy and spectacle on this scale, all of it appearing to draw on earlier tradition, may have been a process that evolved rather than was consciously aimed at. But once it had become clear that a constitutional monarchy was the ideal symbol of the nation and its domains, then for the rulers of the greatest empire the world had ever seen it followed that pomp was its natural accompaniment. Appropriately, it was a process that had begun with Queen Victoria's gradual emergence from her self-imposed seclusion after the death of Prince Albert in 1861. When designated Empress of India in 1876, an "Imperial Assemblage" was held the following year in Delhi. On the site where the Indian Mutiny had been finally suppressed in 1858, 70 Indian princes expressed their loyalty to the Viceroy, the queen's direct representative. As the Viceroy put it: "The further east you go, the greater becomes the importance of a bit of bunting." (It

The highpoint of British imperial pretensions was represented by the Delhi Durbar (above). Iconic and idealistic, George V and Queen Mary personified the seemingly permanent edifice that was British rule in India.

wasn't a flawless success: a number of people were trampled to death after a 101-gun salute stampeded the elephants.)

The discovery of how spectacle could underpin the monarchy, in turn reinforcing the self-esteem of the nation, was substantially enhanced with Queen Victoria's Golden and Diamond Jubilees in 1887 and 1897. However novel most of their forms, both reflected what was widely assumed to be time-honoured tradition; and both were conceived as public spectacles on a deliberately lavish scale. It was also in 1897 that colonial troops were used for the first time — "dusky warriors" as *The Illustrated London News* called them. (The success of the spectacle also inspired A.C. Benson to write the words to *Land of Hope and Glory*.)

George V's coronation had an important follow-up six months later when he and the queen travelled to what had been the Mogul capital of India, Delhi, subsequently proclaimed the new capital of British India, for the Delhi Durbar, a ritual exchange of gifts and loyalties between ruler and ruled. For five days, swelter-

The queen at the Trooping of the Colour in 2001 (above). The ceremony, which has celebrated the sovereign's official birthday since the 17th century, has its origins in the Middle Ages when knights and other nobles carried flags into battle to allow their position to be easily seen in the heat and smoke of conflict. The ceremony today is the annual highpoint of royal pageantry.

The funeral of the Queen Mother in March 2002 was simultaneously moving and uplifting (above). Impeccably organized, it saw the full weight of royal ceremonial deployed at its most commanding. Only the most stony-hearted could fail to have been moved.

ing under the Indian sun, George V and Queen Mary, dressed in their coronation robes, received the submission of India's princes. Even after the king and queen had left, "… tens of thousands of Indians … made obeisance … many kneeling, touching the railings, and prostrating themselves in the dust."

"What lay behind this splendid pageantry, what force was symbolised in the quiet, dignified figure receiving the acclaim of his Indian subjects?" asked *The Times of India*. "Stability … fixity of purpose and continuity of purpose" was its answer. It turned out to be quite wrong. It had been intended that every new British monarch would preside over a similar Durbar: George V was the first and last. His heir, Edward VIII, was not king long enough to be crowned let alone to visit India as its ruler. George VI, was immediately sucked into the European crisis racked up by Hitler. And by the time his successor, Elizabeth II, came to the throne, she was no longer ruler of India. The heyday of imperial pageantry lasted less than 20 years.

Yet in Britain at least, pageantry and the monarchy — for all

that many of its forms were of recent invention — had become inseparable. The coronation of George VI was every bit as gorgeous as that of his father; that of Elizabeth II, in which ancient forms were deliberately exploited to celebrate the country's final emergence from the austerity of the Second World War, almost more so. Further, whether Trooping the Colour or at the State Opening of Parliament, the two annual occasions when the full might of royal pageantry are set out at their most opulent, the monarchy is seen at its most imposing. Notably, the funeral of the Queen Mother in 2002, admittedly planned long in advance, struck exactly the tone of solemnity and ceremonial splendour that Lord Salisbury feared was permanently beyond the throne.

GEORGE VI 1936–52

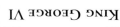

BORN: December 14 1895
ACCEDED: December 11 1936: crowned May 12 1937, Westminster Abbey

*Duke of York,
Earl of Inverness
and Baron Killarney,
King of the United King-
dom of Great Britain
and Northern Ireland
and the British
Dominions beyond the
Seas, Emperor of India
(until 1947)*

George VI (above), shy, stuttering and uncertain, may not have been cut out to be king but no one could claim he discharged his responsibilities with anything less than fortitude. It is a striking tribute to him that, once free from the shadow of his elder brother Edward VIII, he set the monarchy back on its feet.

If never exactly hearty, George VI nonetheless had a clear taste for wholesome outdoor life. In 1926, he played in the doubles at Wimbledon (right). He and his partner, Louis Greig, lost 6-1, 6-2, 6-3. More successfully in 1921 he established the Duke of York's camps, an attempt to introduce working-class city children to the discip-lines and rewards of Scouting.

IF THERE WAS NEVER A MORE RELUCTANT KING THAN GEORGE VI, THERE WAS CERTAINLY NEVER A MORE DUTIFUL ONE. SUCCEEDING AT A MOMENT OF SUPREME CRISIS FOR THE THRONE AFTER HIS BROTHER'S ABDICATION, GEORGE FORCED HIMSELF TO PERFORM PUBLIC DUTIES THAT A SEVERE STAMMER MADE A TORMENT. HE SET THE NATION A STALWART EXAMPLE IN SELF-SACRIFICE IN THE SECOND WORLD WAR.

ISITING HIS MOTHER ON DECEMBER 9 1936, two days before Edward VIII's abdication, the future George VI, his completely unlooked-for reign now imminent, "broke down and sobbed like a child". His terror was understandable. Less than a month before, the duke of York, as he then was, had had no idea he was so close to the throne. Not only had he had little or no formal preparation for the task, he was in all respects, save one, scarcely suited for it anyway. Yet it was this one virtue – a refusal to shirk even the most painful duty – that would restore the stability of the throne and make his reign, if not great, then at the very least admirable.

As a child, Prince Albert, as he had been chris-tened, was slow and awkward, prone to illness, bad at his lessons and given to rages. He also developed a stammer that he never lost. With public speaking being a key part of kingship, it was a heavy burden to carry.

Like his father George V, he was destined for the Navy. Unlike him, his career was not distinguished. At Osborne Naval College he was 68th out of 68. Later, at Dartmouth, he came 61st out of 68. Gastritis, appendicitis and seasickness made his naval career stop-start at best, though he was present at the Battle of Jutland in May 1916.

He is of course a fairly reactionary person.

Hugh Gaitskell MP on George VI

Marriage in 1923 to Lady Elizabeth Bowes-Lyon was the making of him. Intelligent and charming, she proved an ideal wife and a permanent support. Their undemanding domestic life, complemented by the births of Princess Elizabeth in 1926 and Princess Margaret in 1930, was contented and settled. That the duke of York was rarely in the public spotlight was, to him, a blessing.

Almost his first act as George VI – a name adopted to emphasize the continuity he hoped his reign would restore – was to sever all links with his brother. For a hesitant man, it was an uncharacteristically

There can be no question that his wife and children provided George VI with an emotional stability he had never known as a child. "We four," as he touchingly called his family, were at the heart of his life. Theirs may have been an incontestably royal existence, but its humanity was never in doubt. This painting (above), showing the royal family at Royal Lodge, Windsor in 1940, is by James Gunn.

1908	1916	1920	1921	1923	1926	1930	1936
Enters Osborne Naval College	*Serves at Battle of Jutland on HMS Collingwood*	*Created duke of York*	*Founds Duke of York's camps to enable working-class children to learn Scouting*	*Marriage to Lady Elizabeth Bowes-Lyon*	*Birth of Princess Elizabeth, future Elizabeth II*	*Birth of Princess Margaret*	*Abdication of Edward VIII; accession of George VI*

GEORGE VI 1936–52

■ ○		*British-held, 1936*
		Dominion in 1936, independent member of the Commonwealth by 1952
■ ○		*Administered by a British Empire power (under League of Nations mandate, 1936 or UN trusteeship, 1945*
⧄		*Independent by 1952, with details*
■ ○		*Under British administration following WWII, with date of termination where applicable*
—		*Frontiers, 1952*

Demands for independence, above all in India, proved irresistible. Its loss in 1947 presaged the almost total ending of the British empire (map above). By the end of George VI's reign, Britain's claim to great power status were looking increasingly threadbare, a central fact that well-meaning attempts to promote the Commonwealth in place of the empire could not disguise

The bombing of Buckingham Palace in September 1940 prompted Queen Elizabeth's famous comment: "At last we can look the East End in the face." The king and queen's determination to share their subjects' suffering was almost their most admirable quality. They made hundreds of visits to bombed cities, their sympathy with the suffering of the victims entirely genuine. Here (left), the king and queen inspect the bomb damage at Buckingham Palace.

firm stance, almost certainly instigated by Queen Elizabeth. But as an exercise in damage limitation it was a success. Normal royal business had been restored.

The first years of the king's reign were overshadowed by the threat of war, which George VI was desperate to avoid. It is clear that he was naive – suggesting he send telegrams to Hitler and Mussolini; inviting Neville Chamberlain onto the balcony of Buckingham Palace after the Munich Agreement , but it is even more clear that when war came he did more than just his bit. Uncharismatic he may have been, but the king's determination to stick out the war alongside his subjects, not least his refusal to leave London even at the height of the Blitz, firmly endeared him to the country. At the end of the war, it was wholly appropriate that Buckingham Palace became the focus of wild national rejoicing, a delirious crowd repeatedly calling the king and queen back onto the balcony.

The remaining years of his reign, a successful visit to South Africa in 1947 aside, were darkened by continuing austerity, the break-up of empire, above all Indian independence in 1947, and the king's ill-health. Queen Elizabeth would maintain that the king's death in 1952 at only 56 had been brought on by the strain of kingship. She may have been right. But for George VI there was the consolation of having done his duty.

1938	1939	1940	1945	1947	1948	1951
Royal visit to France cements Anglo-French relations (June); Munich Agreement (Sept.)	*Royal visit to Canada and America cements Anglo-America relations (May–June). German invasion of Poland (Sept.): the Second World War*	*National Government under Winston Churchill (May). Buckingham Palace bombed (Sept.). George Cross and George Medal for civilian gallantry introduced*	*Axis defeat: end of the Second World War. Labour government elected: introduces nationalization and welfare state*	*Indian and Pakistani independence. Royal Family visit South Africa. Marriage of Princess Elizabeth to Duke of Edinburgh*	*Illness forces cancellation of royal visit to New Zealand*	*Conservatives returned under Winston Churchill. King's left lung removed*

QUEEN ELIZABETH II

ELIZABETH II FROM 1952

IN FEBRUARY 2002, ELIZABETH II BECAME ONLY THE FIFTH BRITISH MONARCH TO REIGN FOR OVER 50 YEARS. IF HER REIGN HAS GENERATED CONTROVERSY, IT IS THE INSTITUTION OF MONARCHY ITSELF OR OTHER MEMBERS OF HER FAMILY THAT HAVE COME UNDER ATTACK: THE QUEEN HERSELF, THROUGH HER OBVIOUS CONSCIENTIOUSNESS, HAS SCARCELY PUT A FOOT WRONG.

BORN: April 21 1926
ACCEDED: February 6 1952; crowned June 2 1953, Westminster Abbey

⁕ ⁕ ⁕ ⁕ ⁕ ⁕ ⁕

Queen of the United Kingdom of Great Britain and Northern Ireland and of Her Other Realms and Territories and Head of the Commonwealth

The coronation of Elizabeth II in 1953 was widely seen as the moment of Britain's final emergence from the deprivation of the Second World War. The belief in the country's imminent regeneration was palpable. Simultaneously forward-looking yet rooted in tradition, Elizabeth, here (above) photographed in her coronation robes by Cecil Beaton in 1953, was cast as the symbol of a reborn Britain.

QUEEN ELIZABETH CAME TO THE THRONE amid a welter of largely spurious talk about a "new Elizabethan age". With wartime austerity finally behind it, the country, under its young, attractive and obviously capable new queen, was widely expected to embark on a period of confident national pride fully the equal of that under Elizabeth I. In the event, almost the precise opposite happened. Thirty years of seemingly irreversible relative economic and military decline followed. At the same time, in little more than ten years from the mid-1950s, Britain divested itself of what, at Elizabeth's accession, had still been a substantial global empire. Symbolically, in 1958 "Empire Day" was renamed "Commonwealth Day". The former colonies did, it is true, nearly all become members of the British Commonwealth of Nations, with the queen as its head. Almost as rapidly, however, it became clear that the Commonwealth, in the words of a noted historian, was little more than "a marginalized talking-shop with very little political clout".

Over the same period, though its institutions survived largely intact, the country's values were revolutionized. Britain in 1950 was recognizably the same deferent country it had been in 1900; by 1977, the queen's Silver Jubilee, it had become an aggressive, consumer-driven society in which popular culture had emerged as a major force.

The queen can hardly be blamed for being slow to appreciate the significance of the changes taking place around her. Not many others were properly

In 1945, much against her father's wishes, Princess Elizabeth conspicuously supplemented her patriotic duty by joining the Auxiliary Transport Service, the ATS (right). Her service may have lasted only a month, but as a demonstration of the young princess's determination to share her people's burden it was a notable public relations success.

aware of them either. When Lord Altrincham criticized her in 1957 for being out of touch, he aroused a storm of public controversy. But there is no question but that he was right – or that his attitude has since come to be widely shared. Yet finding ways to make the monarchy less remote without sacrificing its essential dignity has proved difficult. In part, and in considerable contrast to her mother, the queen has never had the kind of personality that naturally lends itself to easy public informality. Yet at the same time, it is undeniable that for many people it is precisely the queen's obvious and impeccable formality that is her strongest asset.

Her discharge of her constitutional duties has been flawless. It is a remarkable tribute to her sense of duty that even after 50 years on the throne, and despite inevitable press speculation, she has never once let slip her views on any matter of public policy. However widely it may be assumed that her natural political instincts are to the Right, her conduct towards the four Labour administrations that her reign has seen has been one of complete constitutional propriety, precisely as it has been towards Conservative

I declare before you all that my whole life, whether it be long or short, shall be devoted to your service and the service of our great Imperial family to which we all belong

21st birthday speech by Princess Elizabeth, April 1947

1939	1945	1947	1948	1950	1953
First meeting with Prince Philip, Dartmouth	Joins Auxiliary Transport Service	Marries Prince Philip, the duke of Edinburgh	Birth of Prince Charles	Birth of Princess Anne	Coronation attracts television audience of 20 million

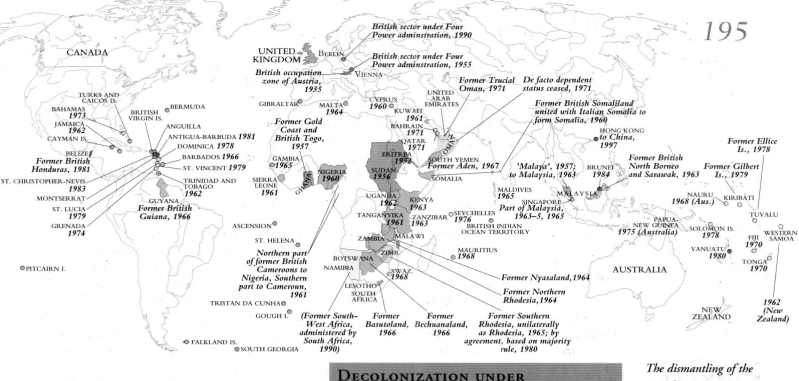

CANADA
UNITED KINGDOM
British sector under Four Power adminstration, 1990
BERLIN
British sector under Four Power adminstration, 1955
VIENNA
British occupation zone of Austria, 1955
Former Trucial Oman, 1971
De facto dependent status ceased, 1971
TURKS AND CAICOS IS.
BAHAMAS 1973
BERMUDA
GIBRALTAR
MALTA 1964
CYPRUS 1960
KUWAIT 1961
UNITED ARAB EMIRATES
Former British Somaliland united with Italian Somalia to form Somalia, 1960
JAMAICA 1962
BRITISH VIRGIN IS.
ANGUILLA
ANTIGUA-BARBUDA 1981
BAHRAIN 1971
HONG KONG to China, 1997
Former Ellice Is., 1978
CAYMAN IS.
DOMINICA 1978
Former Gold Coast and British Togo, 1957
QATAR 1971
ERITREA 1952
Former British North Borneo and Sarawak, 1963
Former Gilbert Is., 1979
BELIZE Former British Honduras, 1981
BARBADOS 1966
GAMBIA 1965
NIGERIA 1960
SUDAN 1956
SOUTH YEMEN Former Aden, 1967
'Malaya', 1957; to Malaysia, 1963
BRUNEI 1984
NAURU 1968 (Aus.)
KIRIBATI
ST. CHRISTOPHER-NEVIS 1983
ST. VINCENT 1979
TRINIDAD AND TOBAGO 1962
SIERRA LEONE 1961
SOMALIA
MALDIVES 1965
MALAYSIA
TUVALU
MONTSERRAT
GUYANA Former British Guiana, 1966
UGANDA 1962
KENYA 1963
SINGAPORE Part of Malaysia, 1963–5, 1965
ST. LUCIA 1979
TANGANYIKA 1961
ZANZIBAR 1963
SEYCHELLES 1976
BRITISH INDIAN OCEAN TERRITORY
PAPUA-NEW GUINEA 1975 (Australia)
SOLOMON IS. 1978
FIJI 1970
WESTERN SAMOA
GRENADA 1974
ASCENSION
ZAMBIA
MALAWI
MAURITIUS 1968
VANUATU 1980
TONGA 1970
ST. HELENA
Northern part of former British Cameroons to Nigeria, Southern part to Cameroun, 1961
ZIMB.
AUSTRALIA
BOTSWANA
NAMIBIA
SWAZ. 1968
Former Nyasaland,1964
PITCAIRN I.
LESOTHO
SOUTH AFRICA
Former Northern Rhodesia,1964
TRISTAN DA CUNHA
GOUGH I.
(Former South-West Africa, administered by South Africa, 1990)
Former Basutoland, 1966
Former Bechuanaland, 1966
Former Southern Rhodesia, unilaterally as Rhodesia, 1965; by agreement, based on majority rule, 1980
NEW ZEALAND
1962 (New Zealand)
FALKLAND IS.
SOUTH GEORGIA

DECOLONIZATION UNDER ELIZABETH II

Under British administration following World War II, with date of termination

Gained independence during the 1950s, with details

Gained independence during the 1960s, with details

Gained independence during the 1970s, with details

Gained independence during the 1980s and '90s, with details

Gained independence from former dominions, with details

British claim for area abandoned to the benefit of Saudi Arabia

British-held territory, 2004

At only 13, Princess Elizabeth seems to have made up her mind to marry her third cousin, Prince Philip Mountbatten, the impoverished but gallant grandson of George I of Greece. Created Duke of Edinburgh on their wedding day in November 1947, he has proved to be a solid if occasionally unpredictable fixture in the royal family. His reputation for tactlessness pales besides his loyalty to his wife, the Queen. Here (left), the couple pose after announcing their engagement.

The dismantling of the British empire was extraordinarily swift and, on the whole, orderly. By the late 1960s, Britain had given up all its African colonies as well as its remaining territories in Southeast Asia (map above). *Independence for its remaining island territories, chiefly in the Caribbean, Indian Ocean and Pacific duly followed. The last Crown Colony to be surrendered, in 1997, was Hong Kong.*

administrations. This in itself is a potent argument in favour of constitutional monarchy.

On those rare occasions when the queen has taken a more active part in popularizing her image, the results have been tepid at best. The 1969 BBC documentary, *Royal Family*, purportedly an intimate portrait of the queen and her family, was a very stilted affair. For the most part, therefore, it is other younger members of the family who have taken the lead in generating a new royal image. The results have been generally discouraging.

That said, the marriage of Prince Charles to Lady Diana Spencer in 1981 in a blaze of global publicity did for a time look as though it would genuinely rejuvenate the royal family's fading image. Prince Andrew's marriage to Sarah Ferguson in 1986 briefly sparked a further burst of monarchical fer-

vour. Yet the apparent stuffiness of the Queen would turn out to be very much more appealing than either the extravagance of some younger royals – nowhere more obvious than when they appeared in the 1987 television programme *It's a Royal Knockout* – or Princess Diana's elegant glamour.

Much more important, both marriages ended in divorce, the couples separating in 1992, the queen's *annus horribilis*, the same year in which part of Windsor Castle burned down and Princess Anne was divorced from her first husband, Captain Mark Phillips. It was the beginning of a truly traumatic period for the royal family, the whole played out against a background of intrusive and hypocritical press coverage of a kind that even ten years earlier would have been unimaginable. The separation of Charles and Diana in particular became distinctly

1956	1957	1960	1964	1969	1973
Suez Crisis confirms British imperial military impotence	*Ghana becomes first British African colony to be granted independence*	*Harold Macmillan confirms British decolonization with "Wind of Change" speech. Birth of Prince Andrew*	*Labour government elected under Harold Wilson. Birth of Prince Edward*	*"Royal Family" documentaries broadcast. Investiture of Prince Charles as Prince of Wales*	*Marriage of Princess Anne to Mark Phillips (divorced 1992)*

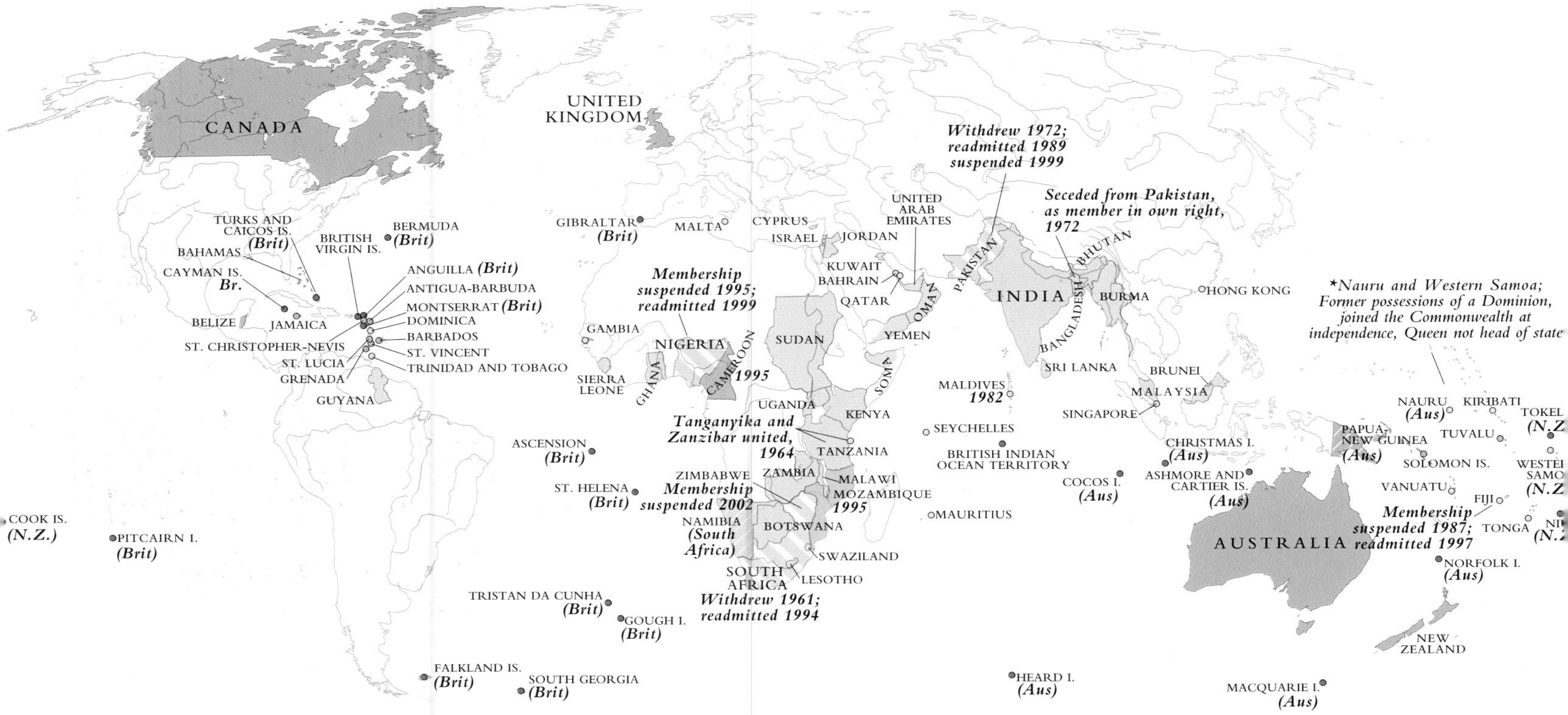

The Map

UNITED KINGDOM

CANADA

Withdrew 1972; readmitted 1989 suspended 1999

Seceded from Pakistan, as member in own right, 1972

TURKS AND CAICOS IS. *(Brit)*
BERMUDA *(Brit)*
BAHAMAS
BRITISH VIRGIN IS.
CAYMAN IS. *Br.*
ANGUILLA *(Brit)*
ANTIGUA-BARBUDA
MONTSERRAT *(Brit)*
DOMINICA
BARBADOS
BELIZE
JAMAICA
ST. CHRISTOPHER-NEVIS
ST. VINCENT
ST. LUCIA
GRENADA
TRINIDAD AND TOBAGO
GUYANA

GIBRALTAR *(Brit)*
MALTA
CYPRUS
ISRAEL
JORDAN
UNITED ARAB EMIRATES
KUWAIT
BAHRAIN
QATAR
OMAN
PAKISTAN
INDIA
BANGLADESH
BHUTAN
BURMA
HONG KONG

*Nauru and Western Samoa; Former possessions of a Dominion, joined the Commonwealth at independence, Queen not head of state

GAMBIA
Membership suspended 1995; readmitted 1999
NIGERIA
SUDAN
YEMEN
SIERRA LEONE
GHANA
CAMEROON *1995*
UGANDA
KENYA
SOMA
SRI LANKA
MALAYSIA
BRUNEI
SINGAPORE
NAURU *(Aus)*
KIRIBATI
TOKEL *(N.Z*
PAPUA NEW GUINEA *(Aus)*
TUVALU
WESTE SAMO *(N.Z*

Tanganyika and Zanzibar united, 1964
TANZANIA
MALDIVES *1982*
SEYCHELLES
BRITISH INDIAN OCEAN TERRITORY
CHRISTMAS I. *(Aus)*
COCOS I. *(Aus)*
ASHMORE AND CARTIER IS. *(Aus)*
VANUATU
FIJI
Membership suspended 1987; readmitted 1997
TONGA
NI *(N.*

ASCENSION *(Brit)*
ZIMBABWE *Membership suspended 2002*
ZAMBIA
MALAWI *1995*
MOZAMBIQUE
ST. HELENA *(Brit)*
NAMIBIA *(South Africa)*
BOTSWANA
MAURITIUS
SWAZILAND
SOUTH AFRICA
LESOTHO
Withdrew 1961; readmitted 1994

AUSTRALIA
NORFOLK I. *(Aus)*

COOK IS. *(N.Z.)*
PITCAIRN I. *(Brit)*
TRISTAN DA CUNHA *(Brit)*
GOUGH I. *(Brit)*
FALKLAND IS. *(Brit)*
SOUTH GEORGIA *(Brit)*
HEARD I. *(Aus)*
MACQUARIE I. *(Aus)*
NEW ZEALAND

The Development of the Commonwealth

- Joined Commonwealth at independence, Queen head of state
- Commonwealth members, Queen not head of state
- Former possession of a Dominion, joined the Commonwealth at independence, Queen head of state
- Former possession of a Dominion, joined the Commonwealth at independence, Queen not head of state
- Joined the Commonwealth, though only a part of the country was a British possession, the Queen is not head of state, with date of joining
- Joined the Commonwealth without past connection to British Empire, the Queen is not head of state, with date of joining
- Former British possessions that refused to join the Commonwealth
- Commonwealth membership suspended, with details
- Possession of a Commonwealth member, with details

Her empire may have gone but there is no doubt about the Queen's fervent belief in the benevolence of the Commonwealth, pale substitute though it is for the Empire proper. In this 1995 photograph (below), taken at the bi-annual Commonwealth heads of government meeting, the Queen, Prince Philip by her side, is shown with the leaders of almost 50 Commonwealth countries.

The development of the Commonwealth was not always smooth (map above). Five countries have been suspended or have left, one of them, Pakistan, twice. A number, mostly in the Middle East, have also declined the opportunity to join the organization. Nonetheless, the Queen is recognized as head of the Commonwealth by all 53 member countries and is head of state of 16, Canada, Australia and New Zealand among them.

In the words of one of my more sympathetic correspondents, it has turned out to be my annus horribilis

Elizabeth II, November 1992

sordid, with both sides attempting to manipulate sympathetic press coverage. Diana proved to have a talent for this, successfully blackening the Windsors as cold-hearted, smug and self-absorbed. Charles meanwhile confessed on television to having had an affair with a married woman and Diana admitted to an affair with an army officer. However conscientiously the queen continued to perform her duties, the royal family was being dragged into the kind of disrepute unknown since the Regency.

It came to a head with the death of Princess Diana in Paris in August 1997. Fleeing a pack of pursuing paparazzi in the company of her Egyptian boyfriend, her car crashed in an underground tunnel. The press turned a genuine tragedy into a further attack on the royal family, whipping up a bizarre outpouring of national hysteria masquerading as grief. For the first time, even the queen began to attract direct criticism: that she had not immediately left Balmoral for London; that, when she did return, the royal standard at Buckingham Palace was not flown at half-mast.

In the circumstances, it was hardly surprising if *bien-pensant* views about the desirability of republicanism began to be aired more widely. The monarchy was attacked as reactionary, class ridden, anachronistic, and incompatible with a forward-looking, modernizing Britain. The decision by the Labour government not to replace the royal yacht,

1975	1977	1978	1979	1981	1982	1986
Constitutional crisis provoked when Governor General of Australia dismisses Labour government under Gough Whitlam	Queen Elizabeth's Silver Jubilee	Princess Margaret divorced from Earl of Snowdon	Queen's cousin Lord Mountbatten assassinated by IRA	Marriage of Prince of Wales to Lady Diana Spencer (divorced 1996)	Falklands War	Marriage of Prince Andrew (Duke of York) to Sarah Ferguson (divorced 1996)

Far from the damp squib it was widely feared it would be, the Queen's Golden Jubilee celebrations in the spring of 2002 were a triumphant reaffirmation of Britain's regard for their queen (right). As the Guardian *newspaper commented, "The Golden Jubilee may have given those of us who seek a radical change in the way Britain is governed food for thought." On the whole, it was something of an understatement.*

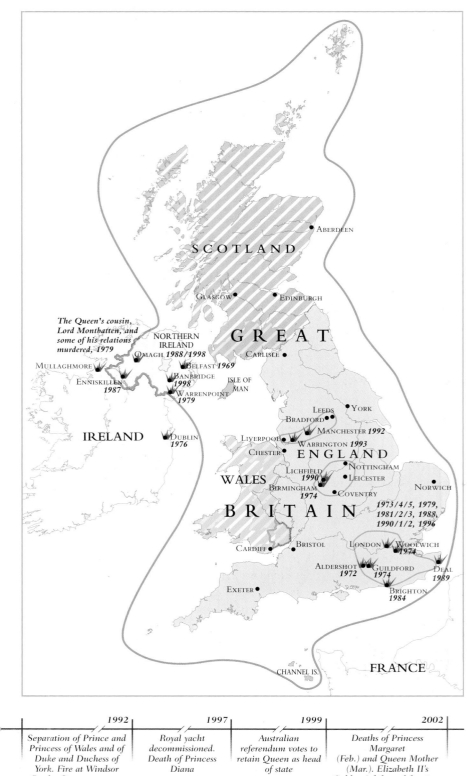

The Queen's cousin, Lord Mountbatten, and some of his relations murdered, 1979

THE UNITED KINGDOM UNDER ELIZABETH II

- *Main areas of immigrant settlement*
- *Worst incidents of Irish republican terrorism since 1969, Home rule suspended 1972, reintroduced 1999*
- *Returned to Wales, 1974*
- *England since 1974*
- *Rejected devolution in 1979 referenda*
- *Voted for devolution in 1997 referenda*
- *Rejected devolution in 1997 referenda*
- *Dependencies of the United Kingdom*
- *United Kingdom and dependencies, 2002*

By far the most important constitutional development in the reign of Elizabeth II has been the move towards the break-up of the United Kingdom (map left). In Northern Ireland, this has been spearheaded by a terror campaign aimed at the forcible union of the province with the Irish Republic. In Wales and Scotland, the former now with its own Assembly, the latter with its own Parliament, the process has been entirely legal. At the same time, the arrival of immigrants from former British possessions has helped create a multi-racial Britain

Britannia, on the grounds of cost was typical of this new, sour mood. In 1999, a republican-inspired referendum to replace the queen as head of state in Australia failed by the narrowest of margins.

Yet the monarchy, the queen above all, retains a unique place in the affections of the nation. This was made clear with the death of the Queen Mother in March 2002, only eight weeks after the death of the queen's younger sister, Princess Margaret. It was underlined even more emphatically with the massive popular success of the queen's Golden Jubilee celebrations in May and June 2002. With upwards of a million people thronging central London, all of a sudden it was republicanism that looked out of step. The essential durability of the monarchy had never been more obvious.

1992	1997	1999	2002
Separation of Prince and Princess of Wales and of Duke and Duchess of York. Fire at Windsor Castle. Queen agrees to pay income tax	*Royal yacht decommissioned. Death of Princess Diana*	*Australian referendum votes to retain Queen as head of state*	*Deaths of Princess Margaret (Feb.) and Queen Mother (Mar.). Elizabeth II's Golden Jubilee celebrations*

You reign with our love

The Sun, *June 2002*

BIBLIOGRAPHY

GENERAL
Brewer's British Royalty, David Williamson, Cassell 1996
Britain's Royal Families: The Complete Genealogy, Alison Weir, Bodley Head 1989
The British Isles – A History of Four Nations, Hugh Kearney CUP 1989
Britons: Forging the Nation 1707–1837, Linda Colley, Yale UP 1992
Complete Guide to the Battlefields of Britain, David Smurthwaite, Webb & Bower, 1984
Conquest, Coexistence and Change: Wales 1063–1415, R.R. Davies, University of Wales Press, 1987
Conquest and Union: Fashioning a British State 1485–1725, ed, S.G. Ellis and S. Barber, Longman 1995
The Historical Atlas of Scotland, ed. P. MacNeill and R. Nicholson, St Andrews 1975
A History of Britain 3000 BC–AD 1603, Simon Schama, BBC 2000
A History of Britain 1603–1776, Simon Schama, BBC 2001
A History of the British Isles, Jeremy Black, Macmillan 1996
A History of Wales, John Davies, Allen Lane 1993
The Isles: A History, Norman Davies, Macmillan 1999
Kings and Queens of Britain, David Williamson, Webb & Bower1991
Kings and Queens of England, ed. Antonia Fraser, Cassell 2000
The Kings and Queens of Scotland, Caroline Bingham, Weidenfeld and Nicolson 1976
The Mammoth Book of British Kings and Queens, Mike Ashley, Robinson 1998
Modern Ireland 1600–1972, R.F. Foster, Penguin 1988
Monarchs of Scotland, Stewart Ross, Lochar Publishing, 1990
The Monarchy and the Constitution, Vernon Bogdanor, OUP 1995
The Oxford Companion to British History, ed. John Cannon, OUP 1997
The Oxford Companion to Irish History, ed. S.J. Connolly, OUP 1998
The Oxford History of Britain, ed. Kenneth O. Morgan, OUP 1999
The Oxford Illustrated History of the British Monarchy, John Cannon and Ralph Griffiths, OUP 1998, p/b 2000
Oxford, The Kings and Queens of Britain, John Cannon and Anne Hargreaves, OUP 2001
Queens of Britain, Norah Lofts, Hodder & Stoughton, 1977
The Royal Encylopedia, ed. Ronald Allison and Sarah Riddell, Macmillan 1991
Royal Fortune: Tax, Money and the Monarchy, Philip Hall, Bloomsbury 1992
The Saxon and Norman Kings, Christopher Brooke, Batsford 1963
Scotland: The Making of the Kingdom, Archibald Duncan, Oliver and Boyd, 1975
Scotland: A New History, Michael Lynch, Pimlico 1991
Scottish Kings, Gordon Donaldson, Batsford 1967
Uniting the Kingdom? The Making of British History, eds. Alexander Grant and Keith J. Stringer, Routledge 1995

CHAPTER 1: MYTHS AND ORIGINS
The Anglo-Saxon Chronicle, translated and ed. Michael Swanton, Dent 1996
An Atlas of Anglo-Saxon England, David Hill, Basil Blackwell 1981
Anglo-Saxon England, Sir Frank Stenton, OUP 1971
The Anglo-Saxon Landscape: The Kingdom of the Hwicce, Della Hooke, Manchester UP 1985
Boudica, Graham Webster, Batsford 1993
The Celts, ed. Nora Chadwick, Pelican 1971
Celt and Saxon: The Struggle for Britain, Peter Beresford Ellis, Constable 1993
The Earliest English Kings, D.P. Kirby, Unwin Hyman 1991
Early Ireland, M.J. O'Kelly, CUP 1989
Ecclesiastical History of the British People, Bede, ed. D.H. Farmer, Penguin 1990
The English Conquest: Gildas and Britain in the 5th Century, Nicholas J. Higham, Manchester UP 1994
An English Empire: Bede and the Early Saxon Kingdoms, N.J. Higham, Manchester UP 1994
The Formation of England 550–1042, H.P.R. Finberg, Hart-Davis MacGibbon 1974
Gallic Wars, Julius Caesar, translated H.J. Edwards, Harvard UP 1986

Gildas: the Ruin of Britain and Other Documents, ed. Michael Winterbottom, Phillimore 1978
The History of the Kings of Britain, Geoffrey of Monmouth, translated Lewis Thorpe, Penguin 1976
Ireland Before the Vikings, Gearóid Mac Niocaill, Gill and Macmillan 1972
The Kingdom of Northumbria, 350–1100, Nicholas J. Higham, Alan Sutton 1993
King Arthur: Hero and Legend, Richard Barber, Boydell and Brewer 1994
King Arthur: King of Glamorgan and Gwent, A.T. Blackett and Alan Wilson, M.T. Byrd 1981
Kings and Kingship in Early Scotland, Majorie Anderson, Scottish Academic Press 1973
Kings and Queens of Early Britain, Geoffrey Ashe, Methuen 1982
Macbeth, High King of Scotland 1040–57, Peter Berresford Ellis, Frederick Muller 1980
Nennius: British History and the Welsh Annals, John Norris, Phillimore 1980
Northanhymbre Saga: The History of the Anglo-Saxon Kings of Northumbria, John Marsden, Kyle Cathie 1992
The Origins of Anglo-Saxon Kingdoms, ed. Steven Bassett, Leicester UP 1989
Picts, Gaels and Scots, Sally M. Foster, Batsford 1996
Sutton Hoo: Burial Ground of Kings?, Martin Carver, BM Press 1998

CHAPTER 2: PRE-CONQUEST ENGLAND
Alfred the Great: Asser's Life of King Alfred and Other Contemporary Sources, translated S. Keynes and M. Lapidge, Penguin 1983
Alfred the Great: War, Kingship and Culture in Anglo-Saxon England, Richard P. Abels, Longman 1998
The Anglo-Saxons, ed. James Campbell, Penguin 1991
Cnut: the Danes in England in the Early 11th Century, M.K. Lawson, Longman 1993
Edward the Confessor, Frank Barlow, Yale UP 1997
The English Nobility Under Edward the Confessor, Peter A. Clarke, OUP 1994
Harold: the Last Anglo-Saxon King, Ian W. Walker, Sutton 1997
Hastings, Peter P. Wright, Windrush Press and Interlink Publishing 1997
King Alfred the Great, Alfred P. Smyth, OUP 1996
Kings and Vikings, P.H. Sawyer, Methuen 1982
The Life and Times of Alfred the Great, Douglas Woodruff, Weidenfeld and Nicolson 1984
The Oxford Illustrated History of the Vikings, ed. Peter Sawyer, OUP 2000
The Penguin Historical Atlas of the Vikings, John Haywood, Penguin 1995
1066: The Year of the Three Battles, P.F. McLynn, Pimlico 1996
Wessex in the Early Middle Ages, Barbara Yorke, Cassell 1995

CHAPTER 3: ENGLAND: THE NORMANS
Anglo-Norman England 1066–1666, Majorie Chibnall, Blackwell 1986
Conquest and Colonisation: Normans in Britain 1066–1100, Brian Golding, Macmillan 1994
The Death of Anglo-Saxon England, N.J. Higham, Sutton 1998
The Empress Matilda: Queen Consort, Queen Mother and Lady of the English, Marjorie Chibnall, Blackwell 1993
England Under the Norman and Angevin Kings 1075–1225, Robert Bartlett, Clarendon Press 1982
Hereward, Victor Head, Alan Sutton 1995
The Killing of William Rufus, Duncan Grinnell-Milne, David and Charles 1968
Kings and Lords in Conquest England, R. Fleming, CUP 1994
The Norman Conquest: Its Setting and Impact, Dorothy Whitelock, *et al*, Eyre and Spottiswoode 1966
Robert Curthose, C.W. David, Harvard UP 1920
Stephen and Matilda: The Civil War of 1139–53, Jim Bradbury, Alan Sutton 1996
William the Conqueror, D.C. Douglas, Eyre and Spottiswoode 1964
William the Conqueror, David Bates, George Philip 1989
William the Conqueror, David C. Douglas, Yale UP 1999
William Rufus, Frank Barlow, Methuen 1983

CHAPTER 4: SCOTLAND: FROM DUNKELD TO BRUCE
The Anglo-Norman Era in Scottish History, G.W.S. Barrow, OUP 1980

An Antidote to the English: The Auld Alliance 1295–1560, Norman Macdougall, Tuckwell Press 2001
Independence and Nationhood: Scotland 1306–1469, A. Grant, Edinburgh University Press, 1991
The Kingdom of the Isles, R. Andrew McDonald, Tuckwell Press 1997
The Kingless Kingdom: The Scottish Guardianship of 1286–1306, N. Reid, *Scottish Historical Review* lxi 1982
Kingship and Unity: Scotland 1000–1306, G.W.S. Barrow, Edinburgh UP 1989
Medieval Scotland: The Making of an Identity, Bruce Webster, Macmillan 1997
Robert Bruce and the Community of the Realm, G.W.S. Barrow, Eyre and Spottiswoode 1965
Scotland: The Making of the Kingdom, A.A.M. Duncan, Edinburgh UP 1992
Under the Hammer: Edward I and Scotland 1286–1307, Fiona Watson, Tuckwell Press 1998
The Wars of the Bruces: Scotland, England and Ireland, Colm McNamee, Tuckwell Press 1996

CHAPTER 5: ENGLAND: THE ANGEVINS AND PLANTAGENETS
The Angevin Empire, John Gillingham, Holmes and Meier 1984
Angevin England 1154–1258, Richard Mortimer, Blackwell 1996
Angevin Kingship, John E. Jolliffe, A&C Black 1963
The Crowned Lions: the Early Plantagenet Kings, Caroline Bingham, David and Charles 1978
Edward I, Michael Prestwich, Yale UP 1997
Edward II, Caroline Bingham, Weidenfeld and Nicolson 1973
Eleanor of Aquitaine, Alison Weir, Cape 1999
Eleanor of Aquitaine and the Four Kings, A. Kelly, Harvard UP 1950
Eleanor of Aquitaine: Queen and Legend, D.D.R. Owen, Blackwell 1993
England in the Reign of Edward III, Scott L. Waugh, CUP 1991
Henry Plantagenet, Richard Barber, Boydell Press 1972
Henry II, W.L. Warren, Yale UP 1973
The Hollow Crown: A Life of Richard II, Harold F. Hutchison, John Day 1961
King Edward III, M. Packe, Routledge and Keegan Paul 1983
King John, Maurice Ashley, Weidenfeld and Nicolson, 1972
King John, Ralph V. Turner, Longman 1994
King John, W.L. Warren, Eyre Methuen 1998
The Reign of Edward III, W.M. Ormrod, Tempus Publishing 1999
The Reign of Henry III, D.A. Carpenter, Hambledon Press 1996
Richard I, John Gillingham Weidenfeld and Nicolson 1973
Richard II, Nigel Saul, Yale UP 1999
Richard II and the English Nobility, J.A. Tuck, Arnold 1973
The Three Edwards: Wars and State in England 1272–1377, Michael Prestwich, Routledge 1997

CHAPTER 6: ENGLAND: LANCASTER AND YORK
Edward IV, Charles Ross, Eyre Methuen 1974
Henry IV of England, J.L. Kirby, Constable 1970
Henry V, Peter Earle, Weidenfeld and Nicolson 1972
Henry V: The Practice of Kingship, ed. G. Harriss, OUP 1985
Henry V, Christopher Allmand, Yale UP 1993
Lancaster and York, Alison Weir, Cape 1995
The Princes in the Tower, Alison Weir, Bodley Head 1992
The Reign of Henry VI, R.A. Griffiths, Sutton 1998
The Revolt of Owain Glyn Dwr, R.R. Davies, OUP 1995
Richard III, Charles Ross, Methuen 1981
Richard III: A Medieval Kingship, ed. John Gillingham, St Martin's Press 1993
Richard III: A Study of Service, Rosemary Horrox, CUP 1991
This Son of York, Mary Clive, Macmillan 1973
The Wars of the Roses, Charles Ross, Thames and Hudson 1986
The Wars of the Roses, Desmond Seward, Constable 1995

CHAPTER 7: SCOTLAND: FROM BRUCE TO STUART
Court, Kirk and Community: Scotland 1470–1625, Jenny Wormald, Edinburgh UP 1991

David II, M. Penman, Tuckwell Press 2002
The Early Stewart Kings: Robert II and Robert II, S. Boardman, Tuckwell Press 1996
Edward III and the Scots, R. Nicholson, OUP 1965
James I, M. Brown, Tuckwell Press 2000
James II, C. McGladdery, Edinburgh UP 1990
James IV, Norman Macdougall, Tuckwell Press 1997
James V, King of Scots, Caroline Bingham, Collins 1971
James V: The Personal Rule 1528–42, J. Cameron, Tuckwell Press 1998
Mary, Queen of Scots, Antonia Fraser, Weidenfeld and Nicolson 1969
Medieval Scotland: Crown, Lordship and Community, eds. A. Grant and K.J. Stringer, Edinburgh 1993
The Rough Wooings: Mary, Queen of Scots 1542–51, M. Merriman, Tuckwell Press 2000
Scotland: James V to VII, G. Donaldson, Edinburgh UP 1965
Stewart Style 1513–42: Essays on the Court of James V, ed. J. Handley Williams, Tuckwell Press 1996

CHAPTER 8: ENGLAND AND WALES: THE TUDORS
Anne Boleyn, E. Ives, Blackwell 1986
Bloody Mary: A Life of Mary Tudor, Carroly Erickson, Robson Books, 1997
The Cult of Elizabeth: Elizabethan Portraiture and Pageantry, Roy Strong, Pimlico 1999
Edward VI, Jennifer Loach, Yale UP 1999
The Elizabethan Age: The England of Elizabeth, Roy Strong (2 vols.), Macmillan 1955
Elizabeth, David Starkey, Chatto and Windus 2000
Elizabeth I, Jasper Ridley, Constable 1987
Elizabeth I, Anne Somerset, Weidenfeld and Nicolson 1991
Elizabeth the Queen, Alison Weir, Cape 1998
Henry VII: The First Tudor King, Eric N. Simons, Muller 1968
Henry VIII, Jasper Ridley, Constable 1984
Henry VIII, J.J. Scarisbrick, Yale UP 1968
Images of Tudor Kingship, Sydney Anglo, Seaby 1992
Lady Jane Grey, Hester Chapman, Cape 1962
The Later Tudors, England 1547–1603, Pendry Williams, OUP 1995
The Life and Times of Elizabeth I, Neville Williams, Weidenfeld and Nicolson 1972
The Life and Times of Henry VIII, Robert Lacey, Weidenfeld and Nicolson 1972
Mary Tudor, Jasper Ridley, Weidenfeld and Nicolson 1973
The Reign of Henry VIII: Politics, Policy and Piety, Diarmaid MacCulloch, Macmillan Press 1995
The Royal Palaces in Tudor England: Architecture and Court Life 1460–1547, Simon Thurley, Yale UP 1993
The Six Wives of Henry VIII, Alison Weir, Bodley Head 1991
The Tudor Monarchy, John Guy, Arnold 1997

CHAPTER 9: ENGLAND, WALES, SCOTLAND AND IRELAND: THE STUARTS
Absolute Monarchy and the Stuart Constitution, Lenn Burgess, Yale UP 1996
The Army, James II and the Glorious Revolution, J. Childs, Manchester UP 1980
The Causes of the English Civil War, Nora Carlin, Blackwell 1999
Charles II, Christopher Falkus, Weidenfeld and Nicolson 1972
Charles II: King of England, Scotland and Ireland, R. Hutton, Clarendon Press 1989
The Civil Wars Experienced: Britain and Ireland 1638–61, Martyn Bennett, Routledge 2000
Country and Court, England 1658–1714, J.R. Jones, Arnold 1978
Cromwell: Our Chief of Men, Antonia Fraser, Weidenfeld and Nicholson 1973
Cromwell: An Honourable Enemy, Tom Reilly, Brandon 1999
Cromwell in Ireland, J.S. Wheeler, Palgrave 2000
The Fall of the British Monarchies 1637–42, Conrad Russell, Clarendon Press 1990
The Golden Age Restored: The Culture of the Court 1603–42, Graham Parry, Manchester UP 1981
Great Britain's Solomon: James VI and I in his Three Kingdoms, Maurice Lee, University of Illinois Press 1990
The Interregnum: The Quest for Settlement 1646–60, G.E. Aylmer, Macmillan 1972
James I, C. Durston, Routledge 1993

James I by his Contemporaries, R. Ashton, Hutchinson 1969
James II: A Study in Kingship, John Miller, Methuen 1989
King Charles II, Antonia Fraser, Weidenfeld and Nicolson 1979
King or Covenant?, David Stevenson, Tuckwell Press 1996
King James VI and I, D.H. Willson, Cape 1963
The King's Head: Charles I, King and Martyr, Jane Roberts, Royal Collection 1999
The King's War, 1641–47, C.V. Wedgewood, Collins 1958
The Life and Times of Charles I, D.R. Watson, Weidenfeld and Nicolson 1972
The Life and Times of King James, Antonia Fraser, Weidenfeld and Nicolson 1973
The Mental World of the Jacobean Court, ed. Linda Levy Peck, CUP 1991
Monarchy and Revolution: The English State in the 1680s, J.R. Western, Blandford 1972
A Monarchy Transformed, Britain 1603–1714, Mark Kishlansky, Penguin 1996
Oliver Cromwell, Peter Gaunt, Blackwell 1996
The Personal Rule of Charles I, Kevin Sharpe, Yale UP 1992
Queen Anne, Edward Gregg, Ark 1980
The Right to be King: The Succession to the Crown of England 1603–1714, Howard Nenner, Macmillan 1995
The Reign of James VI and I, ed. A.G.R. Smith, Macmillan 1973
The Restoration, R. Hutton, OUP 1985
The Stuarts, J.P. Kenyon, Batsford 1958
The Stuart Age 1603–1714, Barry Coward, Longman 1994
The Trial of Charles I, C.V. Wedgewood, Collins 1964
William III, S. Baxter, London 1966
William III and the Defence of European Liberty, Stephen Baxter, Longman 1996
The World Turned Upside Down, Christopher Hill, Penguin 1978
Writings and Speeches of Oliver Cromwell, ed. W.C. Abbott, Clarendon 1988

CHAPTER 10: GREAT BRITAIN AND IRELAND: THE HANOVERIANS
Albert, Prince Consort, Robert Rhodes James, Hamish Hamilton 1983
Battle for Empire: The Very First World War 1756–63, Tom Pocock, Michael O'Mara 1998
Crucible of War: The Seven Years War and the Fate of Empire in British North America 1754–66, Fred Anderson, Knopf 2000
Edward VII, Christopher Hibbert, Allen Lane 1976
The 18th Century: The Oxford History of the British Empire, Vol. 2, ed. P.J. Marshall, OUP 1998
The English Constitution, Walter Bagehot, 1867
The First Four Georges, J.H. Plumb, Batsford 1956
George I, Elector and King, Ragnald Hatton, Thames and Hudson 1978
George IV, Prince of Wales, Christopher Hibbert, Longmans 1972
George IV, Regent and King, Christopher Hibbert, Longmans 1973
The Jacobite Risings in Britain, 1689–1746, B.P. Lenman, Eyre Methuen 1980
The Jacobites, F. McLynn, Routledge and Keegan Paul 1985
Jacobitism and the '45, ed. M. Lynch, Historical Association for Scotland 1995
The Letters of Queen Victoria, 9 vols, ed. Christopher Benson et al., John Murray 1907, 1928 and 1932
The Life and Times of Edward VII, Keith Middlemas, Weidenfeld and Nicolson 1972
The Life and Times of George III, John Clarke, Weidenfeld and Nicolson 1972
The Life and Times of George IV, Alan Palmer, Weidenfeld and Nicolson 1972
Memoirs of the Reign of George the Third, Horace Walpole, ed. G.F. Russell-Barker, 1894
Queen Victoria's Family, Dulcie Ashdown, Robert Hale 1975
Queen Victoria: a Personal History. Christopher Hibbert, HarperCollins 2000
Robert Walpole and the Nature of Politics in Early 18th-Century Britain, Jeremy Black, Macmillan 1990
Victoria and Albert, Joanna Richardson, Dent 1977

Victoria R.I., Elizabeth Longford, Weidenfeld and Nicolson 1964
Victoria, the Young Queen, Monica Charlot, Blackwell 1991

CHAPTER 11: GREAT BRITAIN: THE WINDSORS
Edward VIII, Frances Donaldson, Weidenfeld and Nicolson 1973
Edward VIII, Philip Zeigler, Collins 1990
Elizabeth, Sarah Bradford, Heinemann 1996
Elizabeth R., Elizabeth Longford, Weidenfeld and Nicolson 1983
George VI, Sarah Bradford, Fontana 1991
George VI, Patrick Howarth, Hutchinson 1987
King George V, Kenneth Rose Weidenfeld and Nicolson 1983
King George V: His Life and Reign, Harold Nicolson, Constable 1952
King George VI: His Life and Reign, Sir John Wheeler-Bennett, Macmillan 1958
A King's Story, HRH the Duke of Windsor, Cassell 1951
Kings, Queens and Courtiers: Intimate Portraits of the Royal House of Windsor from its Foundation to the Present Day, Kenneth Rose, Weidenfeld and Nicolson 1985
Majesty, Robert Lacey, Hutchinson 1977
The Prince of Wales: A Biography, Jonathan Dimbleby, Little, Brown 1994
The Queen, Kenneth Harris, Weidenfeld and Nicolson 1994
The Queen, Ben Pimlott, HarperCollins 1996

INDEX

A

Aberdeen, Bishops' War, 141; university founded, 117
Abernethy, Malcolm III submits, 60
Abingdon, Battle of, 57; Matilda at, 57
Abolition Act, 173
Acre, 76
Adelaide, Princess of Saxe-Coburg-Meiningen, 172, 173
Adeliza (wife of Henry I), 55
administration, Anglo-Saxon, 31, 33, 34;
    based around castles, 46; under Cnut, 39;
    Domesday Book, 45, 47, 48-9;
    under Henry III, 80;
    Pipe Rolls, 54; royal court, 74-5;
    see also government and parliament
Aelfgifu (wife of Cnut), 38
Aelfweard, King of Wessex, 33
Aelle, King of Sussex, 15
Aeneas, 8
Aethelbald, 13
Aethelred I, 30
Aethelred II (the Unready), 27, 34-5
Agincourt, Battle of, 98, 102
agriculture, George III interest in, 166
Ahlden, Castle of, 158
Alba, kingdom, 20, 22
Albany, Charles Duke of, 140; James Duke of, 138;
    Robert Duke of, 114, 115, 116
Albert (son of George V), see George VI
Albert, Prince Consort (Duke of Saxe-Coburg), 174-8
Albert Victor, Prince, 181, 184
Alcuin (scholar), 28
Alençon, duke of, 132
Alexander I, 60, 61
Alexander II, 62, 63
Alexander III, 59, 62, 63, 73, 85, 86, 113
Alexandra, Princess of Denmark, 180
Alfred (brother of Edward the Confessor), 40
Alfred the Great, 8, 26-7, 30-1; heirs to, 32-5
Alfred Jewel, 31
Alice, daughter of Victoria, 176;
    sister of Philippe II, 76-7
Alphege, Archbishop of Canterbury, 35
Altrincham, Lord, 194
American colonies, 164-7
American Declaration of Independence, 165
American Revolution, 166
Andrew, Duke of York, 195, 197
Angevin, Plantagenet phase, 69
Angevins, 69-97
Angles, arrive in England, 12, 20
Anglesey, Druids defeated, 10
Anglo-Dutch War, 146
Anglo-Norman invasion of Ireland, 72
Anglo-Saxon, administration, 31, 33, 34;
    consolidation under Alfred, 26;
    regain English rule, 38;
    expansion, 16; kingdoms, 9, 12, 13-14, 27;
    Saxon arrival, 13; supremacy ends, 43
Anglo-Saxon Chronicle, The, 12, 23, 28, 35, 54, 56
Angus, earl of, 117
Anjou, count of, 45, 49, 55, 56-7, 69, 70, 80;
    duke of, 105
Annabella (wife of Robert III), 115
Anne, daughter of Elizabeth II, 194, 196;
    daughter of James II, 148
Anne, Queen (sister of Mary II), 69, 153, 154-5, 156-7
Anne of Bohemia, 95
Anne of Cleves, 125, 127
Anne of Denmark, 138
Anselm, Archbishop of Canterbury, 52, 53, 54
anthem, first sung, 36
Antonine Wall, 11
ap Cynan, Gruffydd, 52
ap Gruffudd, Owain, 17
ap Gruffydd, Dafydd, 85-6
ap Gruffydd, Llywelyn, 17, 18, 19, 85-6
ap Gruffydd, Rhys, 17, 19
ap Llywelyn, Dafydd, 19
ap Llywelyn, Gruffydd, 16, 19, 41, 42
Aquitaine, duke of, 70, 76, 88, 90-1, 102
Aragon, in anti-French coalition, 109;
    see also Catherine of Aragon
Arbroath, Declaration of, 64, 65, 114
Ardmannoch, baron of, 138, 140

Argyll, 20, 62; earl of, 148, 149
Arran, earl of (Regent of Scotland), 118
    art, portraits, 96-7, 170-1
Arthur, King, 9, 13
Arthur (brother of Henry VIII), 124
Arthur, Duke of Brittany, 78
Arthur, Prince of Wales (son of Henry VII),
    122, 124, 125
arts, Henry III patronizes, 80
Arundel, earl of, 101; Lord Appellant, 95
Arundel, invasion lands at, 56
Ascham, Roger, 132
Ashdown, Vikings defeated at, 30
Ashingdon, Battle of, 35, 39
Asquith, H.H., 186
Asser, Bishop, 8
Athelstan, King of Wessex, 15, 23, 27, 29, 32-3, 38
Atrebates, in Surrey, 10, 11
Atterbury, Francis Bishop of Rochester, 161
Atterbury Plot, 159
Aughrim, Battle of, 160
Augustus, Emperor, 11
Augustus, Georg, see George I
Auld Alliance, 66-7, 69, 92, 117, 154
Auld Blearie, see Robert II
Australia, government dismissed, 196;
    independence, 187;
    referendum, 197;
    visited, 185
Austrian Succession, War of, 162
Avignon, Pope in, 101
Azay-le-Rideau, Treaty of, 73

B

Bagehot, Walter, 178
Bahamas, Governor of, 191
bailiff, introduction of, 34
Baldwin, Stanley, 190
Balfour, A.J., 179
Balliol, Edward, 67, 91-2, 113, 114-15
Balliol, John, 22, 50, 62-3, 64, 67, 86-7, 90-2
Balmoral, 175, 177
Bán, Donald, see Donald III
Bank of England, founded, 153
Bannockburn, Battle of, 64, 65, 88
Barnet, Battle of, 107, 110
Basilikon Doron, 138
Bastille, fall of, 166
Bath, Edgar crowned, 33
Battenburg, Prince Louis, 182
Battle Abbey, 52
Baugé, French victory at, 66, 103
Bayeux Tapestry, 42-3, 46
Beaton, Cecil, 194
Beaufort, Duke of Somerset, 106
Becket, Thomas Archbishop of Canterbury, 37, 71, 73
Bede (monk), 12, 15
Bedford, duke of, 104
Belach Mugna, Battle of, 24
Bengal, claimed, 163
Benson, A.C., 189
Beowulf, 14, 74
Berengaria of Navarre, 76
Berkley Castle, 89
Bernicia, kingdom, 14, 20
Berwick, English control, 108-9, 110, 113;
    inhabitants slaughtered, 87;
    siege, 67, 92, 102;
    trading burgh, 60;
    Treaty of, 67, 133, 138
Bible, Great, 125, 127;
    King James, 139
Birgham, Treaty of, 63, 86
Bishops' War, 141, 142
Black Death, 92, 93
Black Prince, see Edward the Black Prince
Bland, Dorothea see Jordan, Dorothea
Blenheim, Battle of, 154, 155
Bloodaxe, Eric, 28, 33, 39
Bloodless Revolution, 151, 152-3
Bluetooth, Harold, 34, 39
Bluetooth, Sweyn, 34-5
Bodvoc, King, 11

Boer War, 177
Bognor Regis, 187
Bohemia, King of, 139
Boleyn, Anne, 125, 126-7, 130, 132
Bolingbroke, Henry, see Henry IV
Bolingbroke Castle, 100
Bonaparte, Napoleon, 157
Bone, Henry, 168
Bonnie Prince Charlie, see Charles (Young Pretender)
Book of Common Prayer, 128-9, 140, 142
Book of Martyrs, The, 130
Bordeaux, Edward I court, 85
Boru, King Brian, 25, 29
Boston Tea Party, 164
Bosworth, Battle of, 107, 110, 111, 122
Bothwell, earl of, 118-19, 138
Boudicca, 10, 11
Boulogne, captured, 125;
    Count of, 56;
    Peace of, 131;
    siege, 128
Bouvines, John's defeat at, 78, 79
Bower, Edward, 142
Bowes-Lyon, Lady Elizabeth, 192-3
Boyd, Sir Alexander, 116
Boyne, Battle of, 153, 160
Bracton, Henry, 82
Breda, Declaration of, 146
Brétigny, Treaty of, 93
Brigantes, 10, 11
Brighton Pavilion, 168, 169, 171
Bristol, Black Death in, 93
Britain, legendary kings of, 8;
    origin of name, 8;
    as seafaring nation, 133-5
Britannia, 197
British Commonwealth of Nations, created, 187
British Empire, decolonisation, 195;
    growth, 163-77
Brittany, 45, 73, 122;
    Conan Duke of, 73;
    in anti-French coalition, 109
Bruce, Edward, 64, 65
Bruce, Robert, see Robert I the Bruce
Brude I, 20
Brunanburh, Battle of, 22, 23, 29, 33
Brussels, assassination attempt, 181
Brutus, 8
Buckingham, duke of, 110, 122, 138, 140
Buckingham Palace, 171, 177, 185, 188, 193, 196
Burgh, Sir Edward, 125
Burgundy, 104, 107, 109;
    duke of, 108;
    war declared on, 108
Burton, Thomas, 93
Bute, Lord, 164, 166
Byrhtnoth, Ealdorman, 35

C

Cabot, John, 123
Cade, Jack, 105
Cadiz, raided, 135
Cadwallon, King of Gwynedd, 16
Caernarvon Castle, 88
Caithness, 29, 59
Calais, before Agincourt, 102;
    Armada at, 135;
    English control, 92, 93, 104, 131;
    Field of the Cloth of Gold, 124;
    French defeat, 160;
    in planned invasion, 108;
    in Wars of the Roses, 107o
Caledonii (northern Picts), 11, 20
Cambridge, duke and marquess of, 162;
    earl of, 102, 108
Cameroon, 196
Canada, independence, 176, 187;
    visited by monarch, 185
Canmore, see Malcolm III
Canterbury, archbishop of, 35, 36, 52, 54, 56, 71, 73, 77,
    79, 94, 128, 131, 141, 148;
    Becket's murder, 73;
    Cathedral, 90;

Quitclaim of, 62; sacked, 43, 48;
  Treaty of, 102
Cantiaci, in Kent, 10
Caratacus, 10, 11
Carlisle Castle, 52; Edward I dies at, 87
Carlton House (Buckingham Palace), 169, 171
Caroline of Ansbach, 162, 163
Caroline of Brunswick, 168, 169, 172
Carolingian empire, 50
Carr, Robert Earl of Somerset, 138, 139
Carrick, earl of, see Edward VII and Edward VIII and
  George IV and Robert I the Bruce and
  Robert III
Cartimandua, Queen, 11
Cashel, sacks Dublin, 29;
  kings of, 24;
  sacks Limerick, 29
Cassivellaunus, King, 8, 10-11
Castile, alliance with, 123
Castillon, French victory, 104, 105
castles, destroyed, 71;
  Norman built, 46, 48-9;
  in Wales, 18, 84, 86
Caswallawn, 10
Cateau-Cambrésis, Treaty of, 133
Cathach, Shrine of, 25
Catherine (daughter of Charles VI;
  wife of Henry V), 103
Catherine of Aragon, 123, 124, 126
Catherine of Braganza, 146
Catholic Emancipation Act, 167, 169
Catuvellauni, 8, 10, 11
Caxton, William, 109
Cecil, Robert, 132, 139
Cecil, William, 132
Celts, tribes, 10, 12
Chalus, Richard I dies, 77
Chamberlain, Neville, 192, 193
Charing Cross, Eleanor Cross at, 86
Charlemagne, Emperor, 50, 96
Charles (Bonnie Prince; Young Pretender), 160
Charles, Prince of Wales (son of Elizabeth II), 194, 196
Charles I of England, 37, 97, 136-7, 139,
  140-3, 144-5, 170
Charles II of England, 22, 37, 137, 140,
  144, 145, 146-7, 148, 150-1, 154
Charles IV of France, 66, 89, 90, 92
Charles V of France, 93, 117
Charles VI of France, 98-9, 102-3, 104
Charles VII of France, 67, 103, 104
Charles VIII of France, 111, 123
Charles V of Spain, 131
Charlotte (daughter of George IV), 169, 172
Charlotte (wife of George III),
  see Sophia Charlotte of Mecklenburg-Strelitz
Charter of Liberties, 54
Cheddar, royal palace, 74
Chester, earl of, 16, 54, 56, 84, 90, 94, 102, 140, 162,
  164, 168, 180, 184, 190
Chester, Edgar crowned in, 33
Chesterfield, Lord, 159, 162
children, employment of, 173
Chippenham, Alfred defeated, 30, 31
chivalric codes, 96
Christianity, Cnut's conversion, 39;
  in Ireland, 25;
  Pictish, 20-1;
  spread of, 9, 12, 15, 20, 25;
  see also religion
Chronica Majora, 80
Chronicle of the Princes, 19
Churchill, John Duke of Marlborough, 154, 155, 160,
  162
Churchill, Sarah, 154, 155
Cingris, pharaoh, 8
Civil List Act, 153
civil war, Edward II precipitates,
  88-9; English, 137, 141-5;
  French, 98;
  Henry III, 82, 99;
  Ireland, 65;
  Scotland, 64;
  Stephen--Matilda, 56, 74;
  Wars of the Roses, 67, 99, 105, 106-7, 111, 113
Claim Act, 152
Clarence, duke of, 103, 108-9, 110, 184

Clarence and St Andrews, duke of, 172
Clarendon, assizes of, 72; Constitutions of, 71
Claudius, Emperor, 10, 11
Clement III, Pope, 52, 53
Clerk, Sir John, 155
Cleves, duke of, 127
Clive, Robert, 163
Clontarf, Battle of, 25, 29
Cnut, King, 23, 27, 34-5, 38-9;
  successors, 39
Cnut IV, 47, 49
Coel Hen, commander, 12
coin, Aethelred II's, 34;
  Alfred's, 31;
  Edgar's reform, 33;
  Edward III's reform, 92;
  first British, 11;
  first Scottish, 60;
  Hywel Dda's, 17;
  James II's, 114;
  Norman, 48;
  Offa's, 11, 15;
  Roman, 11;
  Viking, 28
Colchester, 11
college, Eton, 104, 105;
  King's Cambridge, 104, 105
Commius, King, 11
Common Law, 72
Commonwealth, the, 144-5, 194, 197
Commonwealth Day, 194
Comyn, John, 64
Comyn clan, rivals for Scottish throne, 65
Conan, Duke of Brittany (Earl of Richmond), 73
Concord, conflict at, 165
Cong, Cross of, 24
Connaught, overlordship, 24
Conrad II, Emperor, 39
Constantine II, 22-3
Copenhagen, Battle of, 167
Corbridge, defeat of Constantine II, 22
Coritani, tribe, 11
Cork, founded, 24
Cormac of Cashel, The Glossary of, 25
Corn Laws, 174
Cornwall, duke of, 102, 104, 128;
  earl of, 88, 94;
  Irish kingdom in, 24;
  MPs for, 173;
  under Saxon control, 14;
  Warbeck lands at, 122
Cornwall and Rothesay, duke of, 138, 140, 146, 162,
  164, 168, 180, 184
Cornwallis, Gen., 164
Coronation Oath Act, 151
coronation rites, 36-7
Coruña, fleet forced back, 161
Council of Government, 94, 95
Council of Regents, 128
Council of Twelve, 66
Coventry, archbishop of, 47
Cranborne Chase, 49
Cranmer, Thomas Archbishop of Canterbury, 126, 127,
  128-9
Cravant, battle at, 66
Crécy, Battle of, 66, 91, 92-3
Crimean War, 175
Cromwell, Oliver, 137, 143-5, 146
Cromwell, Richard, 145
Cromwell, Thomas, 126, 127
crown jewels, lost, 79
crowns, used in coronations, 37
Croyland Chronicle, 111
crusades, 53, 76-7, 84, 85
Crystal Palace, 174
Culloden, Battle of, 161
Cumbria, annexed by William II, 52, 61
Cunedda of Gwynedd, 16
Cunobelinus, King, 10, 11
Curragh, scandal at, 181
Cymbeline, 11
Cyprus, 76
Czechoslovakia, invaded, 192

D

d'Avranches, Hugh, 16
d'Este, Maria (Mary, wife of James II), 148
Dal Riada, kingdom, 20
Danby, earl of, 147
Danegeld, 34-5
Danelaw, 28
Danes, massacre ordered, 34;
  settle in England, 24
  see also Vikings
Darnley, Lord (Henry Stewart), 118-19, 138
Dartmouth, 192; Royal Naval College, 184, 190
Dauphin of France, see Charles VII and François II
David (son of Robert III), 115
David, Old Testament king, 60
David I, 56, 59, 60, 61, 62, 70
David II, 37, 66, 67, 90-3, 113, 114-15
Dda, King Hywel the good, 16
de Bordeaux, Richard, see Richard II
de Burgh, Hubert, 80
de Lusignan, Hugh, 78
de Montfort, Simon Earl of Leicester, 80-1, 82, 84
de Mowbray, Robert Earl of Northumbria, 60, 61
de la Pole, Michael, 94
des Roches, Peter, 80
de Vere, Richard, 75, 94
de la Zouche, Walter Archbishop of York, 93
Declaration of Indulgence, 148
Declaration of Rights, 151, 152
Defender of the Faith, Henry VIII awarded title, 126
Degastan (Battle of), 21
Deheubarth, kingdom, 16, 17
Deira, kingdom, 14
Delhi Durbar, George V at, 185, 186, 188
Denmark, see Cnut, King
Derby, Charles (Young Pretender) at, 161
Derby, earl of, 100; as Danish borough, 29
Despenser, Hugh le, 88, 89
Dettingen, Battle of, 162
Devereux, Robert Earl of Essex, 132
Disraeli, Benjamin, 176
Dobunni, tribe, 11
Domesday Book, 45, 47, 48-9
Domfront, lord of, 54
Donald II, 22
Donald III (Donald Bán), 60-1
Douglas, Earl of, 113, 114, 115
Dover Castle, 49; James II in, 150; Treaty of, 146, 147
Drake, Francis, 133-5
Drogheda, Cromwell victory, 144
Dublin, Easter Rising, 186;
  founded, 24-5, 28;
  Norse ruler of, 39;
  the Pale, 125;
  sacked, 29
Dudley, Guildford, 129
Dudley, Robert Earl of Leicester, 132
Duke of York's camps, 192
Dunad Fort, 20
Dunbar, Cromwell victory, 144, 146
Duncan I, 60-1
Duncan II, 52, 53, 60-1
Dundee, Viscount, 152
Dunkeld, abbot of, 60; House of, 60-3
Dunsinnan, Malcolm murdered, 60, 61
Durham, grant of land, 60
Dyfed, loyalty to Edward, 32

E

Eadred, King of Wessex, 29, 33
Eadric (brother of Edmund Ironside), 38
Eadwig, King of Wessex, 33
Eahlswith, marries Alfred, 30
Eanred, King of Northumbria, 14
East Anglia, earl of, 46, 48;
  earldom, 38, 39, 41;
  kingdom, 12-13;
  uprising quelled, 48;
  Vikings invade, 28, 30;
  incorporated into Wessex, 32
Easter Rising, 186

Edgar (son of Malcolm III), 53, 60, 61
Edgar the Aetheling, 42, 47, 48, 60
Edgar of Wessex, 23, 27, 33, 36, 96
Edgehill, Battle of, 142
Edinburgh, Charles (Young Pretender) in, 161;
        Darnley murdered, 118;
        duke of, 164, 194-5, 197;
        Holyrood coronations, 22;
        Prayer Book Riots, 140;
        stormed, 110, 116;
        trading burgh, 60;
        Treaty of, 65, 114, 133
Edington, Danes defeated at
Edith (Matilda: wife of Henry I), 54, 55
Edmund, Duke of Somerset, 105, 106
Edmund I, King of Wessex, 23, 33
Edmund the Aetheling, 23
Edmund Ironside, 35, 38, 48
Edmund the Martyr, 95
Edred, King of Wessex, 27
Edric the Wild, 46
Education Act, 117
Edward, son of Elizabeth II, 195;
        son of Henry VI, 107;
        son of Richard III, 111
Edward I, 84-7;
        humiliates Balliol, 62-3-6;
        expels Jews, 84;
        homage paid, 50;
        annexes Isle of Man, 29;
        continues Magna Carta, 78;
        marriages, 86;
        military prowess, 84-7;
        moves Stone of Scone, 22;
        presides over parliament, 82-3;
        taken prisoner, 81;
        subjugates Scotland, 59, 62, 64-5, 66-7, 87;
        succession, 36-7;
        conquest of Wales, 17-19, 69, 85
Edward II, 37, 64-5, 66, 82, 86, 88-9
Edward III, 65-7, 69, 89, 90-3, 98-9, 102, 113, 115
Edward IV, 99, 105, 107, 108-9, 110, 116
Edward V, 37, 99, 107, 110, 111
Edward VI (Prince Edward; son of Henry VIII), 107,
        118, 124, 126, 127, 128-9, 130-1, 132
Edward VII, 157, 174, 177, 179, 180-1, 182
Edward VIII, 37, 183, 184, 185, 187, 189, 190-1
Edward the Atheling, 38, 41
Edward the Black Prince, 69, 90-1
Edward the Confessor, 17, 27, 36-7, 39, 40-1, 42-3, 46,
        80, 95
Edward the Elder, King of Wessex, 16, 22-3, 27, 32, 33
Edward Longshanks, see Edward I
Edwin, Earl of East Anglia, 42-3, 46, 48
Edwin, King of Northumbria, 14, 16
Edwy (son of Edmund Ironside), 38
Egbert, King of Mercia, 13, 15
Egfrith, King of Mercia, 14, 36
Eleanor (sister of Henry III), 80
Eleanor, Infanta of Castile, 86
Eleanor of Aquitaine, 67, 70, 73, 76
Eleanor of Provence (wife of Henry III), 80, 86
Eleanor Crosses, 86
Elizabeth, daughter of Anne Boleyn, 125, 127;
        daughter of James I of England, 139;
        wife of Edward IV (Elizabeth Woodville), 108-9,
        110, 111
Elizabeth I, 96-7, 113, 118-19, 121, 132-5, 138, 150
Elizabeth II, 36, 183, 189, 192, 194-7
Elizabeth of York (daughter of Edward IV), 107, 122-3
Ellendun, Battle of, 13, 14
Eltham, earl of, 164; Palace, 109
Ely, bishop of, 76; marquess of, 164
Emma (wife of Aethelred and Cnut), 35, 38, 42
England, Cnut's rule, 38-9;
        counties, 33;
        Danish settlement, 24;
        divided into earldoms, 39;
        French invasion attempted, 91;
        Henry II invades, 70;
        Robert's failed invasion, 54;
        Romans invade, 10-11;
        Viking raids, 26-30
English Common Law, 51
English Constitution, The, 178
Entente Cordiale, 181

Essex, Robert Earl of, 132, 135
Essex, kingdom of, 9, 13
Essie, Lulach killed at, 61
Eton College, 104, 105
Eustace (son of Stephen), 57
Evelyn, John, 147
Evesham, Battle of, 81, 84
Exclusion Act, 147
Exeter, bishop of, 56;
        sacked, 46

F

Factory Act, 173
Falaise, Treaty of, 62
Falkirk, Battle of, 87
Falklands War, 196
Farne island, 15
Faversham, abbey, 56
Ferguson, Sarah, 195, 197
feudalism, 50-1
Field of the Cloth of Gold, 124
Fine-Hair, King Harald, 29
Fishbourne, Roman palace, 10
Fitzclarence, descendants of William IV, 172
Fitzherbert, Maria, 168, 169
Fitzosbern, William, 16
Fitzroy, Robert Earl of Gloucester, 55, 57
Five Boroughs, 29, 32
flag, Union Jack, 139
Flanders, count of, 43, 49, 54;
        Emma flees to, 39;
        French fleet destroyed, 92, 92;
        Mortimer's army in, 89
Flann Sinna, High King, 24-5, 28
Flodden, Battle of, 67, 113, 117, 124
Fontevrault, tomb, 70, 73
Forest Laws, 49
Forteviot, Vikings raid, 20, 22
Fortriu, 21
Fox, Charles James, 166, 168, 169
Foxe, John, 130
France, Aethelred alliance, 35;
        Auld alliance, 66-7, 69, 92;
        Bastille falls, 166;
        Edward III invasion, 92-3;
        Edward IV's planned invasion, 108, 109;
        feudal system, 50;
        fleet destroyed, 91, 92;
        Henry VIII invades, 124;
        Jacquerie, 92;
        last English possession, 128, 131;
        peace with England, 124;
        planned invasion of England, 66;
        Revolution, 166, 167;
        Scottish alliance, 66-7, 87, 160
François I of France, 66, 116, 124
François II (Dauphin), 118
Frederick (palatine elector), 139
Frederick, Duke of York, 172
Frederick, Prince of Wales, 162-3
French Revolution, 166, 167
Frobisher, 133
Froissart, Jean, 36, 66
Furness, abbey, 56

G

Gaillard, Château, 77
Gaitskell, Hugh, 192
Galloway, 59, 62
Gascony, Black Prince in, 90;
        duke of, 84;
        Edward I in, 84-5, 87;
        Edward III in, 93;
        French control resumes, 105;
        Philippe IV invades, 91;
        province of, 66, 80, 86
Gaul, 13
Gaveston, Piers Earl of Cornwall, 88, 89
Geddington, Eleanor Cross, 86
General Assembly of the Kirk, 139

General Strike, 186, 187
Geoffrey, Count of Nantes, 73
Geoffrey of Anjou, 55, 56-7, 70, 76
Geoffrey of Monmouth, 8, 11, 13
George, Prince of Denmark, 154-5
George I (Georg Augustus), 157, 158-9, 161
George I of Greece, 195
George II, 36, 157, 158, 162-3
George III, 157, 164-7, 168, 171
George IV (Prince of Wales; Prince Regent), 36, 157,
        167, 168-9, 171, 172
George V, 157, 181, 182-3, 184-7, 148-9
George VI, 37, 183-4, 189, 191, 192-3
Gerberoi, Battle of, 47
Germany, Edward VIII admires, 191
Gervais of Canterbury, 56
Ghana, 195
Gibraltar, 154, 155
Gillray, James, 156
Gladstone, 176, 177, 179
Glanville, Ranulph, 72
Glencoe Massacre, 152, 160
Glendower, Owain, see Glyn Dwr, Owain
Gloucester, Henry Duke of, 184;
        Richard Duke of, see Richard III;
        Robert Earl of, 55, 56;
        William Duke of, 154
Gloucester, Abbey, 89;
        duke of, 109, 153;
        Henry III coronation, 80;
        Lord Appellant, 95
Glyn Dwr, Owain, 100-1
Gododdin, kingdom, 20
Godwine, Edith, 40
Godwine, Gyrd, 40, 43
Godwine, Gyrth Earl of East Anglia, 40-1
Godwine, Harold, see Harold II
Godwine, Leofwine, 43
Godwine, Tostig Earl of Northumbria, 41, 42-3, 60
Goidel, 8
Gordon Riots, 165
Gordon-Cumming, Coln. Sir William, 180
Gothfrithson, Olaf, 29, 33
government, Coalition, 187;
        first National, 186;
        king's authority, 82, 102, 123; see also parliament
Gowrie, Lord, 138
Grafton, earl of, 166
Graham, Sir Robert, 115
Grand Coalition, 153
Grand Remonstrance, 143
Gratton, Henry, 166
Gray, Thomas, 160
Great Bible, 125, 127
Great Britain, created, 154, 155
Great Covenant, 142
Great Depression, 186
Great Exhibition, The, 175
Great Fire of London, 147
Great Plague, 147
Greenwich, 170; Treaty of, 118, 128
Gregory VII, Pope, 52
Gregory the Great, Pope, 15
Greville, Lord, 156, 175
Grey, Lady Jane, 129, 130
Grey, Lord, 173
Greyfriars Abbey, Comyn murdered, 64
Guildford, Godwine's court at, 40
Guillaume I le Bâtard, 46
Gunn, James, 192
Gunpowder Plot, 139
Guthrum, the Dane, 28, 30
Guy of Brionne, 46
Guyenne, France recaptures, 105
Gwent, kingdom, 16
Gwynedd, Owain, 19, 70
Gwynedd, kingdom, 16, 17;
        loyalty to Edward, 32, 86

H

Haakon, King of Norway, 63
Hadrian's Wall, 11
Haifa, Battle of, 84

Hainault, mercenaries recruited, 89
Hales, Coln., 148
Hales, Robert, 94
Halfdan, the Dane, 30
Halidon Hill, Battle of, 67, 90, 114
Hampton Court, 124, 159, 170;
        Conference, 138
Handel, 36
Hanover, Sophia Duchess of, 154, 156-7
Hanover, duke and elector of, 158, 162, 164;
        House of, 156-81
Hapsburg empire, 67
Harby, Eleanor Cross, 86
Hardinge, Alex, 191
Hardingstone, Eleanor Cross, 86
Hardrada, Harold King of Norway, 39, 42-3, 46, 60
Harfleur, 102
Harlech Castle, 101
Harley, Robert, 155
Harold I (son of Cnut), 39
Harold II (Harold Godwine, Earl of Wessex), 17, 36, 37,
        38-41, 42-3, 46, 70
Harthacnut, King (son of Cnut), 39, 40
Hastings, Battle of, 43, 46;
        castle, 46;
        Lord, 111
Hatton, Sir Christopher, 135
Hawkins, 133-4
Hebrides, 20, 28-9, 113, 116
Hengest, 9, 12
Henri Grâce à Dieu, 127
Henri II of France (Henry VI), 104, 128
Henri IV of France, 139
Henrietta Maria of France, 140
Henry, brother of Stephen, 56;
        son of James I of England, 139
Henry I, 45, 51, 54-5, 59, 61, 74
Henry II (Henry Plantagenet), 17, 19, 24-5, 36, 57, 59,
        62, 69, 70-3, 76-9, 82
Henry III (Young King), 17, 19, 40, 62, 69, 70, 72, 73,
        78, 80-1, 84, 98
Henry IV (Henry Bolingbroke), 36-7, 69, 95, 98, 99,
        100-1, 102, 106, 115
Henry V, 67, 98, 101, 102-3, 106
Henry V, Holy Roman Emperor, 54, 57, 124
Henry VI (Henri II of France), 98-9, 104-5, 106-7, 123,
        128, 167
Henry VII (Henry Tudor), 69, 99, 107, 110, 111, 120-1,
        122-3
Henry VIII, 51, 67, 82, 96-7, 113, 117, 118, 121, 124-7,
        128, 130, 132
Henry IX, 161
Henry of Anjou (son of Matilda), 57, 61
Henry Percy (Hotspur), 101
Henry Plantagenet, see Henry II
Henry Tudor, see Henry VII
Heptarchy kingdoms, 13
Hereford, earl of, 16, 100
Hertford, earl of (Lord Protector; duke of Somerset), 128
Hewitt, James, 196
Hexham, Lancastrians defeated, 108
Hilliard, Nicholas, 138
Hitler, Adolf, 189, 191, 192-3
Hogarth, 158, 164
Holbein, 97, 124, 127
Holinshead, Raphael, 11
Holy Roman Emperor, see Henry V, Holy Roman
        Emperor
Holyrood, Abbey, 61, 140; Palace, 116
Holyroodhouse, 197
Homildon Hill, Battle of, 115
Hong Kong, 195
Horsa, 9, 12
horse racing, 180
Hotspur (Henry Percy), 101
House of Lords, 144, 185
Howard, Frances, 138
Howard, Katherine, 125, 127
Howard, Thomas Earl of Surrey, 124
Hugh the Younger, 88, 89
Huguenots, 140
Humbleton, Scottish defeat, 100, 101
Hundred Years War, 67, 69, 82, 91-3, 103, 104
Hunt, Leigh, 169
hunting, 47, 49
Huntingdon, earl of, 100

Hwicce, Mercian sub-kingdom, 13
Hyde, Anne, 148

I

Iceni tribe, 10, 11
Immortal Seven, 149, 151, 152
India, emperor of, 180, 184, 190, 192;
        empress of, 176, 179, 188;
        king-emperor of, 185, 186
Indian Mutiny, 175, 189
Indulgence, Declaration of, 147, 148
Infanta of Castile, Eleanor, 86
Infanta of Spain, 139, 140
Ingibiorg (wife of Malcolm III), 61
Instrument of Union, rejected, 139
Inverness, earl of, 184, 192
Iona, abbey, 25; monastery, 15, 20; Vikings sack, 28
Ireland, Anglo-Norman invasion, 72;
        duke of, 75, 94, 122;
        duke of York flees to, 106-7;
        high king, 24, 25, 73;
        Home Rule, 185;
        independence, 166, 186;
        kingdoms, 24;
        legendary kings, 8;
        lords of, 24, 73, 84, 88, 102, 104, 108, 100, 110;
        end of Norse control, 29;
        Plantagenet rule, 69;
        Plantation of, 139;
        regent of, 88, 89, 94;
        Scottish 'liberation', 64, 65;
        settlers, 142;
        Viking invasion, 22, 24;
        William III victories, 152-3
Irish Brigade, 160
Irish Free State, 186
Irish Home Rule, 185
Irish-Jorvik kingdom, 24
Isaacs, Sir Isaac, 187
Isabel (daughter of Warwick), 108
Isabella (wife of Edward II), 88, 89, 90, 98
Isabella of Angoulême, 78
Isabella of Gloucester, 78
Isle of Man, annexed to England, 29;
        king of, 84;
        occupation, 29, 59
Isle of Wight, 177
Ivar the Boneless, 24, 28, 30

J

Jacobite rebellions, 158, 160-1
Jaffa, 76
James (Old Pretender), 154, 160
James I of England (James VI of Scotland), 67, 113, 119,
        136, 138-9
James II of England (James VII of Scotland), 137, 147,
        148-9, 150-1, 152-3, 154, 160
James III of England (James VIII of Scotland), 160
James I of Scotland, 101, 103, 112-13, 114-15
James II of Scotland, 22, 113, 114-15
James III of Scotland, 113, 115, 116-17
James IV of Scotland, 67, 113, 116-17, 122-3, 124
James V of Scotland, 66, 116-17
James VI of Scotland, see James I of England
James VII of Scotland, see James II of England
James VIII of Scotland, see James III of England
Japan, Emperor of, 188
Jarrow, Vikings sack, 28
Jean II of France, 90, 92-3
Jedburgh trading burgh, 60
Jenkins's Ear, War of, 162
Jerusalem, 76-7; Henry IV in, 101
Jews, expulsion of, 84
Joan, daughter of Edward II, 114;
        daughter of Edward III, 93;
        sister of Henry III, 62
Joan of Arc, 67, 104, 105
Joan of Navarre, 102
John (son of George V), 184
John, Earl of Carrick, see Robert III
John, King (brother of Richard I), 19, 24, 50, 62, 69, 70,

73, 76-7, 78-9, 82
John, Lord Latimer, 125
John, Prince of England (Lord of Ireland), 25
John II, Lord of the Isles, 116
John of Gaunt, 93, 94, 95, 99
John of Salisbury, 82
Jordan, Dorothea, 172
Jorvik, 28, 29
Julius Agricola, 11
Julius Caesar, 8, 10-11
Jutland, Battle of, 192

K

Karsh, Yousef, 192
Kelso Abbey, 60
Kenilworth, parliament at, 89
Kensington Palace, 159, 170
Kent, Cantiaci in, 10;
        duchess of, 172, 173;
        duke of, 184;
        earl of, 100;
        Hengest in, 12;
        kingdom of, 13;
        Viking fleet lands, 28
Kett's Rebellion, 128
Kew Palace, 171
Killarney, Baron, 184, 192
Killiecrankie, Jacobite victory, 152, 160
Kilmartin, 20
king, origin of word, 9
King George's War, 162
King William's War, 152, 153
King's College, Cambridge, 104, 105
King's Council (Star Chamber), 122, 123
kingship, see monarchy
Kingston, coronation at, 37
Kingston-upon-Thames, Aethelred II coronation, 34
Königsmark, Philip von, 158

L

La Hogue, French defeat, 153, 160
La Rochelle, English fleet defeated, 93
Labour, Statute of, 93
Lady Jane Grey, 129, 130
Lambeth, Treaty of, 80
Lancaster, duke of, 99, 100, 102;
        earl of, 88, 89
land enclosures, 129
Land of Hope and Glory, 189
Landseer, 175
Lanfranc, Archbishop of Canterbury, 52
Lanfrec of Bec, 47
Langton, 79
language, spoken by Edward I, 84;
        Gaelic supplants Pictish, 23;
        Norse, 29
Latimer, Hugh Bishop of Worcester, 130
Laud, William Archbishop of Canterbury, 141
Launceston, Viscount of, 164
law, 12-man jury, 72;
        Abolition Act, 173;
        Act of Settlement, 153, 156, 191;
        Act of Six Articles, 128;
        Act of Supremacy, 124, 126;
        Act of Uniformity, 128, 133;
        Act of Union, 125, 127, 155, 160, 166;
        Acts of Attainder, 108, 123;
        Alfred overhauls, 31;
        Bill of Rights, 151;
        Building Act, 147;
        Claim Act, 152;
        Cnut overhauls, 39;
        Common, 72;
        Corn Laws, 174;
        Coronation Oath Act, 151;
        Council of Government, 94, 95;
        Danelaw, 28;
        Domesday Book, 45, 47, 48-9;
        Education Act, 117;
        Edward I reforms, 84;

English Common, 51;
Factory Act, 173;
Forest Laws, 49;
Henry II reforms, 70, 72, 82;
Lords Ordainers, 88, 89;
Magna Carta, 50, 62, 69, 80, 82;
Parliament Act, 186;
Petition of Right, 140;
Reform Acts, 173, 175, 178;
Royal Marriages Act, 169;
royal rule, 68;
Septennial Act, 158;
Statute of Westminster, 84;
Swearing and Cursing Act, 145;
Test Act, 147;
time immemorial defined, 84;
Wantage Law Code, 34; Welsh, 16
Lawrence, Thomas, 171
legend, kings, 8-9
Leicester, as Danish borough, 29;
earl of, 100;
Robert Earl of, 132;
Simon Earl of, 80
Leinster, King of, 73;
overlordship, 24
Leir, play based on, 8
Leo X, Pope, 126
Leopold, Duke (of Austria), 76-7
Lewes, Henry III defeated at, 81
Lexington, conflict at, 165
Limerick, sacked, 25, 29;
Treaty of, 160
Limoges, English fleet defeated, 93
Lincoln, bishop of, 56;
as Danish borough, 29;
earl of, 100, 122;
investiture in, 19;
Louis IX defeated, 80;
Ranulf's rebellion, 56;
Stephen defeated, 56
Lindisfarne, monastery, 15;
Vikings sack, 28
Lindisfarne Gospels, 15
Lindsey, Welsh sub-kingdom, 13
Lionel (son of Edward III), 114
literacy, King Alfred, 30
Lithuania, Henry IV in, 101
Lloyd George, 181, 186-7
Llud, gives name to London, 8
Llywelyn the Great, 17, 18, 19, 79
Lochleven, 119
Lollard rising, 100, 102
London, archbishop of, 53;
Balliol in, 62;
Boudicca attacks, 11;
Charing Cross, 86;
Cnut's coronation, 38;
George IV's plans, 169;
Gordon Riots, 165;
Great Fire of, 147;
jubilee celebrations, 197;
Matilda moves to, 56;
Norman occupation, 48;
origin of name, 8;
Peasants' Revolt, 94-5;
revolt against, 106, 131;
Ridley Bishop of, 130;
sacked, 34;
Tower of, 47, 50, 74, 87, 89, 105, 107, 108, 111,
122, 132, 149;
Viking occupation, 35;
Westminster Abbey, 22
Londonderry, siege of, 152-3
Longchamp, William Bishop of Ely, 76, 78
Lord of the North (Richard III), 110
Lords Appellants, 94, 95
Lords Ordainers, 88, 89
Lothian, 22, 23
Louis, Prince of France, 62
Louis VI, 55
Louis VII, 70, 71, 73, 76
Louis IX, 80
Louis XI, 99, 107, 108-9
Louis XIV, 146, 147, 148, 151, 152-3, 154, 161, 170
Louis XV, 160
Louis Philippe of France, 174

Louvain, Count of, 55
Ludlow, 106-7, 111
Lulach (stepson of Macbeth), 60, 61
Lumphanan, Macbeth murdered, 60, 61
Lyme Regis, Monmouth lands at, 149

M

Mac Alpin, Kenneth, 20-2
Mac Alpin, kings of, 61
Mac Erp, King Drust, 20
Macbeth of Moray, 60-1
Macdonald, Alasdair Chief of Glencoe, 152
MacDonald, Ramsay, 186
MacDougall clan, rivals for Scottish throne, 65
Macfinlay, ruler of Moray, see Macbeth of Moray
Macmillan, Harold, 195
MacMurrough, Dermot, 24, 25
Madeleine (daughter of François I), 66, 117
Maetae (southern Picts), 20
Magna Carta, 50, 62, 69, 78-9, 80, 82, 143, 150
Magnus I, King of Norway, 39, 40, 42
Magonsaete, sub-kingdom, 14
Magyar invasions, 68
Maid of Norway, see Margaret Maid of Norway
Maine (France), count of, 70;
county of, 46, 47, 104, 105
Malcolm II, 23, 39, 58, 60-1
Malcolm III (Canmore), 23, 48, 49, 52, 60-1
Malcolm IV, 59, 60, 62-3, 70
Maldon, Battle of, 35
Malmsey, Clarence executed, 109
Malory, Sir Thomas, 13
Malplaquet, Battle of, 154
Mancini, Dominic, 109
Mantes, siege, 47
map, Anglo-Saxon arrival, 13;
Anglo-Scottish conflict, 21, 23, 63, 65;
Anne I, 155;
Charles I, 141;
Charles II, 146;
Cnut's occupation, 38;
Commonwealth, 145, 196;
David I, 61;
dissolution of monasteries, 126;
Edward I, 84, 87;
Edward II, 88;
Edward IV, 109;
Edward VI and Mary I, 131;
Edward VIII, 191;
Elizabeth I, 133, 134;
Elizabeth II, 195, 196, 197;
England pre-conquest, 41;
English civil war, 143;
European politics in 1000, 50;
George I, 159;
George II, 162;
George III, 165;
George IV, 168;
George V, 185;
George VI, 193;
Glorious Revolution, 151;
Henry I, 55;
Henry II, 71, 72;
Henry III, 81;
Henry IV, 100;
Henry VII, 123;
Henry VIII, 125, 126;
Heptarchy kingdoms, 14;
Hundred Years War, 91, 103, 104;
Imperial expansion of England, 125;
Ireland, 24;
Jacobite uprisings, 161;
James I, 139;
James II of England, 149;
John, 79;
Mary Queen of Scots, 119;
Norman, 43, 47;
Richard I, 77;
Richard II, 95;
Richard III, 110;
Roman, 10;
Stephen's England, 57;
Stewarts, 115, 117;

United Kingdom, 197;
Victoria, 176-7;
Viking conflict, 29, 30, 35;
Wales, 17, 18, 84;
Wessex, 32;
William and Mary, 153;
William II, 53
Mar, earl of, 116, 160
March, earl of, 102, 106-7, 108
Marcher lordships, created, 16, 48, 52
Margaret, daughter of George VI, 192, 196, 197;
daughter of Louis VII, 73;
sister of Henry VIII, 67;
sister of Philippe IV, 86;
wife of Malcolm III, 60
Margaret of Anjou (wife of Henry VI), 99, 104, 105,
106, 108
Margaret of Bergundy (sister of Edward IV), 108, 122
Margaret Maid of Norway, 59, 62, 63, 66, 86, 116
Margaret Tudor (daughter of Henry VII)
wife of James IV), 113, 117, 118, 123
Market Bosworth, Battle of, 111
Marlborough, duke of, see Churchill, John Duke of
Marlborough
Marshall, William, 80
Marston Moor, Battle of, 142
Mary, daughter of Catherine of Aragon, 126;
daughter of Charles I, 140;
daughter of James II, 148;
wife of James II, 148
Mary I (Bloody Mary), 130-1
Mary II, 147, 149, 151, 152-3, 154, 170
Mary of Gueldres, 116-17
Mary of Guise, 66, 116, 117, 118
Mary Queen of Scots (Infant Queen), 67, 113, 118-19,
124-5, 128, 133, 135, 138
Mary of Teck, 182, 184
Matilda, daughter of Henry I, 54, 55, 56-7, 61;
wife of Henry I, 54, 55, 70
Mauricius, 12
Mawr, Rhodri the Great, 16
Maximilian I, Holy Roman Emperor, 122
Meath, king of, 73;
overlordship, 24
Meaux, Henry V captures, 103
Medway, Dutch raid, 147
Melbourne, Lord, 175, 178
Mercia, earl of executed, 38;
earldom created, 38, 39;
kingdom, 13, 15;
Offa's Dyke created, 13;
Vikings invade, 28, 30;
Wessex alliance, 30, 32;
West Saxon control, 31
Merciless Parliament, 82
Methven, Scottish army defeated, 64
Middlesex, as Middle Saxon kingdom, 9
Milesian (King of Ireland), 8
Milford Haven, earl of, 162; landing at, 122
Minorca, captured, 163
Model Parliament, 82
Modena, Duke of, 148
monarchy, abdication, 190-1;
abolition of, 144;
authority of, 82, 96-7;
constitutional, 150-1, 173, 174, 178-9;
coronation rites, 36-7;
discrimination against women, 57;
in feudal ages, 50-1;
growth of ceremony, 188-9;
image of, 96-7, 170-1;
limits taxation, 108;
madness in, 98-9;
medieval, 68, 74-5, 96;
radio broadcast, 187;
regalia, 37;
royal court, 74-5, 109;
succession, 27, 68-9, 98, 136-7, 153;
and television, 195
monasteries, dissolution of, 125, 126-7
Monck, George, 145
money, see coin
Monkswell, Lady, 177
Monkwearmouth, Vikings sack, 28
Monmouth, Duke of, 147, 148, 149
Mons Graupius, 11

Montagu, Lady Mary Wortley, 159
Montgomery, Roger, 16
Montgomery, Treaty of, 17
Mor, King Fergus, 20
Moray, 59, 61, 62
Morcar, Earl of Northumbria, 42-3, 46, 48
Mordaunt divorce case, 180
More, Thomas, 124, 125
Mortain, Count of, 56
Morte D'Arthur, Le, 13
Mortimer, Edmund, 101
Mortimer, Roger, 89, 90, 91, 98
Moses, 8
Mount Badon, Battle of, 13
Mountbatten, Lord, assassinated, 196
Mountbatten, Philip, see Philip, Prince (Duke of
    Edinburgh)
Munich Agreement, 192
Munster, earl of, 172;
    Munster, king of, 25;
    Munster, overlordship, 24
Muslim invasions, 68
Mussolini, 193
Mytens, Daniel, 139
myths, 8-9

N

Nantes, Geoffrey Count of, 73
Napoleonic wars, 167
Naseby, Battle of, 143
Nash, John, 169, 171
Nassau-Dillenburg, Count of, 152
Nechtansmere, Battle of, 20
Neerwinden, French victory, 153
Nelson, Lord Horatio, 163, 167
Netherlands, armed support for, 134-5;
    Charles II exiled, 146;
    French war against, 147
Neville, Anne (wife of Richard III), 111
Neville, Richard, see Warwick, Richard Neville Earl of
Neville's Cross, Battle of, 92, 114-15
New Castle, 49
New Forest, 47, 49, 53
New Zealand, independence, 187;
    visited by monarchy, 185
Newcastle, duke of, 166;
    Scots occupy, 142
Newmarket, racecourse, 147
Niall Noígiallachi, High King, 24
Nicholas II, Tsar, 177, 181, 184, 186
Nile, Battle of the, 167
Norfolk, duke of, 119, 127, 134;
    Isabella in, 90
Norman Conquest, of England, 16, 17, 27, 42-3, 44-9, 57;
    of Ireland, 24
Normandy, Aethelred flees to, 35;
    changes in control, 54-5, 56-7, 104, 105;
    conquest by Henry V, 103;
    Edward the Confessor in, 40;
    Henry III renounces, 80;
    Henry Duke of, 54, 55, 70;
    James II Duke of, 148;
    pawned, 53;
    Richard Duke of, 76;
    Robert Duke of, 52-3, 54;
    William II invades, 52-3;
    William Duke of, see William I
Norse, see Viking
North, Lord, 164, 165, 166
Northampton, assizes, 72;
    earl of, 100;
    Treaty of, 90, 91;
    Yorkists capture, 107
Northumberland, earl of (Warwick), 129;
    earls of (Percys), 101-1, 107
Northumbria, earldom, 38, 39, 40;
    Hardrada and Tostig invade, 43;
    kingdom, 13, 14, 20, 23;
    oath of loyalty, 32;
    Robert Earl of, 60, 61;
    Scottish invasion, 38, 52, 60;
    uprising quelled, 48;
    Viking control, 28, 30, 35;

    William I in, 62
Norway, Cnut's conquest of, 38;
    King of, 38, 62, 116;
    Maid of, see Margaret Maid of Norway;
    surrenders western isles, 62
Notre Dame de Paris, 104
Nottingham, as Danish borough, 29;
    Edward I at, 75;
    Edward IV trapped, 108;
    Lord Appellant, 95
Novgorod, 38

O

O'Connor, Rory High King of Ireland, 24, 25, 73
O'Neill, Hugh, 135
Oates, Titus, 147
Odo, Bishop, 42, 52
Offa, King of Mercia, 13, 14, 15, 36
Offa's Dyke, 15, 16
Old Pretender, see James (Old Pretender)
Olney, Treaty of, 35
Orange, William of, see William III
Order of the Garter, Most Noble, 90, 92
Order of Merit, 181
Orkney, ceded by Norway, 113;
    Earl of, 29, 39, 62;
    earldom of, 29;
    King of, 11;
    Thorfinn Earl of, 60;
    Vikings occupy, 20, 22, 28-9
Orléans, Siege of, 104
Ormonde, Charles marquess of, 140
Osborne House, 177;
    Naval College, 192
Oswald, King, 14
Oswy, King, 14, 15
Otto the Great, 36
Ottoman Sultan, 188
Ottuel (brother of Richard Earl of Chester), 54
Oudenarde, Battle of, 162
Overbury, Thomas, 138
Oxford, bishop of, 149;
    Henry II in, 76, 78;
    James II prisoner in, 148;
    Magdalen College, 149;
    Matilda in, 56-7;
    Provisions of, 80, 81, 82;
    Viking occupation, 35

P

Pains, Bill of, 169
Palmerstone, PM, 175
Paris, Matthew, 52, 80
Paris, Edward Duke of Windsor retires to, 191;
    Edward III attacks, 93;
    Henry V in, 103;
    Notre Dame, 104;
    recaptured by Charles VII, 104;
    Treaty of, 66, 80, 164
Parker-Bowles, Camilla, 196
parliament, Cavalier, 146;
    constitutional, 150-1, 186;
    dismissed, 142-3;
    dissolved, 144, 147;
    under Henry VIII, 127;
    Irish, 166;
    king's authority over, 82-3, 102, 142-3, 178;
    Merciless, 82, 94;
    Model, 82;
    Parliament Act, 186;
    reform of, 165, 173, 176, 177, 178;
    Rump, 143, 144-5;
    supremacy of, 137, 151, 156;
    Welsh, 101;
    Welsh representation, 127
Parr, Catherine, 125, 127, 130, 132
Patriot Boys, 163
Peasants' Revolt, 94-5
Peel, Lord Robert, 172, 175, 178
Pembroke, Earl of, 24, 25, 88

Penda, King of Mercia, 14, 16
Pepys, Samuel, 147
Percy, earls of Northumberland, 100-1, 107
Perpetual Peace, Treaty of, 67, 113, 116, 117, 123
Persia, Shah of, 188
Perth, Treaty of, 29
Peter of Blois, 71, 75
Peter of Langtoft, 8
Petition of Right, 140
Pevensey, 46
Philip, Prince (Duke of Edinburgh), 194-5, 197
Philip I of France, 49
Philip II of Spain (son of Charles V), 130, 131, 134
Philippa (wife of Edward III), 93
Philippe II of France, 70, 72, 73, 76-7, 78-9, 80
Philippe III of France, 84-5
Philippe IV of France, 66, 87
Philippe VI of France, 69, 90-2
Phillips, Mark, 195, 196
photography, first, 175
Picquigny, Treaty of, 109
Pictavia, 22
Picts, elimination of, 23;
    Northumbrian expansion, 14;
    symbol stones, 21;
    Viking conflict, 20-3;
    repulsed by Vortigern, 12
Pilgrimage of Grace, 125, 127
Pinkie, Battle of, 118, 128
Pipe Rolls, 54
Pitgaveny, Duncan I killed at, 60, 61
Pitt, William the Elder, 162, 163
Pitt, William the Younger, 166, 167
Pius V, Pope, excommunicates Elizabeth I, 133
plague, in London, 147
Plantagenet, Henry, see Henry II
Plantagenet dynasty, 57, 69, 70-97, 99
Plantation of Ireland, 139
Plassey, Battle of, 163
Poitiers, Black Prince victory, 90, 91, 93;
    Eleanor's court, 70
Poitou, Louis IX gains, 80
Poland, invaded, 193
Pole, Reginald (papal legate; Archbishop of
    Canterbury), 130, 131
Ponsonby, Sir Henry, 174
Pontefract Castle, Richard II murdered, 100
Ponthieu and Montreuil, Count of, 90
Poorstock, 49
Portadown, Protestants killed, 142
Portsmouth, fleet review, 188
Powys, kingdom, 16
Prasutagus, Iceni king, 11
Prayer Book Riots, 140
Pretenders, Yorkist, 122, 123
printing, first book, 109;
    press in Scotland, 116
Proclamation of Rebellion, 165
publication, Bible, 125, 127, 139;
    James I's books, 138

Quebec, captured, 163
Queen Anne's Bounty, 154
Queen Mother, 183, 189, 197
Quitclaim of Canterbury, 62

R

Raedwald, King, 12
Ragnallson, Margad of Dublin, 39
Ramsay, Alan, 164
Ranulf, Earl of Chester, 56
Reading, Vikings at, 30
Reform Acts, 173, 176, 178
Reformation, 67
Regnenses, in Sussex, 10, 11
religion, Bible published, 125, 127, 139;
    Book of Common Prayer, 128-9;
    Catholic primacy, 125;
    Catholicism, 9, 67, 128, 130-4;
    Christianity, 9, 12, 15, 20, 25;
    church feudalism, 50-1;
    Church of England founded, 126;
    conflict with monarchy, 68, 71, 96;

and coronation rites, 36;
Declaration of Indulgence, 148;
dissolution of monasteries, 125, 126-7;
under Henry I, 54-5;
Henry VIII as head, 121, 124-7;
in Ireland, 25;
Jews expelled, 84;
vested in king, 9;
Pictish, 20-1;
Presbyterianism, 143;
Protestantism reinstated, 133;
Protestants burned, 130-1;
punishment for heretics, 100;
reform, 126;
in Scotland, 62, 67;
in Tudor times, 121;
Wales, 101
Renfrew, baron, 168, 180, 190
Rheged, kingdom, 20
Richard, brother of Edward V, 107;
son of Henry I, 54-5;
son of Henry II, 70, 73
Richard, Earl of Chester, 54
Richard I (Lionheart), 62, 73, 74, 76-7, 84
Richard II (Richard de Bordeaux), 36-7, 69, 82, 90,
94-5, 96, 100-1, 102, 106-7
Richard III (Duke of Gloucester), 69, 99, 104, 106, 107,
108, 110-11, 122
Richard IV, 122
Richmond, Conan Earl of (Duke of Brittany), 73
Richmond, George III farm at, 166; Palace, 123
Ridley, Nicholas Bishop of London, 130
Ridolfi plot, 134
Rights, Bill of, 151
Rivers, Lord, 109, 111
Rizzio, David, 118-19
Roanoake (Virginia), 134
Robert, Duke of Albany, 114
Robert, Duke of Normandy (brother of William II),
49, 53, 54
Robert I the Bruce, 64-5, 66, 87, 88, 91, 112, 114
Robert II (Auld Blearie), 66, 69, 112, 113, 114-15
Robert III (John Earl of Carrick; Duke of Albany), 112,
114-15
Robinson, Perdita, 168
Robinson, Ralph, 166
Rochester, Francis Bishop of, 161
Rochester, Robert Viscount, 138
Rochester, castle, 49
Rockingham, Council of, 53;
Lord, 166
Roger, Bishop of Salisbury, 54
Rome, Alfred sent to, 30;
invades Britain, 10-11;
rule collapses, 16;
trade with Britain, 10, 11
Rosebury, Lord, 177
Ross, earl of, 62, 65, 138, 140
Rouen, captured, 103, 105;
Edward IV's birthplace,
108; Joan of Arc burned, 105
Round Table Conference, 185, 186
Row, John, 140
Roxburgh, 102, 113, 114, 115
Royal Academy of Music, established, 159
Royal Escape, 147
Royal Marriages Act, 169
Royal Navy, dominance, 167
royal palace, 74
royalty, image of, 96-7, 170-1
Rufus, William, see William II
Ruthven Raid, 138
Rye House Plot, 147
Ryswick, Treaty of, 153, 160

S

St Aidan, 15
St Albans, 11, 80, 106-7
St Andrew, coronation, 116
St Columba, 20, 25
St Columbanus, 25
St Cuthbert, 15
St Edward, shrine of, 80

St George, 92
St James's Palace, 148, 184
St John, Henry, 155
St Ninian, 20
St Patrick, 24, 25
St Peter, West Minster of, 40
Saladin, 76-7
Salisbury, Lord, 188, 189
Salisbury, bishop of, 54, 56;
cathedral, 80;
countess of, 92;
earl of, 100, 107;
William of Orange reaches, 149, 150
Sandringham, 180, 184
Sandwich, Louis IX defeated at, 80
Sauchieburn, Battle of, 116
Saxe-Coburg, duke of, 175
Saxe-Coburg-Gotha, duke of, 180, 182
Saxons, arrive, 12-13
Schleswig-Holstein, 180
Scone, abbey, 22, 64, 146;
Stone of, 22, 37, 87
Scotia, 8
Scotland, border fixed, 59, 63;
Caledonii Picts, 11;
counties introduced, 59;
Edward I subjugates, 62, 64-5, 66-7;
Edward III controls, 91, 114;
Edward IV invasion, 108;
French alliance, 66-7, 87;
Henry I alliance, 54;
independence of, 63, 91;
Irish kingdom in, 24;
kingship transformed, 58-9;
Lieutenant of the Realm, 115;
Maetae Picts, 20;
Norman authority, 48;
oath of loyalty, 32;
origin of name, 8, 20;
Plantation of Ireland, 139;
Richard III invasion, 110;
succession crisis, 85, 86-7;
regains western isles, 62
Scout movement, 192
Scrope, Richard Archbishop of York, 101
Sedgmoor, Battle of, 149
Seisyllwg, kingdom, 16
Septennial Act, 158
Settlement, Act of, 153, 156, 191
Seven Years War, 163, 165, 166
Seymour, Jane, 125, 127
Seymour, Thomas, 125
Shaftesbury, Earl of, 147
Shakespeare, William, 8, 11, 60, 100, 102
sheriff, introduction of, 34, 59
Sherriffmuir, Battle of, 160
Shetland, 22, 28, 116
Ship Money, 140, 141, 142
Shrewsbury, Battle of, 100;
earl of, 16
Sicily, 76, 80, 85
Simnel, Lambert, 122
Simon of Sudbury, Archbishop of Canterbury, 94
Simpson, Mrs Wallis, 190-1
Siric, Archbishop, 35
Siward, Earl of Northumbria, 60, 61
Six Articles, Act of, 125, 128
Slaigne the Firbolg, 8
slavery, 173
Sluys, French fleet destroyed, 91, 92
Snowdon, baron of, 164;
earl of, 196
Solway Moss, Battle of, 66, 113, 117, 124
Somerled, Lord of Argyll, 62
Somerset, Beaufort Duke of, 106
Somerset, Duke of (Earl of Hertford; Lord Protector),
128-9, 131, 132
Somerset, Edmund Duke of, 105, 106-7
Somerset, Robert Earl of, 139
Sophia, Dowager Duchess of Hanover, 154, 156-7
Sophia Charlotte (mistress of George I), 158
Sophia Charlotte of Mecklenburg-Strelitz (wife of
George III), 164, 167
Sophia Dorethea of Celle, 158
South Africa, George VI visits, 193;
independence, 187

South Sea Bubble, 158, 159
Southampton, French raid on, 92
Spain, Armada, 97, 130, 133-5;
Queen consort of, 130
Spanish Succession, War of, 154, 160
Spencer, Lady Diana, 195, 196, 197
Spenser, Edmund, 135
Spurs, Battle of the, 124
Stamford (Danish borough), 29
Stamfordham, Lord, 182
Stamp Act, 164
Standard, Battle of the, 56, 61
Stanhope, Lord, 159
Statute of Labour, 93
Statute of Westminster, 84
Stephen, King (Stephen of Blois), 45, 55, 56-7, 70, 74
Stewart, Henry, see Darnley, Lord
Stewart, John, see Robert III
Stewart, Robert, see Robert I the Bruce and Robert II
Stewart clan, 69, 114-17
Stirling, Edward I defeated, 87;
as Scottish stronghold, 64;
trading burgh, 60
Stirling Castle, coronation 118, 138;
extended, 116
Stone of Destiny, see Scone, Stone of
Strabo, the geographer, 10
Strafford, Thomas Earl of, 142
Strathclyde, kingdom, 20, 22, 28;
oath of loyalty, 32
Strathmore, submission to Edward I, 64
Stuart, Charles, see Charles (Young Pretender)
Stuart, James, see James II of Scotland
Stuart, James Francis Edward (son of James II),
see James (Old Pretender)
Stuart dynasty, 69, 136-55
succession, principles of royal, 27, 68-9, 98, 136-7, 153
Suetonius, 11
Suez Crisis, 195
Suffolk, earl of (duke of), 105, 106, 123
Sugar Act, 164
Supremacy, Act of, 124, 126
Surrey, Atrebates in, 10;
Thomas Earl of, 124
Sussex, as kingdom, 9, 13;
Regnenses in, 10
Sutherland, Viking occupation, 29
Sutton Hoo, 12, 14, 15
Sweyn, King of Norway (son of Cnut), 39
Sweyn II of Denmark, 47, 48
Sybilla (daughter of Henry I), 61
Synod of Whitby, 15

T

Tara, 22, 24, 29
Tasciovan, King, 11
taxation, on American colonies, 164;
Anglo-Saxon, 34;
collectors executed, 124;
customs revenue, 147;
via Domesday Book, 48, 49;
under Edward III, 90;
Edward IV avoids, 108;
forced loans, 140;
under Henry VII, 122;
for Hundred Years War, 82;
under King John, 79;
monarchy pays tax, 197;
parliament refuses, 139;
poll, 94;
ship money, 140, 141, 142
Tea Act, 164
television, 36
Tempsford, Danes defeated at, 29, 32
Test Act, 147
Tettenhall, Danes defeated at, 29, 32
Tewkesbury, Battle of, 106, 110;
Prince Edward killed, 107
Thérouanne, 124
Thirteen Colonies of British America, 166
Thirty Years War, 139
Thorfinn, Earl of Orkney, 60, 61
Thorkell the Tall, 35, 38

Thornhill, James, 170
Tiberius Claudius Cogidumnus, 10
Tinchebrai, 54
Tirel, Walter, 53
Togidubnus, Regni king, 10
Togodumnus, 11
Tolerance, Act of, 152
Torbay, William of Orange lands, 149, 150, 151, 152
Torrigiano, Pietro, 123
Tostig (brother of Harold), see Godwine, Tostig
Toulouse, campaign to capture, 71;
        count of, 73;
        Henry II attacks, 70, 73
Touraine, Count of, 70
Tournai, 124
tournaments, 74
Tours, Treaty of, 104
Towton, Royalists defeated, 105, 107
trade, English, 108;
        with Flanders, 92;
        Roman, 10, 11;
        Scottish, 60;
        unions, 186;
        Viking, 24
Trafalgar, Battle of, 167
Tranby Croft Scandal, 180, 181
Trinovantes, tribe, 10
Troyes, Treaty of, 103
Tudor, Henry, see Henry VII
Turberry, birth Robert the Bruce, 64
Turgeis, 24
Tyler, Wat, 94

U

Uí Néills, 24, 25
Ulster, earl of, 108, 148;
        'Plantation', 139;
        power centre, 24;
        Unionists in, 186
Uniformity, Act of, 128, 133
Union, Act of, 127, 155, 160, 166
Union Jack, flag introduced, 139
United Kingdom, creation of, 166, 167
university, founded, 101, 117
Urban II, Pope, 52, 53
Utrecht, Treaty of, 155

V

Valentinian, 12
Van Dyke, Anthony, 97, 140, 170
Vawr-Tigherne, 12
Venutius, 11
Verneuil, 67
Versailles, 150, 170, 171
Vexin, territory, 71, 73
Victoria, Queen, 73, 157, 172, 174-7, 148-9, 180, 181, 185, 188-9
Viking, defeat Anglo-Saxons, 34-5;
        defeated at Edington, 28, 31;
        gods, 8;
        Great Army, 28;
        raids, 13, 20, 22-3, 26-31, 32, 33, 34-5;
        settlements, 20, 22;
        threat, 15;
        trade, 24;
        driven from York, 33
Villiers, George Duke of Buckingham, 138, 139
Virgin Queen, see Elizabeth I
Vitalinus, commander, 12
Vitalis, Orderic (the chronicler), 48, 49
Volisios, King, 11
von Schulenburg, Ehrengard Melusine, 158
Vortigern, 9, 12
voting, 173

W

Wade, King, 15
Wakefield, Royalists capture, 107
Wales, border fixed, 127;
        divided into counties, 127;
        divided into shires, 86;
        united with England (Act of Union), 125, 127, 155, 160, 166;
        kingdoms, 16, 24;
        laws, 16;
        Prince of, 17, 19, 85-6, 88, 94, 100-1, 102;
        religion, 101;
        Statute of, 19, 85, 86;
        suppressed, 16-18, 32, 48, 70, 85-7, 100-1, 110;
        university, 101;
        William II invasion, 52
Wallace, William, 64, 87
Wallingford, Treaty of, 57, 70
Walpole, Horace, 164
Walpole, Sir Robert, 158, 159, 160, 163
Walsingham, Francis, 132
Walter, Hubert, 77
Waltham Cross, Eleanor Cross, 86
Walton Orinances, 91
Wantage Law Code, 34
Warbeck, Perkin, 122-3
Wars of the Roses, 67, 99, 105, 106-7, 111, 113
Warwick, Lord Appellant, 95
Warwick, Lord Protector, 128-9
Warwick, Richard Neville Earl of (kingmaker), 99, 105, 107, 108, 122
Wat, King, 15
Waterford, founded, 24
Waterloo, Battle of, 169
Wednesfield, Danes defeated at, 29, 32
Wellington, Duke of, 173
Wells, H.G., 184
Wentworth, Thomas Earl of Strafford, 142
Wessex, earldom, 38, 39, 40;
        Harold Earl of, see Harold II;
        kingdom of, 9, 14, 26-7;
        Mercian alliance, 30, 32;
        supremacy of, 13, 32-3;
        Vikings repulsed, 28, 30-1
Westminster, Statute of, 84
Westminster Abbey, burial, 80, 123;
        construction, 40, 41, 74, 80, 123;
        coronations at, 37;
        pageantry, 188;
        portrait in, 96;
        sanctuary, 111
Wexford, Cromwell victory, 144;
        founded, 24
Whitby, Synod of, 15
White Ship, 54-5, 75
Whithorn Priory, 20
Whitlam, Gough, 196
Wilhelm I, 182
Wilhelm II, 182, 184, 186
Wilkes, John, 164, 166
William (son of Henry I), 54-5
William I (the Conqueror; Duke of Normandy), 16, 17, 37, 40, 41, 42-45, 46-9, 50-1, 59, 61, 74, 82
William I (the Lion), 62, 63
William II (Rufus), 36, 45, 48, 49, 52-3, 54, 60, 61, 75
William III (of Orange), 137, 147, 148, 149-51, 152-3, 154, 160, 170
William IV, 36, 172-3, 178
William of Malmesbury, 56
William Rufus see William II
Wilson, Harold, 195
Winchester, Arthur born at, 122;
        coronation, 40;
        Norman occupation, 48;
        Norman palace, 74;
        Treasury, 52, 53;
        Viking occupation, 35
Windsor, duke of, 190;
        House of, 182-97;
        name change to, 182;
        Norman palace, 74;
        Treaty of, 25

Windsor Castle, 75, 90, 92, 109, 169, 171, 177, 196;
        George III at, 166, 167;
        George IV at, 168
Winterhalter, Franz Xaver, 171
Witan assembly, 27, 33, 82
witchcraft, 102
Woden, 8
Wolfe, James, 163
Wolsely, Cardinal Thomas, 124, 126
Woodstock, manor, 155;
        Treaty of, 17
Woodville, Elizabeth, 108, 110
Worcester, Cromwell victory, 144, 146;
        earl of, 101;
        Hugh Latimer Bishop of, 130;
        John buried at, 79
World War, First, 182, 184-6;
        Second, 183, 189, 192-3
Wren, Christopher, 170
Wulfstan, Archbishop of York, 38
Wyatt, Thomas, 130, 131, 132
Wyclif, John, 94, 100

Y

Yeavering, royal palace, 74
York, archbishop of, 38, 93, 101;
        Danes driven from, 33, 47;
        duke of, 99, 105, 106-7, 108, 111, 140, 147, 148, 152, 172, 184, 192;
        duke's head displayed, 107;
        Treaty of, 62;
        Viking king of, 28, 32-3
Yorktown, British surrender, 165, 166
Young King, see Henry III
Ypwines Fleot (Saxon landing place), 12

Z

Zoffany, Johann, 170, 171